Presented by your
true Friend
J. A. Clark
To J. H. Campbell Esq

Painted by Sir Thos. Lawrence P.R.A. Engd. by Geo. E. Perine N. York

JOHN PHILPOT CURRAN

SPEECHES

OF

JOHN PHILPOT CURRAN,

WHILE AT THE BAR.

EDITED BY

JAMES A. L. WHITTIER,

COUNSELOR AT LAW

SECOND EDITION.

CHICAGO:

CALLAGHAN & COMPANY.

1872.

CONTENTS.

PAGE

Memoir, - - - - - - - - - 1
Statement of the Case of Egan *v.* Kindillan, - - - 15
Mr. Curran's Speech for the Defendant, - - - - 15
Statement of the Case of A. H. Rowan, - - - - 26
Mr. Curran's Speech for the Defendant, - - - - 27
Mr. Curran's Speech on the Motion to set aside the Verdict in the Case of A. H. Rowan, - - - - - - - 88
Statement of the Case of the Droheda Defenders, - - - 105
Mr. Curran's Speech for the Defendants, - - - - 108
Statement of the Case of Doctor Drennan, - - - - 121
Mr. Curran's Speech for the Defendant, - - - - 125
Statement of the Case of the Northern Star, - - - 142
Mr. Curran's Speech for the Defense, - - - - 147
Statement of the Case of the Rev. William Jackson, - - 151
Mr. Curran's Speech for the Defendant, - - - - 154
Statement of the Case of the Dublin Defenders, - - - 175
Mr. Curran's Speech for the Defendants, - - - - 176
Statement of the Case of Peter Finnerty, Publisher of "The Press," 204
Mr. Curran's Speech for the Defense, - - - - 211
Statement of the Case of Patrick Finney, - - - - 258
Statement of the Case of Henry Sheares, - - - - 295
Mr. Curran's Speech for the Defense on the Demurrer to the Indictment, - - - - - - - 300
Statement of the Testimony in the Case of Henry Sheares, - 316
Mr. Curran's Summing-up for the Defense, - - - 323

CONTENTS.

	PAGE
Statement of the Case of Oliver Bond, - - - -	354
Mr. Curran's Speech for the Defendant, - - - -	355
Statement of the Case of Lady Pamela Fitzgerald and her Children, - - - - - - -	384
Mr. Curran's Speech in support of the Petition, - - -	385
Statement of the Case of Napper Tandy, - - - -	402
Mr. Curran's Speech for the Defendant, - - - -	404
Statement of the Case of Sir Henry Hayes, - - -	417
Mr. Curran's Speech for the Prosecution, - - - -	420
Statement of the Case of Hevey *v.* Major Sirr, - - -	451
Mr. Curran's Speech for the Plaintiff, - - - -	451
Statement of the Case of Owen Kirwan, - - - -	475
Mr Curran's Speech for the Defense, - - - -	477
Statement of the Case of John Costly, - - - -	502
Mr. Curran's Speech for the Prosecution, - - - -	502
Statement of the Case of Massy *v.* Headfort, - - -	515
Mr. Curran's Speech for the Plaintiff, - - - -	517
Statement of the Case of Judge Johnson, - - -	544
Mr. Curran's first Speech for the Defendant, - - -	547
Mr. Curran's Second Speech for the Defendant, - -	551

MEMOIR.

Born in the year 1750, his birth-day being the 24th of July, his birth-place, Newmarket, of parents belonging to the middle class of Irish land-holders, there was little in the early youth of John Philpot Curran either remarkable or singular. A playful boy, easily made a dupe by reason of his unthinking credulity, affording thus amusement to his companions, his amiable qualities attracted for him the attention and soon the regard of the parish clergyman, through whose aid his education was rendered more complete than that of other youth of his rank, so that, after the usual preparatory studies, he was entered as a sizar of Trinity College, Dublin, it being understood by all the parties concerned, that he should enter on the ministry of the Church in due season.

But having, on the occasion of excusing himself to the governing body of the University for a flagrant violation of the college laws, evinced great readiness in presenting the side of the case most favorable to himself, he was led to consider whether or not his interests would be advanced by pursuing the studies pertaining to the law, and soon decided so to do. It must not be understood that Curran was an inattentive student. Such was not the case. While he was full of boyish energy, and by no means averse to a participation in the sometimes rude divertisements of his associates, he was of good standing in his classical studies and of fair rank in others. "He studied", says his son and biographer, "the classical writings of antiquity with great ardor, and with eminent success. Nor did his enthusiastic admiration of them ever after subside. Amidst the distractions of business and ambition he was all his life returning with fresh delight to their perusal; and in the last journey that he ever took, Horace and Virgil were his travelling companions."

Curran, like many another eminent man, was fond of attributing much of his success to the influence, the example and the teachings of his mother. And it is pleasant to know that she lived long enough to be a witness of his triumphs, and to share in the fruits of his labors. She was never, however, fully reconciled to his choice of a profession, and on one occasion, when congratulated upon his success, replied—"Oh, yes, it was very fine, but it breaks my heart to think what a noble preacher was lost to the church when John disappointed us all, and insisted on becoming a lawyer." And in her later years, when her friends, to gratify and console her, used to remind her that she had lived to see her favorite child one of the judges of the land, she would still reply—"Don't speak to me of judges. John was fit for anything; and had he but followed our advice, it might hereafter be written upon my tomb that I had died the mother of a bishop."

His collegiate studies being ended, in pursuance of his design to fit himself for legal practice, Curran, in the spring of 1773, repaired to London, where he became a student of law in the Middle Temple. Many letters written by him at this interesting period have been preserved, and one we copy as being very characteristic. It was addressed to one of his earliest friends, then a resident of his native town of Newmarket.

"LONDON, [illegible] CHANDOS STREET, *July* 10, 1773.

"I would have taken a last farewell of my dear Henry from Dublin, if I had not written so shortly before I left it; and indeed I was not sorry for being exempt from a task for which a thousand causes conspired to make me at that juncture unqualified. It was not without regret that I could leave a country, which my birth, education, and connections, had rendered dear to me, and venture alone, almost a child of fortune, into a land of strangers. In such moments of despondence, when fancy plays the self tormentor, she commonly acquits herself to a miracle, and will not fail to collect in a single group the most hideous forms of anticipated misfortune. I considered myself, besides, as resigning for ever the little indulgencies that youth and inexperience may claim for their errors, and passing to a period of life in which the best can scarce escape the rigid severity of censure; nor could the little trivial vanity of taking the reins of my own conduct alleviate the pain of so dear-bought a transition from dependence to liberty. Full of these reflections as I passed the gate, I could not but turn and take a last lingering look of poor Alma Mater; it was the scene of many a boyish folly, and of many an happy hour. I should have felt more confusion at part of the retrospect, had I not been relieved by a recollection of the valuable friendships I had formed there. Though I am far from thinking such a circumstance can justify a passed misconduct, yet I cannot call that time totally a blank in which one has acquired the greatest blessing of humanity. It was with a melancholy kind of exultation I counted over the number of those I loved there, while my heart gave a sigh to each name in the catalogue; nay, even the *fellows,* whom I never loved, I forgave at that moment; the parting tear blotted out every injury, and I gave them as hearty a benediction as if they had deserved it; as for my general acquaintance (for I could not but go the round), I packed their respective little sighs into one great sigh as I turned round on my heel. My old friend and handmaid Betty, perceiving me in motion, got her hip under the *strong-box,* with my seven shirts, which she had rested against the rails during the delay, and screwed up her face into a most rueful caricature, that might provoke a laugh at another time; while her young son Denny, grasping his waistband in one hand and a basket of sea-provisions in the other, took the lead in the procession, and so we journeyed on to George's-Quay, where the ship was just ready to sail. When I entered I found my fellow passengers seated round a large table in the cabin; we were fourteen in number. A young Highland lord had taken the head of the table and the conversation, and with a modesty peculiar to himself, gave a history of his travels, and his intimate connections with the princes of the empire. An old, debauched officer was complaining of the gout, while a woman who sat next to him, (good Heaven! what a tongue), gave a long detail of what her father suffered from that disorder. To do them all justice, they exerted themselves most zealously for the common entertainment. As for my part, I had nothing to say; nor, if I had, was any one at leisure to listen to me; so I took possession of what the captain called a bed, wondering, with Partridge, 'how they could play so many different tunes at the same time without putting each other out!' I was expecting that the sea-sickness would soon give those restless mouths different employment, but in that I was disappointed; the sea was so calm that one only was sick during the passage, and it was not my good fortune that the lot should fall on that devil who never ceased chattering. There was no cure but patience; accordingly I never stirred from my tabernacle (unless to visit my basket) till we arrived at Park-gate. There, after the usual pillage at the custom-house, I laid my box down on the beach, seated myself upon it, and, casting my eyes westward over the Welsh mountains towards Ireland, I began to reflect on the impossibility of getting back without the precarious assistance of others. "Poor Jack"! thought I, "thou wast never till now so far from home but thou mightest return on thine own legs. Here now must thou remain, for where here canst thou expect the assistance of a friend?" Whimsical as the idea was, it had power to affect me; until, at length, I was awaked from this reverie by a figure which approached me with the utmost affability; methought his looks seemed to say, 'why is thy spirit troubled?' He pressed me to go into his house, and to 'eat of his bread' and to 'drink of his drink!' There was so much good-natured solicitude in the invitation 'twas irresistible. I rose, therefore, and followed him, ashamed of my uncharitable despondence. "Surely", thought I, "there is still humanity left amongst us", as I raised my eyes to the golden letters over his door, that offered entertainment and repose to the wearied traveller. Here I resolved to stay for the night, and agreed for a place in his coach next morning to Chester; but finding my loquacions fellow-passenger had agreed for one in the same vehicle, I retracted my bargain, and agreed for my box only. I perceived, however, when I arose next morning, that my box was not sent, though the coach was gone. I was thinking how I should remedy this unlucky disappointment, when my friendly host told me that he could furnish me with a chaise! Confusion light upon him! what a stroke was this! It was not the few paltry shillings that vexed me, but to have my philanthropy till that moment running cheerily through my veins, and to have the current turned back suddenly by the detection of his knavery. Verily, Yorick, even thy gentle spirit, so meekly accustomed to bear and forbear, would have been roused on such an occasion. I paid hastily for my entertainment, and shaking the dust from my feet at his gate, I marched with my box on my shoulder to a waggoner's at the other end of the town, where I entered it for London, and sallied forth toward Chester on foot. I was so nettled at being the dupe of my own credulity, that I was almost tempted to pass an excommunication on all mankind, and resolved never more to trust my own skill in physiognomy. Wrapt up in my speculations,

I never perceived at what a rate I was striding away, till I found myself in the suburbs of Chester quite out of breath, and completely covered with dust and dirt. From Chester I set out that evening in the stage: I slept about four hours the next day at Coventry, and the following evening at five o'clock, was in view of near a hundred and twenty spires, that are scattered from one side of the horizon to the other, and seem almost bewildered in the mist that perpetually covers this prodigious capital. 'Twould be impossible for description to give any idea of the various objects that fill a stranger, on his first arrival, with surprise and astonishment. The magnificence of the churches, hospitals, and other public buildings which everywhere present themselves, would alone be ample subject of admiration to a spectator, though he were not distracted by the gaudy display of wealth and dissipation continually shifting before his eyes in the most extravagant forms of pride and ostentation, or by a hurry of business that might make you think this the source from which life and motion are conveyed to the world beside. There are many places here not unworthy of particular inspection, but as my illness prevented me from seeing them on my first arrival, I shall suspend my curiosity till some future time, as I am determined to apply to reading this vacation with the utmost diligence, in order to attend the courts next winter with more advantage. If I should happen to visit Ireland next summer, I shall spend a week before I go in seeing the curiosities here, (the king, and queen, and the lions); and, if I continue in my present mood, you will see a strange alteration in your poor friend. That cursed fever brought me down so much, and my spirits are so reduced that, faith! I don't remember to have laughed these six weeks. Indeed, I never thought solitude could lean so heavily on me as I find it does: I rise, most commonly, in the morning between five and six, and read as much as my eyes will permit me till dinner time; I then go out and dine, and from that till bed-time I mope about my lodgings and the park. For Heaven's sake send me some news or other (for, surely, Newmarket cannot be barren in such things) that will teach me once more to laugh. I never received a single line from any one since I came here. Tell me if you know anything about Keller: I wrote twice to that gentleman, without being favored with any answer. You will give my best respects to Mrs. Aldworth and her family; to Doctor Creagh's: and don't forget my good friends Peter and Will Connel. Yours sincerely

J. P. C."

"P.S. I will cover this blank edge with entreating you to write closer than you commonly do when you sit down to answer this, and don't make me pay ten pence for a half-pennyworth of white paper."

His course of study and manner of amusing himself in London, he thus describes: — "I have made some additions to my wardrobe, and purchased *a fiddle,* which I had till then denied myself. Do not think however from my mentioning these indulgences, that I have diminished my hours of reading. All I have done by the change, is, employing the time that must otherwise be vacant, in amusement instead of solitude. I still continue to read ten hours every day—seven at law, and three at history and the general principles of politics; and that I may have time enough I rise at half-past four. I have contrived a machine after the manner of an hour-glass, which perhaps you may be curious to know, which wakens me regularly at that hour. Exactly over my head I have suspended two vessels of tin, one above the other. When I go to bed, which is always at ten, I pour a bottle of water into the upper vessel, in the bottom of which is a hole of such a size as to let the water pass through so as to make the inferior reservoir overflow in six hours and a half. I have had no small trouble in proportioning these vessels; and I was still more puzzled for a while, how to confine my head so as to receive the drop, but I have at length succeeded."

In addition to these labors, productive in due season of most satisfactory results, he was a regular attendant on the exercises of the debating clubs which the students of law formed among themselves, and his experience as an amateur debater is similar to that of most other young orators—great diffidence at first, overcome by a single effort, and subsequent facility in public speaking.

In some of the published sketches of Mr. Curran's life it has been stated, that when at the Temple, and afterwards while struggling into notice at the bar, he derived part of his subsistence from contributions to literary works; but for this there is no foundation. During the first year of his residence in London his means were supplied partly by his relatives in Ireland, and partly by some of his more affluent companions, who considered his talents a sufficient security for their advances.

At Michaelmas term, 1775, Curran was called to the Irish bar, and became one of a remarkable coterie of counsellors, who brought to their daily business a degree of enthusiasm, and did their daily work with a freedom from considerations of custom, precedent or formality, very congenial to his nature. The latitude of ornament and digression, once so usual at that bar, had never been known, and would hardly have been tolerated in any other country. Yet, as has been remarked, all this was listened to in Ireland with favor and admiration, though the influence of impassioned oratory and fervid appeals to the feelings or the fancy had little effect upon the decisions of the bench. "The advocate might have excited the smiles or tears of his auditors, but no legal concessions followed. The judges who showed the most indulgence and sensibility to these episodes of fancy, were ever the most conscientious in preserving the sacred stability of law. Into the counsel's mirth or tenderness, no matter how digressive, they entered for the moment, more pleased than otherwise with irregularities that gratified their taste and relieved their labor; but with them the triumph of eloquence was evanescent,—the oration over, they resumed their gravity and firmness, and proved by their ultimate decision that if they relaxed for an instant it was from urbanity, and not from any oblivion of the paramount duties of their station."

In some instances, it is true, where the case on trial had a political aspect, the judges forgot to be impartial, and allowed their prejudices to lead them into displays of feeling towards counsel, not alway screditable to themselves or productive of satisfactory results. This was especially true in the early part of Curran's career, but he made himself respected and feared ere long, and was freed from unpleasantnesses of this kind.

It is related of him that, in one of his first cases, argued before a certain Judge Robinson, who had won an unenviable notoriety as an anonymous pamphleteer, he said, "That he had never met the law as laid down by his lordship in any book in *his* library."—"That may be, sir," said the Judge contemptuously, "but I suspect that *your* library is very small." The young barrister, roused by this sneer at his circumstances, replied, that true it was his library might be small, but he thanked Heaven that among his books there were none of the "wretched publications of the frantic pamphleteers of the day. I find it more instructive, my Lord, to study good works than to compose bad ones; my books may be few, but the title pages give me the writers' names; my shelf is not disgraced by any of such rank absurdity, that their very authors are ashamed to own them." He was here interrupted by the Judge, who said, "Sir, you are forgetting the respect which you owe to the dignity of the judicial character." "Dignity!" exclaimed Curran; "my Lord, upon that point I shall cite you a case from a book of some authority, with which you are, perhaps, not unacquainted. A poor Scotchman,* upon his arrival in London, thinking himself insulted by a stranger, and imagining that he was the stronger man, resolved to resent the affront, and, taking off his coat, delivered it to a bystander to hold; but, having lost the battle, he turned to resume his garment, when he discovered that he had unfortunately lost that also; that the trustee of his habiliments had decamped during the affray. So, my Lord, when the person who is invested with the dignity of the judgment-seat lays it aside for a moment to enter into a disgraceful personal contest, it is in vain, when he is worsted in the encounter, that he seeks to resume it—it is in vain that he endeavors to shelter himself behind an authority which he has abandoned."

Judge Robinson. "If you say another word, sir, I'll commit you."

Curran. "If your Lordship should do so, we shall, both of us, have the consolation of reflecting that I am not the worst thing your Lordship has committed."

The Judge did not commit him; but he was understood to have solicited the bench to interfere, and make an example of the advocate, by depriving him of his gown, and to have received so little encouragement, that he thought it prudent to proceed no farther in the affair.

Curran had probably the usual early experience of lawyers getting into practice, but within five years had an opportunity at once to show his mettle and rise into great popularity by his speech in the case of *Neale v. Dinesuile,* never fully reported, in which the plaintiff, a poor parish priest, brought an action against a wealthy noble-

* The Scotchman alluded to is Strap, in Smollett's Roderick Random.

man, to recover damages for a peculiarly aggravated assault committed by the defendant. On the one side was justice represented by a poor man, and on the other pride of place, great wealth, high social position, and unbounded influence. Curran's speech was equal to the occasion, and he was successful in winning a verdict, and of establishing himself as an advocate of remarkable power, and in gaining the affections of the people, so that popular applause he ever after had to his heart's content. And the fact that he was obliged to fight a duel with one of the relatives of the defendant, on account of language he had used during the trial, and that he acquitted himself bravely, did not lessen either his reputation or popularity.

The celerity of his ascent to distinction in his profession, and in the public estimation, may be inferred from his entrance into the Irish Parliament within seven years from his call to the bar, and his receiving a silk gown about the same time. He entered upon the performance of his legislative duties at a period now historical; when his country was full of disturbances and revolts; the revolution of 1782 scarcely quelled; the government not in unison with the people; the people distrusting and disobeying the government. He early identified himself with the reform or liberal party, and became almost at once a leader of it. While his parliamentary efforts do not equal those at the bar, they are vigorous and effective, and had weight at all times.

In 1786, when in full practice at the bar, he spoke of himself as follows, in a familiar letter:

"Patterson, Chief-Justice of the Common Pleas, has been given over many days, but still holds out. My good friend Carleton succeeds him. Had he got this promotion some time ago, it might have been of use to me, for I know he has a friendship for me; but at present his partiality can add little to whatever advantage I can derive from his leaving about four thousand a year at the bar.

"I understand they have been puffing me off to you from this (Dublin). I have been, indeed, very much employed this term, and I find I have a merit imputed to me of changing a determination which the Chancellor had formed against Burroughs a few days ago. He has really been uncommonly kind and polite to me. This, I believe, is the first time I ever became my own panegyrist, therefore excuse it: I should scarcely mention it for any vanity of mine, if it were not of some little value to others; tot it up therefore on the table of pence, not on the scale of vain glory."

He was now able to purchase land near his native town of Newmarket, and erected thereon a residence suited to his fortunes, where he exercised a generous hospitality. "It may not be a dignified circumstance in his history," says his biographer, "yet it must be mentioned, that his arrival at Newmarket was always considered there as a most important event. Gibbon somewhere observes, that one of the liveliest pleasures which the pride of man can enjoy, is to reappear in a more splendid condition among those who had known him in his obscurity. If Mr. Curran had been proud, he might have enjoyed this pleasure to the full. Upon the occasion of every return to the scene of his childhood, visits and congratulations upon his increasing fame poured in upon 'the counsellor' from every side. 'His visitors' (according to his own description,) 'were of each sex and of every rank, and their greetings were of as many kinds. Some were delivered in English, some in Irish, and some in a language that was a sort of compromise between the two—some were communicated verbally—some by letter or by deputy, the absentees being just at that moment 'in trouble', which generally meant, having been lately committed for some, 'unintentional' misdemeanor, from the consequences of which who could extricate them so successfully as 'the counsellor?' —some came in prose,—some in all the pomp of verse;

for Mr. O'Connor, the roving bard (of whom Mr. Curran used to say, that if his imagination could have carried him as far as his legs did, he would have been the most astonishing poet of the age) was never absent; at whatever stage of their poetical circuit he and his itinerant muse might be, the moment certain intelligence reached them that the master of the Priory had arrived, they instantly took a short cut across the country, and laid their periodical offerings at the feet of him whose high fortune they had of course been the first to predict!

"All these petty honors gratified his heart, if not his pride, and he never fastidiously rejected them. Those who came from the mere ambition of a personal interview he sent away glorying in their reception, and delighted with his condescension and urbanity; to those who seemed inclined 'to carry away anything rather than an appetite', he gave a dinner. The village disturber of the peace had once more the promise that his rescue should be effected at the ensuing assizes, while the needy laureate seldom failed to receive the *'crown'*, which he had 'long preferred to the freshest bays'."

In the prefatory notes to the speeches which follow, will be found such allusions to his professional career as are necessary for a good understanding of his position and his achievements, and the completion of this memoir does not require further allusion to this part of his life. These speeches commend themselves to the reader's attention, by their clearness, vivacity, wealth of language and illustration, the spirit of ardent patriotism, evinced in them, and especially to the legal reader by reason of the unshrinking devotion to the interests of his clients which is always manifest;—the more honorable too in memory of the fact that so many of his speeches were in defence of political prisoners, and virtual arraignments of the existing government, the dispenser alike of patronage and power.

In the year 1806, on the death of Pitt, Fox and the Whigs assumed the control of the English government, and Curran, who deserved much of the new Administration, and in fact had for seventeen years been promised one of the best places in its gift, was given the Mastership of the Rolls for Ireland, a position for which he was by no means fitted. He would have preferred the Attorney-Generalship, but it was given to another. For eight years he performed the duties of his office feeling daily an increasing dislike to them, and his judgments are none of them remarkable. His was not what may be termed a judicial mind. He needed the incentive of the advocate, the ardor of the orator, to bring out his noblest qualities, and his decisions are not remembered, nor his judgeship often alluded to.

He resigned this official position in 1814, on account of impaired health, and the short remainder of his life was spent in London, Paris and Dublin, but he rarely visited the latter place, and his love of country increased by absence. He bitterly felt the injustice that was done her by the government, and one of his latest desires was, to be buried in her soil. Stricken by paralysis, in the summer of 1817, receiving but little relief from a journey to Italy, he died in London on the 14th of October in the same year.

No one among the many who deserve well of Ireland for the love they bore her and the good deeds they did in defence of her honor, has greater claims than Curran, and in the warm hearts of her generous people he is remembered and will be.

And when, in due season, her history is impartially written, his labors will be recognised as those of an ardent patriot, a great advocate, and a whole souled Irishman.

EGAN *v.* KINDILLAN.

Mr. Charles Phillips, from whose "Recollections of Curran" this speech is taken, gives the following account of the case in which it was made. The date is not given.

"The case of "Egan against Kindillan" for seduction, was tried before Lord Avonmore. It was a case of a very singular nature. Miss Egan was a young lady of some accomplishments, and great personal beauty. Mr. Kindillan was then a dashing young officer in a dragoon regiment, nearly related to the late Lord Belvidere. The reader will find the principal circumstances of the trial detailed indignantly in Mr. Curran's speech; but it is necessary to apprize him that Kindillan was first vindictively prosecuted for the offence in a criminal court, and escaped through the great exertions and genius of his immortal advocate, who, however, in the civil action, was only able to mitigate the damages down to £500. After the plaintiff had gone through his case, Mr. Curran proceeded:—"

My lords, and gentlemen of the jury—I am in this case counsel for the defendant. Every action to be tried by a jury, must be founded in principles of law; of that, however, the court only can determine, and upon the judgment of the court, you, gentlemen, may repose with great confidence. The foundation of this action is built upon this principle of law, and this only, that the plaintiff suffered special damage by losing the service of his daughter, who has been taken away from him: for you, gentlemen, will err egregiously, and the court will tell you so, if you imagine that the law has given any retribution by way of damages for all the agony which the father may suffer from the seduction of his child. However, I do not mean to make light of the feelings of a parent; he would be a strange character, and little deserving the attention of a court, who could act in that manner; to see his grey hairs brought with calamity to the grave, and yet hold him out as a subject of levity or contempt. I do no such thing; but I tell you soberly and quietly, that, whatever his feelings may be, it is a kind of misery for which the law does not provide any remedy. No action lies for debauching or seducing a daughter, but only for the loss of her service; at the same time, over and over again, that the only ground is the special circumstance of the loss of her service—at the same time, gentlemen, I agree implicitly in the idea of letting the case go at large to you. In every injury which one man sustains from another, it is right to let all circumstances, which either aggravate or diminish the weight of it, go to the jury. This case has been stated in evidence by two persons. Miss Egan has told, I think, the most extraordinary story—

Lord Chief Baron—The most artless story I ever heard.

Mr. Curran—I do not allude to her credit; I only say I never heard so extraordinary a story, because I never heard of an instance of a young woman, decently bred, arrived at eighteen, going away with a man, after a single conversation; having no previous acquaintance—no express promise; abandoning her father's house, protection, and care, after two conversations, in which there was not one word of marriage; without a previous opportunity of engagement: without a possibility of engaging her affections or seducing her from her father, she embraces the first opportunity which was given to her; therefore, indeed, I am astonished. I said, gentlemen, the case ought rightly to go before you—I tell you why—circumstances which compose the enormity of an offence of this kind can be judged by you. If you receive a man into your house, give him access to any female in your family, and he converts that privilege to abuse her virtue, I know nothing of greater enormity. If you admit a man to your house and your table, and he avails himself of that confidence to abuse the virtue of your daughter or your wife, I know of no length to which the just indignation of a jury might not be carried. But if there be no such criminality on the part of the defendant? if he was rather the follower than the mover of the transaction? His conduct may be palliated, it cannot be condemned. Look at this case, even as stated by the witness herself. Who was the seducer? Mr. Kindillan! Where was the single act to inspire her with a single hope, that he intended to marry her? Why steal away from her father's house—why go to a public inn, at a common

2

seaport, even at that age, and with that degree of understanding you see her possess? She confesses she suspected there was no design of marriage; that at Aungier-street he spent a night with her, and no design of marriage; they cohabited week after week, and no conversation of marriage till they leave their mother country, and arrive at the Isle of Man—and then from whom does it move? not from her who might have talked even with a degree of pride, if she thought he took her away from her father:—"You have robbed me of a father, under the promise of becoming my husband—give me that protector!" No: you find it moving from him, from his apprehension of her dissatisfaction. If you can believe that, what kind of education must she have received? She throws herself into the arms of the first officer she ever saw; flies into a hackney-coach, and goes to another country, and never talks of marriage till she arrives there. To talk of the loss of a father is a very invidious subject; every father must feel an argument of that kind. But it is not because that one man suffers, another must pay. It is in proportion to his own guilt that he must be punished, and therefore it is that the law denies the right of the father to receive compensation. It is an injury which can rarely arise, when the father has discharged the precedent part of his duty. It is wise, therefore, that the law should refuse its sanction to an action of that sort, because it calls upon the father to guard against that event, for which he knows he can have no reparation. It guards more against the injury by discountenancing the neglect which may give it birth; it refuses a compensation to reward his own breach of duty. Only see what would be the consequence if the law gave its sanction to an action of this sort. This man is in the army. I am not here to preach about morals; I am talking to men who may regret that human nature is not more perfect than it is, but who must take men as they are. This man goes to a watering-place; he sees this young woman, full of giddiness and levity—no vice possibly, but certainly not excusable in any female; see how she conducts herself. "Have you considered the proposal?" "No," says she, "our acquaintance is too short;"—but the second conversation, and she is gone. How would any of you, gentlemen, think of your child, if she picked up a young buck whom she never saw before? what would your wife say, if she was told her daughter had picked up a man she did not know? But you know mankind—you know the world. What would you think of a woman, unmarried, who held a conversation on these terms? If at Philipsborough you addressed a young woman, with whom not a word of marriage passed, and yet she accompanied you without hesitation,—would you suppose her a girl of family and education, or would you not rather suppose her to be one of those unfortunate, uneducated creatures, with whom a conversation very different from that of marriage takes place? This, then, is the situation of the defendant; he yields, more seduced than seducing. It is upon this the father calls to you for damages! For an injury committed—by whom? from what cause? From the indiscreet behaviour, the defective education, and neglected mind of his daughter. He can have no feeling, or he would not have exposed both her and himself; or, if he have any feelings, they are such as can be gratified by you, gentlemen of the jury—they are such as can be calmed by money! He can find more enjoyment in pecuniary compensation, than in other species of retribution! I speak harshly—I am obliged to do so; I feel it. It is to be decided by you with liberality and justice between such a father and the defendant. I am stating these things, supposing you believe her. Her story is well delivered—it would be extraordinary if it were not, when it has been so often repeated. The defendant was tried for his life, and twelve men upon their oaths acquitted him of the charge, though the fact was sworn to by her. Her sufferings and her beauty may make an impression upon your minds; but, gentlemen, you are not come here to pity, but to give a verdict; not from passion, but which may be the calm result of deliberation between party and party. There is a kind of false determination of mind, which makes dupes of judicial men upon cases which involve more sentiment than speculation. If you can feel any such sensation in your minds, glowing and heating to a degree of violence in which reason may be consumed, let me entreat you to guard against its falling upon the head which ought not to suffer. We are not to determine by zeal, but judge by discretion. It is not her tears, her heavings, her sighs, that must influence your sentence. She has been brought up a second time by her father, and exhibited before you, the unhappy object of vice and of wantonness. She has thus been exhibited by that father, whose feelings are represented as so tender—an exhibition which ought to have been avoided by a sincere parent. But let me expose the silly trap, that you may not be the dupes of such artifice. It was a simple case: it could have been proved without her testimony; the leaving her father's house could have been proved by many; and of the finding her in the defendant's possession there was sufficient evidence, and the service could be proved as well by any person as herself. But the circumstances are proper for consideration: give me leave to say, there are no circumstances more proper for consideration than the motives of the man who brings the action. What his conduct was, appears by her own evidence; she goes away with a man—he is seized and called upon to marry her, under the terror of a prosecution for his life, a species of inducement such as never was heard of. Let it not be told, that a case of this kind,—that the unsolicited elopement of a young, unfortunate woman yielding to criminal desires, going off with an officer upon a first acquaintance, is an example to be held up by a court and jury, or to be sanctioned by a verdict; that a loose girl, coming back from the cloyed appetite of her paramour, should make welcome her return to her father's house by the golden showers of compensation. If you wish to hold up examples to justify elopements of your children, establish it by your verdict! and be answerable for the consequence; you will resolve yourselves into a fund for unportioned wantons, whose fathers will draw upon you for fortunes; you will establish an example. I am not ashamed to be warm—I do not sell my warmth though I may my talents; but give me leave to tell you that an example of this kind, where no abuse of confidence can be pleaded, no treachery alleged, would go thus far, that every miserable female who parades about your streets, in order to make a miserable livelihood by the prostitution of her person, will come forward under the imposing character of a witness, because there is scarce any of them who has not a father that may bring an action. Let me warn you against another case: you will establish an example by which the needy father is encouraged, first, to force the man into marriage under the apprehension of a prosecution, or afterwards to compel him from the dread of a verdict, unless you think that the man could be reconciled to marry a girl he is tired of, and who has added perjury to the rest of her conduct. It is hard to talk of perjury; but how will they answer for the verdict of twelve honest men upon their oaths? Impeach her credit, because she is swearing this day to the fact, in opposition to the verdict of twelve men; she swore to it upon the prosecution, because of terror from her father, expecting to receive death from his hands, unless she warded it off by perjury. Have you not heard her swear that he forced her into the King's Bench with a knife in his hand? After he has failed to affect the life of the defendant, he makes a desperate attempt at his property, through the means of a jury—is this a case for a jury? She goes off unsolicited, she seeks the opportunity, and yet Mr. Kindillan is to be the victim! A young man who meets a woman, goes to a tavern, and indulges his appetites at the expense of the peace, quietness, and happiness of a family, you may wish to see reformed; but be he whose son he may, he cannot be punished in this way for such conduct. Will you lay your hands on your hearts and say, whether the defendant has been more to blame than Miss Egan herself? She has suffered much—her evidence shows it; at first from her terror of her father, now in preserving her consistency, to see her exposed as she was on the table. But has the defendant suffered nothing? Is it suffering nothing to be put in fear of his life? to have the horrors of a prison to encounter? Is it nothing, what he must have suffered in point of property? He comes now, to resist this last attempt, after all the others, to drive him, by robbing him of his property, to marry the daughter. Would you, gentlemen, advise your sons to marry under such circumstances? I put it boldly to you—answer it, and your answer will be your verdict. After ten weeks' voluntary cohabitation, would you advise him to marry? or would you ensure a reasonable prospect of conjugal fidelity afterwards? Let me not take up your time; we will call witnesses to discredit what she has sworn; let me say in excuse for her, for what she said upon her oath, that she came forward under the terror of her father's power. Certain it is, that a sense of female honour should not have had mòre influence upon her when in the other court, where she was vindicating herself, than here where she comes to put money into her father's pocket. The consequence of large damages is this: you will encourage every man to neglect the education of his child; making a fortune by dropping a seed of immorality in the mind of the female, which may ripen into that tree of enormity, that will be cut down, not to be cast into the fire, but for the father's benefit. A girl of eighteen, whose father forced her upon this table, whose sufferings have been brought upon her by the leprosy of her morals, is not to be countenanced. If you wish to point out the path to matrimony through dishonour, and you think it better that your daughter should be led to the altar from the brothel, than from the parent's arms, you may establish that by your verdict. If you think it better to let the unfortunate author of her own misery benefit by the example she may hold up, you will do it by such a verdict as your understanding, not your passion, dictates.

HAMILTON ROWAN.

29th January, 1794.

The Government proclamation, in the Autumn of '92, against the Volunteers who had assumed French forms, was answered by the United Irishmen, in an address, written by Dr. Drennan, and signed by Rowan, as secretary. For this, Rowan and Drennan were prosecuted. Rowan wanted Thomas Addis Emmet, and the Hon. Simon Butler, members of the society, to defend him; but they preferred Curran.

To the information Mr. Rowan pleaded issue—Not Guilty; and the court appointed Wednesday, the 29th day of January, 1794, for the trial of the said issue.

The Attorney-General (Arthur Wolfe) stated the case. The following passage from his statement describes the proclamation and meeting:—

"The troops are summoned to meet, the guards are summoned to assemble, and the first battalion of National Guards were to have paraded, clothed like Frenchmen. The night before, the Lord Lieutenant had summoned the council of the kingdom; upon that night a proclamation issued, stating that there were intentions to assemble men in arms, with seditious signs, and apprehending danger from their so assembling. It prohibited their meeting. The proclamation issued on a Saturday night, and it produced that satisfaction which all good men desirous of order seek to enjoy; and they felt once more the pleasurable assurance that they had a government. Appalled by this proclamation, the corps did not meet on the 8th December, as it was intended, though some few were seen dressed in the National Guard uniform, parading the streets, with a mob, crowding at their heels; but, however, nothing followed."

"A few days after—I am not aware of the particular day—but a few days after the issuing the proclamation, the society assembled. The proclamation was upon the 7th, the address I speak of was published the 16th of December; the meeting, therefore, must have been between the 7th and the 16th of December. The society, I say, assembled, and they agreed upon a certain address to the Volunteers of Ireland, and Dr. Drennan is there stated to have been in the chair and the traverser secretary. At that meeting the address to the Volunteers was agreed upon, which is the libel charged against Mr. Rowan, as being guilty of publishing it. Under that address, this was to be done. The Volunteers of Dublin were to be called into action, and those papers were to be dispersed among them. For that purpose, the several Volunteer corps at that time existing in Dublin were summoned to assemble in a house in Cope-street, belonging to Purdon, a fencing-master, upon the 16th of December. Accordingly upon that day, the several corps of Volunteers did go with side-arms to this fencing-school in Cope-street. The traverser was, I believe, at the head of one of these corps; another very celebrated name was at the head of another of them, James Napper Tandy. Who was at the head of the others I am not able to inform you. But in the afternoon of the 16th of December, several Volunteers, with uniforms and side-arms, assembled in the fencing-school. In this fencing-school, gentlemen, there was a gallery, and into that gallery there was such public access, that what passed below may be said to have passed in the face of the world."

Witnesses were examined, who fully connected Rowan with the document, and then CURRAN thus spoke for the defence:—

GENTLEMEN of the jury, when I consider the period at which this prosecution is brought forward; when I behold the extraordinary safe-guard of armed soldiers resorted to, no doubt for the preservation of peace and order;* when I catch, as I cannot but do, the throb of public anxiety which beats from one end to the other of this hall; when I reflect on what may be the fate of a man of the most beloved personal character, of one of the most respectable families of our country—himself the only individual of that family—I may almost say of that country—who can look to that possible fate with unconcern? Feeling, as I do, all these impressions, it is in the honest simplicity of my heart I speak, when I say, that I never rose in a court of justice with so much embarrassment as upon this occasion.

If, gentlemen, I could entertain a hope of finding refuge for the disconcertion of my mind in the perfect composure of yours—if I could suppose that those awful vicissitudes of human events, which have been stated or alluded to, could leave your judgment undisturbed, and your hearts at ease, I know I should form a most erroneous opinion of your character. I entertain no such chimerical hope—I form no such unworthy opinion. I expect not that your hearts can be more at ease than my own—I have no right to expect it; but I have a right to call upon you, in the name of your country, in the name of the living God, of whose eternal justice you are now administering that portion

* A few moments before Mr. Curran entered into his client's defence, a guard was brought into the Court-House by the Sheriff (Gifford).

which dwells with us on this side of the grave, to discharge your breasts, as far as you are able, of every bias of prejudice or passion, that if my client be guilty of the offence charged upon him, you may give tranquillity to the public, by a firm verdict of conviction; or, if he be innocent, by as firm a verdict of acquittal; and that you will do this in defiance of the paltry artifices and senseless clamours that have been resorted to, in order to bring him to his trial with anticipated conviction. And, gentlemen, I feel an additional necessity in thus conjuring you to be upon your guard, from the able and imposing statement which you have just heard on the part of the prosecution. I know well the virtues and talents of the excellent person who conducts that prosecution;* I know how much he would disdain to impose on you by the trappings of office; but I also know how easily we mistake the lodgment which character and eloquence can make upon our feelings, for those impressions that reason, and fact, and proof, only ought to work upon our understandings.

Perhaps, gentlemen, I shall act not unwisely in waiving any further observation of this sort, and giving your minds an opportunity of growing cool and resuming themselves, by coming to a calm and uncoloured statement of mere facts, premising only to you, that I have it in strictest injunction from my client, to defend him upon facts and evidence

* The late Lord Kilwarden, then Attorney-General Wolfe.

only, and to avail myself of no technical artifice or subtlety that could withdraw his cause from the test of that inquiry which it is your province to exercise, and to which only he wishes to be indebted for an acquittal.

In the month of December, 1792, Mr. Rowan was arrested on an information, charging him with the offence for which he is now on his trial. He was taken before an honourable personage now on that bench, and admitted to bail.*

He remained a considerable time in this city, soliciting the present prosecution, and offering himself to a fair trial by a jury of his country. But it was not then thought fit to yield to that solicitation; nor has it now been thought proper to prosecute him in the ordinary way, by sending up a bill of indictment to a grand jury.

I do not mean by this to say that informations *ex-officio* are always oppressive or unjust;† but I cannot but observe to you, that when a petty jury is called upon to try a charge not previously found by the grand inquest, and supported by the naked assertion only of the King's prosecutor, that the accusation labours under a weakness of probability which it is difficult to assist. If the charge had no cause of dreading the light—if it was likely to find the sanction of a grand jury—it is not easy

* The Honourable Justice Downes, afterwards Lord Downes, and Chief Justice of the King's Bench.

† M'Nally notes that in Curran's private opinion they were.

to account why it deserted the more usual, the more popular, and the more constitutional mode, and preferred to come forward in the ungracious form of an *ex-officio* information.

If such a bill had been sent up and found, Mr. Rowan would have been tried at the next commission; but a speedy trial was not the wish of his prosecutors. An information was filed, and when he expected to be tried upon it, an error, it seems, was discovered in the record. Mr. Rowan offered to waive it, or consent to any amendment desired. No, that proposal could not be accepted: a trial must have followed. That information, therefore, was withdrawn, and a new one filed; that is, in fact, a third prosecution was instituted upon the same charge. This last was filed on the 18th day of last July.

Gentlemen, these facts cannot fail of a due impression upon you. You will find a material part of your inquiry must be, whether Mr. Rowan is pursued as a criminal, or hunted down as a victim. It is not, therefore, by insinuation or circuity, but it is boldly and directly that I assert, that oppression has been intended and practised upon him, and by those facts which I have stated, I am warranted in the assertion.

His demand, his entreaty to be tried, was refused, and why? A hue and cry was to be raised against him; the sword was to be suspended over his head; some time was necessary for the public mind to become heated by the circulation of artful clamours of anarchy and rebellion: these same clamours which, with more probability, but not more success, had been circulated before through England and Scotland. In this country the causes and the swiftness of their progress were as obvious as their folly has since become, to every man of the smallest observation. I have been stopped myself with—"Good God, sir, have you heard the news?" "No, sir, what?" "Why one French emissary was seen travelling through Connaught in a post chaise, and scattering from the window, as he passed, little doses of political poison, made up in square bits of paper; another was actually surprised in the fact of seducing our good people from their allegiance, by discourses upon the indivisibility of French robbery and massacre, which he preached in the French language, to a congregation of Irish peasants."

Such are the bugbears and spectres to be raised to warrant the sacrifice of whatever little public spirit may remain amongst us. But time has also detected the imposture of these "Cock-lane apparitions;" and you cannot now, with your eyes open, give a verdict, without asking your consciences this question:—Is this a fair and honest prosecution? is it brought forward with the single view of vindicating public justice, and promoting public good? And here let me remind you, that you are not convened to try the guilt of libel, affecting the personal character of any private man. I know no case in which a jury ought to be more severe, than where personal calumny is conveyed through a vehicle which ought to be consecrated to public information. Neither, on the other hand, can I conceive any case in which the firmness and the caution of a jury should be more exerted, than when a subject is prosecuted for a libel on the state. The peculiarity of the British constitution (to which, in its fullest extent, we have an undoubted right; however distant we may be from the actual enjoyment), and in which it surpasses every known government in Europe, is this, that its only professed object is the general good, and its only foundation the general will: hence the people have a right, acknowledged from time immemorial, fortified by a pile of statutes, and authenticated by a revolution that speaks louder than them all, to see whether abuses have been committed, and whether their properties and their liberties have been attended to as they ought to be.

This is a kind of subject by which I feel myself overawed when I approach it; there are certain fundamental principles which nothing but necessity should expose to public examination; they are pillars, the depth of whose foundation you cannot explore, without endangering their strength; but let it be recollected, that the discussion of such subjects should not be condemned in me, nor visited upon my client: the blame, if any there be, should rest only with those who have forced them into discussion. I say, therefore, it is the right of the people to keep an eternal watch upon the conduct of their rulers; and in order to that, the freedom of the press has been cherished by the law of England. In private defamation, let it never be tolerated; in wicked and wanton aspersion upon a good and honest administration, let it never be supported. Not that a good government can be exposed to danger by groundless accusation, but because a bad government is sure to find, in the detected falsehood of a licentious press, a security and a credit, which it could never otherwise obtain.

I said a good government cannot be endangered; I say so again; for whether it be good or bad, it can never depend upon assertion: the question is decided by simple inspection; to try the tree, look at its fruit: to judge of the government, look at the people. What is the fruit of a good government? the virtue and happiness of the people. Do four millions of people in this country gather those fruits from that government, to whose injured purity, to whose spotless virtue and violated honour this seditious and atrocious libeller is to be immolated upon the altar of the constitution? To you, gentlemen of the jury, who are bound by the most sacred obligation to your country, and your God, to speak nothing but the truth, I put the question—do the people of this country gather those fruits?—are they orderly, industrious, religious, and contented?—do you find them free from bigotry and ignorance, those inseparable concomitants of systematic oppression? Or, to try them by a test as unerring as any of the former, are they united? The period has now elapsed in which considerations of this extent would have been deemed improper to a jury: happily for these countries, the legislature of each has lately changed, or, perhaps to speak more properly, revived and restored the law respecting trials of this kind.* For the space of thirty or forty years, a usage had prevailed in Westminster hall, by which the judges assumed to themselves the decision of the question, whether libel or not; but the learned counsel for the prosecution is now obliged to admit that this is a question for the jury only to decide. You will naturally listen with respect to the opinion of the court, but you will receive it as a matter of advice, not as a matter of law; and you will give it credit, not from any adventitious circumstances of authority, but merely so far as it meets the concurrence of your own understandings.

Give me leave now to state the charge, as it stands upon the record: it is, "that Mr. Rowan, being a person of a wicked and turbulent disposition, and maliciously designing and intending to

* Erskine and Fox procured this amendment, or restoration of the law of libel.

excite and diffuse among the subjects of this realm of Ireland, discontents, jealousies, and suspicions of our Lord the King and his government, and disaffection and disloyalty to the person and government of our said Lord the King, and to raise very dangerous seditions and tumults within this kingdom of Ireland, and to draw the government of this kingdom into great scandal, infamy, and disgrace, and to incite the subjects of our said Lord the King, to attempt, by force and violence, and with arms, to make alterations in the government, state, and constitution of this kingdom, and to incite his Majesty's said subjects to tumult and anarchy, and to overturn the established constitution of this kingdom, and to overawe and intimidate the legislature of this kingdom by an armed force;" did "maliciously and seditiously" publish the paper in question.

Gentlemen, without any observation of mine, you must see that this information contains a direct charge upon Mr. Rowan; namely, that he did, with the intents set forth in the information, publish this paper; so that here you have, in fact, two or three questions for your decision. First, the matter of fact of the publication; namely, did Mr. Rowan publish that paper? If Mr. Rowan did not in fact publish that paper, you have no longer any question on which to employ your minds: if you think that he was in fact the publisher, then, and not till then, arises the great and important subject to which your judgments must be directed. And that comes shortly and simply to this. Is the paper a libel? and did he publish it with the intent charged in the information? For, whatever you may think of the abstract question, whether the paper be libellous or not, and of which paper it has not even been insinuated that he is the author, there can be no ground for a verdict against him, unless you also are persuaded that what he did was done with a criminal design.

I wish, gentlemen, to simplify, and not to perplex; I therefore say again, if these three circumstances conspire, that he published it, that it was a libel, and that it was published with the purposes alleged in the information, you ought unquestionably to find him guilty: if, on the other hand, you do not find that all these circumstances concurred; if you cannot upon your oaths say that he published it: if it be not in your opinion a libel; and if he did not publish it with the intention alleged: I say, upon the failure of any one of these points, my client is entitled, in justice, and upon your oaths, to a verdict of acquittal.

Gentlemen, Mr. Attorney-General has thought proper to direct your attention to the state and circumstances of public affairs at the time of this transaction; let me also make a few retrospective observations on a period at which he has but slightly glanced; I speak of the events which took place before the close of the American war.

You know, gentlemen, that France had espoused the cause of America, and we became thereby engaged in a war with that nation.

"Heu nescia mens hominum futuri!"

Little did that ill-fated monarch know that he was forming the first causes of those disastrous events, that were to end in the subversion of his throne, in the slaughter of his family, and the deluging of his country with the blood of his people. You cannot but remember that, at a time when we had scarcely a regular soldier for our defence, when the old and young were alarmed and terrified with apprehensions of descent upon our coasts, that Providence seemed to have worked a sort of miracle in our favour. You saw a band of armed men come forth at the great call of nature, of honour, and their country. You saw men of the greatest wealth and rank; you saw every class of the community give up its members, and send them armed into the field, to protect the public and private tranquillity of Ireland. It is impossible for any man to turn back to that period, without reviving those sentiments of tenderness and gratitude, which then beat in the public bosom; to recollect amidst what applause, what tears, what prayers, what benedictions, they walked forth amongst spectators, agitated by the mingled sensations of terror and of reliance, of danger and of protection, imploring the blessings of heaven upon their heads, and its conquest upon their swords.

That illustrious, and adored, and *abused* body of men, stood forward and assumed the title, which I trust the ingratitude of their country will never blot from its history, — "THE VOLUNTEERS OF IRELAND."

Give me leave now, with great respect, to put this question to you:—Do you think the assembling of that glorious band of patriots was an insurrection? Do you think the invitation to that assembling would have been sedition? They came under no commission but the call of their country; unauthorized and unsanctioned, except by public emergency and public danger. I ask, was that meeting insurrection or not? I put another question:—If any man then had published a call on that body, and stated that war was declared against the state; that the regular troops were withdrawn; that our coasts were hovered round by the ships of the enemy; that the moment was approaching, when the unprotected feebleness of age and sex, when the sanctity of habitation, would be disregarded and profaned by the brutal ferocity of a rude invader; if any man had then said to them— "Leave your industry for a while, that you may return to it again, and come forth in arms for the public defence:" I put the question boldly to you (it is not the case of the Volunteers of that day; it is the case of my client at this hour, which I put to you), would that call have been then pronounced in a court of justice, or by a jury on their oaths, a criminal and seditious invitation to insurrection? If it would not have been so then, upon what principle can it be so now? What is the force and perfection of the law? It is, the permanency of the law; it is, that whenever the fact is the same, the law is also the same; it is, that the letter remains written, monumented and recorded, to pronounce the same decision, upon the same facts, whenever they shall arise. I will not affect to conceal it: you know there has been artful, ungrateful, and blasphemous clamour raised against these illustrious characters, the saviours of the king of Ireland. Having mentioned this, let me read a few words of the paper alleged to be criminal: "You first took up arms to protect your country from foreign enemies, and from domestic disturbance. For the same purposes, it now becomes necessary that you should resume them."

I should be the last man in the world to impute any want of candour to the right honourable gentleman, who has stated the case on behalf of the prosecution; but he has certainly fallen into a mistake, which, if not explained, might be highly injurious to my client. He supposed that this publication was not addressed to those ancient volunteers, but to new combinations of them, formed upon new principles, and actuated by different motives. You have the words to which this construction is imputed upon the record; the meaning of his mind can be collected only from those words which he has made use of to convey it. The guilt imputable to him can only be inferred from the meaning ascribable to those words. Let his meaning then be fairly collected by resorting to them. Is there a foundation to suppose that this address was directed to any such body of men as has been called a banditti (with what justice it is unnecessary to inquire), and not to the old Volunteers?

As to the sneer at the words *citizen soldiers*, I should feel that I was treating a very respected friend with an insidious and unmerited kindness, if I affected to expose it by any gravity of refutation. I may, however, be permitted to observe, that those who are supposed to have disgraced this expression by adopting it, have taken it from the idea of the British constitution, "that no man in becoming a soldier ceases to be a citizen." Would to God, all enemies as they are, that that unfortunate people had borrowed more from that sacred source of liberty and virtue; and would to God, for the sake of humanity, that they had preserved even the little they did borrow! If ever there could be an objection to that appellation, it must have been strongest when it was first assumed.* To that period the writer manifestly alludes; he addresses "those who first took up arms." "You

* In the resolutions and addresses of the old Volunteers, at and prior to 1783, the terms *citizen soldiers* and *citizen soldiery*, were no uncommon appellations.

first took up arms to protect your country from foreign enemies and from domestic disturbance. For the same purposes, it now becomes necessary that you should resume them." Is this applicable to those who had never taken up arms before? "A proclamation", says this paper, "has been issued in England for embodying the militia, and a proclamation has been issued by the Lord Lieutenant and Council of Ireland, for repressing all seditious associations. In consequence of both these proclamations, it is reasonable to apprehend danger from abroad, and danger at home." God help us from the situation of Europe at that time; we were threatened with too probable danger from abroad, and I am afraid it was not without foundation we were told of our having something to dread at home.

I find much abuse has been lavished on the disrespect with which the proclamation is treated, in that part of the paper alleged to be a libel. To that my answer for my client is short: I do conceive it competent to a British subject, if he thinks that a proclamation has issued for the purpose of raising false terrors; I hold it to be not only the privilege, but the duty of a citizen, to set his countrymen right, with respect to such misrepresented danger; and until a proclamation in this country shall have the force of law, the reason and grounds of it are surely at least questionable by the people. Nay, I will go farther; if an actual law had passed, receiving the sanction of the three estates, if it be exceptionable in any matter, it is warrantable to any man in the community to state, in a becoming manner, his ideas upon it. And I should be at a loss to know, if the positive laws of Great Britain are thus questionable, upon what grounds the proclamation of an Irish government should not be open to the animadversion of Irish subjects.

"Whatever be the motive, or from whatever quarter it arises," says this paper, "alarm has arisen." Gentlemen, do you not know that to be fact? It has been stated by the Attorney-General, and most truly, that the most gloomy apprehensions were entertained by the whole country. "You, Volunteers of Ireland, are therefore summoned to arms, at the instance of government, as well as by the responsibility attached to your character, and the permanent obligations of your institution." I am free to confess, if any man, assuming the liberties of a British subject to question public topics, should, under the mask of that privilege, publish a proclamation, inviting the profligate and seditious, those in want, and those in despair, to rise up in arms to overawe the legislature—to rob us of whatever portion of the blessing of a free government we possess; I know of no offence involving greater enormity. But that, gentlemen, is the question you are to try. If my client acted with an honest mind and fair intention, and having, as he believed, the authority of government to support him in the idea that danger was to be apprehended, did apply to that body of so known and so revered a character, calling upon them by their former honour, the principles of their glorious institution, and the great stake they possessed in their country: if he interposed, not upon a fictitious pretext, but a real belief of actual and imminent danger, and that their arming at that critical moment was necessary to the safety of their country, his intention was not only innocent, but highly meritorious. It is a question, gentlemen, upon which you only can decide; it is for you to say, whether it was criminal in the defendant to be misled, and whether he is to fall a sacrifice to the prosecution of that government by which he was so deceived. I say again, gentlemen, you can look only to his own words as the interpreters of his meaning; and to the state and circumstances of his country, as he was made to believe them, as the clue to his intention. The case, then, gentlemen, is shortly and simply this; a man of the first family, and fortune, and character, and property among you reads a proclamation, stating the country to be in danger from abroad, and at home; and, thus alarmed, thus, upon the authority of the prosecutor, alarmed, applies to that august body, before whose awful presence sedition must vanish, and insurrection disappear. You must surrender, I hesitate not to say, your oaths to unfounded assertion, if you can submit to say, that such an act, of such a man, so warranted, is a wicked and seditious libel.

If he was a dupe, let me ask you, who was the impostor? I blush and shrink with shame and detestation from that meanness of dupery and servile complaisance, which could make that dupe a victim to the accusation of an impostor.

You perceive, gentlemen, that I am going into the merits of this publication before I apply myself to the question which is first in order of time, namely, whether the publication, in point of fact, is to be ascribed to Mr. Rowan or not. I have been unintentionally led into this violation of order. I should effect no purpose of either brevity or clearness, by returning to the more methodical course of observation. I have been naturally drawn from it by the superior importance of the topic I am upon, namely, the merit of the publication in question.

This publication, if ascribed at all to Mr. Rowan, contains four distinct subjects: the first, the invitation to the volunteers to arm: upon that I have already observed; but those that remain are surely of much importance, and, no doubt, are prosecuted, as equally criminal. The paper next states the necessity of a reform in parliament: it states, thirdly, the necessity of an emancipation of the Catholic inhabitants of Ireland; and, as necessary to the the achievement of all these objects, does, fourthly, state the necessity of a general delegated convention of the people.

It has been alleged, that Mr. Rowan intended

by this publication, to excite the subjects of this country to effect an alteration in the form of your constitution. And here, gentlemen, perhaps you may not be unwilling to follow a little farther than Mr. Attorney-General has done, the idea of a late prosecution in Great Britain, upon the subject of a public libel. It is with peculiar fondness I look to that country for solid principles of constitutional liberty and judicial example. You have been pressed in no small degree with the manner in which this publication marks the different orders of our constitution, and comments upon them. Let me show you what boldness of animadversion of such topics is thought justifiable in the British nation, and by a British jury. I have in my hand the report of the trial of the printers of the *Morning Chronicle*, for a supposed libel against the state, and of their acquittal; let me read to you some passages from that publication, which a jury of Englishmen were in vain called upon to brand with the name of libel:—

"Claiming it as our indefeasible right to associate together, in a peaceable and friendly manner, for the communication of thoughts, the formation of opinions, and to promote the general happiness, we think it unnecessary to offer any apology for inviting you to join us in this manly and benevolent pursuit; the necessity of the inhabitants of every community endeavouring to procure a true knowledge of their rights, their duties, and their interests, will not be denied, except by those who are the slaves of prejudice, or interested in the continuation of abuses. As men who wish to aspire to the title of freemen, we totally deny the wisdom and the humanity of the advice, to approach the defects of government with 'pious awe and trembling solicitude.' What better doctrine could the pope or the tyrants of Europe desire? We think, therefore, that the cause of truth and justice can never be hurt by temperate and honest discussions; and that cause which will not bear such a scrutiny, must be systematically or practically bad. We are sensible that those who are not friends to the general good, have attempted to inflame the public mind with the cry of 'Danger,' whenever men have associated for discussing the principles of government; and we have little doubt but such conduct will be pursued in this place; we would therefore caution every honest man, who has really the welfare of the nation at heart, to avoid being led away by the prostituted clamours of those who live on the sources of corruption. We pity the fears of the timorous, and we are totally unconcerned respecting the false alarms of the venal.

"We view with concern the frequency of wars. We are persuaded that the interests of the poor can never be promoted by accession of territory, when bought at the expense of their labour and blood; and we must say, in the language of a celebrated author, 'We, who are only the people, but who pay for wars with our substance and our blood, will not cease to tell kings,' or governments, 'that to them alone wars are profitable; that the true and just conquests are those which each makes at home, by comforting the peasantry, by promoting agriculture and manufactures, by multiplying men and the other productions of nature; that then it is that kings may call themselves the image of God, whose will is perpetually directed to the creation of new beings. If they continue to make us fight, and kill one another in uniform, we will continue to write and speak, until nations shall be cured of this folly.

"We are certain our present heavy burdens are owing, in a great measure, to cruel and impolitic wars, and therefore we will do all on our part, as peaceable citizens, who have the good of the community at heart to enlighten each other, and protest against them.

"The present state of the representation of the people calls for the particular attention of every man who has humanity sufficient to feel for the honour and happiness of his country, to the defects and corruptions of which we are inclined to attribute unnecessary wars, &c. We think it a deplorable case when the poor must support a corruption which is calculated to oppress them; when the labourer must give his money to afford the means of preventing him having a voice in its disposal; when the lower classes may say—'We give you our money, for which we have toiled and sweat, and which would save our families from cold and hunger; but we think it more hard that there is nobody whom we have delegated, to see that it is not improperly and wickedly spent: we have none to watch over our interests; the rich only are represented.' An equal and uncorrupt representation would, we are persuaded, save us from heavy expenses, and deliver us from many oppressions; we will therefore do our duty to procure this reform, which appears to us of the utmost importance.

"In short, we see, with the most lively concern, an army of placemen, pensioners, &c., fighting in the cause of corruption and prejudice, and spreading the contagion far and wide.

"We see, with equal sensibility, the present outcry against reforms, and a proclamation (tending to cramp the liberty of the press, and discredit the true friends of the people), receiving the support of numbers of our countrymen.

"We see burdens multiplied, the lower classes sinking into poverty, disgrace, and excesses, and the means of those shocking abuses increased for the purpose of revenue.

"We ask ourselves, 'Are we in England?' Have our forefathers fought, bled, and conquered for liberty? And did they not think that the fruits of their patriotism would be more abundant in peace, plenty, and happiness?

"Is the condition of the poor never to be improved?

"Great Britain must have arrived at the highest degree of national happiness and prosperity, and our situation must be too good to be mended, or the present outcry against reform and improvements is inhuman and criminal. But we hope our condition will be speedily improved, and to obtain so desirable a good, is the object of our present association: an union founded on principles of benevolence and humanity; disclaiming all connexion with riots and disorder, but firm in our purpose, and warm in our affections for liberty.

"Lastly, we invite the friends of freedom throughout Great Britain to form similar societies, and to act with unanimity and firmness, till the people be too wise to be imposed upon; and their influence in the government be commensurate with their dignity and importance. *Then shall we be free and happy.*"

Such, gentlemen, is the language which a subject of Great Britain thinks himself warranted to hold, and upon such language has the corroborating sanction of a British jury been stamped by a verdict of acquittal. Such was the honest and manly freedom of publication; in a country, too, where the complaint of abuses has not half the foundation it has here. I said I loved to look to England for principles of judicial example; I cannot but say to you that it depends on your spirit, whether I shall look to it hereafter with sympathy or with shame. Be pleased, now, gentlemen, to consider whether the statement of the imperfection in your representation has been made with a desire of inflaming an attack upon the public tranquillity, or with an honest purpose of procuring a remedy for an actually existing grievance.

It is impossible not to revert to the situation of the times; and let me remind you, that whatever observations of this kind I am compelled thus to make in a court of justice, the uttering of them in this place is not imputable to my client, but to the necessity of defence imposed upon him by this extraordinary prosecution.

Gentlemen, the representation of our people is the vital principle of their political existence; without it they are dead, or they live only to servitude; without it there are two estates acting upon and against the third, instead of acting in co-operation with it; without it, if the people are oppressed by their judges, where is the tribunal to which their judges can be amenable? without it, if they are trampled upon and plundered by a minister, where is the tribunal to which the offender shall be amenable? without it, where is the ear to hear, or the heart to feel, or the hand to redress their sufferings? Shall they be found, let me ask you, in the accursed bands of imps and minions that bask in their disgrace, and fatten upon their spoils, and flourish upon their ruin? But let me not put this to you as a merely speculative question. It is a plain question of fact: rely upon it, physical man is everywhere the same; it is only the various operations of moral causes that gives variety to the social or individual character and condition. How otherwise happens it that modern slavery looks quietly at the despot, on the very spot where Leonidas expired? The answer is, Sparta has not changed her climate, but she has lost that government, which her liberty could not survive.

I call you, therefore, to the plain question of fact. This paper recommends a reform in parliament: I put that question to your consciences; do you think it needs that reform? I put it boldly and fairly to you, do you think the people of Ireland are represented as they ought to be? Do you hesitate for an answer? If you do, let me remind you, that until the last year, three millions of your countrymen have, by the express letter of the law, been excluded from the reality of actual, and even from the phantom of virtual representation. Shall we then be told that this is only the affirmation of a wicked and seditious incendiary? If you do not feel the mockery of such a charge, look at your country; in what state do you find it? Is it in a state of tranquillity and general satisfaction. These are traces by which good are ever to be distinguished from bad governments, without any very minute inquiry or speculative refinement. Do you feel that a veneration for the law, a pious and humble attachment to the constitution, form the political morality of the people? Do you find that comfort and competency among your people, which are always to be found where a government is mild and moderate, where taxes are imposed by a body who have an interest in treating the poorer orders with compassion, and preventing the weight of taxation from pressing sore upon them?

Gentlemen, I mean not to impeach the state of your representation; I am not saying that it is defective, or that it ought to be altered or amended; nor is this a place for me to say, whether I think that three millions of the inhabitants of a country whose whole number is but four, ought to be admitted to any efficient situation in the state. It may be said, and truly, that these are not questions for either of us directly to decide, but you cannot refuse them some passing consideration at least; when you remember that on this subject the real question for your decision is, whether the allegation of a defect in your constitution is so utterly unfounded and false, that you can ascribe it only to the malice and perverseness of a wicked mind, and not to the innocent mistake of an ordinary understanding; whether it may not be mistake; whether it can be only sedition.

And here, gentlemen, I own I cannot but regret,

that one of our countrymen should be criminally pursued, for asserting the necessity of a reform, at the very moment when that necessity seems admitted by the parliament itself; that this unhappy reform shall, at the same moment, be a subject of legislative discussion and criminal prosecution. Far am I from imputing any sinister design to the virtue or wisdom of our government; but who can avoid feeling the deplorable impression that must be made on the public mind, when the demand for that reform is answered by a criminal information!

I am the more forcibly impressed by this consideration, when I consider, that when this information was first put on the file, the subject was transiently mentioned in the House of Commons. Some circumstances retarded the progress of the inquiry there, and the progress of the information was equally retarded here. On the first day of this session, you all know, that subject was again brought forward in the House of Commons, and, as if they had slept together, this prosecution was also revived in the Court of King's Bench, and that before a jury taken from a panel partly composed of those very members of parliament, who, in the House of Commons, must debate upon this subject as a measure of public advantage, which they are here called upon to consider as a public crime.*

* The names of several members of parliament were included in the panel.

This paper, gentlemen, insists upon the necessity of emancipating the Catholics of Ireland, and that is charged as part of the libel. If they had waited another year, if they had kept this prosecution impending for another year, how much would remain for a jury to decide upon, I should be at a loss to discover. It seems as if the progress of public information was eating away the ground of the prosecution. Since the commencement of the prosecution, this part of the libel has unluckily received the sanction of the legislature. In that interval our Catholic brethren have obtained that admission, which, it seems, it was a libel to propose; in what way to account for this, I am really at a loss. Have any alarms been occasioned by the emancipation of our Catholic brethren? has the bigoted malignity of any individuals been crushed? or has the stability of the government, or that of the country been weakened; or is one million of subjects stronger than four millions? Do you think that the benefit they received should be poisoned by the sting of vengeance? If you think so, you must say to them—"You have demanded emancipation, and you have got it; but we abhor your persons, we are outraged at your success, and we will stigmatize by a criminal prosecution the adviser of that relief which you have obtained from the voice of your country." I ask you, do you think, as honest men, anxious for the public tranquillity, conscious that there are wounds not yet completely cicatrized, that you ought to speak this language at this time, to men who are too much disposed to think that in this very emancipation they have been saved from their own parliament by the humanity of their sovereign? Or do you wish to prepare them for the revocation of these improvident concessions? Do you think it wise or humane at this moment to insult them, by sticking up in a pillory the man who dared to stand forth as their advocate? I put it to your oaths; do you think that a blessing of that kind, that a victory obtained by justice over bigotry and oppression, should have a stigma cast upon it by an ignominious sentence upon men bold and honest enough to propose that measure? to propose the redeeming of religion from the abuses of the church, the reclaiming of three millions of men from bondage, and giving liberty to all who had a right to demand it; giving, I say, in the so much censured words of this paper, giving "UNIVERSAL EMANCIPATION!" I speak in the spirit of the British law, which makes liberty commensurate with, and inseparable from British soil; which proclaims even to the stranger and sojourner, the moment he sets his foot upon British earth, that the ground on which he treads is holy, and consecrated by the genius of UNIVERSAL EMANCIPATION. No matter in what language his doom may have been pronounced; no matter what complexion incompatible with freedom, an Indian or an African sun may have burnt upon him; no matter in what disastrous battle his liberty may have been cloven down; no matter with what solemnities he may have been devoted upon the altar of slavery; the first moment he touches the sacred soil of Britain, the altar and the god sink together in the dust; his soul walks abroad in her own majesty; his body swells beyond the measure of his chains, that burst from around him; and he stands redeemed, regenerated, and disenthralled, by the irresistible genius of UNIVERSAL EMANCIPATION.

A sudden burst of applause from the court and hall, which was repeated for a considerable length of time, interrupted Mr. CURRAN. Silence being at length restored, he proceeded:—

Gentlemen, I am not such a fool as to ascribe any effusion of this sort to any merit of mine. It is the mighty theme, and not the inconsiderable advocate, that can excite interest in the hearer. What you hear is but the testimony which nature bears to her own character; it is the effusion of her gratitude to that Power which stamped that character upon her.

And permit me to say, that if my client had occasion to defend his cause by any mad or drunken appeals to extravagance or licentiousness, I trust in God I stand in that situation that, humble as I am, he would not have resorted to me to be his advocate. I was not recommended to his choice by any connexion of principle or party, or even private friendship; and saying this, I cannot but add, that I consider not to be acquainted with such a man as Mr. Rowan, a want of personal good fortune. But upon this great subject of reform and emancipation, there is a latitude and boldness of remark, justifiable in the people, and necessary to the defence of Mr. Rowan, for which the habits of professional studies, and technical adherence to established forms, have rendered me unfit. It is, however, my duty, standing here as his advocate, to make some few observations to you which I conceive to be material.

Gentlemen, you are sitting in a country which has a right to the British constitution, and which is bound by an indissoluble union with the British nation. If you were now even at liberty to debate upon that subject; if you even were not, by the most solemn compacts, founded upon the authority of your ancestors and of yourselves, bound to that alliance, and had an election now to make; in the present unhappy state of Europe, if you had been heretofore a stranger to Great Britain, you would now say—We will enter into society and union with you:—

"Una salus ambobus erit, commune periculum."

But to accomplish that union, let me tell you, you must learn to become like the English people. It is vain to say you will protect their freedom, if you abandon your own. The pillar whose base has no foundation, can give no support to the dome under which its head is placed; and if you profess to give England that assistance which you refuse to yourselves, she will laugh at your folly, and despise your meanness and insincerity. Let us follow this a little further—I know you will interpret what I say with the candour in which it is spoken. England is marked by a natural avarice of freedom, which she is studious to engross and accumulate, but most unwilling to impart; whether from any necessity of her policy, or from her weakness, or from her pride, I will not presume to say, but so is the fact; you need not look to ourselves.

In order to confirm this observation, I would appeal to what fell from the learned counsel for the crown,—"that notwithstanding the alliance subsisting for two centuries past between the two countries, the date of liberty in one goes no further back than the year 1782."

If it required additional confirmation, I should state the case of the invaded American, and the subjugated Indian, to prove that the policy of England has ever been, to govern her connexions more as colonies than as allies; and it must be owing to the great spirit indeed of Ireland, if she shall continue free. Rely upon it, she will ever have to hold her course against an adverse current; rely upon it, if the popular spring does not continue strong and elastic, a short interval of debilitated nerve and broken force will send you down the stream again, and re-consign you to the condition of a province.

If such should become the fate of your constitution, ask yourselves what must be the motive of your government? It is easier to govern a province by a faction, than to govern a co-ordinate country by co-ordinate means. I do not say it is now, but it will always be thought easiest by the managers of the day, to govern the Irish nation by the agency of such a faction, as long as this country shall be found willing to let her connexion with Great Britain be preserved only by her own degradation. In such a precarious and wretched state of things, if it shall ever be found to exist, the true friend of Irish liberty and British connexion will see, that the only means of saving both must be, as Lord Chatham expressed it, "the infusion of new health and blood into the constitution." He will see how deep a stake each country has in the liberty of the other; he will see what a bulwark he adds to the common cause, by giving England a co-ordinate and interested ally, instead of an oppressed, enfeebled, and suspected dependant; he will see how grossly the credulity of Britain is abused by those who make her believe that her interest is promoted by our depression; he will see the desperate precipice to which she approaches by such conduct; and with an animated and generous piety, he will labour to avert her danger.

But, gentlemen of the jury, what is likely to be his fate? The interest of the sovereign must be for ever the interest of his people, because his interest lives beyond his life: it must live in his fame; it must live in the tenderness of his solicitude for an unborn posterity; it must live in that heart-attaching bond, by which millions of men have united the destinies of themselves and their children with his, and call him by the endearing appellation of king and father of his people.

But what can be the interest of such a government as I have described? Not the interest of the king—not the interest of the people; but the sordid interest of the hour; the interest in deceiving the one, and in oppressing and defaming the other; the interest of unpunished rapine and unmerited favour: that odious and abject interest, that prompts them to extinguish public spirit in punishment or in bribe, and to pursue every man, even to death, who has sense to see, and firmness enough to abhor and to oppose them. What, therefore, I say, will be the fate of the man who embarks in an enterprise of so much difficulty and danger? I will not answer it. Upon that hazard has my client put every thing that can be dear to man, his fame, his fortune, his person, his liberty, and his children; but with what event your verdict only can answer, and to that I refer your country.

There is a fourth point remaining. Says this paper,—"For both these purposes, it appears necessary that provincial conventions should assemble, preparatory to the convention of the Protestant people. The delegates of the Catholic body are not justified in communicating with individuals, or even bodies, of inferior authority; and therefore an assembly of a similar nature and organization is necessary to establish an intercourse of sentiment, an uniformity of conduct, an united cause, and an united nation. If a convention on the one part does not soon follow, and is not soon connected with that on the other, the common cause will split into the partial interests; the people will relax into inattention and inertness; the union of affection and exertion will dissolve; and, too probably, some local insurrection, instigated by the malignity of our common enemy, may commit the character, and risk the tranquillity of the island, which can be obviated only by the influence of an assembly arising from, and assimilated with the people, and whose spirit may be, as it were, knit with the soul of the nation. Unless the sense of the Protestant people be, on their part, as fairly collected and as judiciously directed; unless individual exertion consolidates into collective strength; unless the particles unite into one mass, we may perhaps serve some person or some party for a little, but the public not at all. The nation is neither insolent, nor rebellious, nor seditious; while it knows its rights, it is unwilling to manifest its powers; it would rather supplicate the administration to anticipate revolution by well-timed reform, and to save their country to themselves."

Gentlemen, it is with something more than

common reverence, it is with a species of terror that I am obliged to tread this ground. But what is the idea, put in the strongest point of view? We are willing not to manifest our powers, but to supplicate administration to anticipate revolution, that the legislature may save the country, in mercy to itself.

Let me suggest to you, gentlemen, that there are some circumstances, which have happened in the history of this country, that may better serve as a comment upon this part of the case, than any I can make. I am not bound to defend Mr. Rowan, as to the truth or wisdom of the opinions he may have formed. But if he did really conceive the situation of the country such, as that the not redressing her grievances might lead to a convulsion; and of such an opinion not even Mr. Rowan is answerable here for the wisdom, much less shall I insinuate any idea of my own upon so awful a subject; but if he did so conceive the fact to be, and acted from the fair and honest suggestion of a mind anxious for the public good, I must confess, gentlemen, I do not know in what part of the British constitution to find the principle of his criminality.

But, be pleased further to consider, that he cannot be understood to put the fact on which he argues on the authority of his assertion. The condition of Ireland was as open to the observation of every other man, as to that of Mr. Rowan. What then, does this part of the publication amount to? In my mind, simply to this:

"The nature of oppression in all countries is such, that although it may be borne to a certain degree, it cannot be borne beyond that degree. You find that exemplified in Great Britain; you find the people of England patient to a certain point, but patient no longer. That infatuated monarch, James II., experienced this. The time did come, when the measure of popular sufferings and popular patience was full—when a single drop was sufficient to make the waters of bitterness to overflow. I think this measure in Ireland is brimful at present; I think the state of the representation of the people in parliament is a grievance; I think the utter exclusion of three millions of people is a grievance of that kind, that the people are not likely long to endure, and the continuation of which may plunge the country into that state of despair, which wrongs, exasperated by perseverance, never fail to produce." But to whom is even this language addressed? Not to the body of the people on whose temper and moderation, if once excited, perhaps not much confidence could be placed; but to that authoritative body, whose influence and power would have restrained the excesses of the irritable and tumultuous, and for that purpose expressly does this publication address the Volunteers.

"We are told that we are in danger. I call upon you, the great constitutional saviours of Ireland, to defend the country to which you have given political existence, and to use whatever sanction your great name, your sacred character, and the weight you have in the community, must give you, to repress wicked designs, if any there are. We feel ourselves strong—the people are always strong; the public chains can only be rivetted by the public hands. Look to those devoted regions of southern despotism: behold the expiring victim on his knees, presenting the javelin, reeking with his blood, to the ferocious monster who returns it into his heart. Call not that monster the tyrant; he is no more than the executioner of that inhuman tyranny, which the people practise upon themselves, and of which he is only reserved to be a later victim than the wretch he has sent before. Look to a nearer country, where the sanguinary characters are more legible—whence you almost hear the groans of death and torture. Do you ascribe the rapine and murder in France to the few names that we are execrating here? or do you not see that it is the frenzy of an infuriated multitude, abusing its own strength, and practising those hideous abominations upon itself? Against the violence of this strength, let your virtue and influence be our safeguard."

What criminality, gentlemen of the jury, can you find in this? What, at any time; but I ask you, peculiarly at this momentous period, what guilt you can find in it? My client saw the scene of horror and blood which covers almost the face of Europe: he feared that causes, which he thought similar, might produce similar effects; and he seeks to avert those dangers, by calling the united virtue and tried moderation of the country into a state of strength and vigilance. Yet this is the conduct which the prosecution of this day seeks to punish and stigmatize; and this is the language for which this paper is reprobated to-day, as tending to turn the hearts of the people against their sovereign, and inviting them to overturn the constitution.

Let us now, gentlemen, consider the concluding part of this publication. It recommends a meeting of the people, to deliberate on constitutional methods of redressing grievances. Upon this subject I am inclined to suspect that I have in my youth taken up crude ideas, not founded, perhaps, in law; but I did imagine that, when the bill of rights restored the right of petitioning for the redress of grievances, it was understood that the people might boldly state among themselves that grievances did exist; I did imagine it was understood that people might lawfully assemble themselves in such manner as they might deem most orderly and decorous. I thought I had collected it from the greatest luminaries of the law. The power of petitioning seemed to me to imply the right of assembling for the purpose of deliberation. The law requiring a petition to be presented by a limited number, seemed to me to admit that the petition might be prepared by any number whatever, provided, in doing so, they did not commit any breach or violation of the public peace. I know that there has been a law passed in the Irish parliament of last year, which may bring my former opinion into a merited want of authority. The law declares that no body of men may delegate a power to any smaller number, to act, think, or petition for them. If that law had not passed, I should have thought that the assembling by a delegate convention was recommended, in order to avoid the tumult and disorder of a promiscuous assembly of the whole mass of the people. I should have conceived, before that act, that any law to abridge the orderly appointment of the few, to consult for the interest of the many, and thus force the many to consult by themselves, or not at all, would, in fact, be a law not to restrain but to promote insurrection. But that law has spoken, and my error must stand corrected.

Of this, however, let me remind you: you are to try this part of the publication by what the law was then, not by what it is now. How was it understood until last session of parliament. You had, both in England and Ireland, for the last ten years, these delegated meetings. The Volunteers of Ireland, in 1783, met by delegation: they framed a plan of parliamentary reform; they presented it to the representative wisdom of the nation. It was not received; but no man ever dreamed that it was not the undoubted right of the subject to assemble in that manner. They assembled by delegation at Dungannon; and to show the idea then entertained of the legality of their public conduct, that same body of Volunteers was thanked by both houses of parliament, and their delegates most graciously received at the throne. The other day you had delegated representatives of the Catholics of Ireland, publicly elected by the members of that persuasion, and sitting in convention in the heart of your capital, carrying on an actual treaty with the existing government, and under the eye of your own parliament, which was then assembled; you have seen the delegates from that convention carry the complaints of their grievances to the foot of the throne, from whence they brought back to that convention the auspicious tidings of that redress which they had been refused at home.

Such, gentlemen, have been the means of popular communication and discussion, which, until the last session, have been deemed legal in this country, as, happily for the sister kingdom, they are yet considered there.

I do not complain of this act as any infraction of popular liberty; I should not think it becoming in me to express any complaint against a law, when once become such. I observe only, that one mode of popular deliberation is thereby taken utterly away, and you are reduced to a situation in which you never stood before. You are living in a country, where the constitution is rightly stated to be only ten years old—where the people have not the ordinary rudiments of education. It is a melancholy story, that the lower orders of the people here have less means of being enlightened than the same class of people in any other country. If there be no means left by which public measures can be canvassed, what will be the consequence? Where the press is free, and discussion unrestrained, the mind, by the collision of intercourse, gets rid of its own asperities; a sort of insensible perspiration takes place in the body politic, by which those acrimonies, which would otherwise fester and inflame, are quietly dissolved and dissipated. But now, if any aggregate assembly shall meet, they are censured; if a printer publishes their resolutions, he is punished: rightly, to be sure, in both cases, for it has been lately done. If the people say, let us not create tumult, but meet in delegation, they cannot do it; if they are anxious to promote parliamentary reform in that way, they cannot do it; the law of the last session has for the first time declared such meetings to be a crime.

What then remains? The liberty of the press *only*—that sacred palladium, which no influence, no power, no minister, no government, which nothing, but the depravity, or folly, or corruption of a jury, can ever destroy. And what calamities are the people saved from, by having public communication left open to them? I will tell you, gentlemen, what they are saved from, and what the government is saved from; I will tell you also to what both are exposed by shutting up that communication. In one case, sedition speaks aloud and walks abroad: the demagogue goes forth—the public eye is upon him—he frets his busy hour upon the stage; but soon either weariness, or bribe, or punishment, or disappointment, bears him down, or drives him off, and he appears no more. In the other case, how does the work of sedition go forward? Night after night the muffled rebel steals forth in the dark, and casts another and another brand upon the pile, to which, when the hour of fatal maturity shall arrive, he will apply the torch. If you doubt of the horrid consequence of suppressing the effusion even of individual discontent, look to those enslaved countries where the protection of despotism is supposed to be secured by such restraints. Even the person of the despot there is never in safety. Neither the fears of the despot, nor the machinations of the slave, have any slumber—the one anticipating the moment of peril, the other watching the opportunity of aggression. The fatal crisis is equally a surprise upon both: the decisive instant is precipitated without warning—by folly on the one side, or by frenzy on the other; and there is no notice of the treason, till the traitor acts. In those unfortunate countries—one cannot read it without horror—there are officers, whose province it is, to have the water which is to be drunk by their rulers, sealed up in bottles, lest some wretched miscreant should throw poison into the draught.

But, gentlemen, if you wish for a nearer and more interesting example; you have it in the history of your own revolution. You have it at that memorable period, when the monarch found a servile acquiescence in the ministers of his folly—when the liberty of the press was trodden under foot—when venal sheriffs returned packed juries, to carry into effect those fatal conspiracies of the few against the many—when the devoted benches of public justice were filled by some of those foundlings of fortune, who, overwhelmed in the torrent of corruption at an early period, lay at the bottom, like drowned bodies, while soundness or sanity remained in them; but, at length, becoming buoyant by putrefaction, they rose as they rotted, and floated to the surface of the polluted stream, where they were drifted along, the objects of terror, and contagion, and abomination.*

In that awful moment of a nation's travail, of

* "It may not be ungratifying to hear the manner in which this passage was suggested to the speaker's mind. A day or two before Mr. Rowan's trial, one of Mr. Curran's friends showed him a letter that he had received from Bengal, in which the writer, after mentioning the Hindoo custom of throwing the dead into the Ganges, added, that he was then upon the banks of that river, and that, as he wrote, he could see several bodies floating down its stream. The orator, shortly after, while describing a corrupted bench, recollected this fact, and applied it as above."—*Life of Curran, by his Son*, vol. i., p. 316.

the last gasp of tyranny, and the first breath of freedom, how pregnant is the example! The press extinguished, the people enslaved, and the prince undone. As the advocate of society, therefore—of peace—of domestic liberty—and the lasting union of the two countries—I conjure you to guard the liberty of the press, that great sentinel of the state, that grand detector of public imposture; guard it, because, when it sinks, there sinks with it, in one common grave, the liberty of the subject, and the security of the crown.

Gentlemen, I am glad that this question has not been brought forward earlier; I rejoice, for the sake of the court, of the jury, and of the public repose, that this question has not been brought forward till now. In Great Britain, analagous circumstances have taken place. At the commencement of that unfortunate war which has deluged Europe with blood, the spirit of the English people was tremblingly alive to the terror of French principles; at that moment of general paroxysm, to accuse was to convict. The danger looked larger to the public eye, from the misty region through which it was surveyed. We measure inaccessible heights by the shadows which they project, where the lowness and the distance of the light form the length of the shade.

There is a sort of aspiring and adventurous credulity, which disdains assenting to obvious truths, and delights in catching at the improbability of circumstances, as its best ground of faith. To what other cause, gentlemen, can you ascribe, that in the wise, the reflecting, and the philosophic nation of Great Britain, a printer has been gravely found guilty of a libel, for publishing those resolutions to which the present minister of that kingdom had actually subscribed his name? To what other cause can you ascribe, what in my mind is still more astonishing, in such a country as Scotland—a nation cast in the happy medium between the spiritless acquiescence of submissive poverty, and the sturdy credulity of pampered wealth—cool and ardent—adventurous and persevering—winging her eagle flight against the blaze of every science, with an eye that never winks, and a wing that never tires—crowned, as she is, with the spoils of every art, and decked with the wreath of every muse, from the deep and scrutinizing researches of her Hume, to the sweet and simple, but not less sublime and pathetic, morality of her Burns—how, from the bosom of a country like that, genius, and character, and talents, should be banished to a distant barbarous soil, condemned to pine under the horrid communion of vulgar vice and base-born profligacy, for twice the period that ordinary calculation gives to the continuance of human life?*

* Alluding to Scotland, where sentence of transportation for fourteen years, had been passed upon Mr. Muir, Mr. Palmer, and others. Recently public monuments have been erected to these patriots in Edinburgh and London.

But I will not further press an idea that is so painful to me, and I am sure must be painful to you. I will only say, you have now an example, of which neither England nor Scotland had the advantage; you have the example of the panic, the infatuation, and the contrition of both. It is now for you to decide, whether you will profit by their experience of idle panic and idle regret; or whether you meanly prefer to palliate a servile imitation of their frailty, by a paltry affectation of their repentance. It is now for you to show, that you are not carried away by the same hectic delusions, to acts, of which no tears can wash away the fatal consequences, or the indelible reproach.

Gentlemen, I have been warning you by instances of public intellect suspended or obscured; let me rather excite you by the example of that intellect recovered and restored. In that case which Mr. Attorney-General has cited himself—I mean that of the trial of Lambert, in England—is there a topic of invective against constituted authorities, is there a topic of abuse against every department of British government, that you do not find in the most glowing and unqualified terms in that publication, for which the printer of it was prosecuted, and acquitted by an English jury? See, too, what a difference there is between the case of a man publishing his own opinion of facts, thinking that he is bound by duty to hazard the promulgation of them, and without the remotest hope of any personal advantage, and that of a man who makes publication his trade. And saying this, let me not be misunderstood. It is not my province to enter into any abstract defence of the opinions of any man upon public subjects. I do not affirmatively state to you that these grievances, which this paper supposes, do in fact, exist; yet I cannot but say, that the movers of this prosecution have forced this question upon you. Their motives and their merits, like those of all accusers, are put in issue before you; and I need not tell you how strongly the motive and merits of any informer ought to influence the fate of his accusation.

I agree most implicitly with Mr. Attorney-General, that nothing can be more criminal than an attempt to work a change in the government by armed force; and I entreat that the court will not suffer any expression of mine to be considered as giving encouragement or defence to any design to excite disaffection, to overawe or to overturn the government. But I put my client's case upon another ground: if he was led into an opinion of grievances, where there were none, if he thought there ought to be a reform, where none was necessary, he is answerable only for his intention. He can be answerable to you in the same way only that he is answerable to that God, before whom the accuser, the accused, and the judge, must appear together; that is, not for the clearness of his understanding, but for the purity of his heart.

Gentlemen, Mr. Attorney-General has said, that Mr. Rowan did by this publication (supposing it to be his) recommend, under the name of equality, a general indiscriminate assumption of public rule, by every the meanest person in the state. Low as we are in point of public information, there is not, I believe, any man, who thinks for a moment, that does not know that all which the great body of the people of any country can have from any government, is a fair encouragement to their industry, and protection for the fruits of their labour. And there is scarcely any man, I believe, who does not know, that if a people could become so silly as to abandon their stations in society, under pretence of governing themselves, they would become the dupes and the victims of their own folly. But does this publication recommend any such infatuated abandonment, or any such desperate assumption? I will read the words which relate to that subject—"By liberty, we never understood unlimited freedom; nor by equality, the levelling of property, or the destruction of subordination." I ask you, with what justice, upon what principle of common sense, you can charge a man with the publication of sentiments the very reverse of what his words avow, and that, when there is no collateral evidence, where there is no foundation whatever, save those very words, by which his meaning can be ascertained? Or, if you do adopt an arbitrary principle, of imputing to him *your* meaning, instead of his own, what publication can be guiltless or safe? It is a sort of accusation that I am ashamed and sorry to see introduced in a court acting on the principles of the British constitution.

In the bitterness of reproach it was said, "Out of thine own mouth will I condemn thee." From the severity of justice I demand no more. See if, in the words that have been spoken, you can find matter to acquit or to condemn—"By liberty, we never understood unlimited freedom; nor by equality, the levelling of property, or the destruction of subordination. This is a calumny invented by that faction, or that gang, which misrepresents the King to the people, and the people to the King—traduces one half of the nation, to cajole the other—and, by keeping up distrust and division, wishes to continue the proud arbitrator of the fortune and fate of Ireland. Here you find that meaning, disclaimed as a calumny, which is artfully imputed as a crime.

I say, therefore, gentlemen of the jury, as to the four parts into which the publication must be divided, I answer thus. It calls upon the Volunteers. Consider the time, the danger—the authority of the prosecutors themselves for believing that danger to exist—the high character, the known moderation, the approved loyalty of that venerable institution—the similarity of the circumstances between the period at which they were summoned to take arms, and that in which they have been called upon to reassume them. Upon this simple ground, gentlemen, you will decide, whether this part of the publication was libellous and criminal, or not.

As to reform, I could wish to have said nothing upon it; I believe I have said enough. If Mr. Rowan, in disclosing that opinion, thought the state required it, he acted like an honest man. For the rectitude of the opinion he was not answerable; he discharged his duty in telling the country that he thought so.

As to the emancipation of the Catholics, I cannot but say that Mr. Attorney-General did very wisely in keeping clear of that subject. Yet, gentlemen, I need not tell you how important a figure it was intended to make upon the scene; though, from unlucky accidents, it has become necessary to expunge it during the rehearsal.*

Of the concluding part of this publication, the convention which it recommends, I have spoken already. I wish not to trouble you with saying more upon it. I feel that I have already trespassed much upon your patience. In truth, upon a subject embracing such a variety of topics, a rigid observance either of conciseness or arrangement could, perhaps, scarcely be expected. It is, however, with pleasure I feel I am drawing to a close, and that only one question remains, to which I would beg your attention.

* Referring to the Emancipation Act of 1793.

Whatever, gentlemen, may be your opinion of the meaning of this publication, there yet remains a great point for you to decide upon: namely, whether, in point of fact, this publication be imputable to Mr. Rowan, or not?—whether he did publish it, or not? Two witnesses are called to that fact—one of the name of Lyster, and the other of the name of Morton. You must have observed that Morton gave no evidence upon which that paper could have even been read; he produced no paper—he identified no paper—he said that he got some paper, but that he had given it away. So that, in point of law, there was no evidence given by him, on which it could have gone to a jury; and, therefore, it turns entirely upon the evidence of the other witness. He has stated that he went to a public meeting, in a place where there was a gallery crowded with spectators, and that he there got a printed paper, the same which has been read to you. I know you are well acquainted with the fact, that the credit of every witness must be considered by, and rest with the jury. They are the sovereign judges of that; and I will not insult your feelings by insisting on the caution with which you should watch the testimony of a witness that seeks to affect the liberty, or property, or character, of your fellow-citizens. Under what circumstances does this evidence come before you. The witness says he has got a commission in the army, by the interest of a lady, from a person then high in administration. He told you that he made a memorandum upon the back of that paper, it being his general custom, when he got such papers, to make an indorsement upon them—that he did this from mere fancy—that he had no intention of giving any evidence on the subject—he "took it with no such view." There is something whimsical enough in this curious story. Put his credit upon the positive evidence adduced to his character. Who he is I know not—I know not the man; but his credit is impeached. Mr. Blake was called; he said he knew him. I asked him, "Do you think, sir, that Mr. Lyster is or is not a man deserving credit upon his oath?" If you find a verdict of conviction, it can be only upon the credit of Mr. Lyster. What said Mr. Blake; Did he tell you that he considered him a man to be believed upon his oath? He did not attempt to say that he did. The best he could say was, that he "would hesitate." Do you believe Blake? Have you the same opinion of Lyster's testimony that Mr. Blake has? Do you know Lyster? If you do know him, and know that he is credible, your knowledge should not be shaken by the doubts of any man. But if you do not know him, you must take his credit from an unimpeached witness, swearing that he would hesitate to believe him. In my mind, there is a circumstance of the strongest nature that came out from Lyster on the table. I am aware that a most respectable man, if impeached by surprise, may not be prepared to repel a wanton calumny by contrary testimony. But was Lyster unapprized of this attack upon him? What said he? "I knew that you had Blake to examine against me—you have brought him here for that purpose." He knew the very witness that was to be produced against him—he knew that his credit was impeached—and yet he produced no person to support that credit. What said Mr. Smyth? "From my knowledge of him, I would not believe him upon his oath."

Mr. Attorney-General—I beg pardon, but I must set Mr. CURRAN right. Mr. Lyster said he had heard Blake would be here, but not in time to prepare himself.

Mr. CURRAN—But what said Mrs. Hatchell? Was the production of that witness a surprise upon Mr. Lyster? Her cross-examination shows the fact to be the contrary. The learned counsel, you see, was perfectly apprized of a chain of private circumstances, to which he pointed his questions. This lady's daughter was married to the elder brother of the witness Lyster. Did he know these circumstances by inspiration? No; they could come only from Lyster himself. I insist, therefore, that the gentleman knew his character was to be impeached; his counsel knew it, and not a single witness has been produced to support it. Then consider, gentlemen, upon what ground can you find a verdict of conviction against my client, when the only witness produced to the fact of publication is impeached, without even an attempt to defend his character? Many hundreds, he said, were at that meeting. Why not produce one of them, to swear to the fact of such a meeting? One he has ventured to name; but he was certainly very safe in naming a person, who, he has told you, is not in the kingdom, and could not, therefore, be called to confront him.

Gentlemen, let me suggest another observation or two, if still you have any doubt as to the guilt or innocence of the defendant. Give me leave to suggest to you what circumstances you ought to consider, in order to found your verdict. You should consider the character of the person accused; and in this your task is easy. I will venture to say, there is not a man in this nation more known than the gentleman who is the subject of this prosecution; not only by the part he has taken in public concerns, and which he has taken in common with many, but still more so, by that extraordinary sympathy for human affliction, which, I am sorry to think, he shares with so small a number. There is not a day that you hear the cries of your starving manufacturers in your streets, that you do not also see the advocate of their sufferings—that you do not see his honest and manly figure, with uncovered head, soliciting for their relief—searching the frozen heart of charity for every string that can be touched by compassion, and urging the force of every argument and every motive, save that which his modesty suppresses, the authority of his own generous example. Or if you see him not there, you may trace his steps to the private abode of disease, and famine, and despair—the messenger of heaven, bringing with him food, and medicine, and consolation. Are these the materials of which you suppose anarchy and public rapine to be formed? Is this the man on whom to fasten the abominable charge of goading on a frantic populace to mutiny and bloodshed? Is this the man likely to apostatize from every principle that can bind him to the state—his birth, his property, his education, his character, and his children? Let me tell you, gentlemen of the jury, if you agree with his prosecutors, in thinking that there ought to be a sacrifice of such a man on such an occasion—and upon the credit of such evidence you are to convict him—never did you, never can you give a sentence, consigning any man to public punishment, with less danger to his person or to his fame: for where could the hireling be found to fling contumely or ingratitude at his head, whose private distresses he had not endeavoured to alleviate, or whose public condition he had not laboured to improve?

I cannot, however, avoid reverting to a circumstance that distinguishes the case of Mr. Rowan from that of the late sacrifice in a neighbouring kingdom.*

* Scotland, from whence Messrs. Muir, Palmer, and others were transported for sedition.

The severer law of that country, it seems—and happy for them that it should—enables them to remove from their sight the victim of their infatuation. The more merciful spirit of our law deprives you of that consolation; his sufferings must remain for ever before our eyes, a continual call upon your shame and your remorse. But those sufferings will do more; they will not rest satisfied with your unavailing contrition—they will challenge the great and paramount inquest of society—the man will be weighed against the charge, the witness, and the sentence—and impartial justice will demand, why has an Irish jury done this deed? The moment he ceases to be regarded as a criminal, he becomes of necessity an accuser; and let me ask you, what can your most zealous defenders be prepared to answer to such a charge? When your sentence shall have sent him forth to that stage which guilt alone can render infamous, let me tell you, he will not be like a little statue upon a mighty pedestal, diminishing by elevation; but he will stand a striking and imposing object upon a monument, which, if it does not (and it cannot) record the atrocity of his crime, must record the atrocity of his conviction.

Upon this subject, therefore, credit me when I say, that I am still more anxious for you than I can possibly be for him. I cannot but feel the peculiarity of your situation. Not the jury of his own choice, which the law of England allows, but which ours refuses; collected in that box by a person certainly no friend to Mr. Rowan*—certainly not very deeply interested in giving him a very impartial jury. Feeling this, as I am persuaded you do, you cannot be surprised, however you may be distressed, at the mournful presage with which an anxious public is led to fear the worst from your possible determination. But I will not, for the justice and honour of our common country, suffer my mind to be borne away by such melancholy anticipation. I will not relinquish the confidence that this day will be the period of his sufferings; and, however mercilessly he has been hitherto pursued, that your verdict will send him home to the arms of his family, and the wishes of his country. But if, which heaven forbid! it hath still been unfortunately determined, that because he has not bent to power and authority, because he would not bow down before the golden calf, and worship it, he is to be bound and cast into the furnace; I do trust to God, that there is a redeeming spirit in the constitution, which will be seen to walk with the sufferer through the flames, and to preserve him unhurt by the conflagration.

Upon leaving the court, Mr. Curran was drawn home by the populace, who took the horses from his carriage.

At the close of Curran's speech there was another shout of admiration and sympathy, which Lord Clonmel with difficulty stopped. The Attorney-General (most irregularly) spoke in

* Gifford, the Sheriff.

defence of his own character, against the charge of oppressive delay, and then Prime-Sergeant the Hon. James Fitzgerald replied to CURRAN. Lord Clonmel (Chief Justice) charged the jury violently against Rowan. In this charge he used the following words, omitted in the editions of the trials, but given in Curran's Memoirs, by his Son, vol. i., p. 347:—

"One hundred and fifty Volunteers, or United Irishmen, and not one comes forward! Many of them would have been proud to assist him (the traverser). *Their silence speaks a thousand times more strongly than any cavilling upon this man's credit—the silence of such a number is a volume of evidence in support of the prosecution.*"

Justice (afterwards Lord) Downes also charged, and the Jury, in ten minutes, found a verdict of Guilty. The following scene then occurred:—

"Lord Clonmel—Do the Counsel for the defendant desire four days' time to move in arrest of judgment?

"Mr. CURRAN—The only instructions I have from my client are to disclaim any application of that kind; he does not wish to take advantage of errors in the record, if any there be; but is now ready to attend to receive what sentence the court may be pleased to pronounce.

"Lord Clonmel—(After conferring with the other judges)—We will not pronounce judgment till four days. Mr. Sheriff, take care of your prisoner.

"The Counsel for Mr. Rowan here objected, that he was not a prisoner—he had not been in custody; he had not given bail upon this information; he was bound in no recognizance; was served with no process; he had appeared to the information by attorney; he pleaded by attorney; the issue was tried after the manner of a civil action, a word merely of the record being read, and the defendant was not given in charge to the jury, as the practice is, where he appears in custody. Mr. Rowan attended the trial, it is true, but the court had no judicial cognizance of him; the information could have been tried in his absence; he attended as a common auditor, and the witness being called upon to point him out at the desire of the bench, might have been a satisfaction to them to see that the witnesses were speaking of the same person, but it was altogether unprecedented in such cases as the present. Mr. Rowan was ready for sentence; he claims no indulgence, does not insist upon the four-day rule; but if the court, for their own accommodation, choose to defer the sentence for four days, they have no legal authority for sending Mr. Rowan to prison, until sentence is pronounced, or the usual and accustomed process issued against him.

"Lord Clonmel—If the Attorney-General consents, I have no objection.

"The Attorney-General had left the court, and the Solicitor for the Crown remained silent.

"Lord Clonmel—The defendant is a convict, as such he is a prisoner; the law must have its course. Adjourn the court.

"Accordingly the court was adjourned.

"Mr. Rowan was conveyed to the New Prison, attended by both the Sheriffs, and a formidable array of horse and foot guards."—*Mac Nevin's State Trials,* p. 122.

February 3rd, 1794.

Affidavits were read in court, to prove that one of the jury was avowedly hostile.

February 4th, 1794.

The Recorder applied to set aside the verdict given in the case of Archibald Hamilton Rowan, Esq. The application was grounded upon different affidavits sworn in court, charging, 1st—One of the jurors with a declaration against Mr. Rowan, previous to trial. 2ndly—Partiality in one of the high sheriffs. 3rdly—That John Lyster, the principal evidence, was not to be believed upon his oath; he, as the affidavits stated, having been guilty of perjury. And 4thly—upon which the learned gentleman rested his case — the misdirection of the court.

After much discussion, Mr. CURRAN followed on the same side, and said:—

It was an early idea, that a verdict in a criminal case could not be set aside *inconsulto rege;* but the law had stood otherwise, without a doubt to impeach its principle, for the last two reigns. Common sense would say, that the discretion of the court should go at least as far in criminal as in civil cases, and very often to go no further would be to stop far short of what was right, as in those great questions where the prosecution may be considered either as an attempt to extinguish liberty, or as a necessary measure for the purpose of repressing the virulence of public licentiousness and dangerous faction; where there can be no alternative between guilt or martyrdom; where the party prosecuted must either be considered as a culprit sinking beneath the punishment of his own crimes, or a victim sacrificed to the vices of others. But when it clearly appears that the party has fallen a prey to persecuting combination, there remains but one melancholy question—how far did that combination reach?

There have been two cases lately decided in this very court; the King and Pentland, where the motion was made and refused; and the King and Bowen, where it was granted; both of which show, that captious sophistry and technical pedantry have here, as well as in England, given way to liberal and rational inquiry; and that the court will not now, in their discretion, refuse a motion of this kind, unless they can, at the same time, lay their hands upon their hearts, and say, they believe in their consciences, that justice has been done: such was the manly language of one of your lordships [Mr. Justice Downes], and such the opinion of the court on a former occasion.

He then cited 7 Modern 57, as referred to in Bacon *tit.* Trial, to show, that where there was good ground of challenge to a juror, not known at the trial, it was sufficient cause for setting aside the verdict.

In England they have a particular act of parliament, entitling the party to strike a special jury to try the fact, and then he has time between the striking and the trial to question the propriety of that jury; here my client had no information, till the instant of trial, who his jurors were to be.

There are certain indulgences granted at times, perhaps by the connivance of humanity, which men who are not entitled to demand them in an open court, obtain, nevertheless, by sidelong means; and perhaps the little breach which affords that light to the mind of the man accused, is a circumstance concerning which the court would feel pain, even if called upon to say, that it should in all cases be prevented; but to overturn principles and authorities, for the purpose of oppressing the subject, is what this court will never do.

The first of the affidavits I shall consider, is that of the traverser. I do not recollect whether it states the sheriff, in avowed terms, to be an emissary or a hireling agent of the castle, therefore I do not state it from the affidavit; but he swears that he does believe that he did labour to bring into the box a jury full of prejudices, and of the blackest impressions; instead of having, as they ought, fair and impartial minds, and souls like white paper.

This sheriff now stands in court; he might have denied it, if he would, he had an opportunity of answering it; but he has left it an undenied assertion—he was not certainly obliged to answer it; for no man is bound to convict himself. But there is a part of that charge which amounts at least to this:—"Your heart was poisoned against me, and you collected those to be my judges, who, if they could not be under the dominion of bad dispositions, might be, at least, the dupes of good." The most favourable thing that can be said is this, you sought to bring against me honest prejudices, but you brought against me wicked ones. The very general charge that he sought for persons who, he knew, were most likely to bring prejudices with them into the jury box, is a part of the affidavit that it was incumbent on him to answer if he could.

I do not contend, that what is charged in the affidavit would have been a ground of principal challenge to the array; but I hold it to be the better opinion, that a challenge to the array for favour does well lie in the mouth of the defendant.

The ancient notion was, you shall not challenge the array for favour, where the King is a party; the King only can challenge for favour; for the principle was, that every man ought to be favourable to the crown; but, thank God, the advancement of legal knowledge, and the growing understanding of the age, have dissipated such illiberal and mischievous conceptions.

But I am putting too much stress upon such technical, discarded, and antiquated scruples. The true question has been already stated from the authority of Mr. Justice Downes, and that question is—"Has justice been done?"

It is a matter upon which scarce any understanding would condescend to hesitate, whether a man had been fairly tried, whose triors had been collected together by an avowed enemy, whose conduct had been such as to leave no doubt that he had purposely brought prejudiced men into the box.

In every country where freedom obtains, there must subsist parties. In this country, and Great Britain, I trust there never will be a time when there shall not be men found zealous for the actual government of the day. So, on the other hand, I trust there will never be a time, when there will not be found men zealous and enthusiastic in the cause of popular freedom, and of the public rights. If, therefore, a person in public office suffers his own prejudices, however honestly anxious he may be for a prosecution carried on by those to whom he is attached, to influence him so far as to choose men, to his knowledge devoted to the principles he espouses, it is an error which a High Court of Judicature, seeking to do right justice, will not fail to correct.

A sheriff, in such a case, might not have perceived the partiality of his conduct, because he was surveying through the medium of prejudice and habitual corruption; but it is impossible to think that this sheriff meant to be impartial; it is an interpretation more favourable than his conduct will allow of; if he deserves any credit at all, it is for not answering the charge made against him; at the same time, that, by not answering it, he has left unimpeached the credit of the charge itself.

The sheriff here tendered some form of an affidavit, which the court would not allow to be sworn or read, for the same reason, that those sworn and tendered by the defendant's counsel, had been before refused. Mr. Curran, however, consented to its being sworn and read, which the Attorney-General declined, being unacquainted with the contents, and uninstructed as to its tendency; it, therefore, was not sworn.

Mr. Curran proceeded—Is this, then, the way to meet a fair application to the court, to see whether justice has been done between the subject and the crown? I offer it again, let the affidavit be read. And let me remind the court, that the great reason for sending a cause back to a jury is, that new light must be shed upon it; and how must your lordships feel, when you see that indulgence granted to the conscience of the jury denied to the court?

Mr. Attorney-General—I am concerned that any lawyer should make a proposition in the manner Mr. CURRAN has done; he proposes to have an affidavit read, provided we consent that others, which the court have already refused, should be now read.* I did not hear it offered; but is it to be presumed that I will consent to have an affidavit read, about which I know nothing? Yesterday, without any communication with a human being, I did say, that I conceived it unnecessary to answer any of the affidavits, thinking that they were not sufficient to ground the application made to the court. And it is presumed I am so mad as to consent to the reading of affidavits which I have not seen.

Some altercation here took place, when Lord Clonmel, Chief Justice, interposed, and said, that the counsel had certainly a right to argue it on the ground that the sheriff was biassed, and did return a jury prejudiced against the traverser.

Mr. CURRAN was about to observe upon the expression of one of the jury, sworn to in another affidavit, "that there would be no safety in the country, until the defendant was either hanged or banished," when it was asked by the court, whether the time of its coming to the knowledge of the traverser, that the sheriff was biassed, was stated in his affidavit?

Mr. CURRAN—He was in prison, and could not have the attendance of those counsel whose assistance he had in court; and, besides, from the nature of the circumstances, it was impossible he could

* Mr. Attorney-General, it may be proper to observe, mistook Mr. Curran's proposal, which was an unqualified offer to have Mr. Gifford's affidavit read.

have been sufficiently apprized of its consequences, for he saw not that panel till the day of the trial, when he could not have had time to make any inquiry into the characters, dispositions, or connexions of the jury.

If triors had been appointed to determine the issue, favourable or not, what would have been their finding? Could they say upon their oaths, that he was not unfavourable to that party against whom he could make such a declaration?

Favour is not cause of principal challenge, which, if put upon a pleading, would conclude the party. Favour is that which makes the man, in vulgar parlance, unfit to try the question. And as to the time these facts came to his knowledge, he has sworn that he was utterly ignorant of them at the time of his coming into court to take his trial.

I will not glance at the character of any absent noble person, high in office; but let it be remembered, that it is a government prosecution, and that the witness has, from a low and handicap situation, scraped himself into preferment, perhaps—for I will put the best construction upon it—by offering himself as a man honestly anxious for the welfare of his country; in short, it is too obvious to require any comment, what the nature of the whole transaction has been, that he got his commission as a compensation *pro labore impendendo*, and came afterwards into court, to pay down the stipulated purchase.

Had this then been an unbiassed jury, was there not something in all these circumstances, that might have afforded more deliberation than that of one minute per man, for only so long was the jury out? and, had this been a fair witness, would he have lain down under a charge which, if true, ought not only to damn this verdict, but his character for ever? What would a corps of brother-officers think of a person, charged upon oath with the commission of two wilful perjuries, and that charge remaining undenied? Here is an undenied charge, in point of fact; and although I do not call upon the court to say, that this is a guilty and abominable person, yet surely the suspicion is strongly so, and must be considered. This was at least a verdict where the evidence went to the jury, under slighter blemishes than it will if my client has the advantage of another trial; for then he will put it out of the power of man to doubt, that this witness has been perjured—this witness, who has had notice both here and at the trial, of the aspersions on his character, and yet has not called a human being to say that he entertained a contrary opinion of him.

Was he known anywhere? Did he crawl unobserved to the castle? Was it without the aid or knowledge of any body that that gaudy plumage grew on him, in which he appeared in court? If he was known for any thing else than what he is stated to be, it was, upon that day, almost a physical impossibility, in a court-house, which almost contained the country, not to have found some person, to give some sort of testimony, respecting his general character. For though no man is bound to be ready at all times to answer particular charges, yet every man is supposed to come with his public attestation of common and general probity. But he has left that character, upon the merits of which my client is convicted, unsupported, even by his own poor corporal swearing. You are called upon, then, to say, whether, upon the evidence of a being of this kind, such a man as that is to be convicted, and sentenced to punishment, in a country where humanity is the leading feature even of the criminal law.

I have now to deal with the evidence of the second witness. A man coming to support the credit of another collaterally, is himself particularly pledged; then, what was his testimony? He did not know whether Mr. Gifford was concerned in the newspaper! And now, you have the silence of Gifford himself, in not answering Mr. Rowan's affidavit, to contradict that. And next, he did not know whether his own cousin-german was the relation of their common uncle! I call upon you, my lords, in the name of sacred justice and your country to declare whether the melancholy scenes and murderous plots of the Meal-tub and the Rye-house are to be acted over again; and whether every Titus Oates that can be found is to be called into your courts, as the common vouchee of base and perjured accusation.

I also conceive, my lords, that the direction of the court was not agreeable to the law of Ireland. The defence of my client was rested upon this; that there was no evidence of the fact of publication; upon the incredibility of the fact; and the circumstances of discredit in the character of the witness: yet the court made this observation: "Gentlemen, it scarcely lies in the mouth of Mr. Rowan to build a defence upon objections of this kind to the characters of witnesses, because the fact was public; there were many there; the room was crowded below, the gallery was crowded above; and the publicity of the fact enabled him to produce a number of witnesses to falsify the assertion of the prosecutor, if, in fact, it could be falsified!" Is that the principle of criminal law? Is it a part of the British law, that the fate of the accused shall abide, not the positive establishment of guilt by the prosecutor, but the negative proof of innocence by himself? Why has it been said in foolish old books, that the law supposes the innocence of every man, till the contrary is proved? How has it happened that that language has been admired for its humanity, and not laughed at for its absurdity, in which the prayers of the court are addressed to heaven, for the safe deliverance of the man accused? How comes it that so much public time is wasted in going into evidence of guilt, if the bare accusation of a man did call upon him to go into evidence of his innocence? The force of the observation is this. Mr. Rowan impeaches the credit of a witness, who has sworn that he saw him present, and doing certain acts, at a certain meeting; but it is asked, has he substantiated that discredit, by calling all the persons who were present to prove his absence from that meeting, which is only stated to have existed by a witness whom he alleges to have perjured himself? I call upon the example of judicial character; upon the faith of that high office, which is never so dignified as when it sees its errors and corrects them, to say, that the court was for a moment led away, so as to argue from the most seductive of all sophisms, that of the *petitio principii.*

See what meaning is to be gathered from such words: we say the whole that this man has sworn, is a consummate lie; show it to be so, says the court, by admitting a part of it to be true. It is a false swearing; it is a conspiracy of two witnesses against this defendant; well, then, it lies upon him to rebut their testimony, by proving a great deal of it to be true! Is conjecture, then, in criminal cases, to stand in the place of truth and demonstration? Why were not some of those (I will strip the case of the honour of names which I respect), but why were not some of those, who knew that these two persons were to be brought forward, and that there were to be objections to their credit, if, as it is stated, it happened in the presence of a public crowd, rushing in from motives of curiosity, why were not numbers called on to establish that fact? On the contrary, the court have said to this effect: Mr. Rowan, you say you were not there; produce any of those persons with whom you were there, to swear you were not there! You say it was a perjury; if so, produce the people, that he has perjured himself in swearing to have been there! But as to your own being there, you can easily show the contrary of that, by producing some man that you saw there! You say you were not there? Yes. There were one hundred and fifty persons there: now produce any one of those to swear they saw you there!

It is impossible for the human mind to suppose a case, in which infatuation must have prevailed in a more progressive degree, than when a jury are thus, in fact, directed to receive no refutation nor proof of the perjury of the witness, but only of his truth. We will permit you to deny the charge, by establishing the fact: we will permit you to prove that they swore falsely to your being there, by producing another witness to prove to a certainty that you were there.

Mr. CURRAN was here interrupted by Lord Chief Justice Clonmel.

Lord Clonmel—The reasoning of the court was strong upon that point: this is a transaction stated by the witness to have happened in open day, in a crowded assembly, in the capital, amidst a number of persons dressed in the uniform of Hamilton Rowan. There has been nothing suddenly brought forward to surprise the traverser; yet what has he done? Did he offer, as in the common course, to prove an alibi? It is stated to be at such a day, the witness swears at such an hour; the place is sworn to have been full of people, of Mr. Rowan's friends; but if there was even a partial assembly, it would be easy still to produce some one of those persons who were present, to say, that the fact did not happen which has been sworn to; or if you say Mr. Rowan was not there, it is easier still to prove it, by showing where he was; as thus: I breakfasted with him, I dined with him, I supped with him; he was with me, he was not at Purdon's; disprove that assertion, by proving an affirmation inconsistent with it.

Mr. CURRAN—I beg leave to remind the court of what fell from it. "He may call," said the court, "any of those persons; he has not produced one of them;" upon this, I think, a most material point does hang. "He might have called them, for they were all of his own party."

Lord Clonmel—That is, if there were such persons there; or if there was no meeting at all, he might have proved that.

Mr. CURRAN—There was no such idea put to the jury, as whether there was a meeting or not: it was said they were all of his party, he might have produced them; and the non-production of them was a "volume of evidence" upon that point. No refinement can avoid this conclusion, that even as your lordship now states the charge, the fate of the man must depend upon proving the negative.

Until the credit of the witness was established, he could not be called upon to bring any contrary evidence. What does the duty of every counsel dictate to him, if the case is not made out by his adversary or prosecutor? Let it rest; the court is bound to tell the jury so, and the jury are bound to find him not guilty. It is a most unshaken maxim, that *nemo tenetur prodere seipsum.* And it would indeed be a very inquisitorial exercise of power, to call upon a man to run the risk of confirming the charge, under the penalty of being convicted by *nil dicit.* Surely, at the criminal side of this court, as yet, there has been no such judgment pronounced. It is only when the party stands mute from malice, that such extremes can be resorted to. I never before heard an intimation from any judge to a jury, that bad evidence, liable to any and every exception, ought to receive a sanction from the silence of the party. The substance of the charge was neither more nor less than this: that the falsehood of the evidence shall receive support and credit from the silence of the man accused. With anxiety for the honour and religion of the law, I demand it of you, must not the jury have understood that this silence was evidence to go to them? is the meaning contained in the expression, "a volume of evidence," only insinuation? I do not know where any man could be safe; I do not know what any man could do to screen himself from prosecution; I know not how he could be sure, even when he was at his prayers before the throne of heaven, that he was not passing that moment of his life, on which he was to be charged with the commission of some crime, to be expiated to society by the forfeiture of his liberty or of his life; I do not know what shall become of the subject, if a jury are to be told that the silence of the man charged is a "volume of evidence" that he is guilty of the crime: where is it written? I know there is a place where vulgar frenzy cries out, that the public instrument must be drenched in blood; where defence is gagged, and the devoted wretch must perish. But even there, the victim of such tyranny is not made to fill, by voluntary silence, the defects of his accusation; for his tongue is tied, and therefore no advantage is taken of him by construction; it cannot be there said that his not speaking is a volume of evidence to prove his guilt.

But to avoid all misunderstanding, see what is the force of my objection: is it, that the charge of the court cannot receive a practicable interpretation, that may not terrify men's minds with ideas such as I have presented? No; I am saying no such thing: I have lived too long, and observed too much, not to know, that every word in a phrase is one of the feet upon which it runs, and how the shortening or lengthening of one of those feet will alter the progress or direction of its motion. I am not arguing that the charge of the court cannot by any possibility be reconciled to the principles of law; I am agitating a more important question; I am putting it to the conscience of the court, whether a jury may not have probably collected the same meaning from it which I have affixed to it; and whether there ought not to have been a volume of explanation, to do away the fatal consequences of such mistake.

On what sort of a case am I now speaking; on one of that kind with which it is known the public heart has been beating for many months; which, from a single being in society, has scarcely received a cool or tranquil examination. I am making that sort of application which the expansion of liberal reason and the decay of technical bigotry have made a favoured application.

In earlier times, it might have been thought sacrilege to have meddled with a verdict once pronounced; since then, the true principles of justice have been better understood; so that now, the whole wisdom of the whole court will have an opportunity of looking over that verdict, and setting right the mistake which has occasioned it.

Mr. Curran made other observations, as well in corroboration of his own remarks, as in answer to the opposite counsel, of which it is impossible to give an exact detail, and concluded:—

You are standing on the scanty isthmus that divides the great ocean of duration, on one side of the past, on the other of the future; a ground that, while you yet hear me, is washed from beneath our feet. Let me remind you, my lords, while your determination is yet in your power, "*Dum versatur adhuc intra penetralia Vestæ*," that on that ocean of future you must set your judgment afloat. And future ages will assume the same authority which you have assumed; posterity feel the same emotions which you have felt, when your little hearts have beaten, and your infant eyes have overflowed, at reading the sad history of the sufferings of a Russell or a Sidney.

Similar applause followed this speech. On the 5th the crown counsel argued at much length against the application, and on the 7th Clonmel and Boyd gave judgment against it; and then Boyd sentenced Rowan to a fine of £500, and two years' imprisonment, from the 29th of January, 1794, and to find security, himself in £2,000, and two sureties in £1,000 each. Rowan escaped, and went to France.*

* See Mac Nevin's State Trials, Madden's United Irishmen, and Rowan's Autobiography, edited by Dr. Drummond.

DROGHEDA DEFENDERS.

SPRING ASSIZES, DROGHEDA, APRIL 23RD, 1794.

THE Lords' Committee of 1793 thus describes the Defenders:—

"The people at this time called Defenders are very different from those who originally assumed that appellation, and are all, as far as the Committee could discover, of the Roman Catholic persuasion; in general poor ignorant labouring men, sworn to secrecy, and impressed with an opinion that they are assisting the Catholic cause; in other respects they do not appear to have any distinct particular object in view, but they talk of being relieved from hearth-money, tithes, county cesses, and of lowering their rents. They first appeared in the county of Louth in considerable bodies in April last; several of them were armed; they assembled mostly in the night, and forced into the houses of Protestants, and took from them their arms. The disorders soon spread through the counties of Meath, Cavan, Monaghan, and other parts adjacent; at first they took nothing but arms, but afterwards they plundered the houses of every thing they could find."

Premising that the Protestants were the rich class in these districts, we feel no difficulty in recognizing the same grievances and consequent outrages which have existed in Munster from the beginning of the last century to this day; but the Secret Committee tried to connect them with Catholic gentlemen, and the crown prosecutors tried to trace them to United Irish organization,* and French gold.

* See Mac Nevin's State Trials and Madden's United Irishmen.

On Monday, the 21st of April 1794, Roger Hamill, James Bird, Casimir Delahoyde, Patrick Kenny, Matthew Read, Bartholomew Walsh, and Patrick Tiernan were put to the Bar and arraigned, before the Honourable Mr. Justice Downes, one of the Judges of his Majesty's Court of King's Bench, upon the following

INDICTMENT.

County of the town of Drogheda, to wit. } The Jurors for our Lord the King, upon their oath say and present that Patrick Kenny, of Drogheda, yeoman, Matthew Read of the same, yeoman, Bartholomew Walsh of the same, yeoman, Patrick Tiernan, of Turfeckan, in the county of Louth, yeoman, Roger Hamill, James Bird and Casimir Delahoyde, all of Drogheda, in the county of the town of Drogheda, merchants, being wicked, seditious, and evil-minded persons, and of wicked and turbulent dispositions, and contriving, designing, and intending unlawfully, unjustly, maliciously, turbulently and seditiously, the peace of our said Lord the King and the common tranquillity of this his realm of Ireland to disquiet, molest, and disturb, and, as far as in them lay, to stir up, cause, incite and procure sedition, insurrection, and rebellion within this realm, and to bring the government of our said Lord the King within this realm into manifest danger, on the 14th day of December, in the thirty-third year of the reign of our sovereign Lord George the Third, King of Great Britain and soforth, at Drogheda, in the county of the town of Drogheda, and on divers other days and times, as well before as after, with force and arms their aforesaid wicked, malignant, and seditious purposes and designs to fulfil and effect, did then and there together with divers other wicked, seditious, and ill-minded persons to the jurors of our Lord the King at present unknown, meet, assemble, agree, conspire, confederate and treat of and about the accomplishing and effecting of their aforesaid malignant and seditious purposes and designs, and of, for, and about causing, procuring, inciting and effecting an insurrection and rebellion within the realm of Ireland; and for, about, and concerning the raising, providing, and procuring of arms and armed men to be ready and prepared in different places within this realm, their aforesaid wicked, malignant, seditious, and rebellious designs and purposes to effect, accomplish and fulfil, in contempt of the laws of this realm, to the evil example of all others in the like case offending, and contrary to the peace of our said Lord the King, his crown and dignity.

And the jurors of our Lord the king, do further present and say, that the said Patrick Kenny, Matthew Read, Bartholomew Walsh, and Patrick Tiernan, James Bird, Roger Hamill, and Casimir Delahoyde, being such wicked, ill-minded, and seditious persons as aforesaid, and wickedly, factiously, and seditiously, contriving and intending the peace of our said Lord the King, and the common tranquillity of this his realm of Ireland to molest, disquiet, and disturb, and to cause and incite a wicked rebellion within this realm, and the laws and government of our said Lord the King to bring into danger, on the said 14th day of December, in the said thirty-third year of the reign of our said Lord the King, and at divers other days and times, as well before as after, at Drogheda aforesaid, in the county of the said town of Drogheda aforesaid, with force and arms, did then and there wickedly, factiously, seditiously and contemptuously meet, associate, consult, conspire, confederate and agree together, and to and with divers other wicked and ill-disposed persons to the jurors aforesaid at present unknown, of, for, concerning, and about the raising, causing, and levying of insurrection, rebellion, and war against our said Lord the King, within this his realm of Ireland; and of, for, concerning, and about the procuring and providing of arms and armed men, to be prepared within this realm, their aforesaid wicked, malignant, and diabolical designs and purposes aforesaid to accomplish and effect; in contempt of the laws of this realm, and to the evil example of all others in the like case offending, and contrary to the peace of our said Lord the King, his crown and dignity.

To this indictment the accused traversed, and the court ordered their trial for the following day.

On Wednesday, the 23rd of April, 1794, the several traversers before mentioned were again put to the bar in order of trial.

After several witnesses were examined, CURRAN said:—

BEING counsel for the traversers, Mr. Bird, Mr. Hamill, and Mr. Delahoyde, now on trial, I find it necessary, without proceeding further, to offer to your lordships and this very respectable jury, some general observations on the extraordinary case of my clients, and the singular preposterousness of the charges in this accusation, as laid before you in evidence.

It is an accusation, that, of its nature, must involve a black degree of enormity in any country. It implies a criminal intention, that if carried into effect must loosen every bond of society, and plunge that country which should unhappily be the theatre of such atrocity, into the most inconceivable state of calamity and wretchedness, no matter how rich and prosperous might be its previous condition. The existence of a state is like the existence of life in man; and to take existence from the political body is similar to taking the life of an individual; with this difference, that the consequence of the one is so vastly superior to that of the other, that to determine the proportionate criminality, would be as visionary as impossible.

The charge against my clients is, that they are enemies to their country and its government; that they are adverse to its settlement, its peace, and its prosperity: that they have formed plans to spread general discontent, confusion and divisions, for the purpose of destroying the advantages derived to the nation from a state of well-ordered tranquillity; and that, for carrying such an abominable project into execution, they have employed for their agents, the greatest miscreants in society!

It is that sort of guilt that, at countenancing which, every man of character and sensibility must recoil. But it is for you, gentlemen, to consider, that an offence of such great enormity is not lightly to be believed, and requires to be proved by the strongest evidence.

It is not my intention at present to enter into any very minute observations on the evidence which has been this day laid before you; if that shall be necessary, one of the learned gentlemen here will do so.

There are few general circumstances upon which to observe, from the facts related in evidence. The state of the country, for some time past, and particularly the state of that body of your fellow-subjects against whom suspicion and calumny seem to have been directed, are circumstances that must here be observed upon, and cannot fail of exciting in your minds some of the tenderest feelings.

In last year's parliament, one of the most glorious triumphs that ever this country witnessed, was obtained by that body, over the blackest prejudice and injustice, exasperated by imaginary wrongs. That fatal disunion, from which for centuries great individual calamity and public disquietude had arisen, had the axe laid to its root by the senate of the nation. And there was no good man in the community, that did not look to the consequences of it to be the security of the peace, industry, and happiness of the country, and an exemption from the calamities of the nations around us. Upon such a great occasion, there must necessarily be diversity of opinions; but I am sorry to say, that prejudices are not yet removed from persons of a lower description.

There was, at that time, an obloquy thrown out against the Committee of our Catholic brethren sitting at Dublin; but I speak in the presence of a Protestant jury and a Protestant judge, and I say that in history there is no example of any such proceeding being carried on with more decorous tranquillity and strictly legal propriety. Their orderly, decent, and respectful perseverance was crowned with that success, which, it was imagined, would confer happiness on themselves, and on those that were to come after them. It was expected the disturbances which had been occasioned by a ruinous system of law would be done away; and that there would be a coalition of all parties, formed into one united phalanx, and feeling that their country could never be prosperous and happy, without a general participation of freedom to all its people.

A privileged order in a state may, in some sort, be compared to a solitary individual separated from the society, and unaided by the reciprocal converse, affections or support of his fellow-men. It is like a tree standing singly on a high hill, and exposed to the rude concussions of every varying blast, devoid of fruit or foliage. If you plant trees around it to shade it from the inclemency of the blighting tempest, and secure to it its adequate supply of sun and moisture, it quickly assumes all the luxuriance of vegetation, and proudly rears its head aloft, fortified against the noxious gales which agitate and wither the unprotected brambles lying without the verge of the plantation.

Upon this principle acted the dying man whose family had been disturbed by domestic contentions. Upon his death-bed he calls his children around him; he orders a bundle of twigs to be brought; he has them untied; he gives to each of them a single twig; he orders them to be broken—and it is done with facility. He next orders the twigs to be united in a bundle, and orders each of them to try their strength upon it. They shrink from the task as impossible. Thus, my children, continued the old man, it is UNION alone that can render you secure against the attempts of your enemies, and preserve you in that state of happiness which I wish you to enjoy.

Such should be the effects of the liberty conferred by the act of the last session of parliament; and such I believe they would be, if not for the misconceptions of a lower description of people, who may have imagined that a more respectable order of persons had the same passions and dispositions as themselves. I cannot attribute the accusation altogether to the irregular proceedings going forward for some time in this part of the country, but rather to vague charges, which I have read with concern, brought against a description of persons, the calamities of whose ancestors must have peculiarly influenced to a demeanour directly the contrary.

However ruinous the charges against the individuals may be, that alone does not terminate the mischief. These reports will go abroad—they will be carried to the seat of government; and it is impossible to say what impressions may be made there to the disadvantage of a great portion of our countrymen. But would to God the powers in England were present this day, to hear the charges made against a respectable body of persons, and the manner in which they have been *attempted* to be proved.

It belongs to me to speak only of three persons—Mr. Bird, Mr. Hamill, and Mr. Delahoyde. It is not the unhoused villain and profligate vagabond upon whom you sit in judgment. It is the opulent and respectable merchant—the man who owes every thing to his public character. This is the description of men to be tried.

It cannot possibly be imagined, that the plan had been formed to excite previous prejudices in their favour. If it was, the manner of their arrest and subsequent treatment shows them to have been much disappointed. Mr. Bird was taken out of his bed at eleven o'clock at night, and brought to the capital under a military guard, after a very uncomfortable imprisonment of one night in the Town-house. He was not indulged in the common decencies of imprisonment—nor suffered to enjoy the visits of his friends!—an indulgence permitted to the most flagitious criminals however low the description. Pen and ink were denied him; and he was brought to the capital, and there lodged among the vilest malefactors. He applied to the court of King's Bench to be admitted to bail, fancying from his character he would be admitted. That was denied him. From this, it might be imagined that there was some respectable witness or prosecutor of character to criminate him. You have all seen and heard them.

I certainly consider, that when crimes of this kind are committed, it must be neçessary that some of the parties concerned should turn approver. I am well aware, that to shut out such from examination, would be to stop public justice; but yet, I did imagine, that in the present case some respectable witness would come forward to disclose the turpitude of the offence. To support the enormous charges in the indictment, one Murphy has been produced. But, as gentlemen who are chosen to decide on a matter, upon the issue of which the safety of a great part of the population of Ireland depends, I ask you, is there safety for the life of any man, if the testimony of such a witness has weight in a court of justice? Upon his examination he declared to the learned judge, that he had been examined before at Dundalk, and acknowledged that there the jury showed no respect to his evidence, and, therefore, he did not wish to be examined. On the evidence of a man having such apprehensions of himself, a jury should decide with extreme caution. The man to be believed by a respectable jury against respectable persons, is Murphy, confessedly a robber by character, tried twice in another county upon charges of a flagitious nature, and discharged out of court by proclamation. If you believe him, you must credit the testimony of a man who acknowledges himself to have fired shots into the house of Mr. M'Clintock, with an intent to commit murder.

When the prosecutor lodged these examinations, it appears, he was in gaol, in actual custody. It is now for you to consider, whether, in your unbiassed judgment, the story hangs well together. Mr. Bird and Mr. Hamill, it is well known, exerted themselves much in forwarding the cause of the Roman Catholics. You are told these gentlemen formed committees in ale-houses—that they there associated with the vilest miscreants, to assassinate the Protestants of the land, at a time when the object they had in view was going on prosperously in the legislature of the nation! Is it likely that, at such a period, they would form a plot for the extermination of their Protestant fellow-subjects? Such a supposition is contrary to common sense. Is it likely, that a country reduced to such an unhappy state, that manufacturers are in a state of requisition for the fabrication of arms, should be considered an eligible market for their purchase? It is to me peculiarly nauseous to take up much of your time in describing the character of a wretch like Murphy; I shall, therefore, proceed to the matter most worthy of your consideration. Some of the jury who sit here to-day sat in this court yesterday. They must have heard the observations made by the learned judge who presided. "If (said the learned judge) a witness forswears himself in any material circumstance, making a substantive part of the accusation upon which the prosecution is grounded, the rest of his evidence, although it may be true, should be discredited." I speak this in the recollection of several gentlemen present. If I have stated it wrong, I am sure they will set me right. Gentlemen, I now call upon you to put this principle in practice. Murphy swore in his examinations that he saw money distributed at the committee upon several times and occasions, and that all the persons charged gave the examinant money at several times. Does not all this appear from his own evidence to be false?

Gentlemen, upon such an occasion as this, there is no man but may be drawn beyond the line of calm discussion. For that reason, I have studiously endeavoured to argue the subject coolly, and, therefore, to come to a cool examination of facts. Did Murphy, in his examination, swear he got money from all the traversers at the bar, and did he, on the table, swear he got money but from one? And is there any jury that will be so base as to found a conviction upon such evidence? I am well aware, gentlemen, that nothing is more strongly corroborative of the truth of an evidence, than little accidental deviation in immaterial circumstances. The present must appear to you, however, quite a contrary case.

What has he said of arms? In his examination it is stated that he saw a box of arms landed at Annagassin, and distributed. What has he said himself on the table? That he did not see them distributed, but laid against a wall. Is this no material circumstance in the prosecution? If you ask is it material, I tell you it is. It is a part of the charge, for procuring and distributing arms for the abolition of the Protestant government. I speak in the presence of the court, and in the presence of a right honourable gentleman, my personal respect for whom prevents me from saying what he knows I think of his conduct. The procuring of arms for the purpose specified is a circumstance highly material to the prosecution; it amounts to an act of High Treason. I mention this, to show, upon that fact, you have certain evidence of perjury. You have better evidence of the fact, than if he had been indicted for perjury—you have the man confronted by his own oath. When a man swears two ways upon the same fact, it is physically impossible that he should not be perjured.

There is another person brought forward as a witness in this prosecution, whose state in society it is difficult to ascertain. He was indicted—tried—convicted—pardoned—enlisted—deserted—retaken—brought to gaol—and becomes an approver! If, gentlemen, you apply the same rule to this man, you are to consider has he also perjured himself in a material fact. Gentlemen, it is for you to exercise your judgment in this affair. I had not the informations. It was impossible for me to know any thing about Tiernan—impossible for me to be acquainted with the fact of his having lodged an information against him, as he denied it on the table. In the information read by his lordship, the examinant says, he knew the place of Tiernan's abode—that he has been acquainted with him intimately for six years—and saw him frequently at the Defenders' committees, in company with the traversers. What is his evidence now? Directly the reverse. You have heard him swear that he never saw Tiernan at any of the meetings. You have heard more—you have heard him swear that he never swore so. His lordship asked him, could he have sworn to that effect and forgotten it? He swears positively not. Here is a direct and irreconcileable contradiction between his examination, sworn before a magistrate, and his testimony on this table. And here, gentlemen, you must be convinced that it is impossible he could be forsworn in so material a fact, if not intentionally. You must see clearly that he is deliberately forsworn.

Indeed, if it was not known by unfortunate experience, and particularly in many recent instances, it could scarcely be conceived that such abominable turpitude could find place in any human being. It could scarcely be conceived, that any being, endued with a rational and immortal soul, would deliberately come forward to forswear himself in a court of justice, and, in the face of heaven, to "bear false witness against his neighbour," under such circumstances, as if credited, must cause the life of the accused to be forfeited. Such acts can only proceed from minds the most obdurate. If you see this done in the present case, you must consider it a crime against a great body of your fellow-subjects, and tending directly to disunite the people. It must be of high consideration to you, that when you acquit, you will be able to say, you do not merely acquit because you cannot condemn;

but you acquit from a secondary motive, of discountenancing the persecution of any particular description of people.

The gentlemen here to-day at your bar are merchants—men, whose most valuable property is the integrity of their characters. They have correspondents in foreign countries—in Great Britain, for instance. What effect, then, must it have, when read in foreign newspapers, that such and such men were taken up, to be tried for rebellion against the laws of the country where they live? How will any merchant in England be able to discover, whether they may not really be guilty of the crime against society with which they are charged?

I know, from recent experience, that an acquittal, however honourable, does not wipe off the aspersion which such charges cast on men's characters. I have particularly experienced it in a neighbouring county. I have there been asked, did not I think Fay had a lucky escape! I am aware, gentlemen, you must have a conviction that what has been brought forward in evidence is false; but where allegations of this sort are made, it is proper to try them in the most public manner. I know your characters, and I think you will not content yourselves with a mere acquittal. It should not be alone; it should be accompanied by something calculated to do away the unjust imputations upon the characters of the accused. If, however, you consider further evidence necessary, or feel any dissatisfaction upon your minds, we can produce two or three witnesses.

CURRAN examined several witnesses, the Attorney-General replied, the judge charged, and the jury, in a few minutes, returned a verdict of *Not Guilty.*

The following slip from the back of this Report may be interesting:—

"On Wednesday, the 23rd of April, 1794, came on also the trial of James Skelton, Esq., M.D., of the town of Drogheda, on an Indictment for having, on the 30th day of January, in the 33rd year of his Majesty's reign, taken an unlawful oath, to be a true Defender, not being compelled thereto by any necessity.

"To this indictment Mr. Skelton pleaded the general issue—Not Guilty.

"No evidence being produced on behalf of the crown,

"Mr. CURRAN said—As I understand the learned counsel on behalf of the crown do not mean to bring forward any evidence on the present trial, I must consider that circumstance to be an unanswerable justification of the gentleman accused.

"Mr. M'Cartney—My lord, we have reasons for not bringing them forward.

"Mr. Skelton was then acquitted, and discharged."

DOCTOR DRENNAN.

June 25th, 1794.

WILLIAM DRENNAN, Esq., M.D., was one of the ablest writers and truest patriots during the long struggle for Irish independence. One of his earliest works was Orellana, or the Letters of an Irish Helot, published in 1779, advocating a free constitution, and written with a passionate vigour, which greatly aided the cause, and made the writer famous. He was an intimate of Tone's, who speaks highly of his powers and resolve,—was an early member of the United Irish Society,—and, as we have seen in the introduction to Curran's defence of Rowan, was the writer of the famous counter-proclamation, beginning "Citizen Soldiers!" He was chairman of the meeting (of which Rowan was secretary), at which that document was passed, and was indicted for a seditious libel for having published it. The indictment was found by the City of Dublin Grand Jury in Easter Term, 1794, and contained nine counts, but only two were relied on. viz., the 2nd count, charging him with publishing the libel in "The Hibernian Journal, or Chronicle of Liberty," on the 17th of December, 1793, and the 8th count, charging publication generally.

To this indictment, Dr. Drennan was in the same term called upon to plead.

The Hon. Mr. Butler, and Mr. Emmet, applied to the court for four days' time to plead, and a copy of the indictment.

The Attorney-General, on behalf of the crown, opposed the motion for time to plead, which he insisted was never allowed in case of an indictment. As to the copy of the indictment, if Dr. Drennan had, as his counsel contended, a right to it, he would obtain it, of course, without any such application as this now made.

The court was of opinion with the Attorney-General; and Dr. Drennan, having been arraigned, traversed the indictment.

The 25th of June (in Trinity term) was appointed for the trial.

Wednesday, June 25, 1794.

The court sat at half-past ten. Mr. Justice Boyd, having been taken ill, did not preside.

Dr. Drennan appeared in court with his bail.

The High Sheriffs returned the *venire facias,* with a panel thereto annexed. The panel having been called over, and twenty-six gentlemen having answered to their names, the Clerk of the Crown proceeded to swear the jury.

Sir John Trail, Knight, was called.

Mr. CURRAN—My lord, I understand that this gentleman has declared an opinion on the subject of this prosecution.

Right Hon. Attorney-General—I wonder to see these things practised again. I thought they would be ashamed of such artifices. I am sure the learned gentleman has been instructed to do this. These things are intended to go abroad, and have an effect on the public mind. If this is a cause of challenge—if it is law, that this is cause of challenge—let it be made; let us have the opinion of the court upon it.

Mr. CURRAN—My lord, I stand upon nothing but the rule of law. If what I said be fact, surely he is not a proper juror to try the cause. If he has a preconceived opinion on the subject, I would put the question in the mode which the law warrants, by swearing the juror. It is true, he is not bound to answer anything to his prejudice; but it cannot be to his prejudice to say that he has formed an opinion. Forming an opinion is not a culpable matter in our law; I, therefore, desire to have him sworn.

The Attorney-General—The gentleman has a right to challenge if he has good ground.

Mr. Curran—I move, my lord, that Sir John Trail may be sworn to answer.

Lord Clonmel—It cannot be done; it is not a legal practice.

Mr. Justice Downes—I looked into the books on this point on a former occasion. It is laid down expressly, in Hawkins, that this ought not to be done.

Mr. Curran—I cannot support the objection by any other evidence than the gentleman's own.

Attorney-General — Surely you might by your informer's testimony.*

Sir John Trail was sworn.
Robert Alexander, merchant, sworn.
Mark White, merchant, sworn.
William Lindsay, merchant, sworn.
Benjamin Woodward, merchant, sworn.
Mark Bloxham, merchant, sworn.
Peter Roe, merchant, sworn.
William Beeby, merchant, sworn.
Jeffrey Foot, merchant, sworn.
James Hamilton, merchant, sworn.
William Little, merchant, sworn.
William Galway, merchant, sworn.

The indictment was then read by the Clerk of the Crown, and Dr. Drennan given in charge to the jury.

The several counts were deliberately read, and the different copies of the libel scrupulously and accurately compared with the record by the traverser's counsel. No variance however appeared.

Mr. Ruxton opened the indictment.

The Attorney-General stated the case for the prosecution, and called five witnesses to prove that Drennan was chairman of the meeting at which the address was passed, and that it was published by his (Drennan's) direction. The chief witness

* Trail proved the propriety of the challenge by his audacious speech at the close of the trial.

was William Paulet Carey, printer and publisher of tho "National Evening Star." The Prime-Sergeant examined him in a series of leading questions, to which Curran objected, and got favourable decisions, *after* the questions were answered. Curran cross-examined him at great length, making him contradict himself, and fail in his evidence of the identity of the document read by Drennan and that in the indictment. It appeared that the address was printed in a hand-bill by one M'Allister, but this could not be got. However, Carey acknowledged that he was a United Irishman; that after the address, he had in the society proposed taking up arms, but had been resisted by Dr. Drennan, and that being under prosecution, the society had failed to support him, for which reason he was hostile to its members, and especially to Dr. Drennan.

"Mr. Thomas M'Donnell was also examined, to prove tho printing in the "Hibernian Journal," but broke down under the direct examination.

The first witness for the defence was Thomas Traynor, who answered Mr. Fletcher as follows:—

Do you know Mr. William Paulet Carey? I do.

What are you, Sir? I am a merchant, and live in Poolbeg-street.

Had you ever any conversation with Carey respecting the traverser? I had; I was mentioning to some person that I thought Carey was much aggrieved; and that I would set on foot a subscription for his relief—

How long since is this? This was about the 1st of April last; I did not know Carey before; he waited on me next day; he told me he was much obliged to me for my intention—that he had been much aggrieved by the United Society of Irishmen—but that if they would pay his bail, he would quit the kingdom; he added, that he did not like either to turn informer against Drennan or lose his liberty, and that a few guineas would be of infinite service to him.

Did he threaten the traverser at all? He said that if he did leave the kingdom, he would give Drennan a *flailing* before he went; said I, "Drennan is a delicate little man, and a stroke from a strong man would kill him;" he answered that, "By Jesus, he would think it no crime to assassinate such a villain, who had ruined his peace for ever, and made a motion to expel him from the United Society of Irishmen, just at the time they should have supported him;" some time after this I heard Dr. Drennan was taken up.

Did you see Carey at any time after? He never came near me since.

Attorney-General—You may go down. Mr. Traynor; I shall not cross-examine you.

After some other evidence for the defence, Curran spoke as follows:—

My Lord, and Gentlemen of the Jury—I am of counsel for Doctor Drennan, the traverser; and, gentlemen, I do not, for the sake of my client, regret that my state of health prevents me trespassing long on your time, or that of the court; for my heart tells me, that if he is reduced to stand in need of any effort from talent, that it is impossible, under the circumstances of the case, that he can hope for any assistance from an advocate, where, if there is any danger of conviction, it must arise from what passes in the minds of the jury, and not from any thing which has passed in this court.

It may be a loss to the traverser that he is not aided by the personal exertions of those who are connected with him by habits of life and uniformity of pursuits. Such a person I am not; to him I am a perfect stranger. I never, to my knowledge, exchanged a word with him, save once in the public street. I never was under the same roof with him that I know of; and the reason why I yielded to an ordinary application to become his counsel, was, because I had been personally defamed for acting as counsel in the defence of another, who was charged with the same libel. I felt that my character in the world, little as it may be, was owing all to my professional talents; and I feel that, if a barrister can act so mean and despicable a part as to decline, from personal apprehension, the defence of any man accused, he does not deserve to be heard in any court of justice.

I will state shortly what I conceive the question to be, and the evidence brought in support of the charge.

The indictment is, that Dr. Drennan, the traverser, did publish the libel, and that he did print and publish the paper, with the base and seditious intentions there stated. To this he has pleaded not guilty; and one question to be tried is, did he in point of fact, publish the paper? The next, upon which I shall trouble you but very little, is as to the nature of the paper—whether it is a seditious libel or not?

The law of libels in this country and in Great Britain has lately, (by the perseverance and exertions of two men—Mr. Fox and Mr. Erskine—being at last crowned with success), undergone a most fortunate change.

There is said, gentlemen, to be an instinct in

animals, which directs them to those medicines which relieve their disorders; and it seems as if, in the public malady of the three kingdoms, this only medicine had been discovered, and carried into effect by this law.

For part of the court which I address, I have infinite regard and esteem. To extend that profession would, perhaps, be as presumptuous, as it would flatter my vanity; but let me not by this be understood to profess any contrary feeling. I merely disavow the arrogance of affecting to feel, where I have no claim to any interest.

But, gentlemen, the law has taken the power of decision in those cases from the court, and vested it in you. And you are not only to inquire into the fact of publication, but into the question of "libel or not." Upon the latter question I have said I would make a few observations; but I will be frank with you, and will say, that if you have any disposition to believe the fact of publication, I would advise the traverser to prepare with a fatal facility to receive your opinion, that the paper is whatever the prosecutors please to call it. For, if you believe it, it must be from some perversion of mind—some gangrene of principle, with which I disdain to hold parlance or communication; and this I say, from a proud conviction, that there will be no law in this country, when such monstrous facts are swallowed by juries, and the country disgraced by such convictions.

As to the liberty of the press, I have heard and I have read of some things relative to it lately, at which I am truly astonished. I have heard, that an English Attorney-General could say, "that the guilt or innocence of a man depends on the candour with which he writes." I feel that this must have been an imposition, I cannot believe that it could have been said. The liberty of the press does not consist in reasoning right—in candour—or in weighing the preponderancy of arguments, as a grocer weighs his wares; it is founded in the principle, that government is established for the happiness of the people—that the people have a kind of superintendant, or inquisitorial power, to watch over government, that they may be satisfied that the object is truly sought. The liberty of the press is not for expressing merely argument, but to convey the feelings of personal discontent against the government, that the passions of the governors may be checked; and if any one is bold enough to tell them they over-bound their duty, they may be tortured into rectitude, by being held up as objects of odium, abomination, horror, or ridicule.

I you confine the liberty of the press to fair argument—if you condemn, as libellous, every publication, where invective may be a little too warm—where it may go beyond the enormity, or the complaint beyond the grievance—you destroy it.

Every man knows what is a public crime; the

maliciously pointing out grievances so as to disturb the quiet of the country: such a crime will never find protection from a court or a jury. If the traverser did intend "to diffuse among the subjects of this realm, discontents, jealousies, and suspicions of our sovereign lord the king, and his government; disaffections and disloyalties to his person and government; and to raise very dangerous seditions and tumults within this kingdom," &c., he ought to be found guilty—if he did not, he is entitled to acquittal. Having said this, I dismiss the subject; because, I trust in God, so fatal an example to the liberties of this country, as a condemnation upon such evidence, will never be given.

What has Carey sworn?—that he was at a meeting on the 14th of December; that Dr. Drennan was there; that the question was put on an address; that he himself was desired to publish that address; that the manuscript could not be given him, but that he should take it from the *Dublin Journal** of the next Monday; that he sent for that paper; a great deal of his evidence went to proving the *Star*, but that was not read, and is out of the question. The question is therefore narrowed to the publication in the *Dublin Journal;* is there any evidence that this was the paper read in the

* "It is evident that Mr. Curran meant the *Hibernian Journal*, but these were certainly his words." The foregoing note appears in the pamphlet report, which is plainly hostile to Drennan and his counsel throughout.

society? No. What is it?—Carey has told you—indeed he told you the impossibility of his swearing it; I read the address in the paper—he could not swear even to the substance, he could not tell that it was the same. Coiling and twining about me, as you saw that wretched man, he could not prove this; therefore, all the evidence on this part comes to this, that Dr. Drennan did produce some address in that meeting, but of what it contained you have no evidence before you. And, as to the publication in the *Hibernian*, the evidence is so vague, that it can give no aid whatever to the former proof; so that the evidence stops at the meeting in Back-lane.

I asked Carey what address he was desired to publish—he answered, that agreed to by the society; what proof have you that he did so?—it will be ingeniously endeavoured to impress upon your minds, that a general power to publish was given by the traverser to Carey, and that he thereby made himself personally liable for Carey's acts.

The consequence of such a doctrine as that a man could commit himself for any future publication, made without his privity, would be so wild and desperate, that it is unnecessary to do more than offer it to you in its true light.

But Carey has pinned the authority to a particular publication of the particular paper read in the society. What question are you trying? are you trying the traverser for every possible publication which might have been sent to M'Donnell's paper? do you live in a country where such unlimited power is given to informers? Suppose Carey to have taken from M'Donnell's paper a libel which Dr. Drennan never saw—he is, by this doctrine, responsible—is it not too ridiculous; and does it not come to this, that Carey was tied down to publish that particular paper read in the society, and no other; has he said then that it was the same paper which appeared in the *Dublin Journal?* where is the evidence that it was the same paper, and where is the guilt of Dr. Drennan?

But, it will be said, by his declaration of an intent to publish it, he made himself answerable. Did he give it to M'Donnell to be published by him? or, to take a previous question, did M'Donnell publish it himself? Has he said so? No such thing. But, what did he tell you?—that any other printer might have published the paper produced, if he had had the materials; but it is highly probable that he printed it. What! is a man to be sent for two years to gaol, because you believe it *highly probable* that M'Donnell published this paper? Are you prepared by any impression whatsoever, so far to humble your minds, as to swear that M'Donnell did publish this very paper, though the man himself cannot say so? Where is your honesty, or where is your common sense, if they can be *flattened* down into a verdict founded on nothing but your own credulity?

If Dr. Drennan had given the paper to M'Donnell the acts of the printer might derive credit from the original author; as it is, see how far this would be carrying constructive authority. What, my lord, is the act of the third person?—Is it the law, that the act of a printer, with the witness Lestrange, should affect the traverser, who knew nothing of the transaction? The argument is, that the delivery by M'Donnell to Lestrange was, no doubt, a publication by the traverser; but I say that nothing he does or says can affect Dr. Drennan.

Suppose I were charged with committing murder, and that I had employed the crier of the court for the purpose; if he did the fact by my directions, he is guilty; but no confession of his can be evidence against me. So the publication of M'Donnell, with the authority of Dr. Drennan, might be evidence; but no declaration of M'Donnell's can be evidence. The argument is, that M'Donnell admitted the fact, by giving the paper to the stamp officer; but was this admission on oath? Is what he said to a petty officer of stamps to be evidence against my client? But M'Donnell does not recollect this transaction—he does not, on his oath, confirm the statement by Lestrange—and yet you are desired to take Lestrange's evidence of what M'Donnell did. If you do, purposes may, indeed, be answered; and we have heard that there are many prosecutions in *petto*—many persons over whom the arm of the law is only suspended.

This may be policy, to keep the abandoned informer haunting the slumbers of the innocent man; but it is for you to consider, is such a time as this proper for it. In the present melancholy of the public mind, how far will it heal the grief which afflicts society? Or, will it not rather answer the immediate and selfish objects of those whom a small gale may waft to that point, where the recollection of the country and its situation will never assail their ears?

But of the *probability* of this evidence how shall I speak? What does it depend on? The integrity of the man who swears it. Do you think, gentlemen, that in every case an oath is a sufficient measure to weigh down life and liberty?—where a miscreant swears guilt against a man, must you convict him?

The declaration that the paper would appear in the *Hibernian Journal* stands on the single evidence of Carey. Was he consistent with himself? If he did not appear to you upon that table a perjured man, believe every word he said. This man was under two prosecutions for this and another libel; this charge is to rest as well on his memory as his credit. He received a summons, signed by the Lord Chief Justice of Ireland!! Do you believe, gentlemen, that Lord Clonmel's name was to it? Examine Mr. Kemmis.

What is the answer? That he thought it was—he could not answer—he was sure it was. And this man, who comes to tell of words *spoken* two years ago, makes this silly mistake about the Chief Justice's name. Again, "Who are you?" "I was under prosecution"—"I was a member of the society"—"I do not know whether I would have prosecuted or not, if they had kept their word." Three different things he swore as to my lord's name:—he did recollect; next, he did not; and, last of all, he could not tell. Does he not appear that kind of man, on whose evidence no man ought to be convicted? Scarce ever have I known a conviction on the mere evidence of an informer. But see what motives this man has: under prosecution for the same crime, he has not only his own safety to consult, but the most avowed and rancorous malice to Doctor Drennan. He swore he had none. Did you not hear of his declaration of vengeance? A gentleman comes and swears that he said he thought it no crime to assassinate Drennan, for a refusal to support him under a criminal prosecution—to support the man who proposed to the society to arm against the government.

I asked him why he proposed this? Merely to try character. Was he himself sincere? He was!—he was perfectly sincere; and yet it was a mere fetch to try character!

As to the influence of his situation on his evidence, what did he say?—he was not sure of a pardon, but he hoped for one. If you give credit to this man, you make a fine harvest for informers; a fine opportunity you give to every ruffian in society; and you may go home in the comfortable conviction, that it is far from impossible that the next attack shall be on yourselves; and if your wives are superstitious, or your children undutiful, you may have them going to fortune-tellers to inquire "when Mr. Carey shall be unmuzzled against you."

So far as Bell's testimony was appealed to, he contradicted Carey. He did not believe that the words of the address stood any part of the paper read, and no human being has given evidence of the general substance. Bell contradicted him again; for he said there were no orders made to print it in any paper. And what did Wright say? That it was after the publication in the *Hibernian Journal* that Carey complained to him of having been neglected, and asked should he publish the paper. "How shall I publish it?" says he; "the *Evening Post* is nonsense." Says Wright, "take it from the *Hibernian Journal*." Here is the positive oath of this unimpeached witness contradicting Carey's evidence. Unfortunate, perjured man, he makes a complaint that he received no instructions; he complains of the whole society. Gentlemen, do you believe Wright?

But there is a way in which you may get out of this. It will be said, "God forbid that a man should not perjure himself in one or two little points, and tell truth in the whole;" an old woman may say, that oaths are but wind—he might tell truth at other times. Did you ever, gentlemen, hear of a point in which a perjured witness might be believed? Yes, there is one—when he says he is perjured. The principle is as strong in our hearts, as if it had been written by the finger of that God who said, *"thou shalt not bear false witness."* The law of the country has said that the man once convicted of false swearing shall not a second time contaminate the walls of a court of justice; and it is the very essence of a jury, that if a man appears (though not yet marked out by the law as a perjurer) to have soiled his nature by the deliberate commission of this crime, that moment his credit shall cease with the jury—his evidence shall be blotted from their minds, and leave no trace but horror and indignation.

I feel the hardship of their situation, when grave and learned men are brought forward to support such a prosecution. I have great respect for them—for some of them I have had it from my boyish days—but this respect does not prevent my saying, that, as officers of state, their private worth is not to weigh with you. It is for their credit to deceive you. They have no power to control a prosecution—if one is commanded, they must carry it on; and when they talk of their character, what do they say?—"If the evidence is insufficient, take a little of our dignity to eke it out." What their feelings are is nothing to you, gentlemen; they may have feelings of another kind to compensate for them.

But while I lament this, I will show that your sympathy is not called forth for nothing. Why do we hear such expressions as these—"I speak under the authority of a former jury?" Has that verdict been given in evidence? No. Could it govern you if it had? No. Here you see the necessity of an appeal to official dignity. We heard of clubs formed in this city; we had no evidence of them that their object was to separate the countries. Does this appear? To pull the king from his throne; what can I say, but "how does this appear." Not a word of it has been proved; and here let me mention the impolicy of such expressions, and say that the frequent recital of such circumstances will rather reconcile profligate minds to them than deter them.

As to the Society of United Irishmen, I have had the misfortune, from my strong reprobation of their conduct, to incur much contumelious animadversion. But where is their desperate purpose to be found? Is it in the rejection of Carey's proposal to arm? Does this show their design to pull the king from the throne, or to separate the countries? But it comes down to the *horrible blasphemy* of reviling the police. To make their case more hideous and more aggravated, you are told of their blaspheming the *sanctified* police—the *holy, prudent,* and *economical* police.

Did they suppose that they were addressing the liquorish loyalty of a guzzling corporation? Or do you suppose, gentlemen, that there is a collation of *custards* prepared for you when you leave the jury-box, when they wished to excite your compassion for the *abused* police? But it is said, that they not only attack existing establishments, but sully the character of the *unborn* militia, that they hurl their shafts against what was to be raised the next year. "So, *Gossip*," says the flatterer to *Timon*. "What," says he, "I did not know you had children." "Nay, but I will marry, shortly, and my first child shall be called Timon, and then we shall be gossips." So this wizard, Drennan, found out that a militia was to be raised the next year, and he not only abused the corporation but the police and the militia.

Do they think you are such buzzards—such blind creatures—do they think you are only fit to go to school—or rather to go where one part would be punished, for no other reason, than its exact similarity to the other?

I protest I have been eighteen years at this bar, and never, until this last year, have I seen such witnesses supporting charges of this kind with such abandoned profligacy. In one case, where men were on trial for their lives, I felt myself involuntarily shrinking under your lordships' protection, from the miscreant who leaped upon the table, and announced himself a witness. I had hoped the practice would have remained in those distant parts of the country where it began; but I was disappointed. I have seen it parading through the capital, and I feel that the night of unenlightened wretchedness is fast approaching, when a man shall be judged before he is tried—when the advocate shall be libelled for discharging his duty to his client; that night of human nature, when a man shall be hunted down, not because he is a criminal, but because he is obnoxious.

Punish a man in the situation of Dr. Drennan, and what do you do? what will become of the liberty of the press? you will have the newspapers filled with the drowsy adulations of some persons who want benefices, or commissions in the revenue, or commissions in the army; here and there, indeed, you may chance to see a paragraph of this kind:—

"*Yesterday came on to be tried, for the publication of a seditious libel, Dr. William Drennan. The great law-officer of the crown stated the case in the most candid and temperate manner. During his speech every man in court was in an agony of horror; the gentlemen of the jury—many of them from the rotation office, were all staunch whigs, and friends to government. Mr. Carey came on the table, and declared that he had no malice against the traverser, and most honourably denied the assertion in his next breath. It was proved, much to his honour, that he had declared his intention to assassinate the traverser. The jury listened with great attention. Mr. Curran, with his usual ability, defended the traverser;*"—for he must have been ably defended. "*Dr. Wright was produced, a bloody minded United Irishman—*

he declared, he could not say but that Dr. Drennan was the author of the libel; and that the types were very like each other in the face. An able speech was made in reply by his Majesty's Prime-Sergeant. He said, with the utmost propriety, that the jury knew little of him, if they supposed him to prosecute without a perfect conviction of the traverser's guilt; that Mr. Curran's great abilities had been spent in jests on the subject; that the perjuries were mere little inconsistencies, the gentleman having much on his mind. He made many pertinent observations on the aspersions thrown out on the corporation of Dublin.

"Here Mr. Curran interposed, and assured him he intended no such aspersions. The Prime-Sergeant declared he thought he had heard them. That, as to the Police, they were a most honourable body of men; that a number of looking-glasses, and other articles of furniture, were highly necessary for them; and as to the militia, the attack on that was abominable, for that it was shameful to asperse a body intended to be raised by government next year.

"The Jury—a most worshipful, worthy jury, retired for a few minutes, and returned with a verdict of GUILTY, *much to the satisfaction of the public."*

To this sort of language will you reduce the freedom of public discussion, by a conviction of the traverser: and if the liberty of the press is destroyed for a supposed abuse, this is the kind of discussion you will have.

The Prime-Sergeant replied angrily. Lord Clonmel charged strongly, that the document was a libel, but with some fairness as to Carey's contradictions, and the doubt thereby thrown on the fact of Drennan's having ordered the publication. Justices Downes and Chamberlain concurred with Earl Clonmel, and at 10 o'clock at night the jury retired. At a quarter past 11 they came into court, and (the judges being absent) in reply to the officer, the foreman, Sir John Trail, said the verdict was *Not Guilty*. A burst of applause followed, whereon the foreman retired, and returned and gave in to one of the judges the verdict, with the following comment:—

"My lords, as I consider this a trial of the first importance to the peace of the country, and the happiness of society, I must conceive such indecent conduct as we have experienced, to bespeak a spreading pernicious spirit, which, by an exertion of power, ought to be suppressed. For my own part, timidity has no influence on my mind—I act without fear—I despise the resentment, and disregard the approbation of an unruly and seditious rabble; and I can assure them, they have no cause for exultation in meeting favour from the jury; for they regret at seeing a criminal they cannot reach, and guilt which they cannot punish."

The other counts were then severally put to the jury, and a verdict of *Not Guilty,* received upon all.

NORTHERN STAR.

28*th May*, 1794.

THE following introduction that can be given to CURRAN'S very short speech in this case is that prefixed to the pamphlet report of the trial:—

"The measures which government have taken against the proprietors of the *Northern Star* having excited a considerable share of public curiosity, and it being of importance that the nature and extent of proceedings by information, on the part of the crown, should be generally known, a brief narrative of the prosecution, previous to the following trial, cannot but be interesting.

"The alarming circumstances with which this business commenced are worthy of particular notice. The following account of the ARREST is, therefore, copied from the *Northern Star* of January 2, 1793:—

"'For several days past, rumours prevailed that government meditated an attack on the proprietors of this paper. The reports gained considerable ground on Sunday last; and on the evening of that day a troop of light dragoons, which had been stationed at Banbridge, arrived here, in consequence of an express from this town. At the same time, all the out companies belonging to the regiment quartered here were ordered in with all possible dispatch.

"'These menacing appearances, in a time of perfect peace, and without any previous tumult or disturbance whatever to give the faintest colour of propriety to, or necessity for, such a measure, induced in the proprietors a doubt, whether some very extraordinary act of arbitrary power was not intended against them, the more especially as a general officer had been sent here to take the command of the troops in this part of the kingdom.

"'Under these impressions, one of the proprietors wrote a letter to the sovereign of this town early on Monday morning, of which the following is a copy:—

"'Belfast, December 31, 1792.

"'Mr. Sovereign—It is affirmed that a troop of light horse came to this town last night, and that more are on their way, in consequence of an application from you, as chief magistrate, demanding aid in the execution of certain warrants or orders against individual inhabitants of the town; and it is farther said, that you have represented the town to be in such a state, that said orders could not be executed without the protection of a strong military force.

"'Now, sir, as an inhabitant of Belfast, anxious to maintain the high character of the town—as a Volunteer, who has, in conjunction with my companions, manifested an ardent desire to support the civil magistrate in the due execution of the law—but above all, as a proprietor of a newspaper, which is said to be one object of attack on the present occasion—I call upon you to do away so foul a calumny on the town, over the peace of which you preside; I call upon you to avow the fact, *that the civil power of Belfast is capable of supporting the magistrate in the legal execution of his office;* and in my latter capacity, I will add, that the printer of the paper I allude to, will instantly and cheerfully submit to and obey any *legal* summons, order, or arrest. But any proceeding against him contrary to the law of the land will be resisted, and he will throw himself in such a case for protection on his fellow-citizens, who have declared that they will maintain law, peace, and order, equally against "a *mob* or a *monarch,* a riot or a proclamation."

"'Candour—a regard to your character—but more particularly to the peace and character of the town of Belfast, demand of me this communication.

"'I am, Sir, yours truly, &c.

"'To the Rev. W. Bristow, Sovereign of Belfast.

"'Just as this letter was dispatching to the chief magistrate, he called on the gentleman who wrote it—told him there was an order or warrant in town, for the purpose of holding the proprietors to bail, for a certain publication in the *Northern Star,* of the 5th of December last; and that he would earnestly recommend a peaceable obedience to the law, in order that the matter might come fairly to issue. It was replied, that if the order was in the nature of a judge's warrant or any other *legal* proceeding, it would meet a prompt obedience. The sovereign said that the order was strictly legal, and by no means a proceeding of an extraordinary nature.

"'On reading the letter, the sovereign *most solemnly* declared, that the calling in the troops was not a measure of his, and even done without his knowledge—that the officer from the King's Bench was instructed not to use force—and, farther, that he (the sovereign) was determined not to use military aid on any such occasion.

"'It was then stated, that, as the proprietors were numerous, and all, less or more, engaged in mercantile pursuits, it would be at once a cruel and unnecessary exercise of power to hurry them away eighty-two miles, from their homes and their business, to enter into a recognizance in Dublin; that they were now ready to do so before the chief magistrate, or would surrender at due time, before the justices of the King's Bench, previous to the time of trial.

"'The sovereign, struck with the force of these remarks, took some time to consider, and, finally, agreed to write to government, requesting power might be sent to him, and such other magistrates as might be thought proper, to take bail of the proprietors in Belfast, they, at the same time, pledging themselves to appear in Dublin, for the purpose of giving security, in case this application should prove fruitless.

"'After the business was thus arranged, the officer who had the warrant was admitted, and received the *voluntary submission* of the proprietors, in the presence of the sovereign.'

"The application from the chief magistrate having been refused by government, the proprietors repaired to Dublin, and entered into recognizances on the 7th of January, before Lord Chief Justice Clonmel, themselves in £100, and two sureties in £50 each. When before his lordship, it was entreated that the proprietors might be informed what the publication was for which they had been arrested? His lordship said it was for a publication inserted in the *Northern Star* of the 5th of December, but did not recollect precisely of what nature is was. Counsel then asked his lordship for a copy of the warrant, which was refused.

"Next term the King's Attorney-General filed *six* informations against the proprietors, for having inserted so many seditious publications, including one inserted on the 5th of December. The assizes shortly after succeeded; but Mr. Attorney-General did not think proper to come to trial on any of the informations. During the next term (Easter) no step whatever was taken; but early in Trinity Term, a *seventh* information was filed, for publishing the resolutions of the town of Belfast in the preceding December.

"During this term, the Court of King's Bench was moved, on the part of the defendants, that their recognizances should be vacated, inasmuch as the Attorney-General had proceeded by information, instead of indictment; that he had not come to a trial, although an assizes had intervened; and that the recognizances only related to the execution and warrant on which they had been bound over. This application was refused.

"On the 19th of July, the proprietors' agent was served with notice of trial on *two* out of the *seven* informations, at the ensuing assizes for the county of Antrim, the publication of the 5th of December *not* being one. In consequence of this notice, the proprietors prepared for their trial, engaged a respectable bar, gave out their briefs, and had Mr. Curran retained, to come down specially on the occasion from Dublin; but on the 3rd of August (only five days before the assizes), they were informed that the crown lawyers *did not think fit to proceed.*

"In Michaelmas Term, 1793, the Attorney-General came into court and moved, *as a matter of right,* for a trial at bar, on the 4th of February, 1794. To this motion the court acceded. The Attorney-General did not give any reason why the sheriff, jury, and defendants should be taken to Dublin, to try a cause which originated in the county of Antrim.

"A motion, on behalf of the proprietors, during this term, had the effect of obtaining an order to the crown solicitor, that he would give notice what information he meant to proceed upon.

"On the 1st of February last, the Court of King's Bench (on an application on behalf of the defendants) ordered the trial to stand for the 19th of May, at bar, the Attorney-General refusing to permit it to be tried at Carrickfergus, the last assizes.

"On the 19th of May, the jury were called; but the cause was ordered to stand over for Friday, owing to a civil action, which was then pending in the court; and on Friday, after some slight opposition on the part of the defendants, it was for the same reason farther postponed until Wednesday, the 28th, when it proceeded, as is hereafter related.

"And thus has terminated a prosecution upon *one* out of the *seven* informations filed, which has been attended (from the peculiar manner in which it has been carried on) with an expense, perhaps exceeding that of any criminal prosecution upon record; the fees alone for obtaining copies of the informations, stamps and fees of office, and license for Mr. Curran to plead against the crown, have been little short of ONE HUNDRED POUNDS!!!"

On Wednesday, the 28th of May, 1794, this cause came on to be tried at the bar of the court of King's Bench, before Lord Chief Justice Clonmel and Mr. Justice Downes.

The Attorney-General stated the case, and called evidence to prove proprietorship and publication. An argument arose out of the evidence as to the proof of proprietorship, on which, in reply to the crown, CURRAN said:—

I regret that we are come to such an era in criminal justice, that four gentlemen of high distinction should be gravely listened to, in arguing whether there was a shadow of evidence to go to a jury against twelve of the King's subjects, to charge them with a very heinous crime. I insist that, according to the ordinary practice, where a number of parties are included in a criminal charge, those against whom there is no evidence should be sent to the jury with directions to acquit them, that those who are to be tried may have the benefit of their evidence, if it should be necessary. The counsel for the crown have set out upon erroneous principles; they seem to take the question to be, whether these people are proprietors or not. There is no law of this country by which every man entitled to share the profits of a certain trade shall be criminally responsible for the exercise of that trade by his agent. If several people employ a ship, and the navigator of it shall commit piracy or treason upon the high seas, shall those who are entitled to share the profits be criminally responsible? Is that the principle of Irish law? If not, it is absurd to say that this question depends upon the proprietorship of the parties, or has any thing to do with it. There is no rule of law better established than that distinction between being criminally and civilly responsible for the acts of an agent. If a servant of his own head commit a criminal act, his master certainly will not be involved in the crime, however he might be if it was fully proved to be by his express command, for then the employer would be involved in the guilt. But the bare act is not *prima facie* evidence to charge the master; nothing short of evidence of commandment can do that. Otherwise there could be no safety in society, and every man here might, for what he never knew, be answerable for as many crimes as he had servants. By intendment of law, the master is only supposed to give authority for that which is lawful; unless there is some privity or commandment shown, there is no evidence of guilt in the master. I should be ashamed to insist further from the very elementary principles of a study in which I have been employed for seventeen years. Evidence that these men whose names have crowded the information, are proprietors of a newspaper, is not evidence that they are guilty of a deed not done by themselves. The act of parliament itself makes a clear distinction between the printer and proprietor, and the proprietors come under a clause or designation different from the publisher or printer. This irresistibly shows the fallacy attempted to be imposed upon the court. The stating a man's name and residence and other collateral circumstances, is not for the purpose of making him be considered as printer or publisher, but to let in certain lights which may be advantageous to the public, or any individual who shall be aggrieved.

This affidavit, made pursuant to the act of parliament, states Rabb to be the sole printer; and yet it is offered in evidence, to show that others were the printers or publishers: it is true these gentlemen have not made an affidavit to the contrary, although it might have been a wise thing for them to have made a purgative and preventative affidavit every day as to the case cited: I meant to have quoted it in our favour, as directly establishing the principle, that their barely being entitled to receive a portion of the profits, or being proprietors, is not evidence of their being printers or publishers, but that there must be evidence of the act charged to be criminal being done by the party himself or by his immediate commandment. In Topham's case there was evidence of buying a paper at the office when he was sole proprietor, there was besides an affidavit, of payment for the stamps used, in printing this very paper; there it was clearly done with his privity, under his control; here it is clear that there has been no evidence given of personal interference so as to amount to such authority or command as would render any of the parties criminally liable.

After other counsel were heard, the jury, under direction of the court, found a verdict of acquittal for all the *proprietors* except John Rabb, the actual printer. The case was then proceeded with against him. Mr. Dobbs defended him on the ground that the publication was not a libel. Clonmel and Downes charged against the prisoner, and the jury, "after five minutes consideration, brought in their verdict—Guilty."

REV. WILLIAM JACKSON.

April 23rd, 1795.

Mr. W. H. Curran, in the Memoirs of his Father, thus describes Jackson:—

"Mr. Jackson was a clergyman of the Established Church; he was a native of Ireland, but he had for several years resided out of that country. He spent a part of his life in the family of the noted Duchess of Kingston, and is said to have been the person who conducted that lady's controversy with the celebrated Foote. At the period of the French Revolution he passed over to Paris, where he formed political connexions with the constituted authorities. From France he returned to London, in 1794, for the purpose of procuring information as to the practicability of an invasion of England, and was thence to proceed to Ireland on a similar mission. Upon his arrival in London, he renewed an intimacy with a person named Cockayne, who had formerly been his friend and confidential attorney. The extent of his communications, in the first instance, to Cockayne, did not exactly appear. The latter, however, was prevailed upon to write the directions of several of Jackson's letters, containing treasonable matters, to his correspondents abroad; but in a little time, either suspecting or repenting that he had been furnishing evidence of treason against himself, he revealed to the British minister, Mr. Pitt, all that he knew or conjectured relative to Jackson's objects. By the desire of Mr. Pitt, Cockayne accompanied Jackson to Ireland, to watch and defeat his designs; and as soon as the evidence of his treason was mature, announced himself as a witness for the crown. Mr. Jackson was accordingly arrested, and committed to stand his trial for high treason.

"Mr. Jackson was committed to prison in April, 1794, but his trial was delayed, by successive adjournments, till the same month in the following year. In the interval, he wrote and published a refutation of Paine's Age of Reason, probably in the hope that it might be accepted as an atonement. He was convicted, and brought up for judgment on the 30th of April, 1795."

He was indicted for treason in the Summer of 1794; but, sometimes for the crown, and at others for the prisoner, the trial was postponed till the 23rd of April, 1795.

The Attorney-General led the prosecution. His chief witness was Cockayne, an English attorney. Among the papers proved was this remarkable VIEW OF IRELAND, by Tone:—

"The situation of Ireland and England is fundamentally different in this: the government of England is national—that of Ireland, provincial. The interest of the first is the same with that of the people; of the last, directly opposite. The people of Ireland are divided into three sects—the Established Church, the Dissenters, and the Catholics. The first—infinitely the smallest portion—have engrossed, besides the whole church patronage, all the profits and honours of the country exclusively, and a very great share of the landed property. They are, of course, aristocrats, adverse to any change, and decided enemies of the French Revolution. The Dissenters—who are much more numerous—are the most enlightened body of the nation; they are steady Republicans, devoted to liberty, and, through all the stages of the French Revolution, have been enthusiastically attached to it. The Catholics—the great body of the people—are in the lowest degree of ignorance, and are ready for any change, because no change can make them worse. The whole peasantry of Ireland, the most oppressed and wretched in Europe, may be said to be Catholic. They have within these two years received a certain degree of information, and manifested a proportionate degree of discontent, by various insurrections, &c. They are a bold, hardy race, and make excellent soldiers. There is nowhere a higher spirit of aristocracy than in all the privileged orders, the clergy and gentry of Ireland, down to the very lowest; to countervail which, there appears now a spirit rising in the people which never existed before, but which is spreading most rapidly, as appears by the Defenders, as they are called, and other insurgents. If the people of Ireland be 4,500,000, as it seems probable they are, the Established Church may be reckoned at 450,000; the Dissenters at 900,000; the Catholics at 3,150,000. The prejudices in England are adverse to the French nation under whatever form of government. It seems idle to suppose the present rancour against the French is owing merely to their being Republicans; it has been cherished by the manners of four centuries, and aggravated by continual wars. It is morally certain that any invasion of England would unite all ranks in opposition to the invaders. In Ireland—a conquered, oppressed, and insulted country—the name of England and her power is universally odious, save with those who have an interest in maintaining it; a body, however, only formidable from situation and property, but which the first convulsion would level in the dust. On the contrary, the great bulk of the people of Ireland would be ready to throw off the yoke in this country, if they saw any force sufficiently strong to resort to for defence until arrangements could be made: the Dissenters are enemies to the English power from reason and from reflection; the Catholics, from a hatred of the English name. In a word, the prejudices of one country are directly adverse to the other—directly favourable to an invasion. The government of Ireland is only to be looked upon as a government of force; the moment a superior force appears, it would tumble at once, as being founded neither in the interests nor in the affections of the people. It may be said, the people of Ireland show no political exertion. In the first place, public spirit is completely depressed by the recent persecutions of several. The convention act, the gunpowder, &c., &c., declarations of government, parliamentary unanimity, or declarations of grand juries—all proceeding from aristocrats, whose interest is adverse to that of the people, and who think such conduct necessary for their security—are no obstacles; the weight of such men falls in the general welfare, and their own tenantry and dependants would desert and turn against them. The people have no way of expressing their discontent *civiliter*, which is, at the same time, greatly aggravated by those measures; and they are, on the other hand, in that semi-barbarous state, which is, of all others, the best adapted for making war. The spirit of Ireland cannot, therefore, be calculated from newspaper publications, county meetings &c., at which the gentry only meet and speak for themselves. They are so situated that they have but one way left to make their sentiments known, and that is by war. The church establishment and tithes are very severe grievances, and have been the cause of numberless local insurrections. In a word, from reason, reflection, interest, prejudice, the spirit of change, the misery of the great bulk of the nation, and, above all, the hatred of the English name, resulting from the tyranny of near seven centuries, there seems little doubt but an invasion and sufficient force would be supported by the people. There is scarce any army in the country, and the militia, the bulk of whom are Catholics, would, to a moral certainty, refuse to act, if they saw such a force as they could look to for support."

CURRAN said:—

MY lords, and gentlemen of the jury! I am sure the attention of the court must be a good deal fâtigued. I am sure, gentlemen of the jury, that your minds must of necessity be fatigued also. Whether counsel be fatigued or not, is matter very little worth the observation that may be made upon it. I am glad that it is not necessary for me to add a great deal to the labour, either of the court, or the jury. Of the court I must have some knowledge—of the jury, I certainly am not ignorant. I know it is as unnecessary for me to say much, or, perhaps, anything, to inform the court, as it would be ridiculous to affect to lecture a jury of the description I have the honour to address. I know I address a court, anxious to expound fairly and impartially the law of the country, without any apprehension of the consequences and effect of any prosecution. In the jury I am looking to now, I know I address twelve sensible and respectable men of my country, who are as conscious as I am of the great obligation to which they have pledged themselves by their oath, to decide upon the question fairly, without listening to passion, or being swayed by prejudice—without thinking of anything except the charge which has been made, and the evidence which has been brought in support of that charge. They know, as well as I do, that the great object of a jury is to protect the country against crimes, and to protect individuals against all accusation that is not founded in truth. They will remember—I know they will remember, that the great object of their duty is, according to the expression of a late venerated judge, in another country, that they are to come into the box with their minds like white paper, upon which prejudice, or passion, or bias, or talk, or hope, or fear, has not been able to scrawl any thing; that you, gentlemen!

come into the box, standing indifferent as you stand unsworn.

In the little, gentlemen, that I shall take the liberty of addressing to you, I shall rest the fate of it upon its intrinsic weight. I shall not leave the case in concealment. If there be no ground on which the evidence can be impeached, I will venture to say I will neither bark at it, nor scold it, in lieu of giving it an answer. Whatever objection I have to make, shall be addressed to your reason. I will not say they are great, or conclusive, or unanswerable objections. I shall submit them to you nakedly as they appear to me. If they have weight, you will give it to them. If they have not, a great promise, on my part, will not give anticipated weight to that whose debility will appear when it comes to be examined.

Gentlemen, you are empannelled to try a charge. It consists of two offences, particularly described in the indictment. The first question is, what is the allegation? In the first branch, the prisoner is indicted upon a statute, which inflicts the pains and penalties of high treason upon any man who shall compass or imagine the King's death. The nature of the offence, if you required any comment on it, has been learnedly, and, I must add, candidly commented upon by Mr. Attorney-General in stating the case. The second part is, that the prisoner did adhere to the King's enemies. By the law of this country, there are particular rules, applicable to cases of prosecutions for high treason, contradistinguished from all the other branches of the criminal law. The nature of the offence called for this peculiarity of regulation. There is no species of charge to which innocent men may more easily be made victims, than that of offences against the state, and therefore it was necessary to give an additional protection to the subject. There is an honest impulse in the natural and laudable loyalty of every man, that warms his passions strongly against the person who endeavours to disturb the public quiet and security; it was necessary, therefore, to guard the subject against the most dangerous of all abuses—the abuse of a virtue, by extraordinary vigilance. There was another reason: There is no charge which is so vague and indefinite, and yet would be more likely to succeed, than charging a man as an enemy to the state. There is no case in which the venality of a base informer could have greater expectation of a base reward. Therefore, gentlemen, it was necessary to guard persons accused from the over hasty virtue of a jury on the one hand, and on the other from being made the sacrifice of the base and rank prostitution of a depraved informer. How has the law done this? By pointing out in terms, these rules and orders that shall guide the court, and bind the jury in the verdict they shall give. The man shall be a traitor, if he commits the crime, but it must be a crime of which he should be proveably attaint, by overt acts. And in order that there be an opportunity of investigation and defence, the features of the overt acts should be stated of public record in the very body of the indictment. Justly do I hear it observed, that there cannot be devised a fairer mode of accusation and trial than this is. Gentlemen, I have stated to you how the foundation of it stands in both countries, touching the mode of accusation and trial. I have to add to you, that in Great Britain it has been found necessary still further to increase the sanction of the jury, and the safety of the prisoner, by an express statute in King William's time. By that law it is now settled in that great country, that no man shall be indicted or convicted, except upon the evidence of two witnesses, and it describes what sort of evidence that shall be; either two witnesses swearing directly to the same overt act laid in the indictment, or two witnesses, one swearing to one overt act, and the other to another overt act of the same species of treason. So that, in that country, no man can be found guilty, except upon the evidence of two distinct credible witnesses—credible in their testimony, distinct in their persons, and concurring in the evidence of acts of one and the same class of treason; for it must be to the same identical treason, sworn to by both witnesses; or one witness deposing to one act of treason, and the other to another act of the same class of treason. That is the settled law of the neighbouring kingdom, and I state it emphatically to you to be the settled law; because far am I from thinking, that we have not the blessing of living under the same sanction of law—far am I from imagining that the breath which cannot even taint the character of a man in England, shall here blow him from the earth—that the proof, which in England would not wound the man, shall here deprive him of his life—that though the people in England would laugh at the accusation, yet here it shall cause the accused to perish under it. Sure I am that in a country where so few instances of a foul accusation of this sort have occurred, the judges of the court will need little argument to give effect to every thing urged to show that the law is the same in Ireland as in England.

Lord Clonmel—Do you mean to argue that the statute of William is in force in Ireland?

Mr. Curran.—No, my lord; not that the statute of William is in force—but I mean to argue, that the necessity of two witnesses in the case of treason is as strong here as in England. It is the opinion of Lord Coke, founded upon a number of authorities; the opinion of Lord Coke, referring to a judicial confirmation of what he says; the opinion of Lord Coke controverted, if it can be said to be controverted, by the modest and diffident dissent of Sir Michael Foster. It is laid down by Lord Coke, that he conceives it to be the established law, that two witnesses are necessary to convict:

3 Inst. 26. "It seemeth that by the ancient common law, one accuser or witness was not sufficient to convict any person of high treason—and that two witnesses be required, appeareth by our books, and I remember no authority in our books to the contrary." I know of no judicial determination in our books to the contrary of what Lord Coke here states: the common law is grounded upon the principles of reason. I consider the statutes of Edward VI., and William III., as statutes which had become necessary from the abuses occasioned by a departure from the common law. After the statute of Edward VI., expressly declaring the necessity of two witnesses, the courts had fallen into perhaps a well-intentioned departure from the meaning of the statute of Edward VI., so far that the place of two witnesses was supplied in evidence by any thing that the court thought a material additional circumstance in the case; and to the time of William III., such a departure had prevailed, and this was thought sufficient to discharge every thing respecting the obligations of the statute. It became necessary, therefore, to enact, and by that enactment to do away the abuse of the principle of the common law, by expressly declaring that no man should be indicted or convicted except by two witnesses to one overt act, or one witness to one act, and a second to another act of high treason of the same species. And there seems to me to be a sound distinction between the

case of high treason, and of any other crime. It is the only crime which every subject is sworn against committing: it is the only crime which any subject is sworn to abstain from. In every other case the subject is left to the fear of punishment which he may feel, or to the dictates of his conscience to guard himself against transgressing the law; but treason is a breach of his oath of allegiance, and is so far like the case of perjury: and, therefore, in the case of treason no man should be convicted by the testimony of a single witness, because it amounts to no more than oath against oath: so that it is only reasonable there should be another to turn the scale; and therefore it is that I conceive Lord Coke well warranted in laying down this rule, a rule deduced from general justice, and even from the law of God himself. Gentlemen, what I am now stating, I offer to the court as matter of law.

But what were these witnesses? Witnesses in all cases beyond exception in their personal circumstances, and in their personal credit. Therefore it is the law, that no man shall be found guilty of any offence that is not legally proved upon him by the sworn testimony of credible witnesses. Gentlemen, I have submitted my humble ideas of the law—I have stated the charge which the prisoner is called upon to answer: let me now state the overt acts, which in this particular case are necessary to be proved. The first is, that the prisoner did traitorously come to, and land in, Ireland, to procure information concerning the subjects of Ireland, and to send that information to the persons exercising the government in France, to aid them in carrying on the war against the King. I do not recollect that Cockayne said one single word of the prisoner's coming here for such a purpose. The second overt act is, that the prisoner did traitorously intend to raise and levy war; and incite persons to invade Ireland with arms and men; that he did incite Theobald Wolfe Tone to go beyond seas to incite France to invade this kingdom; that he did endeavour to procure persons to go to France; and that he agreed with other persons, that they should be sent to France for the same purpose. Having stated these overt acts which are laid in the indictment, you will be pleased to recollect the evidence given by Cockayne. Cockayne did not say that the prisoner came over here for any such purpose as the overt act attributes to him. Then, as to the overt act, of endeavouring to procure persons to go to France for the purpose of giving information to the enemy; the witness said he met Mr. M'Nally; he had known him in England; Jackson was a clergyman; he had known him also. Cockayne had professional business with Mr. M'Nally. Mr. M'Nally paid them a courtesy which any decent person would have been entitled to. They dined at his house, and met three or four persons there; they talked of the politics of

Ireland; of the dissatisfaction of the people; but not a syllable of what is stated in the indictment; not one word of any conspiracy; Cockayne did not pretend to be able to give any account of any specific conversation. He went to Newgate; Rowan was then in confinement; he sometimes went by himself: sometimes met Tone, sometimes Jackson; he gave you an account of encouragement; what was it? Was there any thing to support this indictment? Let me remind you that you are to found your verdict on what the witness says and you believe, and not on what learned counsel may be instructed to state. Then what does the witness say? He admits that he did not hear all the conversation. The crying injustice must strike you, of making a man answerable for a part of a conversation, where the witness did not hear it all; but take it as he has stated it, unqualified and unconstrued: how high was he wrought up by it? He heard talk of somebody to go to France; he was to carry papers; he heard an expression of instructions to the French. What French—what instructions? It might be to French manufacturers; it might be to French traitors; it might be to the French King; it might be to the French convention. Do I mean to say that there was nothing by which a credulous or reasonable man might not have his suspicion raised, or that there was nothing in three or four men huddling themselves together in Newgate, and talking of an invasion? No; but my reasoning is this—that your verdict is to be founded on evidence of positive guilt established at the hazard of the personal punishment of the witness; you are not to pick up the conjectures either of his malignity or credulity. I say that this man stands in defiance of your verdict, because it will be affected by nothing but that irresistible evidence on which alone it ought to be founded. But what was the fact which Tone was to do, or any other person? It was an illegal one. By a late act, an English subject going to France is liable to six months' imprisonment. By a clause in the same statute the crime of soliciting a person to go is also punishable. The encouraging any person to go to that country was, therefore, exposing him to danger, but whether it was a motive of trade, or smuggling, or idle adventure, is not the question for you. It is whether the intention was to convey an incitement to the French to make a descent on this kingdom, and endeavour to subvert the constitution of it. You have a simple question before you—has even the prosecutor sworn that he endeavoured to do so? I think not. The next overt act charged is, that he did compose and write a letter in order to be sent to William Stone, in which he traitorously desired Stone to disclose to certain persons in France the scheme and intention of Jackson, to send a person to inform them of the state of Ireland, for the purpose of giving support and effect to a hostile invasion of this country. You have heard these letters read. You must of necessity look on them in one or two important and distinct points of view. The first, perhaps, that will naturally strike you is, what are these letters? Do they sustain the allegations of the overt act? Are they letters requiring Stone to inform the Convention of this country being in such a state as to encourage an invasion? Does that paper support this allegation? God help us! gentlemen of the jury. I know not in what state the property or life of any man will be if they are always to be at the mercy, and to depend on the possibility of his explaining either the real or pretended circumstances on which he corresponds with persons abroad. The letters are written apparently upon mercantile subjects—he talks of manufactures of a firm, of prices changed, of different families, of differences among them, of overtures to be accepted of, of disputes likely to be settled by means of common mediation; what is the evidence on which you can be supported in saying that manufactures mean treason—that Nicholas means the war minister of France—the sister-in-law Ireland—that "the firm has been changed," means Danton has been guillotined, but that makes no alteration in the state of the house, meaning the circumstances of the revolution—that the change of prices and manufactures means any thing else necessary to give consistency to the charge of treason. Give me leave to say that this ludicrous and barbarous consequence would follow from a rule of this sort, the idlest letter might be strained to any purpose. The simplicity of our law is, that a man's guilt should be proved by the evidence of witnesses on their oaths, which shall not be supplied by fancy, nor elicited by the ingenuity of any person making suggestions to the wretched credulity of a jury that should be weak enough to adopt them. I come now to this. A letter produced imports on the face of it to be a letter of business, concerning manufactures—another concerning family differences. In which way are they to be understood? I say with confidence, better it should be to let twenty men, that might have a criminal purpose in writing letters of this kind, escape, than fall into the dreadful alternative of making one man a victim to a charge of this kind not supported by such proof as could bring conviction on the mind of a rational jury.

I do not think it necessary to state to you minutely the rest of these allegations of the overt acts. The charge against the prisoner is supported, and this is perhaps the clearest way of calling your attention to the evidence, either by the positive evidence of Cockayne as to these facts, or by the written evidence which stands also on his testimony alone. Touching actual conspiracy he said nothing: somebody was to go to France—he knew not for what—he had an idea on his mind for what it was—but never from any communication with Jackson. There have been other letters read in evidence. Two of them contained duplicates of a sort of representation of the supposed state of Ireland. Cockayne says that he got the packet from Jackson, that he himself wrote the directions; one addressed to Amsterdam, the other to Hamburgh. They were read, and they contain assertions, whether true or false I do not think material, of the state of this country:—if material at all, material only in their falsehood. The public are satisfied that these allegations are false. It is known to every man in this country, and must be known with great satisfaction by every honest man, that it is not in that state that could induce any but the most adventurous and wicked folly to try an experiment upon it. It is unnecessary for me to comment on the opinions contained in that paper; there is a matter more material, and calling more loudly for your attention. It is stated to be written with the purpose of inviting the persons governing in France to try a descent upon Ireland. This paper is evidence to support that charge; you have heard it read. On what public subject have you ever heard six men speak, and all to agree? Might not a stranger, in a fit of despondency, imagine that an invasion might have a fatal effect on this country? It is not impossible but if ten men were to make a landing some mischief might happen. Then, again, what do I mean to argue? Is it that this letter bears no marks of the design imputed to it? No such thing. It is a letter that the most innocent man might write, but it is also such a one as a guilty man might write, but unless there was clear evidence of his guilt, he would be entitled to your verdict of acquittal. Though it was not expressly avowed, yet I cannot help thinking that it was meant to lay some little emphasis on certain names which I have met with in the newspapers—I am sure I have met the name of Laignelot in the debates of the convention—I have met the names of Horne Tooke and Stone in the English papers. I have read that Horne Tooke was tried for high treason and acquitted—that Stone made his escape into Switzerland. I believe it is said that there is a person of that name in confinement in England at present. But let me tell you, you are not to draw any inferences from circumstances of this kind against the prisoner: let me tell you, it is the guilt of the man, and not the sound of names, by which his fate is to be decided.

Other papers have been read. One seems to contain some form of addresses. A letter said to come from Stone has been read to you. The letter to Beresford, said to be written by Jackson, has also been read to you. I have stated the material parts of the evidence. I have endeavoured to submit my poor idea of the rule by which you ought to be guided. I see only one remaining topic to trouble you upon; it appears to me to be a topic of the utmost importance. And, gentlemen, it is this. Who is the man that has been examined to support this charge? One witness! I beseech you to have that engraven on your minds. The charge, in all its parts, stands only on the evidence of Cockayne; there is no other evidence of any conversation, there is not a material letter read in this case that does not rest upon Cockayne's evidence, and that I am warranted in this assertion you will see to a demonstration when I remind the court that he was the only witness, as I recollect, called to prove the hand-writing of Jackson. On his testimony alone must depend the fact of their being his hand-writing, of the inuendoes imputed to them, or the purpose with which they were sent.

Gentlemen, I am scarcely justified in having trespassed so long on your patience. It is a narrow case. It is a case of a man charged with the highest and most penal offence known by our law, and charged by one witness only. And let me ask who that witness is. A man, stating that he comes from another country, armed with a pardon for treasons committed in Ireland, but not in England whence he comes. What! were you never on a jury before? Did you ever hear of a man forfeiting his life on the unsupported evidence of a single witness, and he an accomplice by his own confession? What! his character made the subject of testimony and support!—take his own vile evidence for his character. He was the foul traitor of his own client. What do you think now of his character? He was a spy upon his friend. He was the man that yielded to the tie of three oaths of allegiance, to watch the steps of his client for the bribe of government, with a pardon for the treasons he might commit; and he had impressed on his mind the conviction that he was liable to be executed as a traitor. Was he aware of his crime?—his pardon speaks it. Was he aware of the turpitude of his character?—he came with the cure; he brought his witness in his pocket. To what? To do away an offence which he did not venture to deny, that he had incautiously sworn that which was false in fact, though the jury did not choose to give it the name of wilful and corrupt perjury. Gracious God! Is it, then, on the evidence of a man of this kind, with his pardon in his pocket, and his bribe—not yet in his pocket—that you can venture to convict the prisoner. He was to be taken care of. How so? Jackson owed him a debt—"I was to do the honourable business of a spy and informer, and to be paid for it in the common way; it was common *acreable* work—treason and conspiracy; I was to he paid for it by the sheet." Do you find men doing these things in common life? I have now stated the circumstances by which, in my opinion, the credit of Cockayne ought to be reduced to nothing in your eyes. But I do not rest here. Papers were found in the chamber of Mr. Jackson; the door was open—and, by the bye, that carelessness was not evidence of any conscious guilt; the papers were seized. That there were some belonging to Jackson is clear, because he expressed an anxiety about some that are confessed not to have any relation to the subject of this day's trial. I asked Cockayne, if he had any papers in Jackson's room the night before he was arrested? He said not. I asked him, if he had told any person that he had? He said not. Gentlemen, the only witness I shall call, will be one to show you that he has in that sworn falsely. And let me here make one observation to you, the strength and good sense of which has been repeated an hundred times, and, therefore, rests on better authority than mine. Where a witness swears glibly to a number of circumstances, where it is impossible to produce contradictory proof, and is found to fail in one, it shall overthrow all the others. And see how strongly the observation applies here: he swore to a conversation with Jackson as to what he said and did, well knowing that Jackson could not be a witness to disprove that, unless the good sense of the jury should save his life, and enable him to become, in his turn, a prosecutor for the perjury. If on a point of this kind this man should be found to have forsworn himself, it cannot occasion any other sentiment but this, that if you have felt yourselves disposed to give any thing like credit to his evidence where he has sworn to facts which he must have known, it is the keystone of the arch in his testimony, and if you can pluck it from its place, the remainder of the pile will fall in ruins about his head.

I will produce that witness—but, before I sit down, permit me, gentlemen of the jury, to remind you, that if every word which Cockayne has here sworn were sworn in Westminster-Hall, the judges would immediately have said—There is not any thing for the jury to decide upon; the evidence of the indictment rests on him alone; there is no second witness. So does the transaction of the letters, for De Joncourt's testimony could not have satisfied the statute; it was not evidence to the same overt act as affecting Jackson personally, nor was it evidence of any distinct overt act; it was merely that species of evidence, the abuse of which had been the cause of introducing the statute of William; a mere collateral concomitant evidence. The overt act was writing and putting into the post-office; that was sworn to by Cockayne, and if he deserved credit, would go so far as to prove the fact by one witness. See what the idea of the statute is; it is that it must be an overt act brought home to the prisoner by each of the two witnesses swearing to it. If De Joncourt's evidence stood single, it could not have brought any thing home to Jackson. Cockayne swore the superscription was his writing; he put the letters into the office. De Joncourt said nothing but that he found in the office a letter which he produced, and which Cockayne said was the one he had put into it.

This observation appears to collect additional strength from this circumstance. Why did they not produce Tone? It is said they could not. I say they could. It was as easy to pardon him as to pardon Cockayne. But whether he was guilty or not, is no objection. Shall it be said that the argument turns about and affects Jackson as much as it does the prosecutor? I think certainly not. Jackson, I believe it has appeared in the course of the evidence, and is matter of judicial knowledge to the court, has lain in prison for twelve months past, from the moment of his trial. If he is conscious that the charge is false, it is impossible for him to prove that falsehood; he was so circumstanced as that he could not procure the attendance of witnesses; a stranger in the country, he could not tell whether some of the persons named were in existence or not.

I have before apologized to you for trespassing upon your patience, and I have again trespassed —let me not repeat it. I shall only take the liberty of reminding you, that if you have any doubt, in a criminal case doubt should be acquittal; that you are trying a case which if tried in England would preclude the jury from the possibility of finding a verdict of condemnation. It is for you to put it into the power of mankind to say, that that which should pass harmlessly over the head of a man in Great Britain shall blast him here;—whether life is more valuable in that country than in this, or whether a verdict may more easily be obtained here in a case tending to establish pains and penalties of this severe nature.

The trial lasted till four o'clock in the morning, when Jackson was found Guilty. He was brought up for judgment on the 30th of April, but he died in the dock, of arsenic which he had taken. It is noticeable that the rule of allowing one witness to convict for treason in Ireland, as established by this case, enabled the government to obtain their convictions in '98.

DUBLIN DEFENDERS.

December 22nd, **1795.**

TRIAL OF JAMES WELDON, FOR HIGH TREASON,

Before the Court holden under a Commission of Oyer and Terminer, and general Gaol delivery, in and for the County of the City of Dublin, in Ireland, on Monday, December 21st, and Tuesday, December 22nd. **36** *Geo. III.,* **A. D. 1795.**

COMMISSION.—MONDAY, DECEMBER 14TH, 1795.

IN the latter end of the month of August, 1795, several persons were taken into custody in the city of Dublin, upon charges of High Treason, and in the ensuing commission of Oyer and Terminer held in October, bills of indictment were preferred against them, and others not then in custody, which were returned by the grand jury to be true bills.

The prisoners in custody were then brought to the bar of the court, for the purpose of having counsel and agents assigned.

In the interval between the October commission and the December, a person of the name of James Weldon was apprehended upon a charge of High Treason, and he, together with such as had been previously in custody, were served with copies of the indictments and the captions thereof, five days before the first day of this commission.

This day the prisoners who had been in custody at the last commission were severally arraigned, and pleaded Not Guilty.

On the 21st of December several arguments took place as to the jury, and on the 22nd the trial came on. The Attorney-General stated the case, and examined many witnesses, but especially one William Lawler, a gilder. The crown examination was leading and unfair throughout. CURRAN said:—

My lords, and gentlemen of the jury, I am of counsel in one of those cases in which the humanity of our law is, very fortunately, joined with the authority and wisdom of the court in alliance with me for the purposes of legal protection. Gentlemen, I cannot, however, but regret, that that sort of laudable and amiable anxiety for the public tranquillity, which glows warmest in the breasts of the best men, has, perhaps, induced Mr. Attorney-General to state some facts to the court and the jury, of which no evidence was attempted to be given. And I make the observation only for this purpose, to remind you, gentlemen, that the statement of counsel is not evidence—to remind you, that you are to give a verdict, upon this solemn and momentous occasion, founded simply upon the evidence which has been given to you; for such is the oath you have taken. Gentlemen, I make the observation, not only in order to call upon you to discharge any impressions not supported by testimony, but to remind you also of another incontrovertible maxim, not only of the humane law of England, but of eternal justice upon which that is founded—that the more horrid and atrocious the nature of any crime charged upon any man is, the more clear and invincible should be the evidence upon which he is convicted. The charge here is a charge of the most enormous criminality that the law of any country can know —no less than the atrocious and diabolical purpose of offering mortal and fatal violence to the person of the Sovereign, who ought to be sacred. The prisoner is charged with entertaining the guilty purpose of destroying all order, and all society, for the well-being of which the person of the King is held sacred. Therefore, gentlemen, I presume to tell you, that in proportion as the crime is atrocious and horrible, in the same proportion ought the evidence to convict be clear and irresistible. Let me, therefore, endeavour to discharge the duty I owe to the unfortunate man at the bar (for unfortunate I consider him, whether he be convicted or acquitted), by drawing your attention to a consideration of the facts charged, and comparing it with the evidence adduced to support it.

The charge, gentlemen, is of two kinds—two species of treason founded upon the statute 25 Edward III. One is, compassing the King's death; the other is a distinct treason—that of adhering to the King's enemies. In both cases, the criminality must be clearly established, under the words of the statute, by having the guilty man convicted of the offence, by provable evidence of overt acts. Even in the case, and it is the only one, where by law the imagination shall complete the crime, there that guilt must be proved, and can be provable only by outward acts, made use of by the criminal, for the effectuation of his guilty purpose. The overt acts stated here are, that he associated with traitors unknown, with the design of assisting the

French, at war with our government, and therefore a public enemy. 2ndly, consulting with others, for the purpose of assisting the French. 3rdly, consulting with other traitors to subvert the government. 4thly, associating with Defenders to subvert the Protestant religion. 5thly, enlisting a person stated in the indictment to assist the French, and administering an oath to him for that purpose. 6thly, enlisting him to adhere to the French. 7thly, corrupting Lawler to become a Defender. 8thly, enlisting him by administering an oath, for similar purposes. In order to warrant a verdict convicting the prisoner, there must be clear and convincing evidence of some one of these overt acts, as they are laid. The law requires that there should be stated upon record such an act as in point of law will amount to an overt act of the treason charged, as matter of evidence, and the evidence adduced must correspond with the fact charged. The uniform rule which extends to every case applies to this, that whether the fact charged be sustained by evidence is for the conscience and the oath of the jury, according to the degree of credit they give to the testimony of it. In treason, the overt act must sustain the crime, and the evidence must go to support the overt act so stated. If this case were tried at the other side of the water, it does not strike me that the very irrelevant evidence given by Mr. Carleton could have supplied what the law requires—the concurring testimony of two witnesses. I cannot be considered, indeed I should be sorry, to put any sort of comparison between the person of Mr. Carleton and the first witness who was called upon the table. Gentlemen of the jury, you have an important province indeed —the life or death of a man—to decide upon. But previous to that, you must consider what degree of credit ought to be given to a man under the circumstances of that witness produced against the prisoner. It does appear to me, that his evidence merits small consideration in point of credibility. But even if he were as deserving of belief as the witness that followed, and that his evidence were as credible as the other's was immaterial, I shall yet rely confidently, that every word, if believed, does leave the accusation unsupported. Gentlemen, I will not affront the idea which ought to be entertained of you, by warning you not to be led away by those phantoms which have been created by prejudice, and applied to adorn the idle tales drunk down by folly, and belched up by malignity. You are sensible that you are discharging the greatest duty that law and religion can repose in you, and I am satisfied you will discard your passions, and that your verdict will be founded, not upon passion or prejudice, but upon your oaths and upon justice. Consider what the evidence in point of fact is—Lawler was brought by Brady and Kennedy to Weldon, the prisoner, in Barrack-street;. what Brady said to him before, if it had been of moment in itself, I do not conceive can possibly be extended to him, who did not assent to the words, and was not present when they were uttered. Lawler was carried to the prisoner at the bar to be sworn; and here give me leave to remind you. what was the evidence—to remind you that the expressions proved do not bear that illegal import which real or affected loyalty would attach to them, and therefore you will discharge all that cant of enthusiasm from your minds. I wish that I were so circumstanced as to be entitled to an answer, when I ask Mr. Attorney-General, what is the meaning of the word Defender? I wish I were at liberty to appeal to the sober understanding of any man, for the meaning of that tremendous word. I am not entitled to put the question to the counsel or the court—but I am entitled to call upon the wise and grave consideration of the court to say whether the zeal of public accusation has affixed any definite meaning to the word? I would be glad to know, whether that expression, which is annexed to the title of the highest magistrate, marking his highest obligation, and styling him the DEFENDER of the religion of the country, in common parlance acquired any new combination, carrying with it a crime, when applied to any other man in the community? Let me warn you, therefore, against that sort of fallacious lexicography which forms new words, that undergoing the examination of political slander or intemperate zeal are considered as having a known acceptation. What is the word? A word that should be discarded, when it is sought to affix to it another meaning than that which it bears in the cases where it is used. Let me remind you that a Defender, or any other term used to denote any confraternity, club, or society, like any other word, is arbitrary, but the meaning should be explicit. And therefore with regard to this trial, you are to reject the word, as having no meaning, unless, from the evidence, you find it has in the mind of the party a definite explication; for observe that the witness, such as he is—such as he was, with all his zeal for the furtherance of justice, which he was once ready to violate by the massacre of his fellow-subjects—with all his anxiety for his sovereign's safety, whom he was once ready to assassinate, he, I say, has not told you, that either Brady or Kennedy, or any other person, said what the principles were that denoted a Defender. But I will not rest the case of my client upon that ground. No; it would be a foolish kind of defence, because words might be used as a cloak, and therefore might be colourably introduced. You, gentlemen, are then to consider what this oath, this nonsensical oath, which so far as it is intelligible is innocent, and so far as it is nonsense, can prove nothing; you are to consider, whether innocent and nonsensical as it may appear, it was yet a cover and a bond for treasonable association. It is not in my recollection, that any evidence was given, that the oath was conceived in artfully equivocal expressions, for forming, under the sanction of loyal language, a treasonable association. Is one of the parties laughing, evidence that it was treasonable, or the bond of a criminal confederation? It is not. Is it treasonable to say, "that were the King's head off to-morrow, the allegiance to him would be at an end?" It is not. The expressions may bring a man into disrepute—to lead the mind of a jury into a suspicion of the morality of the man who used them—but nothing more. It may be asked, why should there be any thing insidious? Why but to cover a treasonable purpose, are all these suspicious circumstances? It is not for me, nor is it the prisoner's duty, to account for them in defending himself against this charge, because circumstances are not to render innocence doubtful; but it is full proof establishing the guilt and the treason indubitably which the law requires. Therefore I submit that even if the evidence could be believed, it does not support the overt acts. Was there a word of violating the person of the King? Any affected misrepresentation or any abuse of government? Have you heard a word stated of the King not being an amiable King? Any words contumeliously uttered respecting his person—disrespectful of his government—expressive of any public grievance to be removed, or good to be attained? Not a word of such a subject—nothing of the kind is proved by this solitary witness, in all his accuracy of detail.

Was there any proposition of assisting the French, in case they invaded this kingdom? To support that charge a nonsensical catechism is produced. There it is asked, "Where did the cock crow when all the world heard him?" What kind of old women's stories are these to make an impression upon your minds? Well, but what does that mean? Why, can you be at a loss? It means to—kill the King! Look at the record—it charges the persons with compassing the King's death, and the question about the crowing of a cock is the evidence against them.

Gentlemen, you all know, for you are not of ordinary description, that the statute of Edward III. was made to reduce vague and wandering treasons —to abolish the doctrine of constructive treason, and to mark out some limited boundaries, clear to a court and jury. If a man has been guilty of disrespect in point of expression to the government or the crown, the law has ascertained his guilt and announced the punishment. But all the dreadful uncertainty intended to be guarded against by the statute, and which before the passing of the statute had prevailed in case of treason, and which had shed upon the scaffold some of the best blood in England, would again run in upon us, if a man were to suffer an ignominious death under such circumstances as the present,—if equivocal expressions should be taken as decisive proof, or if dubious words were to receive a meaning from the zeal of a witness, or the heat, passion, or prejudice of a jury. The true rule by which to ascertain what evidence should be deemed sufficient against a prisoner is, that no man should be convicted of any crime except upon the evidence of a man subject to an indictment for perjury, where the evidence is such as if false, the falsehood of it may be so proved as to convict the witness of perjury. But what indictment could be supported for a laugh, a shrug, or a wink? Was there any conversation about killing the King? No: but there was a laugh—there was an oath to which we were sworn—and then—there was a wink; by which I understood, we were swearing one thing, and meant another. Why, gentlemen, there can be no safety to the honour, the property, or the life of a man, in a country where such evidence as this shall be deemed sufficient to convict a prisoner. There is nothing necessary to sweep a man from society, but to find a miscreant of sufficient enormity, and the unfortunate accused is drifted down the torrent of the credulity of a well-intending jury. See how material this is; Weldon was present at only one conversation with the witness. It is not pretended by the counsel for the crown, that the guilt as to any personal evidence against Weldon does not stand upon the first conversation. Was there a word upon that conversation of adhering to the King's enemies? It was stated in the case, and certainly made a strong impression, that Lawler was enlisted, in order to assist the French. I heard no such evidence given. The signs of what he called Defenders were communicated to him; the oath which he took was read, and he was told there would be a subsequent meeting, of which the witness should receive notice from Brady.

Gentlemen, before I quit that meeting at Barrack-street, let me put this soberly to you, What is the evidence upon which the court can leave it to you to determine that there is equivocation in the oath? It must be in this way: you are to consider words in the sense in which they are spoken, and in writings words are to be taken in their common meaning. Words have sometimes a technical sense for the purposes of certainty: they may also be made the signs of arbitrary ideas, and therefore I admit a treasonable meaning may be attached to words which, in their ordinary signification, are innocent. But where is the evidence, or what has the witness said to make you believe, that these words in the oath were used in any other than in the common, ordinary acceptation? Not a word, as I have heard. Weldon can be affected only personally, either, first, upon acts by himself, or by other acts brought home to him from the general circumstances of the case. I am considering it in that two-fold way, and I submit, that if it stood upon the evidence respecting the conduct of the prisoner at Barrack-street alone, there could not be a doubt as to his acquittal. It is necessary, therefore, that I should take some further notice of the subsequent part of the evidence. The witness stated, that Weldon informed him, that there would be another meeting, of which he, the witness, should have notice. He met Brady and Kennedy: they told him there was a meeting at Plunket-street; and here give me leave to remind the court, that there is no evidence that there was any guilty purpose in agitation to be matured at any future meeting—no proposal of any criminal design. There ought to be evidence to show a connexion between the prisoner and the subsequent meeting, as held under his authority. It is of great moment to recollect, that before any meeting Weldon had left town, and, in the mention of any meeting to be held, let it be remembered he did not state any particular subject, as comprehending the object of the meeting. What happened? There certainly was a meeting at Plunket-street; but there was not a word of assisting the French—of subverting the religion—of massacring the Protestants—of any criminal design whatever. There was not any consultation upon any such design. I make this distinction, and rely upon it, that where consultations are overt acts of this or that species of treason, it must be a consultation by the members composing that meeting; because it would be the most ridiculous nonsense, that a conversation addressed from one individual to another, not applied to the meeting, should be called a consultation: but, in truth, there is no evidence of anything respecting the French, except in Stoney-batter. There, for the first time, the witness says he heard any mention of the French. Here, gentlemen of the jury, let me beseech you to consider what the force of the evidence is. Supposing that what one man said there to another about assisting the French, to have been criminal, shall Weldon, who was then for a week a hundred miles from the scene, be criminally affected by what was criminally done at Stoney-batter? It is not only that he shall be criminally affected by what was criminally done, but even to the shedding of his blood, shall he be affected by what any individual said, who casually attended that meeting! Have you any feeling of the precipice to which you are hurried, when called upon to extend this evidence in such a manner?—without any one person being present with whom the prisoner had any previous confederation! You will be very cautious, indeed, how you establish such a precedent. How did Weldon connect himself with any other meeting? Why, he said, there will be another meeting, you shall have notice—it would be going a great way to affect him in consequence of that. I lay down the law with confidence, and I say there is no doctrine in it so well ascertained and established, as that a man is to be criminally affected only by his own acts—the man to be charged must be charged with overt acts of his own. There is no law—no security—no reason in that country where a man can be mowed down by foolishly crediting the evidence, not of acts of his own, but of the acts of others, constructively applied to him, who did not attend the meeting, nor was even aware of it. If a man was to be exposed to the penalties of treason hatched and perpetrated in his absence, every member of society becomes liable to be cut off by mere suspicion. I say, no man could go to his bed with an expectation of sleeping in it again if he were liable to be called upon to answer a charge of suspicious words, spoken when he was a hundred miles off, by miscreants with whom he had no connexion. Good God! gentlemen, only take asunder the evidence upon which you are called upon to take away the life of this man:—"You, Weldon, are chargeable, and shall answer with your blood, for what was done at Stoney-batter." "Why, that is very hard, gentlemen, for I was not there—I was an hundred miles off." "Yes, but you were there in contemplation of law, consulting about the abominable crimes of compassing the King's death, and adhering to his enemies." "How, gentlemen, could I be there?—I knew not that there was any such meeting—I was not present at it." "Aye, but you were there in contemplation of law, because you told Lawler, that Brady would inform him, when there would be a meeting in Thomas-street; and because you told him so, you shall be answerable with your life for what is done, at any meeting, at any distance of time, at any place, by strangers whom you have never seen or heard of. You have written your name, you have indorsed the treasonable purpose, and through whatever number of persons it may pass, the growing interest of your crime is accumulating against you, and you must pay it with your blood, when it is demanded of you."

Gentlemen, before we shall have learned to shed blood in sport—while death and slaughter are yet not matter of pastime among us, let us consider maturely, before we establish a rule of justice of this kind. Terrible rules, as we have seen them to be, when weighed upon the day of retribution. I confess it is new to me. Whatever doctrines I have learned, I have endeavoured to learn them from the good sense and humanity of the English law; I have been taught, that no man's life shall be sacrificed to the ingenuity of a scholium, and that even he who has heedlessly dropped the seed of guilt, should not answer for it with his blood, when it has grown, under the culture of other hands, from folly to crime, and from crime to treason; he shall not be called upon to answer for the wicked faults of casual and accidental folly. No, gentlemen; I say it with confidence, the act which makes a man guilty must be his own; or if it be by participation it must be by actual participation, not by construction; a construction which leads to an endless confounding of persons and things. If I do an act myself, I am answerable for it: if I do it by another, I am answerable also. If I strike the blow, I am answerable: if I send an assassin, and he strikes the blow, it is still my act, and I ought to be charged with the criminality of it. But if I go into a society of men, into a club, or play-house, and a crime be there committed, there is no principle of law which shall bring home to me the guilty conduct of those men which they may pursue at any distance of time. What protection can a miserable man have from my discharging perhaps the ineffectual office of my duty to him, if the rule laid down, that every word he said, or was said by a man with whom he ever had a conversation, shall affect him at any distance of time? Consider what will be the consequence of establishing the precedent, that a man shall always be responsible for the act of the society to which he has once belonged. Suppose a man heedlessly brought into an association where criminal purposes are going forward—suppose there was, what has been stated, a society of men calling themselves Defenders, and answering in fact to the very singular picture drawn of them. Will you give it abroad, that if a man once belongs to a criminal confederacy, his case is desperate—his retreat is cut off—that every man once present at a meeting to subvert the government, shall be answerable for every thing done at any distance of time by this flagitious association? What is the law in this respect? As in the association there is peril, so in the moment of retreat there is safety. What could this man have done? He quitted the city—he went to another part of the kingdom, when the treasonable acts were committed; yes, but he was virtually among them! What constitutes a man virtually present, when he is physically absent? What is the principle of law by which he shall be tried? It can alone be tried by that, by which the mandate or authority of any man is brought home to him. By previously suggesting the crime, by which he becomes an accessary before the fact, and therefore a principal in treason; for by suggesting the crime he proves the concurrence of his will with that of the party committing the crime. This is a maxim of law: that which in ordinary felonies makes a man an accessary, in treason will constitute him a principal, because in treason there are no accessaries. Suppose a meeting held for one purpose, and a totally distinct crime is committed, are those who were at the first meeting accessaries? Certainly not; because they must be procurers of the fact done. To make a man a principal, he must be *quodammodo* aiding and assisting — that is not proved. What, then, is the accessorial guilt? Did the prisoner write to the others? Does he appear to be the leader of any fraternity—the conductor of any treasonable meeting? No such thing. I say when he quitted Dublin he had no intention of giving aid or countenance to any meeting; the connexion between him and the societies ceased, and there is no evidence that he had any knowledge of any of their subsequent acts. Unless there be positive evidence against him, you ought to consider him out of the sphere of any association. But still you make him answerable for what was done. If you do that, you establish a rule unknown to the sense or humanity of the law; making him answerable for what was done, not by himself but by other persons.

Gentlemen, I feel that counsel, anxious as they ought to be, may be led further than they intend; —in point of time I have pressed further than I foresaw upon the patience of the jury and the court. I say the object of this part of the trial is whether the guilt of any thing which happened in that society be in point of law brought home to the prisoner? I have endeavoured to submit that the charge ought to be clear, and the evidence explicit, and that though the meetings at which Lawler attended were guilty, yet the prisoner, being absent, was not affected by their criminality. Give me leave now, with deference, to consider the case in another point of view. I say then, from what has appeared in evidence, the meetings themselves cannot in the estimation of the law be guilty. If these meetings are not provably guilty of treason, there can be no retroactive guilt upon the prisoner, even if the communication between them and him were proved. If there be no direct and original guilt—if they do not that, which, if done by him, would amount to an overt act of treason, *a fortiori*, it cannot extend to him. Therefore, let me suppose, that the prisoner was at the time present at these meetings. Be pleased to examine this, whether if he were, the evidence given would amount to the proof required. I conceive that nothing can be more clear than the distinction between mere casual, indiscreet language, and language conveying a deliberated and debated purpose. To give evidence of overt acts, the evidence must be clear and direct. How is Hensay's case?* A species of evidence was adduced, which it was impossible for any man to deny—actual proof of correspondence found in his own writing and possession. How was it in Lord Preston's case?† Evidence equally clear of a purpose acted upon—going to another country for that treasonable purpose. In every case of which we read memorials in the law, the act is such, that no man could say it is not an overt act of the means used by the party in effectuation of his guilty intent. But I said, that a deliberate purpose, expressed and acted upon, is different from a casual, indiscreet expression. Suppose now, that the meeting were all indicted for compassing the King's death, and that the overt act charged is,

* 19 Howell's State Trials, 1341.
† 12 Howell's State Trials, 646.

that they consulted about giving aid to the King's enemies, actually at war; the guilt of all is the guilt of each—there is no distinction between them. If that meeting held that consultation, they are all guilty of that species of high treason. But if the evidence were, that at that meeting which consisted of as many as are now here, one individual turned about to another, and said, "we must get arms to assist the French, when they come here." Would any reasonable man say, that was a consultation to adhere to the King's enemies?—a mere casual expression, not answered by any one—not addressed to the body. Can it be sustained for a moment in a court of justice, that it was a consultation to effect the death of the King, or adhere to his enemies? No, gentlemen, this is not matter of any deep or profound learning—it is familiar to the plainest understanding. The foolish language of one servant in your hall is not evidence to affect all the other servants in your house—it is not the guilt of the rest. I am aware it may be the guilt of the rest; it may become such. But I rely upon this; I address it to you with the confidence that my own conviction inspires, that your lordships will state to the jury, that a consultation upon a subject is a reciprocation of sentiment upon the same subject. Every man understands the meaning of a consultation; there is no servant that cannot understand it. If a man said to another, "we will conspire to kill the King," no lacquey could mistake it. But what is a consultation? Why such as a child could not mistake if it passed before him. One saying to another, "We are here together, private friends—we are at war—the French may land, and if they do, we will assist them." To make that a consultation there must be an assent to the same thought; upon that assent, the guilt of the consultation is founded. Is that proved by a casual expression of one man, without the man to whom it was directed making any answer, and when, in fact, every other man but the person using the expression was attending for another purpose? But if there be any force in what I have said, as applied to any man attending there, how much more forcible will it appear, when applied to a man who was an hundred miles distant from the place of meeting. If the law be clear, there is no treason in hearing treasonable designs and not consenting thereto (though it be another offence), unless he goes there, knowing beforehand what the meeting was to be. Here, gentlemen, see how careful the law is, and how far it is from being unprovided as to different cases of this kind. If a man go to a meeting, knowing that the object is to hatch a crime, he shall be joined in the guilt. If he go there and takes a part, without knowing previously, he is involved; though that has been doubted. Foster says, "this is proper to be left to the jury, though a party do or say nothing as to the consultation." If, for instance, a man, knowing of a design to imprison the King, go to a meeting to consult for that purpose, his going there is an obvious proof of his assent and encouragement. This is the law, as laid down by one of the most enlightened writers in any science. Compare that doctrine with what Mr. Attorney-General wishes to inculcate, when he seeks to convict the prisoner. There was a meeting in Barrack-street, and it was treason, because they laughed. As Sancho said, they all talked of me, because they laughed. But, then, there is a catechism. Aye, what say you to that? The cock crew in France;—what say you to that? Why, I say, it might be foolish, it might be indecent to talk in this manner. But what is the charge?—that he consulted to kill the King. Where was it he did that?—at Cork! But did he not assist? No; he was not there. But he did assist, because he communicated signs, and thus you collect the guilt of the party, as the coroner upon an inquest of murder, who thought a man standing by was guilty. Why?—because three drops of blood fell from his nose. This was thought to be invincible proof of his guilt. It reminds me also of an old woman who undertook to prove that a ghost had appeared. "How do you know there was a ghost in the room?" "Oh! I'll prove to you there must have been a ghost—for the very moment I went in, I fainted flat on the floor!" So, says Mr. Attorney-General, "Oh, I'll convince you, gentlemen, he designed to kill the King, *for he laughed.*" Weldon was chargeable with all the guilt of the meeting—he laughed when the paper was read, and said, "When the King's head was off, there was an end of the allegiance." In answer to that, I state the humane good sense of the law, that, in the case of the life of a traitor, it is tender in proportion to the abomination of the crime; for the law of England, while it suspended the sword of justice over the head of the guilty man, threw its protection around the innocent, to save his loyalty from the danger of such evidence. It did more—it threw its protection around him whose innocence might be doubted, but who was not proved to be guilty. The mild and lenient policy of the law discharges a man from the necessity of proving his innocence, because otherwise it would look as if the jury were empannelled to condemn upon accusation, without evidence in support of it, but merely because he did not prove himself innocent. Therefore, gentlemen, I come round again to state what the law is. In order to make a general assembling and consultation evidence of overt acts, there must be that assembling; and the guilt must be marked by that consultation, in order to charge any man, who was present and did not say anything concurring, with the guilt of that consultation. It is necessary that he should have notice that the guilty purpose was to be debated upon—that the meeting was convened for that purpose.

But let me recal your attention to this, and you will feel it bearing strongly upon that case. The silence of a man at such a meeting is not criminal to the degree here charged. Then suppose his disclaimer necessary—suppose the law considered every man as abetting what he did not disavow—remember that the wretch now sought to be affected by his silence at a meeting, was one hundred miles distant from it. There might have been a purpose from which his soul had recoiled. Is this then evidence upon which to convict the prisoner? There is no statement of any particular purpose—no summons to confer upon any particular purpose—no authority given to any meeting by a deputy named; and let me remind you, that at the last meeting, if there were the gossipings and communications you have heard, there was not any one man present who attended the first meeting, nor is there any evidence to show that the prisoner had ever spoken to any one man who attended the last meeting, upon any occasion; and yet the monstrous absurdity contended for is, that although Weldon proposed no subject for discussion—although he proposed no meeting—although he did not know that any purpose was to be carried into effect, because he was then one hundred miles off, he is still to suffer for the foolish babble of one individual to another. You are to put all proceedings together, and out of the tissue of this talk, hearsay, and conjecture, you are to collect the materials of a verdict, by which you directly swear that the man is guilty of compassing the King's death. But suppose a man were to suggest a treasonable meeting—that the meeting takes place, and he does not go—the first proposal may amount to an evidence of treason, if it went far enough, and amounted to an incitement. But suppose the meeting held be a distinct one from that which was suggested, and the party does not attend, it appears to me, that the act of that meeting cannot be considered as his overt act. The previous incitement must be clearly established by evidence, and I rely upon it, that the subsequent acts of that meeting, to which I am supposing he did not go—particularly if it be a meeting at which many others were present who were not at the first—I rely upon it, I say, that no declaration of any man (and more decidedly, if it be by a man not privy to the original declaration), can be evidence upon which a jury can attach guilt to the party. It is nothing more than misfeasance, which is certainly criminal, but not to the extent of this charge. To affect any man by subsequent debate, it must be with notice of the purpose, and if the meeting be dictated by himself it is only in that point he can be guilty; because if you propose a meeting for one purpose, you shall not be affected by any other—no matter what the meeting is—however treasonable or bad. Unless you knew before for what purpose they assembled, you cannot be guilty virtually by what they have done.

Gentlemen, I do not see that any thing further occurs to me upon the law of the case, that I have not endeavoured in some way to submit to you. Perhaps I have been going back somewhat irregularly. Gentlemen, there remains only one, and that a very narrow subject of observation. I said that the evidence upon which the life, and the property of a man should be decided and extinguished, ought to be of itself evidence of a most cogent and impressive nature. Gentlemen, does it appear to you that the witness whom you saw upon the table comes under that description? Has he sworn truly? If he has, what has he told you? As soon as he discovered the extent of the guilt he quitted the fraternity. Do you believe that? Hart told him that ALL the Protestants were to be massacred. "I did not like," said he, "the notion of massacring ALL." Here is the picture he draws of himself—he an accomplice in the guilt. I did not ask him—"Have you been promised a pardon?" I did not ask him—"Are you coming to swear by the acre?"—but I appeal to the picture he drew of himself upon the table. What worked his contrition? Is it the massacre of one wretch? He was unappalled at the idea of dipping his hands, and lapping the blood of *part* of the Protestant body—it was only heaps of festering dead that nauseated his appetite, and worked his repentance and conversion. Is your verdict to be founded upon the unsupported evidence of a wretch of that kind? His stomach stood a partial massacre—it was only an universal deluge of blood that made him a convert to humanity! And he is now, the honest, disinterested, and *loyal* witness in a court of justice! What said he further? "As soon as I found from Hart, their schemes, I went to Mr. Cowan." You saw, gentlemen, that he felt my motive in asking the question. "You abandoned them as soon as you found their criminality?" Because, had he answered otherwise, he would have destroyed his credit; but as it is, he has thrown his credit, and the foundation of it, overboard. If Lawler be innocent, Weldon must be so. He saw that, and, therefore, he said he thought it no crime to kill the King. Therefore, gentlemen, my conscience told me, that if he felt no remorse at plunging a dagger into the heart of his King, he would feel no trembling hesitation at plunging a dagger into the breast of an individual subject, by perjured testimony. Those workings of the heart which agitate the feelings at the untimely fate of a fellow-creature touch not him, and he could behold with delight the perishing of that man who had a knowledge of *his* guilt. He has no compunction, and he betrays no reluctance at drinking deep in the torrent of human blood, provided it leaves a remnant of the class. What stipulation can you make between a wretch of that kind and the sacred obligation of an oath? You are to swear upon his oath; a verdict is not to be founded upon your own loyalty—not upon what you have seen or heard spoken disrespectfully of the government or the King. Your honest, pure, and constitutional verdict can be founded only upon that sympathy that you feel between your own hearts and the credibility of the witness. It is a question for you. Will you hazard that oath upon the conscience of such a man? A man influenced by hope and agitated with fear—anxious for life and afraid to die, that you may safely say, "We have heard a witness, he stated facts which we could not believe; he is a wretch, for he thought it no crime to murder his King; and a partial massacre appeared to him to be meritorious!" Is it upon the testimony of that nefarious miscreant—the ready traitor—the prompt murderer—I retract not the expression, if I did, it would be to put in its place a word of more emphatic and combined reprobation; is it upon that evidence, I say, you will pronounce a verdict, establishing the most aggravated degree of criminality known to our law, upon the person of that man, supposed by the law to be innocent, until his guilt be proved? I know not whether the man be a good subject or a bad one: it is not necessary for me to know nor for you to inquire; but I exhort you finally to remember, that in Great Britain, so anxious has the law been to guard against the perfidiousness of such men, that no less than two concurrent witnesses are necessary there in cases of treason. I call not upon you to adopt that law; but to show you the principle, that there should be strong evidence satisfying the mind of a jury. I commit the decision of this case to your consciences, not to your humanity—I commit it to your determination upon the sound principles of justice aud law.

After Mr. CURRAN had sat down, he rose again, and said he had closed without stating any evidence, from a conviction that it would be unnecessary; and added—"It is desired to produce some evidence which I will not oppose in a case of life. There is evidence to show that Lawler is not credible."

CURRAN examined witnesses to this effect, but Weldon was found GUILTY, and though Leary, another prisoner, was acquitted, under precisely similar facts, Weldon was hanged.

FOR PETER FINNERTY,

PUBLISHER OF

"THE PRESS."

[LIBEL.]

December 22nd, 1797.

The Government and the United Irishmen were now face to face, the former armed with a full code of coercion and a large army and unscrupulous agents to support it—the latter with a good cause, the organization given by Tone, and the prospect of French aid. Each party tried to strengthen itself by conciliation and intimidation. Among the instruments were spies "the battalion of testimony" (Bird, Newell, O'Brien, &c.), free quarters, prosecutions, bribery, patronage, and calumny.

One of the best auxiliaries summoned by the United Irishmen was *"The Press"* newspaper.

The first number of it was published in Dublin, on Thursday, the 28th of September, 1797, and was thence continued on Tuesdays, Thursdays, and Saturdays, until Tuesday, the 13th of March, 1798, when the 69th and last number was seized by the government. It was not, like the *Northern Star*, a chronicle of French politics. It was a propagandist organ of Liberal and National opinions, filled with essays, letters, and addresses of great ability. Arthur O'Connor mainly originated it, and he, Thomas Emmet, Drennan, Sampson, &c., wrote it.

Government naturally longed to crush such a paper, as it had done the *Northern Star*, but raw force was premature for Dublin, so they waited for a libel, and, as they gave plenty of provocation, they waited not long. They found one, which irritated them deeply, while it gave them a good opening, in a letter published on Thursday, the 26th of October, 1797, addressed to the Lord Lieutenant, signed "Marcus." Most of the letter is set out in the indictment; so are the legal facts which were the text of it, but it is right to say something more of them.

William Orr was a Presbyterian farmer, resident at Farranshane, in the County of Antrim—a man of pious, gentle, and gallant character; a tall, athletic, and hearty fellow, too, and popular exceedingly. He was arrested in 1796, under the Insurrection Act (passed in the February of that year), for having, in April, 1796, administered the United Irish oath to Hugh Wheatly, a private in the Fifeshire Fencibles. He was indicted at Carrickfergus, on the 17th April, 1797, and tried on Saturday, 16th of September, 1797, before Chief Baron Lord Yelverton. The chief witness was Wheatly, who deposed that Orr acted as chairman or Secretary of a Baronial Committee in Antrim, where Wheatly was induced to go, and was there forced to take the oath. Lindsay, a private in the same corps, swore that he *saw* the oath administered, but did not hear it. Curran and Sampson, Orr's counsel, contended that this was a case for a prosecution for high-treason, but Yelverton decided otherwise, and charged for a conviction. The jury retired at seven at night, and came into court at six o'clock on Sunday morning, and after much confusion (from conscience or intoxication) gave in a verdict of Guilty, with a recommendation to mercy, which Yelverton sent by express to the Castle. On Monday, the 18th, Curran moved for a new trial, on the affidavit of two of the jurors, stating the drunkenness of some of the jurors, and the intimidation used to one of the deponents. He had an affidavit from a third juror, swearing that he was deceived into the verdict, but Orr was sentenced to be hanged on the 7th of October. Orr declared at the close of the trial that he was innocent. Various attempts were made to save him. His brother James signed a declaration of his guilt and a prayer for mercy, in William's name, and got it backed by the gentry; but William disclaimed it. It was also sworn by a Presbyterian clergyman that Wheatly had confessed himself guilty of murder, perjury, and other crimes. In consequence of all this, Orr was thrice respited, and judging from the conciliatory and beseeching tone of *The Press* (No. 5), Government seems to have had an opportunity of making themselves popular, and weakening the United Irishmen by a just leniency. They preferred the harsh course, and on Saturday, the 14th of October, Orr was hanged, outside Carrickfergus, amid a mass of troops. He distributed a written paper, declaring his innocence, and died calmly and nobly. He left five children and a wife, about again to be a mother.

Indignation was nigh universal. Medals with "Remember Orr!" were circulated; his name became a watchword (and continued so, as Sheares' proclamation proves); "The Ministers in Orr's place" was a toast even in England, and Fox spoke of him as a martyr. That he was a United Irishman is clear; but that he gave Wheatly the oath, or was therefore guilty in law, is not probable. Guilty or not, his execution for such a crime, on such evidence, and after such a verdict, was a murder! So it was treated in the letter of "Marcus." The author was a Mr. Deane Swift, a frequent contributor to "*The Press.*"

On Tuesday, the 31st of October, Peter Finnerty was arrested, at 62, Abbey-street, (*The Press* office), for this publication, under a Judge's warrant, and on Friday, the 22nd of December, was tried before Justice Downes at the Commission Court. The indictment stated,

"That at a general assizes and general gaol delivery, holden at Carrickfergus, in and for the county of Antrim, on the 17th day of April, in the thirty-seventh year of the King, before the Honourable Mathias Finucane, one of the judges of his Majesty's court of Common Pleas in Ireland, and the Honourable Denis George, one of the barons of his Majesty's Court of Exchequer in Ireland, Justices and Commissioners assigned to deliver the gaol of our said Lord the King, in and for the county of Antrim, of the several prisoners and malefactors therein, one

William Orr, late of Farranshane, in said county of Antrim, yeoman, was in lawful manner indicted for feloniously administering a certain oath and engagement, upon a book, to one Hugh Wheatly; which oath and engagement imported to bind the said Hugh Wheatly, who then and there took the same, to be of an association, brotherhood, and society, formed for seditious purposes; and also for feloniously causing, procuring, and inducing said Hugh Wheatly, to take an oath of said import last mentioned; and also for feloniously administering to said Hugh Wheatly another oath, importing to bind said Hugh Wheatly not to inform or give evidence against any brother, associate, or confederate, of a certain society then and there formed; and also for feloniously causing, procuring, and seducing said Hugh Wheatly to take an oath of said import last mentioned. And afterwards at Carrickfergus aforesaid, before the Right Honourable Barry Lord Yelverton, Lord Chief Baron of his Majesty's Court of Exchequer in Ireland, and the Honourable Tankerville Chamberlain, one of his Majesty's Justices of his Court of Chief Pleas in Ireland, at a general assizes, &c., on the 16th day of September, in the 37th year of the King, said William Orr, by the verdict of a certain jury of said county of Antrim, between our said Lord the King and said William Orr, taken of and for the felony aforesaid in due manner, was tried, convicted, and attainted, and for the same was duly executed: and that he, the said Peter Finnerty, well knowing the premises, but being a wicked and ill-disposed person, and of unquiet conversation and disposition, and devising and intending to molest and disturb the peace and public tranquillity of this kingdom of Ireland; and to bring and draw the trial aforesaid, and the verdict thereon, for our said Lord the King against this William Orr given, and the due course of law in that behalf had, as aforesaid, into hatred, contempt, and scandal, with all the liege subjects of our said Lord the King to believe that the trial aforesaid was unduly had, and that the said William Orr did undeservedly die in manner aforesaid; and that his

Excellency John Jefferys, Earl Camden, the Lord Lieutenant of this kingdom, after the conviction aforesaid, ought to have extended to the said William Orr, his Majesty's gracious pardon of the felonies aforesaid; and that in not so extending such pardon, he, the said Lord Lieutenant, had acted inhumanly, wickedly, and unjustly, and in a manner unworthy of the trust which had been committed to him by our said Lord the King in that behalf; and that the said Lord Lieutenant in his government of this kingdom, had acted unjustly, cruelly, and oppressively, to his Majesty's subjects therein: And the said Peter Finnerty, to fulfil and bring to effect his most wicked and detestable devices and intentions aforesaid, on the 26th of October, in the 37th year of the King, at Mountrath-street aforesaid, city of Dublin aforesaid, falsely, wickedly, maliciously, and seditiously did print and publish, and cause and procure to be printed and published, in a certain newspaper entitled '*The Press*,' a certain false, wicked, malicious and seditious libel, of and concerning the said trial, conviction, attainder, and execution of the said William Orr, as aforesaid, and of and concerning the said Lord Lieutenant and his government of this kingdom, and his Majesty's Ministers employed by him in his government of this kingdom, according to the tenor and effect following, to wit:—

"'The death of Mr. Orr, (meaning the execution of the said William Orr) the nation has pronounced one of the most sanguinary and savage acts that had disgraced the laws. In perjury, did you not hear, my Lord (meaning the said Lord Lieutenant,) the verdict (meaning the verdict aforesaid) was given? Perjury accompanied with terror, as terror has marked every step of your government (meaning the government of this kingdom aforesaid, by the said Lord Lieutenant.) Vengeance and desolation were to fall on those who would not plunge themselves in blood. These were not strong enough: against the express law of the land, not only was drink introduced to the jury (meaning the jury aforesaid), but drunkenness itself, beastly and criminal drunkenness, was employed to procure the murder of a better man (meaning the said execution of the said William Orr) than any that now surrounds you (meaning the said Lord Lieutenant).'

"And in another part thereof, according to the tenor and effect following, to wit:—

"'Repentance, which is a slow virtue, hastened, however, to declare the innocence of the victim (meaning the said William Orr); the mischief (meaning the said conviction of the said William Orr) which perjury had done, truth now stept forward to repair. Neither was she too late, had humanity formed any part of your counsels (meaning the counsels of the said Lord Lieutenant). Stung with remorse, on the return of reason, part of his jury (meaning the jury aforesaid) solemnly and soberly made oath that their verdict (meaning the verdict aforesaid) had been given under the unhappy influence of intimidation and drink; and in the most serious affidavit that ever was made, by acknowledging their crime, endeavoured to atone to God and to their country, for the sin into which they had been seduced.'

"And in another part thereof, according to the tenor and effect following, to wit:—

"'And though the innocence of the accused (meaning the said William Orr) had even remained doubtful, it was your duty (meaning the duty of the said Lord Lieutenant), my Lord, and you (meaning the said Lord Lieutenant) had no exemption from that duty, to have interposed your arm, and saved him (meaning the said William Orr) from the death (meaning the execution aforesaid) that perjury, drunkenness, and reward, had prepared for him (meaning the said William Orr.) Let not the nation be told that you (meaning the Lord Lieutenant) are a passive instrument in the hands of others; if passive you be, then is your office a shadow indeed. If an active instrument, as you ought to be, you (meaning the said Lord Lieutenant) did not perform the duty which the laws required of you; you (meaning the said Lord Lieutenant) did not exercise the prerogative of mercy; that mercy which the constitution had entrusted to you (meaning the said Lord Lieutenant) for the safety of the subject, by guarding him from the oppression of wicked men. Innocent it appears he (meaning the said William Orr) was; his blood (meaning the blood of the said William Orr) has been shed, and the precedent indeed is awful.'

"And in another part thereof, according to the tenor and effect following, to wit:—

"'But suppose the evidence of Wheatly had been true, what was the offence of Mr. Orr (meaning the said William Orr)? Not that he had taken an oath of blood and extermination, for then he had not suffered; but that he (meaning the said William Orr) had taken an oath of charity and of union, of humanity and of peace, he (meaning the said William Orr) has suffered. Shall we then be told that your government (meaning the government of this kingdom aforesaid, by the said Lord Lieutenant) will conciliate public opinion, or that the people will not continue to look for a better?'

"And in another part thereof, according to the tenor and effect following, that is to say;—

"'Is it to be wondered that a successor of Lord Fitzwilliam should sign the death-warrant of Mr. Orr (meaning the said William Orr)? Mr. Pitt had learned that a merciful Lord Lieutenant was unsuited to a government of violence. It was no compliment to the native clemency of a Camden, that he sent you (meaning the said Lord Lieutenant) into Ireland, and what has been our portion under the change, but massacre and rape, military murders, desolation and terror.'

"And in another part thereof, according to the tenor and effect here following, that is to say:—

"'Feasting in your castle, in the midst of your myrmidons and bishops, you (meaning the said Lord Lieutenant) have little concerned yourself about the expelled and miserable cottager, whose dwelling, at the moment of your mirth, was in flames, his wife and his daughter then under the violation of some commissioned ravager, his son agonizing on the bayonet, and his helpless infants crying in vain for mercy. These are lamentations which stain not the house of carousal. Under intoxicated counsels (meaning the counsels of the said Lord Lieutenant), the constitution has reeled to its centre, justice is not only blind drunk, but deaf, like Festus, to the words of soberness and truth.'

"'And in another part thereof, according to the tenor and effect here following, to wit:—

"'Let, however, the awful execution of Mr. Orr (meaning the execution aforesaid of the said William Orr) be a lesson to all unthinking juries, and let them cease to flatter themselves that the soberest recommendation of theirs, and of the presiding judge, can stop the course of carnage, which sanguinary, and I do not fear to say, unconstitutional laws have ordered to be loosed. Let them remember, that, like Macbeth, the servants of the crown have waded so far in blood, that they find it easier to go on than to go back.'

"In contempt, &c. and against the peace, &c."

The Attorney-General stated the case, and produced witnesses, who proved printing and publication. Mr. Fletcher opened the defence, and called Lord Yelverton and Mr. E. Cooke (Chief Clerk in the Secretary's office) to prove the truth of the libel; but the evidence was soon stopped, as illegal. CURRAN spoke as follows:—

NEVER did I feel myself so sunk under the importance of any cause. To speak to a question of this kind, at any time, would require the greatest talent and the most mature deliberation; but to be obliged, without either of those advantages, to speak to a subject that has so deeply shaken the feelings of this already irritated and agitated nation, is a task that fills me with embarrassment and dismay.

Neither my learned colleague nor myself received any instruction or license until after the jury were actually sworn, and we both of us came here under an idea that we should not take any part in the trial. This circumstance I mention, not as an idle apology for an effort that cannot be the subject of either praise or censure, but as a call upon you, gentlemen of the jury, to supply the defects of my efforts, by a double exertion of your attention.

Perhaps I ought to regret that I cannot begin with any compliment, that may recommend me or my client personally to your favour. A more artful advocate would probably begin his address to you by compliments on your patriotism, and by felicitating his client upon the happy selection of his jury, and upon that unsuspected impartiality in which, if he was innocent, he must be safe. You must be conscious, gentlemen, that such idle verbiage as that, could not convey either my sentiments, or my client's, upon that subject. You know, and we know, upon what occasion you are come, and by whom you have been chosen; you are come to try an accusation professedly brought forward by the state, chosen by a sheriff who is appointed by our accuser.

The Attorney-General, interrupting Mr. CURRAN, said the sheriff was elected by the city, and that the observation was therefore unfounded.

Be it so [continued Mr. CURRAN]: I will not now stop to inquire whose property the city may be considered to be: but the learned gentleman seems to forget, that the election by that city, to whomsoever it may belong, is absolutely void without the approbation of that very Lord Lieutenant, who is the prosecutor in this case. I do therefore repeat, gentlemen, that not a man of you has been called to that box by the voice of my client; that he has had no power to object to a single man among you, though the crown has; and that you yourselves must feel under what influence you are chosen, or for what qualifications you are particularly selected. At a moment when this wretched land is shaken to its centre by the dreadful conflicts of the different branches of the community; between those who call themselves the partizans of liberty, and those that call themselves the partizans of power; between the advocates of infliction and the advocates of suffering; upon such a question as the present, and at such a season, can any man be at a loss to guess to what class of character and opinion, a friend to either party would resort, for that jury, which was to decide between both? I trust, gentlemen, you know me too well to suppose that I could be capable of treating you with any personal disrespect; I am speaking to you in the honest confidence of your fellow-citizen. When I allude to those unworthy imputations of supposed bias, or passion, or partiality, that may have marked you out for your present situation, I do so, in order to warn you of the ground on which you stand, of the point of awful responsibility in which you are placed, to your conscience, and to your country; and to remind you, that if you have been put into that box from any unworthy reliance on your complaisance or your servility, you have it in your power, before you leave it, to refute and to punish so vile an expectation, by the integrity of your verdict; to remind you, too, that you have it in your power to show to as many Irishmen as yet linger in this country, that all law and justice have not taken their flight with our prosperity and peace; that the sanctity of an oath, and the honesty of a juror are not yet dead amongst us; and that if our courts of justice are superseded by so many strange and terrible tribunals, it is not because they are deficient either in wisdom or virtue.

Gentlemen, it is necessary that you should have a clear idea, first, of the law by which this question is to be decided; secondly, of the nature and object of the prosecution. As to the first, it is my duty to inform you, that the law respecting libels has been much changed of late. Heretofore, in consequence of some decisions of the judges in Westminster-hall, the jury was conceived to have no province but that of finding the truth of the inuendos, and the fact of publication; but the libellous nature of that publication, as well as the guilt or innocence of the publication, were considered as exclusively belonging to the court.

In a system like that of law, which reasons logically, no one erroneous principle can be introduced without producing every other that can be deducible from it. If in the premises of any argument you admit one erroneous proposition, nothing but bad reasoning can save the conclusions from falsehood. So it has been with this encroachment of the court upon the province of the jury with respect to libels. The moment the court assumed as a principle that they, the court, were to decide upon every thing but the publication; that is, that they were to decide upon the question of libel or no libel, and upon the guilt or innocence of the intention, which must form the essence of every crime, the guilt or innocence must of necessity have ceased to be material.

You see, gentlemen, clearly, that the question of intention is a mere question of fact.

Now the moment the court determined that the jury was not to try that question, it followed of necessity that it was not to be tried at all; for the court cannot try a question of fact. When the court said that it was not triable, there was no way of fortifying that extraordinary proposition, except by asserting that it was not material. The same erroneous reasoning carried them another step, still more mischievous and unjust: if the intention had been material, it must have been decided upon as a mere fact, under all its circumstances. Of these circumstances, the meanest understanding can see that the leading one must be the truth or the falsehood of the publication; but having decided the intention to be immaterial, it followed that the truth must be equally immaterial, and under the law so distorted, any man in England who published the most undeniable truth, and with the purest intention, might be punished for a crime in the most ignominious manner, without imposing on the prosecutor the necessity of proving his guilt, or his getting any opportunity of showing his innocence.

I am not in the habit of speaking of legal institutions with disrespect; but I am warranted in condemning that usurpation upon the right of juries, by the authority of that statute, by which your jurisdiction is restored. For that restitution of justice, the British subject is indebted to the splendid exertions of Mr. Fox and Mr. Erskine, those distinguished supporters of the constitution and of the law; and I am happy to say to you, that though we can claim no share in the glory they have so justly acquired, we have the full benefit of their success; for you are now sitting under a similar act passed in this country, which makes it your duty and right to decide on the entire question upon the broadest grounds, and under all its circumstances, and, of course, to determine by your verdict, whether this publication be a false and scandalous libel; false in fact, and published with the seditious purpose alleged, of bringing the government into scandal, and instigating the people to insurrection.

Having stated to you, gentlemen, the great and exclusive extent of your jurisdiction, I shall beg leave to suggest to you a distinction that will strike you at first sight; and that is, the distinction between public animadversions upon the character of private individuals, and those which are written upon measures of government, and the persons who conduct them.

The former may be called personal, and the latter political publications. No two things can be more different in their nature, nor in the point of view in which they are to be looked on by a jury. The criminality of a mere personal libel consists in this, that it tends to a breach of the peace; it tends to all the vindictive paroxysms of exasperated vanity, or to the deeper or more deadly vengeance of irritated pride. The truth is, few men see at once that they cannot be hurt so much as they think by the mere battery of a newspaper. They do not reflect that every character has a natural station, from which it cannot be effectually degraded, and beyond which it cannot be raised by the bawling of a news-hawker. If it is wantonly aspersed, it is but for a season, and that a short one, when it emerges, like the moon from a passing cloud, to its original brightness. It is right, however, that the law, and that you, should hold the strictest hand over this kind of public animadversion, that forces humility and innocence from their retreat into the glare of public view; that wounds and terrifies, that destroys the cordiality and the peace of domestic life, and that, without eradicating a single vice, or single folly, plants a thousand thorns in the human heart.

In cases of that kind, I perfectly agree with the law as stated from the bench; in such cases, I hesitate not to think, that the truth of a charge ought not to justify its publication. If a private man is charged with a crime, he ought to be prosecuted in a court of justice, where he may be punished, if it is true, and the accuser, if it is false. But far differently do I deem of the freedom of political publication. The salutary restraint of the former species, which I talked of, is found in the general law of all societies whatever; but the more enlarged freedom of the press, for which I contend, in political publication, I conceive to be founded in the peculiar nature of the British constitution, and to follow directly from the contract on which the British government hath been placed by the Revolution. By the British constitution, the power of the state is a trust, committed by the people, upon certain conditions; by the violation of which, it may be abdicated by those who hold, and resumed by those who conferred it. The real security, therefore, of the British sceptre, is, the sentiment and opinion of the people, and it is, consequently, their duty to observe the conduct of the government;

and it is the privilege of every man to give them full and just information upon that important subject. Hence the liberty of the press is inseparably twined with the liberty of the people.

The press is the great public monitor: its duty is that of the historian and the witness, that *"nil falsi audeat, nil veri non audeat dicere;"* that its horizon shall extend to the farthest verge and limit of truth; that it shall speak truth to the king in the hearing of the people, and to the people in the hearing of the king; that it shall not perplex either the one or the other with false alarm, lest it lose its characteristic veracity, and become an unheeded warner of real danger; lest it should vainly warn them of that sin, of which the inevitable consequence is death. This, gentlemen, is the great privilege upon which you are to decide; and I have detained you the longer, because of the late change of the law, and because of some observations that have been made, which I shall find it necessary to compare with the principles I have now laid down.

And now, gentlemen, let us come to the immediate subject of the trial, as it is brought before you, by the charge in the indictment, to which it ought to have been confined; and also, as it is presented to you by the statement of the learned counsel who has taken a much wider range than the mere limits of the accusation, and has endeavoured to force upon your consideration extraneous and irrelevant facts, for reasons which it is not my duty to explain.

The indictment states simply that Mr. Finnerty has published a false and scandalous libel upon the Lord Lieutenant of Ireland, tending to bring his government into disrepute, and to alienate the affections of the people; and one would have expected, that, without stating any other matter, the counsel for the crown would have gone directly to the proof of this allegation; but he has not done so; he has gone to a most extraordinary length, indeed, of preliminary observation, and an allusion to facts, and sometimes an assertion of facts, at which, I own, I was astonished, until I saw the drift of these allusions and assertions. Whether you have been fairly dealt with by him, or are now honestly with by me, you must be judges.

He has been pleased to say, that this prosecution is brought against this letter signed "Marcus," merely as a part of what he calls a system of attack upon the government, by the paper called "*The Press*." As to this, I will only ask you whether you are fairly dealt with? whether it is fair treatment to men upon their oaths, to insinuate to them, that the general character of a newspaper (and that general character founded merely upon the assertion of the prosecutor), is to have any influence upon their minds, when they are to judge of a particular publication? I will only ask you, what men you must be supposed to be, when it is thought, that even in a court of justice, and with the eyes of the nation upon you, you can be the dupes of that trite and exploded expedient, so scandalous of late in this country, of raising a vulgar and mercenary cry against whatever man, or whatever principle, it is thought necessary to put down; and I shall, therefore, merely leave it to your own pride to suggest upon what foundation it could be hoped, that a senseless clamour of that kind could be echoed back by the yell of a jury upon their oaths. I trust you see that this has nothing to do with the question.

Gentlemen of the jury, other matters have been mentioned, which I must repeat for the same purpose; that of showing you that they have nothing to do with the question. The learned counsel has been pleased to say, that he comes forward in this prosecution as the real advocate for the liberty of the press, and to protect a mild and a merciful government from its licentiousness; and he has been pleased to add, that the constitution can never be lost while its freedom remains, and that its licentiousness alone can destroy that freedom. As to that, gentlemen, he might as well have said, that there is only one mortal disease of which a man can die: I can die the death inflicted by tyranny; and when he comes forward to extinguish this paper, in the ruin of the printer, by a state prosecution, in order to prevent its dying of licentiousness, you must judge how candidly he is treating you, both in the fact and in the reasoning. Is it in Ireland, gentlemen, that we are told licentiousness is the only disease that can be mortal to the press? Has he heard of nothing else that has been fatal to the freedom of publication? I know not whether the printer of the *Northern Star* may have heard of such things in his captivity; but I know that his wife and children are well apprized that a press may be destroyed in the open day, not by its own licentiousness, but by the licentiousness of a military force.

As to the sincerity of the declaration, that the state has prosecuted, in order to assert the freedom of the press, it starts a train of thought,—of melancholy retrospect and direful prospect,—to which I did not think the learned counsel would have wished you to commit your minds. It leads you naturally to reflect at what times, from what motives, and with what consequences, the government has displayed its patriotism, by prosecutions of this sort. As to the motives, does history give you a single instance in which the state has been provoked to these conflicts, except by the fear of truth and by the love of vengeance? Have you ever seen the rulers of any country bring forward a prosecution from motives of filial piety, for libels upon their departed ancestors? Do you read that Elizabeth directed any of those state prosecutions against libels which the divines of her times had written against her Catholic sister, or against the other libels which the same gentlemen had written against her Protestant father? No, gentlemen, we read of no such thing; but we know she did bring forward a prosecution from motives of personal resentment; and we know that a jury was found time-serving and mean enough to give a verdict which she was ashamed to carry into effect.

I said the learned counsel drew you back to the times that have been marked by these miserable conflicts. I see you turn your thoughts to the reign of the second James. I see you turn your eyes to those pages of governmental abandonment, of popular degradation, of expiring liberty, of merciless and sanguinary persecution; to that miserable period, in which the fallen and abject state of man might have been almost an argument in the mouth of the atheist and the blasphemer, against the existence of an all-just and an all-wise First Cause; if the glorious era of the Revolution that followed it had not refuted the impious inference, by showing that if a man descends, it is not in his own proper motion; that it is with labour and with pain; that he can continue to sink only until, by the force and pressure of the descent, the spring of his immortal faculties acquires that recuperative energy and effort that hurries him as many miles aloft; that he sinks but to rise again. It is at that period that the state seeks for shelter in the destruction of the press; it is in a period like that, that the tyrant prepares for an attack upon the people, by destroying the liberty of the press; by taking away that shield of wisdom and of virtue, behind which the people are invulnerable; in whose pure and polished convex, ere the lifted blow has fallen, he beholds his own image, and is turned into stone. It is at those periods that the honest man dares not speak, because truth is too dreadful to be told; it is then humanity has no ears, because humanity has no tongue. It is then the proud man scorns to speak, but, like a physician baffled by the wayward excesses of a dying patient, retires indignantly from the bed of an unhappy wretch, whose ear is too fastidious to bear the sound of wholesome advice, whose palate is too debauched to bear the salutary bitter of the medicine that might redeem him; and therefore leaves him to the felonious piety of the slaves that talk to him of life, and strip him before he is cold.

I do not care, gentlemen, to exhaust too much of your attention, by following this subject through the last century with much minuteness; but the facts are too recent in your mind not to show you, that the liberty of the press and the liberty of the people sink and rise together; that the liberty of speaking and the liberty of acting have shared exactly the same fate. You must have observed in England, that their fate has been the same in the successive vicissitudes of their late depression; and sorry I am to add, that this country has exhibited a melancholy proof of their inseparable destiny, through the various and fitful stages of deterioration, down to the period of their final extinction, when the constitution has given place to the sword, and the only printer in Ireland who dares to speak for the people is now in the dock.

Gentlemen, the learned counsel has made the real subject of this prosecution so small a part of his statement, and has led you into so wide a range—certainly as necessary to the object, as inapplicable to the subject of this prosecution—that I trust you will think me excusable in having somewhat followed his example. Glad am I to find that I have the authority of the same example for coming at last to the subject of this trial. I agree with the learned counsel that the charge made against the Lord Lieutenant of Ireland is that of having grossly and inhumanly abused the royal prerogative of mercy, of which the King is only the trustee for the benefit of the people. The facts are not controverted. It has been asserted that their truth or falsehood is indifferent, and they are shortly these, as they appear in this publication.

William Orr was indicted for having administered the oath of a United Irishman. Every man now knows what the oath is: that it is simply an engagement, first, to promote a brotherhood of affection among men of all religious distinctions; secondly, to labour for the attainment of a parliamentary reform; and thirdly, an obligation of secrecy, which was added to it when the convention law made it criminal and punishable to meet by any public delegation for that purpose.

After remaining upwards of a year in gaol, Mr. Orr was brought to his trial; was prosecuted by the state; was sworn against by a common informer of the name of Wheatly, who himself had taken the obligation; and was convicted under the Insurrection Act, which makes the administering such an obligation felony of death. The jury recommended Mr. Orr to mercy, and the judge, with a humanity becoming his character, transmitted the recommendation to the noble prosecutor in this case. Three of the jurors made solemn affidavit in court, that liquor had been conveyed into their box; that they were brutally threatened by some of their fellow-jurors with criminal prosecution if they did not find the prisoner guilty; and that under the impression of those threats, and worn down by watching and intoxication, they had given a verdict of guilty against him, though they believed him in their consciences to be innocent. That further inquiries were made, which ended in a discovery of the infamous life and character of the informer; that a respite was therefore sent once, and twice, and thrice, to give time, as Mr. Attorney-General has stated, for his Excellency to consider whether mercy *could* be extended to him or not; and that with a knowledge of all these circumstances, his Excellency did finally determine that mercy should not be extended to him;

and that he was accordingly executed upon that verdict.

Of this publication, which the indictment charges to be false and seditious, Mr. Attorney-General is pleased to say, that the design of it is to bring the courts of justice into contempt. As to this point of fact, gentlemen, I beg to set you right.

To the administration of justice, so far as it relates to the judges, this publication has not even an allusion in any part mentioned in this indictment; it relates to a department of justice that cannot begin until the duty of the judge closes. Sorry should I be, that, with respect to this unfortunate man, any censure should be flung on those judges who presided at his trial, with the mildness and temper that became them upon so awful an occasion as the trial of life and death. Sure am I, that if they had been charged with inhumanity or injustice, and if they had condescended at all to prosecute the reviler, they would not have come forward in the face of the public to say, as has been said this day, that it was immaterial whether the charge was true or not. Sure I am, their first object would have been to show that it was false, and readily should I have been an eye-witness of the fact, to have discharged the debt of ancient friendship, of private respect, and of public duty, and upon my oath to have repelled the falsehood of such an imputation.

Upon this subject, gentlemen, the presence of

those venerable judges restrains what I might otherwise have said, nor should I have named them at all, if I had not been forced to do so, and merely to undeceive you, if you have been made to believe their characters to have any community of cause whatever with the Lord Lieutenant of Ireland. To him alone it is confined, and against him the charge is made, as strongly, I suppose, as the writer could find words to express it, that the Viceroy of Ireland has cruelly abused the prerogative of royal mercy, in suffering a man under such circumstances to perish like a common malefactor. For this Mr. Attorney-General calls for your conviction as a false and scandalous libel; and after stating himself every fact that I have repeated to you, either from his statement, or from the evidence, he tells you that you ought to find it false and scandalous, though he almost in words admits that it is not false, and has resisted the admission of the evidence by which we offered to prove every word of it to be true.

And here, gentlemen, give me leave to remind you of the parties before you.

The traverser is a printer, who follows that profession for bread, and who, at a time of great public misery and terror, when the people are restrained by law from debating under any delegated form; when the few constituents that we have are prevented by force from meeting in their own persons, to deliberate or to petition; when every other paper in Ireland is put down by force, or purchased by the administration (though here, gentlemen, perhaps I ought to beg your pardon for stating without authority; I recollect when we attempted to examine as to the number of newspapers in the pay of the castle, that the evidence was objected to); at a season like this, Mr. Finnerty has had the courage, perhaps the folly, to print the publication in question, for no motive under heaven of malice or vengeance, but in the mere duty which he owes to his family, and to the public.

His prosecutor is the King's minister in Ireland; in that character does the learned gentleman mean to say, that his conduct is not a fair subject of public observation? Where does he find his authority for that in the law or practice of the sister country? Have the virtues, or the exalted station, or the general love of his people preserved the sacred person even of the royal master of the prosecutor, from the asperity and intemperance of public censure, unfounded as it ever must be, with any personal respect to his Majesty, in justice or truth? Have the gigantic abilities of Mr. Pitt, have the more gigantic talents of his great antagonist, Mr. Fox, protected either of them from the insolent familiarity, and for aught we know, the injustice with which writers have treated them? What latitude of invective has the King's minister escaped upon the subject of the present war? Is there an epithet of contumely, or of reproach, that hatred or that fancy could suggest, that is not publicly lavished upon them? Do you not find the words, advocate of despotism, robber of the public treasure, murderer of the King's subjects, debaucher of the public morality, degrader of the constitution, tarnisher of the British empire, by frequency of use lose all meaning whatsoever, and dwindle into terms, not of any peculiar reproach, but of ordinary appellation?

And why, gentlemen, is this permitted in that country? I'll tell you why; because in that country they are yet wise enough to see that the measures of the state are the proper subject for the freedom of the press; that the principles relating to personal slander do not apply to rulers or to ministers; that to publish an attack upon a public minister, without any regard to truth, but merely because of its tendency to a breach of the peace, would be ridiculous in the extreme. What breach of the peace, gentlemen, I pray you, is such a case? Is it the tendency of such publications to provoke Mr. Pitt or Mr. Dundas to break the head of the writer, if they should happen to meet him? No, gentlemen; in that country this freedom is exercised, because the people feel it to be their right; and it is wisely suffered to pass by the state, from a consciousness that it would be vain to oppose it; a consciousness confirmed by the event of every incautious experiment. It is suffered to pass from a conviction, that, in a court of justice at least, the bulwarks of the constitution will not be surrendered to the state; and that the intended victim, whether clothed in the humble guise of honest industry, or decked in the honours of genius, and virtue, and philosophy, whether a Hardy or a Tooke, will find certain protection in the honesty and spirit of an English jury.

But, gentlemen, I suppose Mr. Attorney-General will scarcely wish to carry his doctrine altogether so far. Indeed, I remember, he declared himself a most zealous advocate for the liberty of the press. I may, therefore, even according to him, presume to make some observations on the conduct of the existing government. I should wish to know how far he supposes it to extend; is it to the composition of lampoons and madrigals, to be sung down the grates by ragged ballad-mongers to kitchen maids and footmen? I will not suppose that he means to confine it to the ebullitions of Billingsgate, to those cataracts of ribaldry and scurrility, that are daily spouting upon the miseries of our wretched fellow-sufferers, and the unavailing efforts of those who have vainly laboured in their cause. I will not suppose that he confines it to the poetic license of a birth day ode; the *Laureat* would not use such language! In which case I do not entirely agree with him, that the truth or the falsehood is as perfectly immaterial to the law, as it is to the *Laureat*; as perfectly unrestrained by the law of the land, as it is by any law of decency or shame, of modesty or decorum.

But as to the privilege of censure or blame, I am sorry that the learned gentlemen has not favoured you with his notion of the liberty of the press.

Suppose an Irish Viceroy acts a very little absurdly, may the press venture to be respectfully comical upon that absurdity? The learned counsel does not, at least in terms, give a negative to that. But let me treat you honestly, and go further, to a more material point; suppose an Irish Viceroy does an act that brings scandal upon his master, that fills the mind of a reasonable man with the fear of approaching despotism; that leaves no hope to the people of preserving themselves and their children from chains, but in common confederacy for common safety. What is that honest man in that case to do?

I am sorry *the right honourable advocate for the liberty of the press* has not told you his opinion, at least in any express words. I will therefore venture to give you my far humbler thoughts upon the subject.

I think an honest man ought to tell the people frankly and boldly of their peril; and I must say I can imagine no villany greater than that of his holding a traitorous silence at such a crisis, except the villany and baseness of prosecuting him, or of finding him guilty for such an honest discharge of his public duty. And I found myself on the known principle of the revolution of England, namely, that the crown itself may be abdicated by certain abuses of the trust reposed; and that there are possible excesses of arbitrary power, which it is not only the right, but the bounden duty, of every honest man to resist, at the risk of his fortune and his life.

Now, gentlemen, if this reasoning be admitted, and it cannot be denied; if there be any possible event in which the people are obliged to look only to themselves, and are justified in doing so; can you be so absurd as to say, that it is lawful for the people to act upon it when it unfortunately does arrive, but that it is criminal in any man to tell them that the miserable event has actually arrived, or is imminently approaching? Far am I, gentlemen, from insinuating that (extreme as it is) our misery has been matured into any deplorable crisis of this kind, from which I pray that the Almighty God may for ever preserve us! But I am putting my principles upon the strongest ground, and most favourable to my opponents, namely, that it never can be criminal to say any thing of government but what is false; and I put this in the extreme, in order to demonstrate to you, *à fortiori*, that the privilege of speaking truth to the people, which holds in the last extremity, must also obtain in every stage of inferior importance; and that, however a court may have decided, before the late act, that the truth was immaterial in case of libel, since that act, no honest jury can be governed by such principle.

Be pleased now, gentlemen, to consider the grounds upon which this publication is called a libel, and criminal.

Mr. Attorney-General tells you it tends to excite sedition and insurrection. Let me again remind you, that the truth of this charge is not denied by the noble prosecutor. What is it then that tends to excite sedition and insurrection? "The act that is charged upon the prosecutor, and is not attempted to be denied?" And, gracious God! gentlemen of the jury, is the public statement of the King's representative this, "I have done a deed that must fill the mind of every feeling or thinking man with horror and indignation; that must alienate every man that knows it from the King's government, and endanger the separation of this distracted empire: the traverser has had the guilt of publishing this fact, which I myself acknowledge, and I pray you to find him guilty?" Is this the case which the Lord Lieutenant of Ireland brings forward? Is this the principle for which he ventures, at a dreadful crisis like the present, to contend in a court of justice? Is this the picture which he wishes to hold out of himself to the justice and humanity of his own countrymen? Is this the history which he wishes to be read by the poor Irishmen of the South and of the North, by the sister nation, and the common enemy?

With the profoundest respect, permit me humbly to defend his Excellency, even against his own opinion. The guilt of this publication he is pleased to think consists in this, that it tends to insurrection. Upon what can such a fear be supported? After the multitudes that have perished in this unhappy nation within the last three years, unhappiness which has been borne with a patience not paralleled in the history of nations, can any man suppose that the fate of a single individual could lead to resistance or insurrection?

But suppose that it might, what then ought to be the conduct of an honest man? Should it not be to apprize the government of the country and the Viceroy,—you will drive the people to madness, if you persevere in such bloody councils; you will alienate the Irish nation; you will distract the common force; and you will invite the common enemy? Should not an honest man say to the people,—the measure of your affliction is great, but you need not resort for remedy to any desperate expedients. If the King's minister is defective in humanity or wisdom, his royal master, your beloved sovereign, is abounding in both. At such a moment, can you be so senseless as not to feel, that any one of you ought to hold such language; or is it possible you could be so infatuated, as to punish the man who was honest enough to hold it?—or is it possible that you could bring yourselves to say to your country, that at such a season the press ought to sleep upon its post, or to act like the perfidious watchman on his round, that sees the villain wrenching the door, or the flames bursting from the windows, while the inhabitant is wrapt in sleep, and cries out that "'tis past five o'clock, the morning is fair, and all well?"

On this part of the case I shall only put one question to you. I do not affect to say it is similar in all its points; I do not affect to compare the humble fortunes of Mr. Orr with the sainted names of Russell or Sidney; still less am I willing to find any likeness between the present period and the year 1688. But I will put a question to you, completely parallel in principle: When that unhappy and misguided monarch had shed the sacred blood, which their noble hearts had matured into a fit cement of revolution, if any honest Englishman had been brought to trial for daring to proclaim to the world his abhorrence of such a deed, what would you have thought of the English jury that could have said,—we know in our hearts what he said was true and honest, but we will say, upon our oaths, that it was false and criminal; and we will, by that base subserviency, add another item to the catalogue of public wrongs, and another argument for the necessity of an appeal to heaven for redress?

Gentlemen, I am perfectly aware that what I say may be easily misconstrued; but if you listen to me, with the same fairness that I address you, I cannot be misunderstood. When I show you the full extent of your political rights and remedies;

when I answer those slanderers of British liberty, who degrade the monarch into a despot, who pervert the steadfastness of law into the waywardness of will; when I show you the inestimable stores of political wealth, so dearly acquired by our ancestors, and so solemnly bequeathed; and when I show you how much of that precious inheritance has yet survived all the prodigality of their posterity, I am far from saying that I stand in need of it all upon the present occasion. No, gentlemen, far am I indeed from such a sentiment. No man more deeply than myself deplores the present melancholy state of our unhappy country. Neither does any man more fervently wish for the return of peace and tranquillity, through the natural channels of mercy and of justice. I have seen too much of force and of violence to hope much good from the continuance of them on the one side, or the retaliation of them on another. I have of late seen too much of political rebuilding, not to have observed, that to demolish is not the shortest way to repair. It is with pain and anguish that I should search for the miserable right of breaking ancient ties, or going in quest of new relations, or untried adventures. No, gentlemen; the case of my client rests not upon these sad privileges of despair. I trust, that as to the fact, namely, the intention of exciting insurrection, you must see it cannot be found in this publication; that it is the mere idle, unsupported imputation of malice, or panic, or falsehood.

And that as to the law, so far has he been from transgressing the limits of the constitution, that whole regions lie between him and those limits, which he has not trod, and which I pray to heaven it may never be necessary for any of us to tread.

Gentlemen, Mr. Attorney-General has been pleased to open another battery upon this publication, which I do trust I shall silence, unless I flatter myself too much in supposing that hitherto my resistance has not been utterly unsuccessful.

He abuses it for the foul and insolent familiarity of its address. I do clearly understand his idea; he considers the freedom of the press to be the license of offering that paltry adulation which no man ought to stoop to utter or to hear; he supposes the freedom of the press ought to be like the freedom of a king's jester, who, instead of reproving the faults of which majesty ought to be ashamed, is base and cunning enough, under the mask of servile and adulatory censure, to stroke down and pamper those vices of which it is foolish enough to be vain. He would not have the press presume to tell the Viceroy, that the prerogative of mercy is a trust for the benefit of the subject, and not a gaudy feather stuck into the diadem to shake in the wind, and by the waving of the gorgeous plumage to amuse the vanity of the wearer. He would not have it to say to him, that the discretion of the crown as to mercy, is like the discretion of a court of justice as to law; and that in the one case, as well as the other, wherever the propriety of the exercise of it appears, it is equally a matter of right. He would have the press all fierceness to the people, and all sycophancy to power; he would consider the mad and frenetic outrages of authority, like the awful and inscrutable dispensations of Providence, and say to the unfeeling and despotic spoiler, in the blasphemed and insulted language of religious resignation, "the Lord hath given, and the Lord hath taken away, blessed be the name of the Lord."

But let me condense the generality of the learned gentleman's invective into questions that you can conceive. Does he mean that the air of this publication is rustic and uncourtly? Does he mean, that when "Marcus" presumed to ascend the steps of the castle, and to address the Viceroy, he did not turn out his toes as he ought to have done? But, gentlemen, you are not a jury of dancing-masters: or does the learned gentleman mean that the language is coarse and vulgar? If this be his complaint, my client has but a poor advocate.

I do not pretend to be a mighty grammarian, or a formidable critic; but I would beg leave to suggest to you, in serious humility, that a free press can be supported only by the ardour of men who feel the prompting sting of real or supposed capacity; who write from the enthusiasm of virtue, or the ambition of praise, and over whom, if you exercise the rigour of a grammatical censorship, you will inspire them with as mean an opinion of your integrity as of your wisdom, and inevitably drive them from their post; and if you do, rely upon it, you will reduce the spirit of publication, and with it the press of this country, to what it for a long interval has been, the register of births, and fairs, and funerals, and the general abuse of the people and their friends.

Gentlemen, in order to bring this charge of insolence and vulgarity to the test, let me ask you, whether you know of any language which could have adequately described the idea of mercy denied, where it ought to have been granted; or of any phrase vigorous enough to convey the indignation which an honest man would have felt upon such a subject?

Let me beg of you for a moment to suppose that any one of you had been the writer of this very severe expostulation with the Viceroy, and that you had been the witness of the whole progress of this never-to-be-forgotten catastrophe.

Let me suppose that you had known the charge upon which Mr. Orr was apprehended—the charge of abjuring that bigotry which had torn and disgraced his country—of pledging himself to restore the people of his country to their place in the constitution—and of binding himself never to be the betrayer of his fellow-labourers in that enterprise; that you had seen him upon that charge removed from his industry, and confined in a gaol;

that through the slow and lingering progress of twelve tedious months you had seen him confined in a dungeon, shut out from the common use of air and of his own limbs; that day after day you had marked the unhappy captive cheered by no sound but the cries of his family, or the clinking of chains; that you had seen him at last brought to his trial; that you had seen the vile and perjured informer deposing against his life; that you had seen the drunken, and worn-out, and terrified jury give in a verdict of death; that you had seen the same jury, when their returning sobriety had brought back their conscience, prostrate themselves before the humanity of the bench, and pray that the mercy of the crown might save their characters from the reproach of an involuntary crime, their consciences from the torture of eternal self-condemnation, and their souls from the indelible stain of innocent blood.

Let me suppose that you had seen the respite given, and that contrite and honest recommendation transmitted to that seat where mercy was presumed to dwell—that new and before unheard-of crimes are discovered against the informer—that the royal mercy seems to relent, and that a new respite is sent to the prisoner—that time is taken, as the learned counsel for the crown has expressed it, to see whether mercy could be extended or not!—that after that period of lingering deliberation passed, a third respite is transmitted

—that the unhappy captive himself feels the cheering hope of being restored to a family that he had adored, to a character that he had never stained, and to a country that he had ever loved—that you had seen his wife and children upon their knees, giving those tears to gratitude, which their locked and frozen hearts could not give to anguish and despair, and imploring the blessings of Eternal Providence upon his head, who had graciously spared the father, and restored him to his children —that you had seen the olive branch sent into his little ark, but no sign that the waters had subsided.

"Alas!
Nor wife, nor children more shall he behold—
Nor friends, nor sacred home!"

No seraph mercy unbars his dungeon, and leads him forth to light and life; but the minister of death hurries him to the scene of suffering and of shame, where, unmoved by the hostile array of artillery and armed men collected together, to secure, or to insult, or to disturb him, he dies with a solemn declaration of his innocence, and utters his last breath in a prayer for the liberty of his country.

Let me now ask you, if any of you had addressed the public ear upon so foul and monstrous a subject, in what language would you have conveyed the feelings of horror and indignation? Would you have stooped to the meanness of qualified complaint?—would you have checked your feelings to search for courtly and gaudy language?—would you have been mean enough—but I entreat your forgiveness—I do not think meanly of you. Had I thought so meanly of you, I could not suffer my mind to commune with you as it has done; had I thought you that base and vile instrument, attuned by hope and by fear into discord and falsehood, from whose vulgar string no groan of suffering could vibrate, no voice of integrity or honour could speak, let me honestly tell you, I should have scorned to fling my hand across it—I should have left it to a fitter minstrel. If I do not, therefore, grossly err in my opinion of you, I could use no language upon such a subject as this, that must not lag behind the rapidity of your feelings, and that would not disgrace those feelings, if it attempted to describe them.

Gentlemen, I am not unconscious that the learned counsel for the crown seemed to address you with a confidence of a very different kind: he seemed to expect from you a kind and respectful sympathy with the feelings of the Castle, and with the griefs of chided authority. Perhaps, gentlemen, he may know you better than I do. If he does, he has spoken to you as he ought; he has been right in telling you, that if the reprobation of this writer is weak, it is because his genius could not make it stronger; he has been right in telling you, that his language has not been braided and festooned as elegantly as it might—that the has not pinched the miserable plaits of his phraseology, nor placed his patches and feathers with that correctness of millinery which became so exalted a person.

If you agree with him, gentlemen of the jury—if you think that the man who ventures, at the hazard of his own life, to rescue from the deep, the drowning honour of his country, you must not presume upon the guilty familiarity of plucking it up by the locks. I have no more to say; do a courteous thing. Upright and honest jurors, find a civil and obliging verdict against the printer! And when you have done so, march through the ranks of your fellow-citizens to your own homes, and bear their looks as you pass along. Retire to the bosom of your families and your children, and when you are presiding over the morality of the parental board, tell those infants, who are to be the future men of Ireland, the history of this day. Form their young minds by your precepts, and confirm those precepts by your own example—teach them how discreetly allegiance may be perjured on the table, or loyalty be forsworn in the jury-box; and when you have done so, tell them the story of Orr—tell them of his captivity, of his children, of his crime, of his hopes, of his disappointments, of his courage, and of his death; and when you find your little hearers hanging from your lips—when you see their eyes overflow with sympathy and sorrow—and their young hearts bursting with the pangs of anticipated orphanage —tell them that you had the boldness and the justice to stigmatize the monster who had dared to publish the transaction!

Gentlemen, I believe I told you before, that the conduct of the Viceroy was a small part, indeed, of the subject of this trial. If the vindication of his mere personal character had been, as it ought to have been, the sole object of this prosecution, I should have felt the most respectful regret at seeing a person of his high consideration come forward in a court of public justice, in one and the same breath to admit the truth, and to demand the punishment of a publication like the present, to prevent the chance he might have had of such an accusation being disbelieved, and, by a prosecution like this, to give to the passing stricture of a newspaper that life and body, and action and reality, to prove it to all mankind, and make the record of it indelible. Even as it is, I do own I feel the utmost concern that his name should have been soiled, by being mixed in a question of which it is the mere pretext and scape-goat.

Mr. Attorney-General was too wise to state to you the real question, or the object which he wished to be answered by your verdict. Do you remember that he was pleased to say that this publication was a base and foul misrepresentation of the virtue and wisdom of the government, and a false and audacious statement to the world, that the King's government in Ireland was base enough to pay informers for taking away the lives of the people? When I heard this statement to-day, I doubted whether you were aware of its tendency or not. It is now necessary that I should explain it to you more at large.

You cannot be ignorant of the great conflict between prerogative and privilege which hath convulsed the country for the last fifteen years; when I say privilege, you cannot suppose that I mean the privilege of the House of Commons,—I mean the privileges of the people.

You are no strangers to the various modes by which the people laboured to approach their object. Delegations, conventions, remonstrances, resolutions, petitions to the parliament, petitions to the throne.

It might not be decorous in this place to state to you, with any sharpness, the various modes of resistance that were employed on the other side; but you, all of you, seem old enough to remember the variety of acts of parliament that have been made, by which the people were deprived, session after session, of what they had supposed to be the known and established fundamentals of the constitution, the right of public debate, the right of public petition, the right of bail, the right of trial, the right of arms for self-defence; until the last, even the relics of popular privilege became superseded by a military force; the press extinguished;

and the state found its last entrenchment in the grave of the constitution. As little can you be strangers to the tremendous confederations of hundreds of thousands of your countrymen, of the nature and objects of which such a variety of opinions have been propagated and entertained.

The writer of this letter presumed to censure the recal of Lord Fitzwilliam, as well as the measures of the present Viceroy. Into this subject I do not enter; but you cannot yourselves forget that the conciliatory measures of the former noble lord had produced an almost miraculous unanimity in this country; and much do I regret, and sure I am that it is not without pain you can reflect, how unfortunately the conduct of his successor has terminated. His intentions might have been the best; I neither know them nor condemn them, but their terrible effects you cannot be blind to. Every new act of coercion has been followed by some new symptom of discontent, and every new attack provoked some new paroxysm of resentment, or some new combination of resistance.

In this deplorable state of affairs—convulsed and distracted within, and menaced by a most formidable enemy from without—it was thought that public safety might be found in union and conciliation; and repeated applications were made to the parliament of this kingdom, for a calm inquiry into the complaints of the people. These applications were made in vain.

Impressed by the same motives, Mr. Fox brought the same subject before the Commons of England, and ventured to ascribe the perilous state of Ireland to the severity of its government. Even his stupendous abilities, excited by the liveliest sympathy with our sufferings, and animated by the most ardent zeal to restore the strength with the union of the empire, were repeatedly exerted without success. The fact of discontent was denied—the fact of coercion was denied—and the consequence was, the coercion became more implacable, and the discontent more threatening and irreconcilable.

A similar application was made in the beginning of this session in the Lords of Great Britain, by our illustrious countryman,* of whom I do not wonder that my learned friend should have observed, how much virtue can fling pedigree into the shade; or how much the transient honour of a body inherited from man, is obscured by the lustre of an intellect derived from God. He, after being an eye-witness of this country, presented the miserable picture of what he had seen; and, to the astonishment of every man in Ireland, the existence of those facts was ventured to be denied; the conduct of the Viceroy was justified and applauded; and the necessity of continuing that conduct was insisted upon, as the only means of preserving the constitution, the peace, and the prosperity of Ireland. The moment the learned counsel had talked

* Lord Moira.

of this publication as a false statement of the conduct of the government, and the condition of the people, no man could be at a loss to see that the awful question, which had been dismissed from the Commons of Ireland, and from the Lords and Commons of Great Britain, is now brought forward to be tried by a side wind, and, in a collateral way, by a criminal prosecution.

The learned counsel has asserted that the paper which he prosecutes is only part of a system formed to misrepresent the state of Ireland and the conduct of its government. Do you not, therefore, discover that his object is to procure a verdict to sanction the parliaments of both countries in refusing an inquiry into your grievances? Let me ask you, then, are you prepared to say, upon your oath, that those measures of coercion, which are daily practised, are absolutely necessary, and ought to be continued? It is not upon Finnerty you are sitting in judgment; but you are sitting in judgment upon the lives and liberties of the inhabitants of more than half of Ireland. You are to say that it is a foul proceeding to condemn the government of Ireland; that it is a foul act, founded in foul motives, and originating in falsehood and sedition; that it is an attack upon a government, under which the people are prosperous and happy; that justice is administered with mercy; that the statements made in Great Britain are false—are the effusions of party or of discontent; that all is mildness and tranquillity; that there are no burnings—no transportations; that you never travel by the light of conflagrations; that the gaols are not crowded month after month, from which prisoners are taken out, not for trial, but for embarkation! These are the questions upon which, I say, you must virtually decide. It is in vain that the counsel for the crown may tell you that I am misrepresenting the case—that I am endeavouring to raise false fears, and to take advantage of your passions—that the question is, whether this paper be a libel or not—and that the circumstances of the country have nothing to do with it. Such assertions must be vain. The statement of the counsel for the crown has forced the introduction of those important topics; and I appeal to your own hearts whether the country is misrepresented, and whether the government is misrepresented.

I tell you, therefore, gentlemen of the jury, it is not with respect to Mr. Orr, or Mr. Finnerty, that your verdict is now sought. You are called upon, on your oaths, to say, that the government is wise and merciful—the people prosperous and happy; that military law ought to be continued; that the constitution could not with safety be restored to Ireland; and that the statements of a contrary import by your advocates, in either country, are libellous and false.

I tell you these are the questions; and I ask you, if you can have the front to give the expected answer in the face of a community who know the country as well as you do? Let me ask you, how you could reconcile with such a verdict, the gaols, the tenders, the gibbets, the conflagrations, the murders, the proclamations that we hear of every day in the streets, and see every day in the country? What are the prosecutions of the learned counsel himself, circuit after circuit? Merciful God! what is the state of Ireland, and where shall you find the wretched inhabitant of this land! You may find him, perhaps, in a gaol, the only place of security—I had almost said of ordinary habitation! If you do not find him there, you may see him flying with his family from the flames of his own dwelling—lighted to his dungeon by the conflagration of his hovel; or you may find his bones bleaching on the green fields of his country; or you may find him tossing on the surface of the ocean, and mingling his groans with those tempests, less savage than his persecutors, that drift him to a returnless distance from his family and his home, without charge, or trial, or sentence. Is this a foul misrepresentation? Or can you, with these facts ringing in your ears, and staring in your face, say, upon your oaths, they do not exist? You are called upon, in defiance of shame, of truth, of honour, to deny the sufferings under which you groan, and to flatter the persecution that tramples you under foot.

Gentlemen, I am not accustomed to speak of

circumstances of this kind; and though familiarized as I have been to them, when I come to speak of them, my power fails me—my voice dies within me. I am not able to call upon you. It is now I ought to have strength—it is now I ought to have energy and voice. But I have none; I am like the unfortunate state of the country—perhaps, like you. This is the time in which I ought to speak, if I can, or be dumb for ever; in which, if you do not speak as *you* ought, *you* ought to be dumb for ever.

But the learned gentleman is further pleased to say, that the traverser has charged the government with the encouragement of informers. This, gentlemen, is another small fact that you are to deny at the hazard of your souls, and upon the solemnity of your oaths. You are upon your oaths to say to the sister country, that the government of Ireland uses no such abominable instruments of destruction as informers. Let me ask you honestly, what do you feel, when in my hearing, when in the face of this audience, you are called upon to give a verdict that every man of us, and every man of you know, by the testimony of your own eyes, to be utterly and absolutely false? I speak not now of the public proclamation for informers, with a promise of secrecy, and of extravagant reward; I speak not of the fate of those horrid wretches who have been so often transferred from the table to the dock, and from the dock to the pillory; I speak of what your own eyes have seen, day after day, during the course of this commission, from the box where you are now sitting; the number of horrid miscreants, who acknowledged, upon their oaths, that they had come from the seat of government —from the very chambers of the Castle—where they had been worked upon, by the fear of death and the hope of compensation, to give evidence against their fellows; that the mild, the wholesome, and merciful councils of this government are holden over these catacombs of living death, where the wretch that is buried a man, lies till his heart has time to fester and dissolve, and is then dug up a witness!

Is this a picture created by a hag-ridden fancy, or is it fact? Have you not seen him, after his resurrection from that region of death and corruption, make his appearance upon the table, the living image of life and of death, and the supreme arbiter of both? Have you not marked when he entered, how the stormy wave of the multitude retired at his approach? Have you not seen how the human heart bowed to the supremacy of his power, in the undissembled homage of deferential horror? how his glance, like the lightning of heaven, seemed to rive the body of the accused, and mark it for the grave, while his voice warned the devoted wretch of woe and death—a death which no innocence can escape, no art elude, no force resist, no antidote prevent. There was an antidote—a juror's oath!—but even that adamantine chain, that bound the integrity of man to the throne of eternal justice, is solved and molten in the breath that issues from the informer's mouth; conscience swings from her moorings, and the appalled and affrighted juror consults his own safety in the surrender of the victim:—

"Et quæ sibi quisque timebat,
Unius in miseri exitium conversa tulere."

Informers are worshipped in the temple of justice, even as the devil has been worshipped by Pagans and savages—even so in this wicked country, is the informer an object of judicial idolatry—even so is he soothed by the music of human groans—even so is he placated and incensed by the fumes and by the blood of human sacrifices.

Gentlemen, I feel I must have tired your patience; but I have been forced into this length by the prosecutor, who has thought fit to introduce those extraordinary topics, and to bring a question of mere politics to trial, under the form of a criminal prosecution. I cannot say I am surprised that this has been done, or that you should be solicited by the same inducements, and from the same motives, as if your verdict was a vote of approbation. I do not wonder that the government of Ireland should stand appalled at the state to which we are reduced. I wonder not that they should start at the public voice, and labour to stifle or contradict it. I wonder not that at this arduous crisis, when the very existence of the empire is at stake, and when its strongest and most precious limb is not girt with the sword for battle, but pressed by the tourniquet for amputation; when they find the coldness of death already begun in those extremities where it never ends; that they are terrified at what they have done, and wish to say to the surviving parties of that empire, "they cannot say that we did it." I wonder not that they should consider their conduct as no immaterial question for a court of criminal jurisdiction, and wish anxiously, as on an inquest of blood, for the kind acquittal of a friendly jury.

I wonder not that they should wish to close the chasm they have opened, by flinging you into the abyss. But trust me, my countrymen, you might perish in it, but you could not close it; trust me, if it is yet possible to close it, it can be done only by truth and honour; trust me, that such an effect could no more be wrought by the sacrifice of a jury, than by the sacrifice of Orr.

As a state measure, the one would be as unwise and unavailing as the other; but while you are yet upon the brink, while you are yet visible, let me, before we part, remind you once more of your awful situation.

You are upon a great forward ground, with the people at your back, and the government in your front. You have neither the disadvantages nor the excuses of jurors a century ago. No, thank

God! never was there a stronger characteristic distinction between those times, upon which no man can reflect, without horror, and the present. You have seen this trial conducted with mildness and patience by the court. We have now no Jefferies, with scurvy and vulgar conceits, to browbeat the prisoner and perplex his counsel. Such has been the improvement of manners, and so calm the confidence of integrity, that during the defence of accused persons, the judges sit quietly, and show themselves worthy of their situation, by bearing, with a mild and merciful patience, the little extravagancies of the bar, as you should bear with the little extravagancies of the press. Let me then turn your eyes to that pattern of mildness in the bench. The press is your advocate; bear with its excess—bear with every thing but its bad intention. If it come as a villanous slanderer, treat it as such; but if it endeavour to raise the honour and glory of your country, remember that you reduce its power to a nonentity, if you stop its animadversions upon public measures. You should not check the efforts of genius, nor damp the ardour of patriotism. In vain will you desire the bird to soar, if you meanly or madly steal from it its plumage. Beware lest, under the pretence of bearing down the licentiousness of the press, you extinguish it altogether. Beware how you rival the venal ferocity of those miscreants, who rob a printer of the means of bread, and claim from deluded royalty the reward of integrity and allegiance. Let me, therefore, remind you, that though the day may soon come when our ashes shall be scattered before the winds of heaven, the memory of what you do cannot die; it will carry down to your posterity your honour or your shame. In the presence and in the name of that ever living God, I do therefore conjure you to reflect, that you have your characters, your consciences, that you have also the character, perhaps the ultimate destiny of your country, in your hands. In that awful name, I do conjure you to have mercy upon your country and yourselves, and so judge now, as you will hereafter be judged; and I do now submit the fate of my client, and of that country which we have yet in common, to your disposal.

After a short absence, the jury returned "Guilty" on the issue paper.

On the following day, the 23rd of December, Mr. Finnerty was brought up for judgment. Mr. Finnerty stated that he had been taken out of prison to Alderman Alexander's office, and there threatened with public whipping, if he did not give up the author of the libel. He boldly defended the latter, but was respectful to the Bench. Judge Downes sentenced him to two years' imprisonment from the day of his arrest, to stand in the pillory for an hour, pay a fine of £20, and at the expiration of his imprisonment to give security, himself in £500, and two bailsmen in £250 each, for his good behaviour. On the 30th of December, Mr. Finnerty did actually stand in the pillory, and the rest of the sentence was also carried out.

FOR PATRICK FINNEY,

[HIGH TREASON.]

January, 16th, 1798.

On the 31st of May, 1797, Patrick Finney was arrested at Tuite's public house, in Thomas-street. He was indicted for High Treason, at the Commission held in Dublin, in July, 1797; and on Tuesday, the 16th of January, 1798, was brought to trial. The indictment was in substance as follows;—

The first count of the indictment charged—"That Patrick Finney, yeoman, on the 30th day of April, in the 37th year of the King, and divers other days, at the city of Dublin, being a false traitor, did compass and imagine the death of our said Lord the King, and did traitorously and feloniously intend our said Lord the King to kill, murder, and put to death."

The overt acts laid were as follows:—"I. Adhering to the persons exercising the powers of government in France, in case they should invade, or cause to be invaded this kingdom of Ireland, they being enemies to the King, and at war. 2. That the conspirators aforesaid did meet, &c., confer, consult, and deliberate, about adhering to the persons exercising the powers of government in France. 3. Adhering to the persons exercising the powers of government in France. 4. Conspiring that one or more persons should be sent into France, to excite an invasion of Ireland. 5. Conspiring that one or more persons should be sent into France, to excite an invasion of this kingdom, and to make war therein; and for that purpose did ask, levy, and receive, &c., from other traitors, money, to wit, from each £20, to defray the expenses of the persons to be sent. 6. That conspiring, &c., they did send into France four persons unknown, to excite the persons exercising the powers of government in France to invade this kingdom, and make war therein. 7. Conspiring to send, and sending, four persons into France, to persuade invasion, and to aid them in invading, and raising, and making war; and Finney, then and there, demanding and receiving money, viz. £20 to defray the charges of said persons. 8. That said Patrick Finney became a United Irishman for the purpose of assisting the persons exercising the powers of government in France, and being met to the number of forty-eight other traitors, did divide into four splits, each of which contained twelve traitors, and each split did then choose one to be secretary, to consult on behalf thereof with other splits, under the denomination of baronial meetings, for the purpose of adhering and making war, in case of an invasion of Ireland from France, and then and there conspiring an attack upon the Castle of Dublin, &c., and to deprive his Majesty of the stores and ammunition therein; and said Finney, to facilitate such attack, did advise and commend other traitors to view White's Court, &c., and give their opinion to their several splits, so that their secretaries might report the same to their baronial meetings. 9. Adhering to the persons exercising the powers of government in France, &c., and with forty-eight other conspirators, divided into four splits, each containing twelve, each split choosing a secretary to confer for the purpose of adhering to the enemy in case of invasion, and confederating and agreeing that a violent attack should be made on the ordnance stores, &c. 10. Consulting, &c., to procure an invasion. 11. Consulting to raise insurrection, rebellion, and war, in case of invasion of Ireland or Great Britain, from France. 12. Conspiring to assist the persons exercising the powers of government in France, in case of their invading this realm with ships and arms."

There was a second count, for "adhering to the King's enemies within the realm;" and in support of this count, the overt acts laid were exactly the same as those above recited.

The Attorney-General (Wolfe) stated the case, describing the United Irish organization, and alleging their communication with France. He introduced the charge against the prisoner and the chief witness—the eminent informer, Jemmy O'Brien, in these words:—

"A man of the name of James O'Brien, upon the 25th of April, 1797, was passing through Thomas-street, in this city; he met a man who was his acquaintance, named Hyland, standing at the door of one Blake, who kept a public house. The prisoner at the bar, then, as I believe, a stranger to O'Brien, was standing at the door; Hyland asked O'Brien was he *up?*—which is, I presume, a technical expression to signify that a man is a member of the society. They tried O'Brien by the signs, whether he was, or not. They told him that no man's life was safe if he was not *up;* and, particularly the prisoner at the bar, told O'Brien his life would not be safe, if he were not *up:* they desired O'Brien to go into the house, in a room of which eight people were sitting. There, after some discourse, O'Brien was sworn to secrecy, and afterwards he was sworn to that oath which is called the oath of the United Irishmen. They talked much of their strength—of the number of men and arms provided in various parts of the kingdom, so great as to render the attainment of their object certain; and after much other discourse, which it is unnecessary to state, they adjourned their meeting to the house of one Coghran, in Newmarket on the Coombe, to be held the next Sunday, the 30th of April; they agreed that the pass-word to gain admittance at Coghran's should be "Mr. Green." And it appears (for the trade is attended with some profit) that O'Brien was called upon to pay, and did pay the prisoner one shilling for swearing him.

"As soon as O'Brien left the house, and escaped the danger he imagined he was in, he went to Mr. Higgins, a magistrate of the Queen's county, to whom he was known, then in Dublin, and disclosed to him what had passed. Mr. Higgins told O'Brien he was right to reveal the matter, and brought him to Lord

Portarlington, who brought him to one of the committee-rooms of the House of Lords, where he was examined by one of the Lord Lieutenant's secretaries. It was then thought expedient, that attention should be paid to this society, seeing its dangerous tendency, in order to counteract the designs entertained. O'Brien, conceiving that he might be in some danger from a society formed upon such principles, was advised to enlist in one of the regiments of dragoons then quartered in Dublin, and to attend the society, to learn their designs. With this view, O'Brien attended at Coghran's house, in New-market, and was admitted on giving the pass-word, "Mr. Green." He there found the prisoner at the bar, with forty others assembled; he was desired to pay sixpence to the funds of the society; he said he had not then sixpence; they told him he was to return in the evening, and that it made no difference, whether he then paid, or brought it in the evening. Finney informed him and the society that the money collected was to constitute a fund for the purpose of the society; that upon that day there was to be a collection from the United societies in Dublin, sixpence from each man, and that there was to be collected that evening from the various societies, 10,000 sixpences; and he further informed them (for he was an active man at that meeting) that there was to be a great funeral, that of one Ryan, a mill-wright, whose corpse lay at Pimlico, which was to be attended by all the societies in Dublin; that after the funeral, that particular society was again to assemble at the same place, Coghran's."

Various other meetings were stated in a very moderate speech, and O'Brien swore firmly to the facts. Curran cross-examined the man calmly, and tempted him into confidential insolence. The ruffian described his career as the hanger on of an excise officer, drinking and extorting in public houses; he candidly avowed not only that he had practised coining, but he identified a receipt for coining, which he had, in a missionary spirit, given to another person; he admitted that, when told that Mr. Roberts of Stradbally would give evidence against his character, he (having a sword and pistol in his hands,) had said he "would settle him." For this he made a trivial explanation. Peter Clarke swore that on the 31st of May, Finney gave him a copy of the United Irish test, and Lord Portarlington swore that O'Brien told him of one or two of the early meetings. Curran was to have opened the defence; but a principal witness being absent, a chaise was despatched for him, and Mr. Mac Nally set to speak against time." The court had then to adjourn for twenty minutes' rest. Then CURRAN, after examining some persons of the middle class to prove O'Brien's infamy of character, and one to Finney's general loyalty, spoke as follows:—

MY Lords, and Gentlemen of the Jury. In the early part of this trial, I thought I should have had to address you on the most important occasion possible, on this side of the grave, a man labouring for life, on the casual strength of an exhausted, and, at best, a feeble advocate. But, gentlemen, do not imagine that I rise under any such impressions; do not imagine that I approach you sinking under the hopeless difficulties of my cause. I am not now soliciting your indulgence to the inadequacy of my powers, or artfully enlisting your passions at the side of my client. No, gentlemen; but I rise with what of law, of conscience, of justice, and of constitution, there exists within this realm, at my back, and, standing in front of that great and powerful alliance, I *demand* a verdict of acquittal for my client! What is the opposition of

* Mr. M'Nally has marked, on his copy of the speech, that he spoke for an hour and three quarters, and that the speech was reported by "Leonard M'Nally, jun."

evidence? It is a tissue which requires no strength to break through; it vanishes at the touch, and is sundered into tatters.

The right honourable gentleman who stated the case in the first stage of this trial, has been so kind as to express a reliance, that the counsel for the prisoner would address the jury with the same candour which he exemplified on the part of the crown; readily and confidently do I accept the compliment, the more particularly, as in my cause I feel no temptation to reject it. Life can present no situation wherein the humble powers of man are so awfully and so divinely excited, as in defence of a fellow-creature placed in the circumstances of my client; and if any labours can peculiarly attract the gracious and approving eye of heaven, it is when God looks down on a human being assailed by human turpitude, and struggling with practices against which the Deity has placed his special canon, when he said "Thou shalt not bear false witness against thy neighbour; thou shalt do no murder."

Gentlemen, let me desire you again and again to consider all the circumstances of this man's case, abstracted from the influence of prejudice and habit; and if aught of passion assumes dominion over you, let it be of that honest, generous nature that good men must feel when they see an innocent man depending on their verdict for his life; to this passion I feel myself insensibly yielding;

but unclouded, though not unwarmed, I shall, I trust, proceed in my great duty.

Wishing to state my client's case with all possible succinctness which the nature of the charge admits, I am glad my learned colleague has acquitted himself on this head already to such an extent, and with such ability, that any thing I can say will chance to be superfluous: in truth, that honesty of heart, and integrity of principle, for which all must give him credit, uniting with a sound judgment and sympathetic heart, have given to his statement all the advantages it could have derived from these qualities.

He has truly said that "the declaratory act, the 25th of Edward III., is that on which all charges of high treason are founded; and I trust the observation will be deeply engraven on your hearts. It is an act made to save the subject from the vague and wandering uncertainty of the law. It is an act which leaves it no longer doubtful whether a man shall incur conviction by his own conduct, or the sagacity of crown construction: whether he shall sink beneath his own guilt, or the cruel and barbarous refinement of crown prosecution. It has been most aptly called the blessed act; and oh! may the great God of justice and of mercy give repose and eternal blessing to the souls of those honest men by whom it was enacted! By this law, no man shall be convicted of high treason, but on proveable evidence; the overt acts of treason, as explained in this law, shall be stated clearly and distinctly in the charge; and the proof of these acts shall be equally clear and distinct, in order that no man's life may depend on a partial or wicked allegation. It does every thing for the prisoner which he could do himself, it does every thing but utter the verdict, which alone remains with you, and which, I trust, you will give in the same pure, honest, saving spirit, in which that act was formed. Gentlemen, I would call it an omnipotent act, if it could possibly appal the informer from our courts of justice; but law cannot do it, religion cannot do it, the feelings of human nature frozen in the depraved heart of the wretched informer, cannot be thawed!

Law cannot prevent the envenomed arrow from being pointed at the intended victim; but it has given him a shield in the integrity of a jury! Every thing is so clear in this act, that all must understand: the several acts of treason must be recited, and proveable conviction must follow. What is proveable conviction? Are you at a loss to know? Do you think if a man comes on the table, and says, "By virtue of my oath, I know a conspiracy against the state, and such and such persons are engaged in it," do you think that his mere allegation shall justify you in a verdict of conviction? A witness coming on this table, of whatsoever description, whether the noble Lord wo has been examined, or the honourable Judges on the bench, or Mr. James O'Brien, who shall declare upon oath that a man bought powder, ball, and arms, intending to kill another, this is not proveable conviction; the unlawful intention must be shown by cogency of evidence, and the credit of the witness must stand strong and unimpeached. The law means not that infamous assertion or dirty ribaldry is to overthrow the character of a man; even in these imputations, flung against the victim, there is fortunately something detergent, that cleanses the character it was destined to befoul.

In stating the law, gentlemen, I have told you that the overt acts must be laid and proved by positive testimony of untainted witnesses; and in so saying, I have only spoken the language of the most illustrious writers on the law of England.

I should, perhaps, apologize to you for detaining your attention so long on these particular points, but that in the present disturbed state of the public mind, and in the abandonment of principle which it but too frequently produces, I think I cannot too strongly impress you with the purity of legal distinction, so that your souls shall not be harrowed with those torturing regrets which the return of reason would bring along with it, were you, on the present occasion, for a moment to resign it to the subjection of your passions; for these, though sometimes amiable in their impetuosity, can never be dignified and just, but under the control of reason.

The charge against the prisoner is two-fold:

compassing and imagining the King's death, and adhering to the King's enemies. To be accurate on this head is not less my intention than it is my interest; for if I fall into errors, they will not escape the learned counsel who is to come after me, and whose detections will not fail to be made in the correct spirit of Crown prosecution.

Gentlemen, there are no fewer than thirteen overt acts, as described, necessary to support the indictment; these, however, it is not necessary to recapitulate. The learned counsel for the Crown has been perfectly candid and correct in saying, that if any of them support either species of treason charged in the indictment, it will be sufficient to attach the guilt. I do not complain that on the part of the Crown it was not found expedient to point out which act or acts went to support the indictment; neither will I complain, gentlemen, if you fix your attention particularly on the circumstances.

Mr. Attorney-General has been pleased to make an observation which drew a remark from my colleague with which I fully agree, that the atrocity of a charge should make no impression on you. It was the judgment of candour and liberality, and should be yours; nor though you should more than answer the high opinion I entertain of you, and though your hearts betray not the consoling confidence which your looks inspire, yet do not disdain to increase your stock of candour and liberality, from whatsoever source it flows; though the abundance of my client's innocence may render him independent of its exertions, your country wants it all. You are not to suffer impressions of loyalty, or an enthusiastic love for the sacred person of the King, to give your judgments the smallest bias. You are to decide from the evidence which you have heard; and if the atrocity of the charge were to have any influence with you, it should be that of rendering you more incredulous to the possibility of is truth.

I confess I cannot conceive a greater crime against civilized society, be the form of goverment what it may, whether monarchical, republican, or, I had almost said, despotic, than attempting to destroy the life of the person holding the executive authority; the counsel for the Crown cannot feel a greater abhorrence against it than I do; and happy am I, at this moment, that I can do justice to my principles, and the feelings of my heart, without endangering the defence of my client, and that defence is, that your hearts would not feel more reluctant to the perpetration of the crimes with which he is charged, than the man who there stands at the bar of his country, waiting until you shall clear him from the foul and unmerited imputation, until your verdict, sounding life and honour to his senses, shall rescue him from the dreadful fascination of the informer's eye.

The overt acts in the charge against the prisoner

are many, and all apparently of the same nature, but they, notwithstanding, admit of a very material distinction. This want of candour I attribute to the base imposition of the prosecutor on those who brought him forward.

You find at the bottom of the charge a foundation-stone attempted to be laid by O'Brien,—the deliberations of a society of United Irishmen, and on this are laid all the overt acts. I said the distinction was of moment, because it is endeavoured to be held forth to the public, to all Europe, that, at a time like this, of peril and of danger, there are, in one province alone, one hundred and eleven thousand of your countrymen combined for the purpose of destroying the King, and the tranquillity of the country, which so much depends on him, an assertion which you should consider of again and again, before you give it any other existence than it derives from the attainting breath of the informer. If nothing should induce that consideration but the name of *Irishman*, the honours of which you share, a name so foully, and as I shall demonstrate, so falsely aspersed, if you can say that one fact of O'Brien's testimony deserves belief, all that can from thence be inferred is, that a great combination of mind and will exists on some public subject.

What says the written evidence on that subject? What are the obligations imposed by the test-oath of the society of United Irishmen? Is it unjust to get rid of religious differences and distinctions? Would to God it were possible! Is it an offence against the state, to promote a full, free, and adequate representation of all the people of Ireland in parliament? If it be, the text is full of its own comment, it needs no comment of mine. As to the last clause, obliging to secrecy: Now, gentlemen of the jury, in the hearing of the court, I submit to the opposite counsel this question. I will make my adversary my arbiter. Taking the test-oath as thus written, is there any thing of treason in it? However objectionable it may be, it certainly is not treasonable.

I admit there may be a colourable combination of words to conceal a really bad design; but to what evils would it not expose society, if, in this case, to *suppose* were to *decide*. A high legal authority thus speaks on this subject: "Strong, indeed, must the evidence be which goes to prove that any man can mean, by words, any thing more than what is conveyed in their ordinary acceptation." If the test of any particular community were an open one—if, like the London Corresponding Society, it was to be openly published, then, indeed, there might be a reason for not using words in their common application; but, subject to no public discussion, at least not intended to be so, why should the proceedings of those men, or the obligation by which they are connected, be expressed in the phraseology of studied concealment? If men meet in secret, to talk over how best the French can invade this country, to what purpose is it that they take an engagement different in meaning? Common sense rejects the idea!

Gentlemen, having stated these distinctions, I am led to the remaining divisions of the subject you are to consider. I admit, that because a man merely takes this obligation of union, it cannot prevent his becoming a traitor if he pleases; but the question for you to decide on would then be, whether every man who takes it must necessarily be a traitor?

Independent of that engagement, have any superadded facts been proved against the prisoner? What is the evidence of O'Brien? What has he stated? Here, gentlemen, let me claim the benefits of that great privilege which distinguishes trial by jury in this country from all the world. Twelve men, not emerging from the must and cobwebs of a study, abstracted from human nature, or only acquainted with its extravagancies; but twelve men, conversant with life, and practised in those feelings which mark the common and necessary intercourse between man and man, such are you, gentlemen.

How, then, does Mr. O'Brien's tale hang together? Look to its commencement. He walks along Thomas-street, in the open day (a street not the least populous in this city), and is accosted by a man who, without any preface, tells him he'll be murdered before he goes *half* the street, unless he becomes a United Irishman! Do you think this is a probable story? Suppose any of you, gentlemen, be a United Irishman, or a Freemason, or a Friendly Brother, and that you meet me walking *innocently* along, just like Mr. O'Brien, and meaning *no harm*, would you say, "Stop, Mr. Curran, don't go further, you'll be murdered before you go half the street, if you do not become a United Irishman, a Freemason, or a Friendly Brother." Did you ever hear so *coaxing* an invitation to *felony* as this? "Sweet Mr. James O'Brien! come in and save your precious life—come in and take an oath, or you'll be murdered before you go half the street! Do, sweetest, dearest Mr. James O'Brien, come in, and do not risk your valuable existence." What a loss had he been to his King, whom he loves so marvellously! Well, what does poor Mr. O'Brien do? Poor, dear man, he stands petrified with the magnitude of his danger,—all his members refuse their office,—he can neither run from the danger, nor call out for assistance; his tongue cleaves to his mouth, and his feet incorporate with the paving-stones; it is in vain that his expressive eye silently implores protection of the passenger; he yields at length, as men have done, and resignedly submits to his fate. He then enters the house, and being led into a room, a parcel of men *make faces* at him; but mark the metamorphosis; well may it be said, that "miracles will never cease;" he who feared to resist in open air, and in the face of the public, becomes a *bravo* when pent up in a room, and environed by *sixteen* men, and one is obliged to bar the door, while another swears him, which, after some resistance, is accordingly done, and poor Mr. O'Brien becomes a United Irishman, for no earthly purpose whatever, but merely to save his sweet life.

But this is not all,—the pill, so bitter to the percipiency of his loyal palate, must be washed down; and, lest he should throw it off his stomach, he is filled up to the neck with beef and whiskey. What further did they do?

Mr. O'Brien, thus persecuted, abused and terrified, would have gone and lodged his sorrows in the sympathetic bosom of the Major; but to prevent him even this little solace, they made him drunk. The *next* evening they used him in the like barbarous manner; so that he was not only sworn against his will, but,—poor man,—he was made drunk, against his inclination. Thus was he besieged with *united* beefsteaks and whiskey; and against such potent assailants not even Mr. O'Brien could prevail.

Whether all this whiskey that he has been *forced* to drink has produced the effect or not, Mr. O'Brien's loyalty is better than his memory. In the spirit of loyalty he became prophetic, and told Lord Portarlington the circumstances relative to the intended attack on the ordnance stores full three weeks before he had obtained the information through moral agency. Oh! honest James O'Brien, honest James O'Brien! Let others vainly argue on logical truth and ethical falsehood; but if I can once fasten him to the ring of perjury, I will bait him at it, until his testimony shall fail of producing a verdict, although human nature were as vile and monstrous in you as she is in him! He has made a *mistake!* but surely no man's life is safe if such evidence were admissible; what argument can be founded on his testimony, when he swears he has perjured himself, and that any thing he says must be false? I must not believe him at all, and by a paradoxical conclusion, suppose, against "the damnation" of his own testimony, that he is an *honest man!*

Strongly as I feel my interest keep pace with that of my client, I would not defend him at the expense of truth; I seek not to make the witness worse than he is: whatever he may be, God Almighty convert his mind! May his reprobation,—but I beg his pardon,—let your verdict stamp that currency on his credit; it will have more force than any casual remarks of mine. How this contradiction in Mr. O'Brien's evidence occurred, I am at no loss to understand. He started from the beginning with an intention of informing against some person, no matter against whom; and whether he ever saw the prisoner at the time he gave the information to Lord Portarlington, is a question;

but none, that he fabricated the story for the purpose of imposing on the honest zeal of the law officers of the crown.

Having now glanced at a part of this man's evidence, I do not mean to part with him entirely; I shall have occasion to visit him again; but before I do, let me, gentlemen, once more impress upon your minds the observation which my colleague applied to the laws of high treason, that if they are not explained on the statute-book, they are explained on the hearts of all honest men; and, as St. Paul says, "though they know not the law, they obey the statutes thereof." The essence of the charge submitted to your consideration tends to the dissolution of the connexion between Ireland and Great Britain.

I own it is with much warmth and self-gratulation that I feel this calumny answered by the attachment of every good man to the British constitution. I feel,—I embrace its principles; and when I look on you, the proudest benefit of that constitution, I am relieved from the fears of advocacy, since I place my client under the influence of its sacred shade. This is not the idle sycophancy of words. It is not crying "Lord! Lord!" but doing "the will of my Father who is in heaven." If my client were to be tried by a jury of Ludgate-hill shop-keepers, he would, ere now, be in his lodging. The law of England would not suffer a man to be cruelly butchered in a court of justice. The law of England recognizes the possibility of villains thirsting for the blood of their fellow-creatures; and the people of Ireland have no cause to be incredulous of the fact.

In that country, St. Paul's is not more public than the charge made against the poorest creature that crawls upon the soil of England. There must be two witnesses to convict the prisoner of high treason. The prisoner must have a copy of the jurors' names, by whom he may eventually be tried; he must have a list of the witnesses that are to be produced against him, that they may not, vampire like, come crawling out of the grave to drink his blood; but that, by having a list of their names and places of abode, he may inquire into their characters and modes of life, that, if they are infamous, he may be enabled to defend himself against the attacks of their perjury, and their subornation. There must, I say, be two witnesses, that the jury may be satisfied, if they believe the evidence, that the prisoner is guilty; and if there be but one witness, the jury shall not be troubled with the idle folly of listening to the prisoner's defence. If there be but one witness, there is the less possibility of contradicting him; he the less fears any detection of his murderous tale, having only infernal communication between him and the author of all evil; and when on the table, which he makes the altar of his sacrifice, however common men may be affected at sight of the innocent victim, it cannot be supposed that the prompter of his perjury will instigate him to retribution: this is the law in England, and God forbid that Irishmen should so differ, in the estimation of the law, from Englishmen, that their blood is not equally worth preserving. I do not, gentlemen, apply any part of this observation to you; you are Irishmen yourselves, and I know you will act proudly and honestly. The law of *England* renders two witnesses necessary, and one witness insufficient, to take away the life of a man on a charge of high treason. This is founded on the principle of common sense, and common justice; for, unless the subject were guarded by this wise prevention, every wretch who could so pervert the powers of invention, as to trump up a tale of treason and conspiracy, would have it in his power to defraud the Crown into the most abominable and afflicting acts of cruelty and oppression.

Gentlemen of the jury, though from the evidence which has been adduced against the prisoner, they have lost their value, yet had they been necessary, I must tell you, that my client came forward under a disadvantage of great magnitude, the absence of two witnesses very material to his defence; I am not now at liberty to say, what I am instructed would have been proved by May, and Mr. Roberts.

But, you will ask, why is not Mr. Roberts here? Recollect the admission of O'Brien, that he threatened to *settle* him, and you will cease to wonder at his absence, when, if he came, the dagger was in preparation to be plunged into his heart. I said Mr. Roberts was absent, I correct myself; no! in effect he is here: I appeal to the heart of that obdurate man (O'Brien), what would have been his (Roberts's) testimony, if he had dared to venture a personal evidence on this trial? Gracious God! is a tyranny of this kind to be borne with, where law is said to exist? Shall the horrors which surround the informer, the ferocity of his countenance, and the terrors of his voice, cast such a wide and appalling influence, that none dare approach and save the victim, which he marks for ignominy and death!

Now, gentlemen, be pleased to look to the rest of O'Brien's testimony: he tells you there are one hundred and eleven thousand men in one province, added to ten thousand of the inhabitants of the metropolis, ready to assist the object of an invasion! Gentlemen, are you prepared to say that the kingdom of Ireland has been so forsaken by all principles of humanity and of loyalty, that there are now no less than 111,000 men sworn by the most solemn of all engagements, and connected in a deadly combination to destroy the constitution of the country, and to invite the common enemy, the French, to invade it—are you prepared to say this by your verdict? When you know not the intentions or the means of that watchful and insatiable enemy, do you think it would be wise by your verdict of guilty, to say, on the single testimony of a common informer, that you do believe upon your oaths that there is a body consisting of no less a number than 111,000 men ready to assist the French, if they should make an attempt upon this country, and ready to fly to their standard whenever they think proper to invade it? This is another point of view in which to examine this case. You know the distress and convulsion of the public mind for a considerable length of time; cautiously will I abstain from making observations that could refresh the public memory, situated as I am, in a court of justice. But, gentlemen, this is the first, the only trial for high treason, in which an informer gives his notions of the propriety or impropriety of public measures; I remember none —except the trial of that unfortunate wanderer, that unhappy fugitive, for so I may call him, Jackson, a native of this country—guilty he was, but neither his guilt nor innocence had any affinity with any other system. But this is the first trial that has been brought forward for high treason, except that, where such matters have been disclosed; and gentlemen, are you prepared to think well of the burden of embarking your character, high and respectable, on the evidence of an abandoned, and I will show you, a perjured and common informer, in declaring you are ready to offer up to death 111,000 men, one by one, by the sentence of a court of justice? Are you ready to meet it?

Do not suppose I am base or mean enough to say anything to intimidate you, when I talk to you of such an event; but if you were prepared for such a scene, what would be your private reflections were you to do any such thing? Therefore I put the question fairly to you—have you made up your minds to tell the public, that as soon as James O'Brien shall choose to come forward again, to make the same charge against 111,000 other men, you are ready to see so many men, so many of your fellow-subjects and fellow-citizens, drop one by one into the grave, dug for them by his testimony?

Do not think I am speaking disrespectfully of you when I say, that while an O'Brien may be found, it may be the lot of the proudest among you to be in the dock instead of the jury-box. If you were standing there, how would you feel if you found that the evidence of such a wretch would be admitted as sufficient to attaint your life, and send you to an ignominious death? Remember, I do beseech you, that great mandate of your religion—"Do thou unto all men as you would they should do unto you."

Give me leave to put another point to you—what is the reason that you deliberate—that you condescend to listen to me with such attention? Why are you so anxious, if, even from me, any thing should fall tending to enlighten you on the present awful occasion? It is, because, bound by the sacred obligations of an oath, your heart will not allow you to forfeit it. Have you any doubt that it is the object of O'Brien to take down the prisoner for the reward that follows? Have you not seen with what more than instinctive keenness this blood-hound has pursued his victim? how he has kept him in view from place to place, until he hunts him through the avenues of the court to where the unhappy man stands now, hopeless of all succour but that which your verdict shall afford. I have heard of assassination by sword, by pistol, and by dagger; but here is a wretch who would dip the Evangelists in blood; if he thinks he has not sworn his victim to death, he is ready to swear, without mercy and without end: but oh! do not, I conjure you, suffer him to take an oath; the hand of the murderer should not pollute the purity of the gospel: if he will swear, let it be on the *knife,* the proper symbol of his profession!

Gentlemen, I am again reminded of that tissue of abominable slander and calumny with which O'Brien has endeavoured to load so great a portion of the adult part of your country. Is it possible you can believe the report of that wretch, that no less than 111,000 men are ready to destroy and overturn the government? I do not believe the abominable slander. I may have been too quick in condemning this man; and I know the argument which will be used, and to a certain degree, it is not without sense—that you cannot always expect witnesses of the most unblemished character, and such things would never be brought to light if witnesses like O'Brien were rejected altogether. The argument is of some force; but does it hold here? or are you to believe it as a truth, because the fact is sworn to by an abominable and perjured witness? No; the law of England, the so-often-mentioned principle upon which that important statute is framed, denies the admission. An English judge would be bound to tell you, and the learned judges present will tell you, that a single accomplice is not to be believed without strong corroborative confirmation—I do not know where a contrary principle was entertained; if such has been the case, I never heard of it. O'Brien stated himself to have been involved in the guilt of the prisoner, in taking the obligation which was forced on him, and which he was afterwards obliged to wash down; but may not the whole description given by him be false? May he not have fabricated that story, and come forward as an informer in a transaction that never happened, from the expectation of pay and profit? How does he stand? He stands divested of a single witness to support his character or the truth of his assertions, when numbers were necessary for each. You would be most helpless and unfortunate men, if everything said by the witness laid you under a necessity of believing it. Therefore he must be supported either by collateral or confirmatory evidence. Has he been supported by any collateral evidence, confirming what was sworn this day? No. Two witnesses have been examined, they are not additional witnesses to the overt acts; but if either of them should carry any conviction to your minds, you must be satisfied that the evidence given by O'Brien is false. I will not pollute the respectable and honourable character of Lord Portarlington, by mentioning it with the false and perjured O'Brien. Does his lordship tell you a single word but what O'Brien said to him? Because, if his lordship told all here that O'Brien told to him, O'Brien has done the same too; and though he has told Lord Portarlington every word which he has sworn on the table, yet still the evidence given by his lordship cannot be corroborative, because the probability is that he told a falsehood; you must take that evidence by comparison. And what did he tell Lord Portarlington? or, rather, what has Lord Portarlington told you? That O'Brien did state to him the project of robbing the ordnance some time before he could possibly have known it himself. And it is material that he swore on the table that he did not know of the plot till his third meeting with the societies; and Lord Portarlington swears that he told it to him on the first interview with him: there the contradiction of O'Brien by Lord Portarlington is material; and the testimony of Lord Portarlington may be put out of the case, except so far as it contradicts that of O'Brien.

Mr. Justice Chamberlain—It is material, Mr. CURRAN, that

Lord Portarlington did not swear positively it was at the first interview, but that he was inclined to believe it was so.

Mr. CURRAN—Your lordship will recollect that he said O'Brien did not say anything of consequence at any of the other interviews; but I put his lordship out of the question, so far as he does not contradict O'Brien, and he does so. If I am stating anything through mistake, I would wish to be set right; but Lord Portarlington said he did not recollect anything of importance at any subsequent meeting; and as far as he goes, he does beyond contradiction establish the false swearing of O'Brien. I am strictly right in stating the contradiction: so far as it can be compared with the testimony of O'Brien, it does weaken it; and, therefore, I will leave it there, and put Lord Portarlington out of the question—that is, as if he had not been examined at all, but where he differs from the evidence given by O'Brien.

As to the witness Clarke, after all he has sworn, you cannot but be satisfied he has not said a single word materially against the prisoner; he has not given any confirmatory evidence in support of any one overt act laid in the indictment. You have them upon your minds—he has not said one word as to the various meetings—levying money, or sending persons to France; and, therefore, I do warn you against giving it that attention for which it has been introduced. He does not make a second witness. Gentlemen, in alluding to the evidence of

Lord Portarlington, which I have already mentioned, I was bound to make some observations. On the evidence of Clarke I am also obliged to do the same, because he has endeavoured to prejudice your minds by an endeavour to give a sliding evidence of what does not by any means come within this case; that is, a malignant endeavour to impute a horrid transaction—the murder of a man of the name of Thompson—to the prisoner at the bar; but I do conjure you to consider what motives there can be for insinuations of this sort, and why such a transaction, so remote from the case before you, should be endeavoured to be impressed on your minds. Gentlemen, I am not blinking the question; I come boldly up to it; and I ask you, in the presence of the court and of your God, is there one word of evidence that bears the shadow of such a charge, as the murder of that unfortunate man, to the prisoner at the bar? Is there one word to show how he died—whether by force, or by any other means? Is there a word how he came to his end? Is there a word to bring a shadow of suspicion that can be attached to the prisoner? Gentlemen, my client has been deprived of the benefit of a witness, May, (you have heard of it,) who, had the trial been postponed, might have been able to attend; we have not been able to examine him, but you may guess what he would have said—he would have discredited the informer O'Brien. The evidence of O'Brien ought to be supported by collateral circumstances. It is not; and though Roberts is not here, yet you may conjecture what he would have said. But, gentlemen, I have examined five witnesses, and it does seem as if there had been some providential interference carried on in bringing five witnesses to contradict O'Brien in his testimony, as to direct matters of fact, if his testimony could be put in competition with direct positive evidence. O'Brien said, he knew nothing of ordering back any money to Margaret Moore; he denied that fact. The woman was examined—what did she say on the table in the presence of O'Brien? That "an order was made, and the money refunded, after the magistrate had abused him for his conduct." What would you think of your servant, if you found him committing such perjury—would you believe him? What do you think of this fact? O'Brien denies he knew anything of the money being refunded! What does Mrs. Moore say? That after the magistrate had abused him for his conduct, the money was refunded, and that "she and O'Brien walked down stairs together!" Is this an accidental trip, a little stumble of conscience, or, is it not downright, wilful perjury? What said Mr. Clarke? I laid the foundation of the evidence by asking O'Brien, did you ever pass for a revenue officer? I call gentlemen, on your knowledge of the human character, and of human life, what was the conduct of the man? Was it what you would have acted, if you had been called on in a court of justice? Did he answer me candidly? Do you remember his manner? "Not, sir, that I remember; it could not be when I was sober." "Did you do it at all?" What was the answer— "I might, sir, have done it; but I must have been drunk. I never did anything dishonest." Why did he answer thus? Because he did imagine he would have been opposed in his testimony, he not only added perjury to his prevarication, but he added robbery to both. There are thousands of your fellow-subjects waiting to know, if the fact charged upon the nation of 111,000 men ready to assist the common enemy be true; if upon the evidence of an abandoned wretch, a common cheat, a robber, and a perjurer, you will convict the prisoner at the bar. As to his being a coiner, I will not pass that felony in payment among his other crimes, but I will offer it by itself: I will offer it as an emblem of his conscience, copper-washed —I will offer it by itself.

What has O'Brien said? "I never remember that I did pretend to be a revenue officer; but I remember there was a man said something about whiskey; and I remember, I threatened to complain, and he was a little frightened—and he gave me three and three pence!" I asked him, "Did his wife give you anything?" "There was three and three pence between them." "Who gave you the money?" "It was all I got from both of them!" Gentlemen, would you let him into your house as a servant? Suppose one of you wanted a servant, and went to the other to get one; and suppose that you heard that he personated a revenue officer; that he had threatened to become an informer against persons not having licences, in order to extort money to compromise the actions, would you take him as a servant? If you would not take him as servant in exchange for his wages, would you take his perjuries in exchange for the life of a fellow-subject? Let me ask you, how would you show your faces to the public, and justify a barter of that kind, if you were to establish and send abroad his assignats of perjury to pass current as the price of human blood? How could you bear the tyranny your consciences would exercise over you; the dagger that would turn upon your heart's blood, if in the moment of madness you could suffer by your verdict the sword of justice to fall on the head of a victim committed to your sworn humanity, to be massacred in your presence by the perjured and abominable evidence that has been offered! But does it stop there? Has perjury rested there? —No. What said the honest-looking, unlettered mind of the poor farmer? What said Cavanagh? "I keep a public-house,—O'Brien came to me, and pretended he was a revenue officer;—I knew not but it might be so;—he told me he was so—he examined the little beer I had, and my cask of porter." And, gentlemen, what did the villain do? While he was dipping his abandoned tongue in perjury and in blood, he robbed the wretched man of two guineas. Where is he now? Do you wonder he is afraid of my eye? that he has buried himself in the crowd? that he has shrunk into the whole of the multitude, when the witness endeavoured to disentangle him and his evidence? Do you not feel that he was appalled with horror by that more piercing and penetrating eye that looks upon him, and upon me, and upon us all? The chords of his heart bore testimony by its flight, and proved that he fled for the same. But does it rest there? No. Witness upon witness appeared for the prisoner, to whom, I dare say, you will give that credit you must deny to O'Brien. In the presence of God they swore, that they "would not believe him upon his oath, in the smallest matter." Do you know him, gentlemen of the jury? Are you acquainted with James O'Brien? If you do, let him come forward from that crowd where he has hid himself, and claim you by a look. Have you been fellow companions? If you have I dare say you will recognize him. Have I done with him yet? No; while there is a thread of his villany together, I will tatter it, lest you should be caught with it. Did he dare to say to the solicitor for the crown, to the counsel that are prosecuting the prisoner, that "there is some one witness on the surface of the globe that will say, he believes I am not a villain; but I am a man that deserves some credit on my oath in a court of justice?" Did he venture to call one human being to that fact? But why did they not venture to examine the prisoner's witnesses, as to the reasons of their disbelief? What, if I was bold enough to say to any of you, gentlemen, that I did not think you deserved credit on your oath, would not the first question you would ask be the reason for that opinion? Did he venture to ask that question? No. I think the trial has been fairly and humanely carried on. Mrs. Moore was examined; she underwent cross-examination—the object was to impeach her credit. I offered to examine to her character; no—I would not be suffered to do it; they were right in the point of law. Gentlemen, let me ask you another question; —Is the character of O'Brien such, that you think he did not know that any human creature was to attack it? Did you not see him coiling himself in the scaly circles of his perjury, making anticipated battle against the attack, that he knew would be made, and spitting his venom against the man that might have given such evidence of his infamous character if he had dared to appear?

Gentlemen, do you feel now that I was maliciously aspersing the character of O'Brien? What language is strong enough to describe the mixture of swindling and imposition which, in the face of justice, this wretch has been guilty of? Taking on himself the situation of one of the King's officers, to rob the King's subjects of the King's money; but that is not enough for him—in the vileness and turpitude of his character he afterwards wants to rob them of their lives by perjury. Do I speak truly to you, gentlemen, when I have shown you the witness in his real colours—when I have shown you his habitual fellowship with baseness and fraud? He gave a recipe for forging money. "Why did you give it to him?" "He was an inquisitive man, and I gave it as a matter of course." "But why did you do it?" "It was a light, easy way of getting money—I gave it as a humbug." He gave a recipe for forging the coin of the country, because it was a light, easy way of getting money! Has it, gentlemen, ever happened to you in the ordinary passages of life, to have met with such a constellation of atrocities and horrors, and that in a single man? What do you say to Clarke? Except his perjury, he has scarcely ground to turn on. What was his cross-examination? "Pray, sir, were you in court yesterday?" "No, sir, I was not." "Why?" "Mr. Kemmis sent me word not to come." There happened to be several persons who saw him in court: one of them swore it—the rest were ready. Call up "little Skirmish" again.* "Pray, Skirmish, why did you say you were not in court yesterday, when you were? "Why, it was a little bit of a mistake, not being a lawyer. It being a matter of law, I was mistaken." "How did it happen you were mistaken?" "I was puzzled by the hard questions that Mr. M'Nally asked me." What was the hard question he was asked? "Were you in court yester-

* "Little Skirmish," a character in *The Deserter*.

day?" "No; Mr. Kemmis sent me word I need not come?" Can you, gentlemen of the jury, suppose that any simple, well-meaning man would commit such a gross and abominable perjury? I do not think he is a credible man; that is, that he swore truer than Lord Portarlington did, because his lordship stands on a single testimony; he may be true, because he has sworn on both sides; he has sworn positively that he was not in the court yesterday; and he has sworn positively he was! so that, wherever the truth is, he is found in it; let the ground be clean or dirty, he is in the midst of it. There is no person but deserves some little degree of credit; if the soul was as black as night, it would burn to something in hell. But let me not appear to avoid the question by any seeming levity upon it. O'Brien stands blackened by the unimpeached proofs of five positive perjuries. If he was indicted on any one of them, he could not appear to give evidence in a court of justice; and I do call upon you, gentlemen of the jury, to refuse him on his oath that credit which never ought to be squandered on the evidence of an abandoned and self-convicted perjurer.

The charge is not merely against the prisoner at the bar; it takes in the entire character of your country. It is the first question of the kind for ages brought forward in this nation to public view, after an expiration of years. It is the great experiment of the informers of Ireland, to see with what success they may make this traffic of human blood. Fifteen men are now in gaol, depending on the fate of the unfortunate prisoner, and on the same blasted and perjured evidence of O'Brien. I have stated at large the case, and the situation of my client; I make no apology for wasting your time; I regret I have not been more able to do my duty; it would insult you if I were to express any such feeling to you. I have only to apologize to my client for delaying his acquittal. I have blackened the character of O'Brien in every point of view; and, though he anticipated the attack that would be made on it, yet he could not procure one human being even base enough to depose that he was to be believed on his oath.

The character of the prisoner has been given. Am I warranted in saying, that I am now defending an innocent and unfortunate fellow-subject, on the grounds of eternal justice and immutable law? and on that eternal law I do call upon you to acquit my client. I call upon you for your justice! Great is the reward, and sweet is the recollection in the hour of trial, and in the day of dissolution, when casualties of life are pressing close upon your heart, and when, in the agonies of death, you look back to the justifiable and honourable transactions of your life. At the awful foot of eternal justice I do, therefore, invite you to acquit my client; and may God, of his infinite mercy, grant you that great compensation which is a reward more lasting than that perishable crown we read of, which the ancients gave to him who saved the life of a fellow-citizen in battle. In the name of public justice! I do implore you to interpose between the perjurer and his intended victim; and, if ever you are assailed by the villany of an informer, may you find refuge in the recollection of that example, which, when jurors, you set to those that might be called to pass judgment upon your lives; to repel at the human tribunal the intended effects of hireling perjury, and premeditated murder! If it should be the fate of any of you to count the tedious moments of captivity, in sorrow and in pain, pining in the damps and gloom of a dungeon, recollect there is another more awful tribunal than any on earth, which we must all approach, and before which the best of us will have occasion to look back to what little good he has done on this side the grave; I do pray, that Eternal Justice may record the deed you have done, and give to you the full benefit of your claims to an eternal reward, a requital in mercy upon your souls!

After a reply from the Solicitor-General (Toler), Justice Chamberlain and Baron Smith charged, inclining to the prisoner, and in a quarter of an hour the jury returned a verdict of *Not Guilty*. On the 19th, fifteen other persons, who had been indicted on the same charge, were formally tried and acquitted, and, on taking the oath of allegiance, and filing recognizances for good behaviour, were discharged. So ended the first of the 98 trials.

HENRY SHEARES.

[HIGH TREASON.]

SPECIAL COMMISSION, DUBLIN.

4th and 12th July, 1798.

The United Irish Society was formed in 1791, for the achievement of Catholic Emancipation and Parliamentary Reform, and was increased in 1792-3, retaining its original objects. In 1794, the views of Tone and Neilson, who both desired an independent republic, spread; but the formal objects were unchanged, when, on the 10th of May, 1795,* the organization of Ulster was completed. The recal of Lord Fitzwilliam, and the consequent disappointment of the Roman Catholics—the accumulation of coercive laws—the prospect of French alliance, and the natural progress of a quarrel, rapidly spread the influence, and altered the whole character of the Society. The Test of the Society was made more decisive, and less constitutional. In the Autumn of 1796 the organization was made military in Ulster. Twelve neighbours formed a society, whose secretary was called "a petty officer"; the petty officers of five societies elected one of themselves into the lower baronial, as representative and captain of sixty; the members of ten lower baronials sent a delegate to the upper baronial. This last delegate was, therefore, colonel of a battalion of six hundred men. Towards the middle of 1797, this system spread to Leinster. Each baronial sent a delegate to a county committee, and the provincial

* Neilson's Evidence—Report of Secret Committee, Appendix, No. 31.

committee consisted of two or three delegates from each of the counties. The provincial committee ballotted for five members of an executive; the secretary alone examined the ballot, and reported it to the persons elected, but not to the electors.

Though so far back as May, 1796, the then Executive had *formally* communicated with France, through Lord Edward Fitzgerald, it was not till 19th February, 1798, that it was resolved—"That they would not be diverted from their purpose by anything which could be done in parliament."

The Executive consisted then of Dr. MacNevin, Arthur O'Connor, Thomas Addis Emmet, Richard M'Cormick, Oliver Bond, and Lord Edward.

In the Winter of 1796-7, the coming of the French was urged as a reason for immediate insurrection; but it did not prevail. In May, 1797, the order for the execution of the four soldiers of the Monaghan Militia, at Blaris Môr, was regarded by the Militias as a sufficient motive for action; but not so thought the Executive.

In the Summer of 1797, the Militia regiments sent a deputation, offering to seize the Castle. The Northern leaders were for an outbreak; so was Lord Edward. Still nothing was done. And again, in the beginning of '98, the people, subjected to free quarters, whipping, burnings, and transportation, pressed for insurrection; and Lord Edward was disposed to it. Emmet wanted to wait for French aid (though no man was more adverse to, or took more precautions against, French authority in Ireland;) and thus they were, when Reynolds of Kilkea betrayed them to the Government for money.

Arthur O'Connor was arrested at Maidstone, in the act of embarking for France; and, on the 12th of March, a meeting of Leinster delegates, including Oliver Bond, M'Cann, &c., &., were arrested at Oliver Bond's woollen warehouse, in Bridge-street. MacNevin, Thomas Emmet, and Sampson, were in the warrant with Bond; but not being punctual at the meeting, were not taken for some days.

A warrant had, at the same time, been issued against Lord Edward; but he escaped, and lay concealed. The places of MacNevin, Emmet, and O'Connor were filled. John Sheares was one of the New Directory. But Reynolds, though suspected, retained his intimacy. On the 19th of May, just four days before the rising was to take place, Lord Edward was arrested, and on the 21st, the two Sheares were also taken. Thus the insurrection began, without its designers to lead it, and without time to replace them.

On the night of the 23rd May, the stopping of the mail-coaches was the signal for insurrection. Next day the peasantry of Kildare, Wicklow, and parts of Meath rose. They were generally met and defeated, but they succeeded at Prosperous, and partially in other places. On the 26th, the Meath people were defeated at Tara. On the 27th, the Wexford men won the battle of Oulard—the next day, stormed Enniscorthy—on the 30th, got Wexford town by capitulation, and immediately swept the county. On the 5th June, the insurgents stormed Ross, got drunk in the town, and were driven out with much execution; and, on the 9th, another of their masses failed in an attack on Arklow The Wexford insurrection began thenceforth to decline. On the 21st of June, the battle of Vinegar Hill was gained by General Lake. Meantime, the Antrim rising had been stopped by a battle in that town, on the 7th of June; and the success of that of Down, at Saintfield, on the 10th June was over-balanced by the total defeat of Munroe and his Presbyterians at Ballinahinch, on the 12th. Kildare and Wicklow continued a partizan war: and a column of Wexford fugitives forced their way to the Boyne, and there, utterly worn out, were cut to pieces. This was on the 13th of July, the morning when the Sheares were convicted. On the 17th July, Lord Castlereagh announced the final defeat of the Rebellion.*

* If it is added that the French, under Humbert, entered Killala Bay on the 22nd of August—carried Castlebar on the 27th of

Perhaps the reader will forgive these dates, as he may better appreciate, by means of them, the moral atmosphere wherein these next speeches of Curran were spoken.

Henry and John Sheares were the sons of a Cork banker. The elder was a man of fine person—vain and weak face, and vainer and weaker mind—some eloquence and warmth, and showy manners. In '98, he was forty-five years old, and was married to a second wife, by whom he had a large family. John was thirty-two—a man of firmness, feeling, and ready intellect. He was, at the time of his death, engaged to a Miss Steele.

Henry's property was £1,200 a-year, which he encumbered; John's £3,000, on which he lived, after lending his brother money. Miss Steele says he bought "nothing but books." They resided in Baggot-street (now No. 130), and there Henry was arrested. John was arrested at Surgeon Lawless's, in French-street. They had been United Irishmen from 1793, and John was a frequent chairman, and apparently a man of weight in "The Union." He contributed to "*The Press*"—was peculiarly active with his brother in pushing the organization in Cork—and became, as we have seen, one of the Executive, after the arrests at Bond's, in March, '98,

Strange to say, it was not till the 10th of May that they first met their betrayer; but he was a skilful and zealous artist, and in eleven days he contrived to win their intimacy, share their hospitality, gain their secrets, and hand them to the executioner! Unrivalled Armstrong!

This John Warneford Armstrong was a man of good family, and a Captain in the King's County Militia, then stationed at Loughlinstown Camp, between Dublin and Bray. On the 10th May, he went to the shop of Byrne, a bookseller, in Grafton-

August—and surrendered, at Ballinamuck, on the 8th September; and that Hardy's flotilla was taken on the 11th October, with Tone, who died on the 19th of November, the reader will have a short chronology of the "Rebellion of '98."

street, and a member of the United Irish Society. He was in the habit of buying there the books current among the Republicans, and Byrne (a feeble, but not treacherous, man) introduced him to Henry Sheares.* Henry declined communication, and went away; but John (who had before noticed Armstrong in the shop) soon came in, was introduced, and plunged headlong into communication with Armstrong. Frequent interviews followed. The means of taking the Castle, Island-bridge Barracks, and Lehaunstown (Loughlinstown) Camp, were constant topics. On the 20th (Sunday), he dined at Baggot-street, on John's invitation, and with the earnest approval of Lord Castlereagh; was informed by John, on the part of the Executive, that he was to command the King's County force, and discussed many raw, but important, projects. Armstrong had formed the acquaintance to get them in his clutches; they were so, and on the 21st of May they were taken.

On the 26th of June, Chief Justice Lord Carleton, Baron George, and Justices Crookshank, Chamberlain, and Daly, opened the Special Commission. After the Grand Juries for Dublin City and County were sworn, they were addressed by Lord Carleton; and then numerous prisoners were arraigned. True bills were found against Samuel Neilson, Michael Byrne, Henry and John Sheares, John M'Cann, and Oliver Bond. The Court assigned† Mr. Curran and Mr. M'Nally to John Sheares; Mr. Plunket, for Henry Sheares; and Mr. Armstrong Fitzgerald, as agents for both; and then adjourned to the 4th July.

On the 4th July, Lord Carleton, Barons Smith and George, and Justices Crookshank and Daly, sat; and Henry and John

* At Armstrong's request, says the brief; at Byrne's own desire, said Captain Armstrong, in a conversation with Dr. Madden, which will appear in the Third, and most interesting, Series of "The United Irishmen."

† The right to have counsel assigned, and to get a copy of the indictment, was conceded to prisoners by the 5th George III., an act introduced by the father of the Sheares, when a member of the Irish Parliament.

Sheares being put to the bar, their indictment for High Treason was read by the Clerk of the Crown. The first count stated sixteen overt acts. The second count was for associating as United Irishmen, &c.

Mr. M'Nally objected, after some delay, that John Decluzeau, one of the grand jurors who found the bills, was an alien, not naturalized, and filed a plea in court. The Crown replied, and CURRAN supported the plea as follows:—

MY lords, we have looked over this replication, and we find that the gentlemen concerned for the crown have thought proper to plead in three ways. The subject matter of our plea in abatement came very recently to our knowledge. To suppose that an alien had been upon the grand jury finding a bill of indictment involving the duty of allegiance was a rare thing; the suspicion of it came late to our knowledge. It would have been our duty to be prepared, had we known it in time; but as we did not, and as it is a plea of great novelty, we hope the court will not think it unreasonable to give us time till to-morrow to answer this pleading.

The court over-ruled the application

Mr. CURRAN—My lords, before we rejoin, it may be prudent to consider, whether this replication should not be *quashed*. There are three distinct matters in the replication, and they are repugnant to one another. One is, that the juror is *not an alien*; the second and third contain averments that he *is an alien*. Clearly, in civil cases, a party cannot plead double matter, without the leave of the court; even the statute which gives that benefit, does not admit it without a special motion, in order that the court may see whether the pleas can stand together. But even that holds only in civil cases, and by the authority of an act of parliament. Therefore, your lordships will consider, whether a replication of this kind, consisting of three parts, contradictory and repugnant, ought to be answered.

Lord Carleton—In civil cases, certainly, the right of pleading double arises from the act of parliament. As to the objection you now make, you must avail yourself of it in some other way. We will not quash the replication upon motion.

A rejoinder and demurrer of insufficiency were then filed on the part of the prisoners.

Mr. Curran—My lords, it is my duty to suggest such reasons as occur to me in support of the demurrer filed here on the part of the prisoners. My lords, the law of this country has declared that in order to the conviction of any man, not only of any charge of the higher species of criminal offences, but of any criminal charge whatsoever, he must be convicted upon the finding of two juries; first, of the grand jury, who determine upon the guilt in one point of view; and, secondly, by the corroborative finding of the petty jury, who establish that guilt in a more direct manner; and it is the law of this country, that the jurors who shall so find, whether upon the grand, or whether upon the petty inquest, shall be *probi et legales homines omni exceptione majores*. They must be open to no legal objection of personal incompetence. They must be capable of having freehold property; and, in order to have freehold property, they must not be open to the objection of being born under the jurisdiction of a foreign prince, or owing allegiance to any foreign power. Because the law of this country, and, indeed, the law of every country in Europe, has thought it an indispensable precaution, to trust no man with the weight or influence which territorial possession may give him, contrary to that allegiance which ought to flow from every man having property in the country.

This observation is emphatically forcible in every branch of the criminal law; but in the law of treason, it has a degree of force and cogency that fails in every inferior class of offence, because the very point to be inquired into in treason, is the nature of allegiance.

The general nature of allegiance may be pretty clear to every man. Every man, however unlearned he may be, can easily acquire such a notion of allegiance, whether natural and born with him, or whether it be temporary, and contracted by emigration into another country, he may acquire a vague, untechnical idea of allegiance, for his immediate personal conduct.

But I am warranted in saying, that the constitution does not suppose, that any foreigner has any direct idea of allegiance, but what he owes to his original prince. The constitution supposes, and takes for granted, that no foreigner has such an idea of our peculiar and precise allegiance, as qualifies him to act as a juror, where that is the question to be inquired into; and I found myself upon this known principle, that though the benignity of the English law has in many cases, where strangers are tried, given a jury half composed of foreigners and half natives, that benefit is denied to any man accused of treason, for the reason I have stated; because, says Sir W. Blackstone, "aliens are very improper judges of the breach of allegiance." A foreigner is a most improper judge of what the allegiance is which binds an English subject to his constitution. And, therefore, upon that idea of utter incompetency in a stranger, is every foreigner directly removed and repelled from the possibility of exercising a function that he is supposed utterly unable to discharge.

If one Frenchman shall be suffered to find a bill of indictment between our Lord the King and his subjects, by a parity of reasoning, may twenty-three men of the same descent be put into the box, with authority to find a bill of indictment. By the same reason that the court may communicate with one man, whose language they do not know, may they communicate with twenty-three natives of twenty-three different countries and languages.

How far do I mean to carry this? Thus far: that every statute, or means by which allegiance may be shaken off, and any kind of benefit or privilege conferred upon an emigrating foreigner, is for ever to be considered by a court of justice with relation to that natural incompetency to perform certain trusts, which is taken for granted, and established by the law of England. I urge it with this idea, that whether the privilege is conferred by letters patent, making the foreigner a denizen, or whether by act of parliament, making him as a native subject, the letters patent, or act of parliament, should be construed *secundum subjectam materiam;* and a court of justice will take care, that no privilege be supposed to be granted, incompatible with the original situation of the party to whom, or the constitution of the country in which, it is conferred.

Therefore, my lords, my clients have pleaded, that the bill of indictment to which they have been called upon to answer, has been found, among others, by a foreigner, born under a foreign allegiance, and incapable of exercising the right of a juror, upon the grand, or the petty inquest. That is the substance of the plea in abatement. The counsel for the crown have replied, and we have demurred to the second and third parts of the replication.

My lords, I take it to be a rule of law, not now to be questioned, that there is a distinction in our statute laws; some are of a public, some of a private nature.

That part of the legislative edict which is considered as of a public nature, is supposed to be recorded in the breasts of the King's judges. As the King's judges, you are the depositories and the records of the public law of the country.

But wherever a private indulgence is granted, or a mere personal privilege conferred, the King's judges are not the depositories of such laws, though enacted with the same publicity; you are not the repositories of deeds or titles which give men franchises or estates, nor of those statutes which ease a man of a disability, or grant him a privilege. With regard to the individual to whom they relate, they are mere private acts, muniments, or deeds, call them by what name you please; they are to be shown as private deeds, to such courts as it may be thought necessary to bring them forward. Therefore, if there be any act of parliament, by which a man is enabled to say he has shaken off the disability which prevented him from intermeddling in the political or judicial arrangement of the country; if he says he is no longer to be considered as an alien, he must show that act specially to the court in his pleading. The particular authority, whether by letters of denization, or act of parliament, must be set forth, that the court may judge of them, that if it be by act of parliament, the court may see whether he comes within the provisions of the act. This replication does no such thing.

The second and the third parts were intended to be founded upon the statute of Charles II., and also, I suppose, upon the subsequent statute, made to give it perpetuity, with certain additional requisites. The statute of Charles recites, that the kingdom was wasted by the unfortunate troubles of that time; and that trade had decreased, for want of merchants. After thus stating generally the grievances which had afflicted the trade and population of the country, and the necessity of encouraging emigration from abroad, it goes on and says, that strangers may be induced to transport themselves and families, to replenish the country, if they may be made partakers of the advantages and free exercise of their trades, without interruption and disturbance.

The grievance was the scarcity of men; the remedy was the encouragement of foreigners to transport themselves; and the encouragement given was such a degree of protection as was necessary to the full exercise of their trades, in dealing, buying, and selling, and enjoying the fullest extent of personal security. Therefore, it enacts, that all foreigners, of the Protestant religion, and all merchants, &c., who shall, within the *term of seven years,* transport themselves to this country, shall be deemed and reputed natural-born subjects, and *may implead and be impleaded, and prosecute and defend suits.*

The intention was, to give them protection for

the purposes for which they were encouraged to come here; and, therefore, the statute, instead of saying generally they shall be subjects *to all intents and purposes,* specifically enumerates the privileges they shall enjoy. If the legislature intended to make them subjects *to all intents and purposes,* it had nothing more to do than say so. But not having meant any such thing, the statute is confined to the enumeration of the mere hospitable rights and privileges to be granted to such foreigners as come here for special purposes. It states, that he may implead, and shall be answered unto, that he may prosecute and defend suits. Why go on and tell a man, who is *to all intents and purposes* a natural-born subject, that he may implead and bring actions? I say, it is to all intents and purposes absurd and preposterous. If *all* privileges be granted in the first instance, why mention *particular* parts afterwards? A man would be esteemed absurd, who by his grant gave a thing under a general description, and afterwards granted the particular parts. What would be thought of a man who gave another his horse, and then said to the grantee, "I also give you liberty to ride him when and where you please?"

What was the case here? The government of Ireland said, we want men of skill and industry, we invite you to come over, our intention is, that if you be Protestants, you shall be protected: but you are not to be judges, or legislators, or kings.

We make an act of parliament, giving you protection and encouragement to follow the trades for your knowledge in which we invite you; you are to exercise your trade as a natural-born subject. How? With full power to make a bargain and enforce it: we invest you with the same power, and you shall have the same benefit, as if you were appealing to your own natural form of public justice; you shall be here as a Frenchman in Paris, buying and selling the commodities appertaining to your trade.

Look at another clause in the act of parliament, which is said to make a legislator of this man, or a juror, to pass upon the life and death of a fellow-subject, no, not a fellow-subject, but a stranger. It says, "you may purchase an estate, and you may enjoy it, without being a trustee for the crown." Why was that necessary, if he were a subject *to all intents and purposes?*

This statute had continuance for the period of seven years only: that is, it limited the time in which a foreigner might avail himself of its benefits to seven years. The statute 4 George I. revives it, and makes it perpetual. I trust I may say, that whenever an act of parliament is made, giving perpetuity to a former act, no greater force or operation can be given to the latter, than would have been given to the former, had it been declared perpetual at the time of its enactment. An act of that kind is merely to cure the defect of continuance;

therefore, it does no more than is necessary to that end. Then how will it stand? Thus: that any man, who, within seven years after the passing of the act of Charles II. performs the requisites there mentioned, shall have the privileges thereby granted for ever thereafter. The court would assume the office of legislation, not of construction, if they inferred or supplied by intendment, a longer period than seven years; there is nothing in the subsequent act, changing the term of seven years limited in the former; it is not competent to a court of justice to alter or extend the operation of a statute by the introduction of clauses not to be found in it. It is the business of the legislature to enact laws, of the court to expound them.

It is worthy of observation, my lords, that this subsequent statute has annexed certain explicit conditions to be performed by the person who is to take the benefit of the preceding act; for it is provided, that no person shall have the benefit of the former act, unless he take the several oaths appointed to be taken by the latter; among which, is the oath against the Pretender, which is not stated in the replication.

There is a circumstance in the latter act, which, with regard to the argument, is extremely strong, to show, that the legislature did not indend to grant the universal franchise and privilege to all intents and purposes. It revives every part of the former, save that part exempting aliens from the payment of excise. Will it be contended, that an alien should be considered as a natural-born subject *to all intents and purposes*, and yet be exempt from the payment of excise? It is absurd, and impossible.

Put it in another point of view. What is an act of naturalization? It is an encroachment upon the common law rights, which every man born in this country has in it; those rights are encroached upon and taken away by a stranger. The statute therefore should be construed with the rigour of a penal law. The court, to be sure, will see, that the stranger has the full benefit intended for him by the statute; but they will not give him any privilege inconsistent with the rights of the natural-born subjects, or incompatible with the fundamental principles of the constitution into which he is admitted; and I found myself upon this, that after declaring that he shall be considered as a natural-born subject, the act states such privileges only as are necessary to the exercise of trade and the enjoyment of property.

Therefore, it comes back to the observation just now made. Is not any man pleading a statute of naturalization, by which he claims to be considered as a natural-born subject, bound to set forth a compliance with all the requisites pointed out by that statute? He is made a native to a certain extent, upon complying with certain conditions; is he not bound to state that compliance? Here he has not stated them. But I go farther; I say, that every condition mentioned in the statute of Charles should be set forth in the second part of the replication; that he came with an intent of settling; that he brought his family and his stock; that he took the oaths before the proper magistrates; and, after a minute statement of every fact, he should state the additional oath required by the statute George I.

But, my lords, a great question remains behind to be decided upon. I know of no case upon it. I do not pretend to say, that the industry of other men may not have discovered a case. But I would not be surprised, if no such case could be found; if since the history of the administration of justice in all its forms in England, a stranger had not been found intruding himself into its concerns; if through the entire history of our courts of justice, an instance was not to be found, of the folly of a stranger interfering upon so awful a subject as the breach of allegiance between a subject and his king.

My lords, I beg leave upon this part to say, that it would be a most formidable thing, if a court of justice would pronounce a determination big with danger, if they said that an alien may find a bill of indictment involving the doctrine of allegiance. It is permitting him to intermeddle in a business of which he cannot be supposed to have any knowledge. Shall a subject of the Irish crown be charged with a breach of his allegiance upon the saying of a German, an Italian, a Frenchman, or a Spaniard? Can any man suppose any thing more monstrous or absurd, than that of a stranger being competent to form an opinion upon the subject? I would not form a supposition upon it. At a time when the generals, the admirals, and the captains of France are endeavouring to pour their armies upon us, shall we permit their petty detachments to attack us in judicial hostility? Shall we sit inactive and see their skirmishers take off our fellow-subjects by explosions in a jury room?

When did this man come into the country? Is the raft upon which he floated now in court? What has he said upon the back of the bill? What understanding had he of it? If he can write more than his own name, and had wrote *ignoramus* upon the back of the indictment, he might have written truly; he might say, he knew nothing of the matter.

He says he is naturalized; I am glad of it; you are welcome to Ireland, sir; you shall have all the privileges of a stranger, independent of the invitation by which you came; if you sell, you shall recover the price of your wares, you shall enforce the contract; if you purchase an estate, you shall transmit it to your children, if you have any, if not, your devisee shall have it. But you must know, that in this constitution, there are laws binding upon the court as strongly as upon you: the statute itself which confers the privileges you enjoy, makes you incapable of discharging offices. Why? Because they go to the fundamentals of the constitution, and belong only to those men who have an interest in that constitution transmitted to them from their ancestors.

Therefore, my lords, the foreigner must be content; he shall be kept apart from the judicial functions; in the extensive words of the act of parliament, he shall be kept from "all places of trust whatsoever." If the act had been silent in that part, the court would notwithstanding be bound to say, that it did not confer the power of filling the high departments of the state. The alien would still be incapable of sitting in either house of parliament, he would be incapable of advising with the king, or holding any place of constitutional trust whatever. What! shall it be said, there is no trust in the office of a grand juror? I do not speak or think lightly of the sacred office confided to your lordships, of administering justice between the crown and the subject, or between subject and subject: I do not compare the office of a grand juror to that. But, in the name of God, with regard to the issues of life and death, with regard to the consequences of imputed or established criminality, what difference is there, in the importance of the constitution, between the juror who brings in a verdict, and the judge who pronounces upon that verdict the sentence of the law? Shall it be said, that the former is no place of trust? What is the place of trust meant by the statute? It is not merely giving a thing to another, or depositing for safe custody, it means *constitutional trust*, the trust of executing given departments, in which the highest confidence must be reposed in the man appointed to perform them. It means not the trust of keeping a paltry chattel, it means the awful trust of keeping the secrets of the state, and of the king.

Look at the weight of the obligation imposed upon the juror; look at the enormous extent of the danger, if he violate or disregard it. At a time like the present, a time of war, what! is the trust to be confided to the conscience of a Frenchman? But I am speaking for the lives of my clients, and I do not choose, even here, to state the terms of the trust, lest I might furnish as many hints of mischief, as I am anxious to furnish arguments of defence. But shall a Frenchman, at this moment, be entrusted with those secrets upon which your sitting upon that bench may eventually depend? What is the inquiry to be made? Having been a pedlar in the country, is he to have the selling of the country, if he be inclined to do so? Is he to have confided to him the secrets of the state? He *may* remember to have had a *first* allegiance, that he has sworn to it: he might find civilians to aid his perfidious logic, and to tell him, that a secret communicated to him by the humanity of the country which received him, might be disclosed to the older and better matured allegiance sworn to a former power! He might give up the perfidious use of his conscience to the integrity of the older title. Shall the power of calling upon an Irishman to take his trial before an Irish judge, before "the country," be left to the broken speech, the *lingua franca*, of a stranger coming among you and saying, "I was naturalized by act of parliament, and I cannot carry on my trade, without dealing in the blood of your citizens?"

He holds up your statute as his protection, and flings it against your liberty, claiming the right of exercising a judicial function, feeling at the same time the honest love for an older title to allegiance. It is a love which every man ought to feel, and which every subject of this country would feel if he left this country to-morrow, and were to spend his last hour among the Hottentots of Africa. I do trust in God, there is not a man wo hears me, who does not feel that he would carry with him to the remotest part of the globe the old ties which bound him to his original friends, his country, and his king: I do, as the advocate of my clients, of my country—as the advocate for you, my lords, whose elevation prevents you from the possibility of being advocates for yourselves,—for your children, stand up and rely upon it, that this act of parliament has been confined to a limited operation; it was enacted for a limited purpose, and will not allow this meddling stranger to pass upon the life, fame, or fortune of the gentlemen at the bar, —of me, their advocate,—of you, their judges,— or of any man in the nation. It is an intrusion not to be borne.

My lords, you deny him no advantage that strangers ought to have. By extending the statute, you take away a right from a native of the country, and you transfer one to an intermeddling stranger. I do not mean to use him with disrespect; he may be a respectable and worthy man; but whatever he may be, I do, with humble reliance upon the justice of the court, deprecate the idea of communicating to him that high, awful, and tremendous privilege, of passing upon life, of expounding the law in cases of treason; it being a fundamental maxim that strangers will, most improperly, be called upon to judge of breaches of allegiance between a subject and his sovereign.

The objection being over-ruled, the court adjourned.

On Thursday, the 12th July, at nine o'clock, the trial came on. Mr. Webber opened, and the Attorney-General (Toler) stated, the case. Alderman Alexander proved that he found in John's open desk, in Baggot-street, the following paper. (The words in *italics* were interlined; those between crotchets were struck across with a pen):—

"IRISHMEN,

[Your country is free; all those monsters who usurped its government to oppress its people are in our hands, except such as have]

"Your country is free and you are about to be avenged [already] that vile government which has so long and so cruelly oppressed you is no more; some of its most atrocious monsters have already paid the forfeit of their lives, and the rest are in our hands [waiting their fate.] The national flag, ***the sacred green,*** is at this moment flying over the ruins of despotism, and that capital which a few hours past [was the scene] witnessed the debauchery, [the machinations] plots and crimes of your tyrants, is now the citadel of triumphant patriotism ***and virtue.*** Arise, then, united sons of Ireland; arise like a great and powerful people, determined to [live] be free or die; arm yourselves by every means in your power, and rush like lions on your foes; consider, that [in disarming your enemy] for every enemy you disarm, you arm a friend, and thus become doubly powerful; in the cause of liberty, inaction is cowardice, and the coward shall forfeit the property he has not the courage to protect. Let his arms be seized and transferred to those gallant [patriots] *spirits* who want, and will use them; yes, Irishmen, we swear by that eternal justice, in whose cause you fight, that the brave patriot who survives the present glorious struggle, and the family of him who has fallen, or shall fall hereafter in it, shall receive from the hands of a grateful nation an ample recompense out of [those funds] that property which the crimes of our enemies [shall] have forfeited into its hands, and his name [too] shall be inscribed on the national record of Irish revolution, as a glorious example to all posterity; ***but we likewise swear to punish robbery with death and infamy.***

"We also swear that we will never sheathe the sword until every [person] being in the country is restored to those equal rights which the God of nature has given to all men; until an order of things shall be established, in which no superiority shall be acknowledged among the citizens of Erin, but that [which] of virtue and talent [shall entitle to].

"[As for those degenerate wretches who turn their swords against their native country, the national vengeance awaits them. Let them find no quarter unless they shall prove their repentance by speedily deserting, exchanging from the standard of slavery, for that of freedom, under which their former errors may be buried, and they may share the glory and advantages that are due to the patriot bands of Ireland.]

"Many of the military feel the love of liberty glow within their breasts, and have [already to] joined the national standard; receive [those] with open arms, such as shall follow so glorious an example, they can render signal service to the cause of freedom, and shall be rewarded according to their deserts: but for the wretch who turns his sword against his native country, let the national vengeance be visited on him, let him find no quarter, two other crimes demand—

"Rouse all the energies of your souls; call forth all the merit and abilities which a vicious government consigned to obscurity, und under the conduct of your chosen leaders march with a steady step to victory; heed not the glare of [a mercenary] hired soldiery, or *aristocratic yeomanry*, they cannot stand the vigorous shock of freemen, [close with them man to man, and let them see what vigour the cause of freedom can.] Their trappings and their arms will soon be yours, and the detested government of England to which we vow eternal hatred, shall learn that the treasures [she, it] *they* exhaust on [their mercenary] its accoutred slaves for the purpose of butchering Irishmen, shall but further enable us to turn their swords on its devoted head.

"Attack them in every direction by day and by night; avail yourselves of the natural advantages of your country, which are innumerable, *and with which you are better acquainted than they;* where you cannot oppose them in full force, constantly harass their rear and their flanks; cut off their provisions and magazines, and prevent them as much as possible from uniting their forces; let whatever moments you cannot [pass in] devote to fighting for your country, be [devoted to] passed in learning how to fight for it, or preparing the means of war; for war, war alone must occupy every mind, and every hand in Ireland, until its long oppressed soil be purged of all its enemies.

"Vengeance, Irishmen, vengeance on your oppressors. Remember what thousands of your dearest friends have perished by their [murders, cruel plots] *merciless orders;* remember their burnings, their rackings, their torturings, their military massacres, and their legal murders. Remember ORR."

The briefs in this case are still in existence. The present owner of them was, in '98, an apprentice to Mr. A. Fitzgerald, agent for the defence, and was employed to write down the defence, from *John Sheares' dictation.* These briefs (for the 4th and 12th July) possess, therefore, unusual interest. They are clear, masculine, and sagacious. In them John Sheares plainly enough tells his counsel to save his brother at his expense.

The back is torn off the brief for the 4th, which contains the main case for the defence; but the "additional brief, on behalf of the Prisoners," is directed to "George Ponsonby, Esq.," and "with you, J. P. Curran, Wm. C. Plunket, Leonard MacNally;" yet formally Curran only spoke for Henry Sheares.

The brief must have struck dismay into the counsel's heart. Covered in the usual language of advocacy, it disclosed that, on the 10th of May, John had undertaken to find out what United Men were in Armstrong's regiment; that Armstrong entreated secrecy; that the two brothers were called on in Baggot-street, at four o'clock, on the same day, by Armstrong, and there discussed with him the taking of Lehaunstown. On the evening of the 11th, and twice on the 12th, they met. On Sunday, Armstrong dined with them, and John wrote down many names of officers and men, including Captain Crofton, Lieutenant Wilkinson, &c., who could be relied on. A return of the number of organized and of armed men in the different counties was also on the same paper. This paper was found on John's person when he was arrested. It seems to have greatly alarmed him and his agent. It was not only proved, but A. Kearney swore that he and John Sheares were at a meeting in Werburgh-street, where the calculations were made.

Armstrong *may* for a moment have doubted which to sell himself to—the United Irish, or the Castle; for he expressed great anxiety about his commission in case of a revolution, and "to which the prisoner John replied, that it was more probable they would make him Colonel, as Colonel Lestrange was a violent man against them." So it ran first in the brief, but was altered to, "that they ought rather make him Colonel, as Sir Laurence Parsons had resigned."

He had a bargainer's eye on every one—even on Parsons, his patron and benefactor; for he asked John Sheares, if Sir Laurence was "united," and that he'd like to talk to him on the subject.

Here is Armstrong at home with the family on Sunday night, whom he crunched like a shark next day:—

"During dinner, and until the females withdrew, the most perfect picture of domestic happiness, that could soften the most obdurate heart, was presented in the family then collected together. It consisted of the prisoners' mother and sister, and the wife and three young children of the prisoner Henry, on all of whom he doats with the tenderest affection. Yet could not this scene move the prosecutor from his purposed treachery! On the contrary, he was very lively, and seemed to enjoy the ruin he meditated. When the wine had circulated pretty freely, the prosecutor again renewed the political theme—spoke in the harshest terms of the government, and particularly of the Chancellor, Speaker, and some others, whom he termed the prime movers of all the cruelties, military and civil, that were inflicted on the people. Among many other instances which he cited to inflame the passions of the prisoners, he mentioned one that deserves notice. He said he was on guard one night at the Castle, when a guard was demanded of him to quell some tumult in the Liberties; that the orders expressly given by Major Sirr to him were, to desire the officer who was to command the party going on that service, *to be sure to shed blood enough—to spare neither man, woman, nor child—and, at his peril, to take no prisoners;* that he did, accordingly, give those orders, and that the officer entirely disobeyed them, and brought back some prisoners, for which he was violently abused by Major Sirr."

In nothing does John's superiority appear more than in his self-sacrificing care for his brother. Surely this **is a** clear direction to his counsel to save Henry at *any* rate:—

"It is suggested to counsel that as the only means by which any of the overt acts, committed *exclusively* by the said John, can attach upon the said Henry, arise from the alleged conversation, &c., of both the prisoners, in presence of the prosecutor, for the purpose of overturning the government, &c., the entire force of the prisoners' defence should be directed to show, in the first instance, that at these interviews nothing occurred but conversations started by the prosecutor himself, and afterwards distorted by him into criminal consultations; and, secondly, that whatever consultations can be suspected to have passed between the prosecutor and John, Henry had no concern in—none of the overt acts laid in the indictment having been committed in his presence, nor with his concurrence or knowledge. Possessed of complete domestic happiness, he felt it a duty he owed his family and self, to avoid engaging in any political controversy, by which he had already so severely injured them. The same motives actuated the said John to preserve to the said Henry the full advantage of this prudent resolution, though more addicted, from nature and situation, to indulge his own political propensities; he endeavoured to avert from the said Henry any inconvenience or injury that might result from his (the said John's) conduct. But the artifice of the prosecutor baffled him, and apparently connected both in this transaction. Yet when it is considered, that at the first introduction between the prosecutor and the prisoner Henry, which certainly was entirely unsought for by the latter, no political conversation whatsoever took place; that he, Henry, was never present when any of the names of officers or sergeants were written or produced; that at two of the meetings between the prosecutor and John, Henry was absent; that in no instance did Henry take upon him any part, *or promise to do any act,* nor to procure any of the information sought for; that no writing, or other document whatsoever, was found in *his possession;* that though John, his brother, lived in his house, their papers were wholly distinct, and those of each secret and unknown to the other; that it can in no instance be shown that Henry associated with any individual suspected of being concerned in this rebellion."

In reference to the proclamation, after many palliations and speaking of it as a rude and hypothetical "scroll," as it surely was, the brief (or rather John Sheares) says:—

"But what the real object of it was cannot appear, but by explanation and evidence of the writer's opinions, relative to points mentioned therein. (The justification of his opinions on some of these points is considered by the prisoner, in whose desk these papers were found, of more importance than his personal safety.)"

Poor fellow! every one's testimony, man's and woman's, goes to show that he was the more humane, as he was the braver and the more earnest, of the brothers.

There is one other fact about Armstrong, better told in the brief than in any narrative:—

"When taken to the guard-room at the Castle, another instance occurred of the prisoner John's total unconsciousness that any intercourse he had had with the prosecutor was of a criminal nature. While there in custody, the prosecutor entered—expressed his surprise and concern at seeing the prisoner there—inquired if there was any danger of prisoner, or if the government had any charge against him—offered his services in the most friendly manner. Prisoner, instead of suspecting or fearing him, as he naturally would have done, if conscious he could injure him, felt and expressed himself as highly grateful for such friendly attention. Said all he feared was that a certain paper had been found in his desk; that if it was, he would certainly be committed; recommended to the prosecutor to withdraw immediately from the room, lest any injurious suspicion might attach upon him, if seen in conversation with the prisoner; (prisoner thought that prosecutor's anxiety for him made him forget his former caution relative to their acquaintance;) prisoner requested prosecutor that he would call upon his family and pacify their fears, which he promised to do, and departed."

Toler's* speech was as sanguinary and confused as possible.

Armstrong was examined by Saurin, and swore to the facts we have stated (he had no occasion for perjury); and his cross-examination only proved him blood-thirsty, an Atheist, and a traitor.

Application was made for adjournment, but in vain. Mr. G. Ponsonby opened for Henry, and Mr. Plunket for John Sheares. Mr. M'Nally pressed some law points with little effect. Three witnesses were examined, to prove Captain Armstrong an Atheist; two that he was an avowed Republican and rebel. Several witnesses were examined to the character of the Sheares.

It was then twelve at night—the trial had begun at nine; and, worn with fifteen hours of anxiety, in a crowded court, in the midst of the summer, CURRAN rose and said:—

My Lord, before I address you or the Jury, I would wish to make one preliminary observation; it may be an observation only, it may be a request: for myself, I am indifferent, but I feel I am now unequal to the duty—I am sinking under the weight of it. We all know the character of the jury; the interval of their separation must be short, if it

* He had been made Attorney, and Stewart Solicitor-General on the 10th of July.

should be deemed necessary to separate them. I protest I have sunk under this trial. If I must go on, the court must bear with me, the jury may also bear with me: I will go on, until I sink. But after a sitting of sixteen hours, with only twenty minutes' interval, in these times, I should hope it would not be thought an obtrusive request to hope for a few hours' interval for repose, or rather for recollection.

Lord Carleton—What say you, Mr. Attorney-General?

Mr. Attorney-General—My lords, I feel such public inconvenience from adjourning cases of this kind, that I cannot consent. The counsel for the prisoners cannot be more exhausted than those for the prosecution. If they do not choose to speak to the evidence, we shall give up our right to speak, and leave the matter to the court altogether. They have had two speeches already [Mr. Ponsonby had spoken], and leaving them unreplied to is a great concession.

Lord Carleton—We would be glad to accommodate as much as possible. I am as much exhausted as any other; but we think it better to go on.

Mr. Curran—Gentlemen of the jury, it seems that much has been conceded to us. God help us! I do not know what has been conceded to me, if so insignificant a person may have extorted the remark. Perhaps it is a concession that I rise in such a state of mind and body, of collapse and deprivation, as to feel but a little spark of indignation raised by the remark, that much has been conceded to the counsel for the prisoner; much has been conceded to the prisoners! Almighty and merciful God, who lookest down upon us, what are the times to which we are reserved, when we are told, that much has been conceded to prisoners who are put upon their trial at a moment like this, of more darkness and night of the human intellect, than a darkness of the natural period of twenty-four hours; that public convenience cannot spare a respite of a few hours to those who are accused for their lives, and that much has been conceded to the advocate, almost exhausted in the poor remark which he has endeavoured to make upon it.

My countrymen, I do pray you, by the awful duty which you owe your country, by that sacred duty which you owe your character (and I know how you feel it), I do obtest you, by the Almighty God, to have mercy upon my client, to save him, not from guilt, but from the baseness of his accuser, and the pressure of the treatment under which I am sinking.

With what spirit did you leave your habitations this day? with what state of mind and heart did you come here from your families? with what sentiments did you leave your children, to do an act of great public importance, to pledge yourselves at the throne of eternal justice, by the awful and solemn obligation of an oath, to do perfect, cool, impartial and steady justice, between the accuser and the accused? Have you come abroad under the idea, that public fury is clamorous for blood? that you are put there under the mere formality or memorial of death, and ought to gratify that fury with the blood for which it seems to thirst? If you are, I have known some of you, more than one, or two, or three in some of those situations, where the human heart speaks its honest sentiments. I think I ought to know you well, you ought to know me, and there are some of you who ought to listen to what so obscure an individual may say, not altogether without some degree of personal confidence and respect. I will not solicit your attention by paying the greatest compliment which man can pay to man; but I say, I hold you in regard as being worthy of it; I will speak such language as I would not stoop to hold, if I did not think you worthy of it.

Gentlemen, I will not be afraid of beginning with what some may think I should avoid, the disastrous picture which you must have met upon your way to this court. A more artful advocate might endeavour to play with you, in supposing you to possess a degree of pity and of feeling beyond that of any other human being. But I, gentlemen, am not afraid of beginning by warning you against those prejudices which all must possess; by speaking strongly against them; by striking upon the string, if not strong enough to snap it, will wake it into vibration. Unless you make an exertion beyond the power almost of men to make, you are not fit to try this cause. You may preside at such an execution as the witness would extol himself for—at the sentence flowing from a very short inquiry into reason; but you are not fit to discharge the awful trust of honest men, coming into the box, indifferent as they stand unsworn, to pronounce a verdict of death and infamy, or of existence and of honour. You have only the interval between this and pronouncing your verdict to reflect, and the other interval when you are resigning up your last breath, between your verdict and your grave, when you may lament that you did not as you ought.

Do you think I want to flatter your passions? I would scorn myself for it. I want to address your reason, to call upon your consciences, to remind you of your oaths, and the consequence of that verdict, which, upon the law and the fact, you must give between the accuser and the accused. Part of what I shall say must of necessity be addressed to the court, for it is matter of law; but upon this subject, every observation in point of law is so inseparably blended with the fact, that I cannot pretend to say that I can discharge your attention, gentlemen, even when I address the court. On the contrary, I shall the more desire your attention, not so much that you may understand what I shall say, as what the court shall say.

Gentlemen, this indictment is founded upon the statute 25th Edward III.

The statute itself begins with a melancholy observation on the proneness to deterioration which has been found in countries unfortunately to take place in their criminal law, particularly in the law respecting high treason. The statute begins with reciting, that in the uncertainty of adjudications, it became difficult to know what was treason, and what was not; and to remove further difficulty, it professes to declare all species of treason that should thereafter be so considered; and by thus regulating the law, to secure the state and the constitution, and the persons of those interested in the executive departments of the government, from the common acts of violence that might be used to their destruction.

The three first clauses of the statute seem to have gone a great way indeed upon the subject; because the object of the provisions was to protect the person, and I beg of you to understand what I mean by person, I mean the *natural person;* I mean no figure of speech, not the monarch in the abstract, but the natural man. The first clause was made without the smallest relation to the executive power, but solely to the natural body and person. The words are, "when a man doth compass or imagine the death of the King, or of our lady his Queen, or their eldest son and heir, and thereof be, upon sufficient proof, attainted of open deed by men of his condition, he shall be a traitor." This I say relates only to the natural person of the King. The son and heir of the King is mentioned in the same manner, but he has no power; and, therefore, a compassing his death must mean the death of his natural person, and so must it be in the case of the King. To conceive the purpose of destroying a common subject, was once a felony of death, and that was expressed in the same language, compassing and imagining the death of the subject. It was thought right to dismiss that severe rigour of the law in the case of the subject, but it was thought right to continue it in the case of the King, in contradistincton to all the subjects within the realm.

The statute, after describing the persons, describes what shall be evidence of that high and abominable guilt; it must appear by open deed; the intention of the guilty heart must be proved by evidence of the open deed committed towards the accomplishment of the design. Perhaps in the hurry of speaking, perhaps from the mistakes of reporters, sometimes from one, and sometimes from the other, judges are too often made to say, that such or such an overt act is, if proved to have been committed, ground upon which the jury must find the party guilty of the accusation. I must deny the position, not only in the reason of the thing, but am fortified by the ablest writers upon the law of treason. In the reason of the thing, because the design entertained, and act done, are matters for the jury. Whether a party compassed the King's death or not, is matter for the jury: and, therefore, if a certain fact be proved, it is nonsense to say, that such a conclusion *must* follow;

because a conclusion of law would then be pronounced by the jury, not by the court. I am warranted in this by the writers cited by Mr. Justice Foster; and, therefore, gentlemen, upon the first count in the indictment, you are to decide a plain matter of fact, 1st, whether the prisoner did compass and imagine the death of the King? and whether there be any act proved, or apparent means taken, which he resorted to for the perpetration of the crime?

Upon this subject, many observations have already been made before me. I will take the liberty of making one, I do not know whether it has been made before. Even in a case where the overt act stated has of its own nature gone to the person of the King, still it is left to the jury to decide, whether it was done with the criminal purpose alleged, or not. In Russell's case, there was an overt act of a conspiracy to seize the guards; the natural consequence threatened from an act of gross violence so immediately approaching the King's person, might fairly be said to affect his life; but still it was left to the jury to decide, whether that was done for the purpose of compassing the King's death.

I mention this, because I think it a strong answer to those kind of expressions, which in bad times fall from the mouths of prosecutors, neither law nor poetry, but sometimes half metaphysical. Laws may be enacted in the spirit of sound policy, and supported by superior reason; but when only half considered, and their provisions half enumerated, they become the plague of the government, and the grave of principle. It is that kind of refinement and cant which overwhelmed the law of treason, and brought it to a metaphysical death; the laws are made to pass through a contorted understanding, vibratory and confused, and, therefore, after a small interval from the first enactment of any law in Great Britain, the dreams of fancy get around, and the law is lost in the mass of absurd comment. Hence it was that the statute gave its awful declarations to those glossaries; so that if any case arise, apparently within the statute, they were not to indulge themselves in conjecture, but refer to the standard, and abide by the law as marked out for them. Therefore, I say, that the issue for the jury here is to decide in the words of the statute, whether the prisoners did compass the death of the King; and whether they can say, upon their oaths, that there is any overt act proved in evidence, manifesting an intention of injury to the natural person of the King?

I know that the semblance of authority may be used to contradict me: if any man can reconcile himself to the miserable toil of poring over the records of guilt, he will find them marked, not in black, but in red, the blood of the unfortunate, leaving the marks of folly, barbarity, and tyranny. But I am glad that men who in some situations appear not to have had the pulse of honest compassion, have made sober reflections in the hour of political disgrace. Such has been the fate of Lord Coke, who, in the triumph of insolence and power, pursued a conduct which, in the hour of calm retreat, he regretted in the language of sorrow and disappointment. He then held a language which I willingly repeat, "that a conspiracy to levy war, was no act of compassing the murder of the King." There he spoke the language of law and of good sense; for a man shall not be charged with one crime, and convicted of another. It is a narrow and a cruel policy, to make a conspiracy to levy war an act of compassing the King's death; because it is a separate and distinct offence; because it is calling upon the honest affections of the heart, and creating those pathetical effusions, which confound all distinct principles of law, a grievance not to be borne in a state where the laws ought to be certain.

This reasoning is founded upon the momentary supposition that the evidence is true; for you are to recollect the quarter from whence it comes; there has been an attempt by precipitate confession, to transfer guilt to innocence, in order to escape the punishment of the law. Here, gentlemen, there is evidence of levying war, which act, it is said, tends to the death of the King: that is a constructive treason, calculated as a trap for the loyalty of a jury; therefore you should set bounds to proceedings of that kind; for it is an abuse of the law, to make one class of offence, sufficiently punished already, evidence of another. Every court, and every jury, should set themselves against crimes, when they come to determine upon distinct and specified guilt: they are not to encourage a confusion of crimes, by disregarding the distinction of punishments; nor show the effusion of their loyalty, by an effusion of blood.

I cannot but say that when cases of this kind have been under judgment in Westminster-hall, there was some kind of natural reason to excuse this confusion in the reports—the propriety of making the person of the King secure. A war immediately adjoining the precincts of the palace, a riot in London, might endanger the life of the King; but can the same law prevail in every part of the British empire? It may be an overt act of compassing the King's death to levy war in Great Britain; but can it be so in Jamaica, in the Bahama isles, or in Corsica, when it was annexed to the British empire? Suppose at that time a man had been indicted there for compassing the King's death, and the evidence was, that he intended to transfer the dominion of the island to the Genoese, or the French; what would you say, if you were told that was an act by which he intended to murder the King? By seizing Corsica, he was to murder the King? How can there be any immediate attempt upon the King's life, by such a proceeding? It is not possible, and therefore no such consequence can be probably inferred; and, therefore, I call upon you to listen to the court with respect, but I also call upon you to listen to common sense, and consider, whether the conspiring to raise war can in this country be an overt act of compassing the King's death in this country? I will go further: if the statute of Edward III. had been conceived to make a conspiracy to levy war an overt act of compassing the King's death, it would be unnecessary to make it penal by any subsequent statute; and yet subsequent statutes were enacted for that purpose; which I consider an unanswerable argument, that it was not considered as coming within the purview of the clause against compassing the King's death.

Now, gentlemen, you will be pleased to consider what was the evidence brought forward to support this indictment. I do not think it necessary to exhaust your attention by stating at large the evidence given by Captain Armstrong. He gives an account which we shall have occasion to examine, with regard to its credibility. He stated his introduction, first to Mr. Henry Sheares, afterwards to his brother; and he stated a conversation which you do not forget, so strange has it been! But in the whole course of his evidence, so far from making any observation, or saying a word in connexion with the power at war with the King, he expressly said, that the insurrection, by whomsoever prepared, or by what infatuation encouraged, was to be a home exertion, independent of any foreign interference whatever. And, therefore, I am warranted in saying, that such an insurrection does not come within the first clause of the statute. It cannot come within the second, of adhering to the King's enemies; because that means his foreign enemies; and here, so far from any intercourse with them, they were totally disregarded.

Adhering to the King's enemies means co-operating with them, sending them provisions, or intelligence, or supplying them with arms. But I venture to say, that there has not been any one case deciding that any act can be an adherence to a foreign enemy, which was not calculated for the advantage of that enemy. In the case of Jackson, Hensey, and Lord Preston, the parties had gone as far as they could in giving assistance. So it was in Quigley's. But, in addition to this, I must repeat, that it is utterly unnecessary the law should be otherwise; for levying war is, of itself, a crime; therefore it is unnecessary, by a strained construction, to say, that levying war, or conspiring to levy war, should come within any other clause equally penal, but not so descriptive.

But, gentlemen, suppose I am mistaken in both points of my argument; suppose the prisoners (if the evidence were true) did compass the King's death, and adhere to the King's enemies; what are you to found your verdict upon? Upon your oaths; what are they to be founded upon? Upon the oath of the witness: and what is that founded upon? Upon this, and this only, that he does believe that there is an eternal God, an intelligent supreme existence, capable of inflicting eternal punishment for offences, or conferring eternal compensation, upon man, after he has passed the boundary of the grave! But where the witness believes he is possessed of a perishing soul, and that there is nothing upon which punishment or reward can be exerted, he proceeds regardless of the number of his offences, and undisturbed by the terrors of exhausted fancy, which might save you from the fear that your verdict is founded upon perjury. I suppose he imagines that the body is actuated by some kind of animal machinery. I know not in what language to describe his notions. Suppose his opinion of the beautiful system framed by the Almighty hand to be, that it is all folly and blindness, compared to the manner in which he considers himself to have been created; or his abominable heart conceives its ideas; or his tongue communicates his notions. Suppose him, I say, to think so; what is perjury to him? He needs no creed, if he thinks his miserable body can take eternal refuge in the grave, and the last puff of his nostrils can send his soul into annihilation! He laughs at the idea of eternal justice, and tells you that the grave, into which he sinks as a log, forms an entrenchment against the throne of God, and the vengeance of exasperated justice!

Do you not feel, my fellow-countrymen, a sort of anticipated consolation, in reflecting, that Religion—which gave us comfort in our early days, enabled us to sustain the stroke of affliction, and endeared us to one another,—when we see our friends sinking into the earth, fills us with the expectation that we rise again; that we but sleep for a while, to wake for ever? But what kind of communion can you hold, what interchange expect, what confidence place, in that abject slave, that condemned, despaired of wretch, who acts under the idea that he is only the folly of a moment, that he cannot step beyond the threshold of the grave, that that which is an object of terror to the best, and of hope to the confiding, is to him contempt, or despair?

Bear with me, my countrymen; I feel my heart run away with me—the worst men only can be cool. What is the law of this country? If the witness does not believe in God, or a future state, you cannot swear him. What swear him upon? Is it upon the book, or the leaf? You might as well swear him by a bramble, or a coin. The ceremony of kissing is only the external symbol, by which man seals himself to the precept, and says, "May God so help me, as I swear the truth." He is then attached to the divinity, upon the condition of telling truth; and he expects mercy from heaven, as he performs his undertaking. But the infidel!—By what can you catch his soul, or by what can

22

you hold it? You repulse him from giving evidence; for he has no conscience, no hope to cheer him, no punishment to dread!

What is the evidence touching that unfortunate young man? What said his own relation Mr. Shervington? He had talked to him freely, had known him long. What kind of character did he give of him? Paine was his creed and his philosophy. He had drawn his maxims of politics from the vulgar and furious anarchy broached by Mr. Paine. His ideas of religion were adopted from the vulgar maxims of the same man, the scandal of inquiry, the blasphemer of his God as of his King. He bears testimony against himself, that he submitted to the undertaking of reading both his abominable tracts, that abominable abomination of all abominations, Paine's "Age of Reason," professing to teach mankind, by acknowledging that he did not learn himself! working upon debauched and narrow understandings. Why not swear the witness upon the vulgar maxims of that base fellow, that wretched outlaw and fugitive from his country and his God? Is it not lamentable to see a man labouring under an incurable disease, and fond of his own blotches?

"Do you wish" says he, "to know my sentiments with regard to politics? I have learned them from Paine! I do not love a King, and if no other executioner could be found, I would myself plunge a dagger into the heart of George III., because he is a King, and because he is my King. I swear by the sacred missal of Paine, I would think it a meritorious thing to plunge a dagger into his heart, to whom I had devoted a soul, which Mr. Paine says I have not to lend." Is this the casual effusion of a giddy young man, not considering the meaning of what he said? If it were said among a parcel of boarding-school misses, where he might think he was giving specimens of his courage by nobly denying religion, there might be some excuse. There is a latitude assumed upon some such occasions. A little blasphemy and a little obscenity passes for wit in some companies. But recollect it was not to a little miss whom he wished to astonish that he mentioned these sentiments; but a kinsman, a man of boiling loyalty. I confess I did not approve of his conduct in the abstract, talking of running a man through the body; but I admired the honest boldness of the soldier who expressed his indignation in such warm language. If Mr. Shervington swore true, Captain Armstrong must be a forsworn witness; it comes to that simple point. You cannot put it upon other ground. I put it to your good sense, I am not playing with your understandings, I am putting foot to foot, and credit to credit. One or the other of the two must be perjured; which of them is it? If you disbelieve Captain Armstrong, can you find a verdict of blood upon his evidence?

Gentlemen, I go further: I know your horror of crime—your warmth of loyalty. They are among the reasons why I respect and regard you. I ask you, then, will you reject such a witness? or would you dismiss the friend you regarded, or the child you loved, upon the evidence of such a witness? Suppose him to tell his own story:—"I went to your friend, or your child—I addressed myself in the garb of friendship—in the smile of confidence, I courted confidence, in order to betray it—I traduced you, spoke all the evil I could against you, to inflame him—I told him, your father does not love you." If he went to you, and told you all this—that he inflamed your child, and abused you to your friend, and said, "I come now to increase it, by the horror of superadded cruelty," would you dismiss from your love and affection the child or the friend you had loved for years? You would not prejudge them. You would examine the consistency of the man's story—you would listen to it with doubt, and receive it with hesitation.

Says Captain Armstrong—"Byrne was my bookseller; from him I bought my little study of blasphemy and obscenity, with which I amused myself." "Shall I introduce Mr. Sheares to you?"—not saying which. What is done then? He thought it was not right till he saw Captain Clibborn. Has he stated any reason why he supposed Mr. Sheares had any wish at all to be introduced to him?—any reason for supposing that Byrne's principles were of that kind?—or any reason, why he imagined the intercourse was to lead to anything improper?

It is most material that, he says, he never spoke to Byrne upon political subjects; therefore, he knew nothing of Byrne's principles, nor Byrne of his. But the proposal was made, and he was so alarmed, that he would not give an answer till he saw his Captain. Is not this incredible?

There is one circumstance which made an impression upon my mind: that he assumed the part of a public informer, and, in the first instance, came to the field with pledgets and bandages; he was scarcely off the table, when a witness came to his credit. It is the first time that I saw a witness taking fright at his own credit, and sending up a person to justify his character.

Consider how he has fortified it: he told it all to Captain Clibborn! He saw him every evening when he returned like a bee, with his thighs loaded with evidence. What is the defence? That the witness is unworthy of belief. My clients say, their lives are not to be touched by such a man; he is found to be an informer—he marks the victim! You know the world too well, not to know that every falsehood is reduced to a certain degree of malleability by an alloy of truth. Such stories as these are not pure and simple falsehoods: look at your Oateses, your Bedloes, and Dugdales!

I am disposed to believe, shocking as it is, that this witness had the heart, when he was surrounded by the little progeny of my client—when he was sitting in the mansion in which he was hospitably entertained—when he saw the old mother supported by the piety of her son, and the children basking in the parental fondness of the father—that he saw the scene, and smiled at it; contemplated the havoc he was to make, consigning them to the storms of a miserable world, without having an anchorage in the kindness of a father! Can such horror exist, and not waken the rooted vengeance of an eternal God? But it cannot reach this man beyond the grave. Therefore, I uphold him here. I can imagine it, gentlemen, because, when the mind becomes destitute of the principles of morality and religion, all within the miserable being is left a black and desolate waste, never cheered by the rays of tenderness and humanity. When the belief of eternal justice is gone from the soul of man, horror and execution may set up their abode. I can believe that the witness—with what view, I cannot say—with what hope, I cannot conjecture—you may—did meditate the consigning of these two men to death, their children to beggary and reproach, abusing the hospitality with which he was received, that he might afterwards come here and crown his work, having obtained the little spark of truth by which his mass of falsehood was to be animated.

I have talked of the inconsistency of the story. Do you believe it, gentlemen? The case of my client is, that the witness is perjured; and you are appealed to, in the name of that ever-living God, whom you revere, but whom he despiseth, to consider, that there is something to save him from the baseness of such an accuser.

But I go back to the testimony; I may wander from it, but it is my duty to stay with it. Says he: "Byrne makes an important application—I was not accustomed to it; I never spoke to him, and yet he, with whom I had no connexion, introduces me to Sheares—this is a *true brother*." You see, gentlemen, I state this truly—he never talked to Byrne about politics. How could Byrne know his principles? By inspiration? He was to know the edition of the man, as he knew the edition of books. "You may repose all confidence." I ask not is this true; but I say it can be nothing else than false. I do not ask you to say it is doubtful; it is a case of blood, of life or death; and you are to add to the terrors of a painful death, the desolation of a family—overwhelming the aged with sorrow, and the young with infamy. Gentlemen, I should disdain to reason with you; I am pinning your minds down to one point, to show you to demonstration that nothing can save your minds from the evidence of such perjury; not because you may think it may be false, but because it is impossible it can be true. I put into one of the scales of justice that execrable perjury, and I put into the other, the life, the fame, the fortune, the children of my client. Let not the balance tremble as you hold it; and, as you hold it now, so may the balance of eternal justice be held for you.

But is it upon his inconsistency only I call upon you to reject him? I call in aid the evidence of his own kinsmen, Mr. Shervington, and Mr. Drought; the evidence of Mr. Bride and Mr. Graydon. Before you can believe Armstrong, you must believe that all those are perjured. What are his temptations to perjury? The hope of bribery and reward. And he did go up with his sheets of paper in his hand: here is one, it speaks treason—here is another, the accused grows paler—here is a third, it opens another vein. Had Shervington any temptation of that kind? No; let not the honest and genuine soldier lose the credit of it. He has paid a great compliment to the proud integrity of the King, his master, when he did venture, at a time like this, to give evidence, "I would not have come for one hundred guineas." I could not refuse the effusion of my heart, and exclaiming, may the blessings of God pour upon you, and may you never want a hundred guineas!

There is another circumstance. I think I saw it strike your attention, my lords; it was the horrid tale of the three servants whom he met upon the road. They had no connexion with the rebels; if they had, they were open to a summary proceeding. He hangs up one, shoots a second, and administers torture to the body of the third, in order to make him give evidence. Why, my lords, did you feel nothing stir within you? Our adjudications had condemned the application of torture for the extraction of evidence. When a wild and furious assassin had made a deadly attempt upon a life of much public consequence, it was proposed to put him to the torture, in order to discover his accomplices. I scarcely know whether to admire most the awful and impressive lesson given by Felton, or the doctrine stated by the judges of the land. "No," said he, "put me not to the torture; for in the extravagance of my pain, I may be brought to accuse yourselves." What say the judges? "It is not allowable by the law and constitution of England to inflict torture upon any man, or to extract evidence under the coercion of personal sufferings." Apply that to this case: if the unfortunate man did himself dread the application of such an engine for the extraction of evidence, let it be an excuse for his degradation that he sought to avoid the pain of body by public infamy. But there is another observation more applicable:—Says Mr. Drought, "Had you no feeling, or do you think you will escape future vengeance?" "Oh, sir, I thought you knew my ideas too well to talk in that way." Merciful God! Do you think it is upon the evidence of such a man that you ought to consign a fellow-subject to death? He who would hang up a miserable peasant, to gratify caprice, could laugh at remonstrance, and say, "You know my ideas of futurity."

If he thought so little of murdering a fellow-creature, without trial and without ceremony, what kind of compunction can he feel within himself, when you are made the instruments of his savage barbarity? He kills a miserable wretch, looking, perhaps, for bread for his children, and who falls, unaccused, uncondemned. What compunction can he feel at sacrificing other victims, when he considers death as eternal sleep, and the darkness of annihilation. These victims are at this moment led out to public execution; he has marked them for the grave—he will not bewail the object of his own work: they are passing through the vale of death, while he is dozing over the expectancy of annihilation.

Gentlemen, I am too weak to follow the line of observation I had marked out; but I trust I am warranted in saying, that if you weigh the evidence, the balance will be in favour of the prisoners..

But there is another topic, or two, to which I must solicit your attention. If I had been stronger, in a common case, I would not have said so much; weak as I am here, I must say more.

It may be said that the parole evidence may be put out of the case; attribute the conduct of Armstrong to folly, or passion, or whatever else you please, you may safely repose upon the written evidence. This calls for an observation or two. As to Mr. Henry Sheares, that written evidence, even if the hand-writing were fully proved, does not apply to him. I do not say it was not admissible. The writings of Sidney found in his closet were read, justly, according to some; but I do not wish to consider that now. But I say, the evidence of Mr. Dwyer has not satisfactorily established the handwriting of John. I do not say it is not proved to a certain extent; but it is proved in the very slightest manner that you ever saw paper proved: it is barely evidence to go to you; and the witness might be mistaken.

An unpublished writing cannot be an overt act of treason; so it is laid down expressly by Hale and Foster. A number of cases have occurred, and decisions have been pronounced, asserting that writings are not overt acts, for want of publication; but if they plainly relate to an overt act proved, they may be left to the jury for their consideration. But here it has no reference to the overt act laid; it could not be intended for publication until after the unfortunate event of revolution had taken place; and, therefore, it could not be designed to create insurrection. Gentlemen, I am not counsel for Mr. John Sheares, but I would be guilty of cruelty, if I did not make another observation. This might be an idle composition, or the translation of idle absurdity from the papers of another country. The manner in which it was found leads me to think that the more probable. A writing designed for such an event as charged, would hardly be left in a writing-box, unlocked, in a room near the hall-door. The manner of its finding also shows two things; that Henry Sheares knew nothing of it, for he had an opportunity of destroying it, as Alderman Alexander said he had; and further, that he could not have imagined his brother had such a design; and it is impossible, if the paper had been designed for such purposes, that it would not be communicated to him.

There is a point to which I will beseech the attention of your lordships. I know your humanity, and it will not be applied merely because I am exhausted or fatigued. You have only one witness to any overt act of treason. There is no decision upon the point in this country. Jackson's case was the first; Lord Clonmel made allusion to the point; but a jury ought not to find guilty upon the testimony of a single witness. It is the opinion of Foster, that by the common law one witness, if believed, was sufficient. Lord Coke's opinion is, that two were necessary: they are great names; no man looks upon the works of Foster with more veneration than myself, and I would not compare him with the depreciated credit of Coke; I would rather leave Lord Coke to the character which Foster gives him; that he was one of the ablest lawyers, independent of some particulars, that ever existed in England. In the wild extravagance, heat, and cruel reign of the Tudors, such doctrines of treason had gone abroad as drenched the kingdom with blood. By the construction of crown lawyers, and the shameful complaisance of juries, many sacrifices had been made, and, therefore, it was necessary to prune away these excesses, by the statute of Edward VI., and, therefore, there is every reason to imagine, from the history of the times, that Lord Coke was right in saying, not by new statute, but by the common law, confirmed and redeemed by declaratory acts, the trials were regulated.

A law of Philip and Mary was afterwards enacted; some think it was a repeal of the statute of Edward VI.—some think not. I mention this diversity of opinions, with this view, that in this country, upon a new point of that kind, the weight of criminal prosecution will turn the scale in favour of the prisoner, and that the court will be of opinion that the statute 7th Wm. III. did not enact any new thing, unknown to the common law, but redeemed it from abuse. What was the state of England? The King had been declared to have abdicated the throne; prosecutions, temporizing juries, and the arbitrary construction of judges, condemned to the scaffold those who were to protect the crown, men who knew that, after the destruction of the cottage, the palace was endangered. It was not, then, the enactment of any thing new; it was founded on the caution of the times, and derived from the maxims of the constitution. I know the peevishness with which Burnet observed upon that statute; he is reprehended in a modest manner by Foster; but what says Blackstone, of great authority, of the clearest head, and the profoundest reading? He agrees with Montesquieu, the French philosopher:—

"In cases of treason, there is the accused's oath of allegiance to counterpoise the information of a single witness; and that may perhaps be one reason, why the law requires a *double* testimony to convict him: though the principal reason undoubtedly is, to secure the subject from being sacrificed to fictitious conspiracies, which have been the engines of profligate and crafty politicians in all ages."*

Gentlemen, I do not pretend to say that you are bound by an English act of parliament. You may condemn upon the testimony of a single witness. You, to be sure, are too proud to listen to the wisdom of an English law! Illustrious independents! You may murder under the semblance of judicial forms, because you are proud of your blessed independence! You pronounce that to be legally done which would be murder in England, because you are proud! You may imbrue your hands in blood, because you are too proud to be bound by a foreign act of parliament; and when you are to look for what is to save you from the abuse of arbitrary power, you will not avail yourself of it, because it is a foreign act of parliament! Is that the independence of an Irish jury? Do I see the heart of any Englishman move, when I say to him, "Thou servile Briton, you cannot condemn upon the perjury of a single witness, because you

* 4, Blackstone's Commentaries, 353.

are held in by the cogency of an act of parliament."

If power seeks to make victims by judicial means, an act of parliament would save you from the perjury of abominable malice. Talk not of proud slavery to law, but lament that you are bound by the integrity and irresistible strength of right reason; and, at the next step, bewail that the all-powerful author of nature has bound himself in the illustrious servitude of his attributes, which prevent him from thinking what is not true, or doing what is not just. Go, then, and enjoy your independence. At the other side of the water, your verdict upon the testimony of a single witness would be murder. But here you can murder without reproach, because there is no act of parliament to bind you to the ties of social life, and save the accused from the breath of a perjured informer. In England, a jury could not pronounce conviction upon the testimony of the purest man, if he stood alone; and yet, what comparison can that case bear with a blighted and marred informer, where every word is proved to be perjury, and every word turns back upon his soul?

I am reasoning for your country and your children. Let me not reason in vain. I am not playing the advocate; you know I am not—your conscience tells you I am not. I put this case to the Bench: The statute 7 Henry III. does not bind this country by its legislative cogency; and will you declare positively, and without doubt, that it is not common law, the enactment of a new one? Will you say it has no weight to influence the conduct of a jury, from the authority of a great and exalted nation—the only nation in Europe where liberty has seated herself? Do not imagine, that the man who praises liberty is singing an idle song; for a moment, it may be the song of a bird in his cage—I know it may. But you are now standing upon an awful isthmus, a little neck of land, where liberty has found a seat. Look about you—look at the state of the country—the tribunals that dire necessity has introduced. Look at this dawn of law, admitting the functions of a jury; I feel a comfort—methinks I see the venerable forms of Hold and Halo looking down upon us, attesting its continuance. Is it your opinion that bloody verdicts are necessary—that blood enough has not been shed—that the bonds of society are not to be drawn close again, nor the scattered fragments of our strength bound together, to make them of force, but they are to be left in that scattered state, in which every little child may break them to pieces? You will do more towards tranquillizing the country, by a verdict of mercy. Guard yourselves against the sanguinary excesses of prejudice or revenge; and, though you think there is a great call of public justice, let no unmerited victim fall.

Gentlemen, I have tired you—I durst not relax. The danger of my client is from the hectic of the moment, which you have fortitude, I trust, to withstand. In that belief, I leave him to you; and as you deal justice and mercy, so may you find it; and I hope that the happy compensation of an honest discharge of your duty may not be deferred till a future existence, which this* witness does not expect, but that you may speedily enjoy the benefits you will have conferred upon your country.

A verdict of Guilty was returned, and the brothers were executed the next day.

* Armstrong.

FOR OLIVER BOND.

[HIGH TREASON.]

SPECIAL COMMISSION, GREEN-STREET.

24th July, 1798.

THREE days after the Sheares died, John M'Cann was tried, defended by Curran, convicted, and hanged. On the 20th, Byrne was tried, and similarly defended, with a like fate. Curran's speeches are not reported.

On the 23rd of July, Oliver Bond, a woollen-draper, of Bridge-street, and a shrewd, kind man, was put to the bar.

The officer of the court charged the prisoner as follows:—

"Mr. Oliver Bond, you stand indicted, for, that not having the fear of God before your eyes, nor the duty of your allegiance considering, but being moved and seduced by the instigation of the devil, you did, with other false traitors, conspire and meet together, and contriving and imagining with all your strength this kingdom to disturb, and to overturn by force of arms, &c., the government of this kingdom, on the 20th day of May, in the thirty-eighth year of the reign of the present King, in the parish of St. Michael the Archangel, did conspire and meet together about the means of overturning the government; and his Majesty of and from his royal state, power, and government of this country to deprive and put; and that you, Oliver Bond, with other false traitors, did meet together, and make resolutions to procure arms and ammunition, for the purpose of arming men to wage war against our Sovereign Lord the King; and did conspire to overturn by force the lawful government of this kingdom, and to change by force the government thereof; and did assemble and meet together to raise a rebellion in this kingdom; to procure arms to aid and assist in said rebellion; and that you, Oliver Bond, did aid and cause Thomas Reynolds to be a colonel in the county of Kildare, to aid and assist in the said rebellion; and did administer unlawful oaths to said Thomas Reynolds, and to certain other persons, to be United Irishmen, for the purpose of overturning by force the government of this kingdom: and that you, the said Oliver Bond, did collect sums of money to furnish arms and ammunition to the persons in said rebellion, against the duty of your allegiance, contrary to his Majesty's peace, his crown, and dignity, and contrary to the form of the statute in that case made and provided. And whereas a public war, both by land and sea, is and hath been carried on by persons exercising the powers of government in France, that you, the said Oliver Bond, not having the fear of God before your eyes, did aid and assist the French and men of France to invade this kingdom, to overturn by force the government of this kingdom, and to compass and imagine the death of the King, and so forth. On this indictment, you, Oliver Bond, have been this day arraigned, and have pleaded not guilty, and for trial have put yourself on God and your country."

The principal witness was Thomas Reynolds, of Kilkea Castle, in the County Kildare. He had been a silk-mercer in Dublin, and was "united" at an early period. In 1797, he was Treasurer, and a Colonel, of Kildare. Soon after he became one of the Leinster Delegates.

There is nothing peculiar in the indictment, nor did any facts additional to what have been stated in Sheares' case appear.

Curran spoke as follows:—

My lords, and gentlemen of the jury, I am counsel for the prisoner at the bar, and it is my duty to lay his case before you. It is a duty that at any time would be a painful one to me, but at present peculiarly so; having, in the course of this long trial, experienced great fatigue both of mind and of body—a fatigue I have felt in common with the learned judges who preside on the bench, and with my brethren of the bar; I feel, as an advocate, for my client, the duty of the awful obligation that has devolved on me. I do not mean, gentlemen of the jury, to dilate on my own personal fatigues; for I am not in the habit of considering my personal ill state of health, or the anxiety of my mind, in discharging my duty to clients in such awful situations as in the present momentous crisis; I have not been in the habit, gentlemen of the jury, to expatiate to you on personal ill health. In addressing myself to jurors on any common subject, I have been in the habit of addressing myself to the interposition of the Court, or to the good-natured consideration of the jury, on behalf of my client. I have mentioned, indeed, my own enfeebled worn-out body, and my worn-out state of mind, not out of any paltry respect to myself, nor to draw your attention to myself, but to induce you to reflect upon this, that in the weakness of the advocate, the case of my client, the prisoner at the bar, is not implicated; for his case is so strong in support of his innocence, that it is not to be weakened by the imbecility or the fatigue of the advocate.

Gentlemen of the jury, I lament that this case has not been brought forward in a simple, and in the usual way, without any extraneous matter being introduced into it, as I think in justice, and as I think in humanity, it ought to have been. I lament that any little artifices should be employed upon so great and solemn a case as this, more especially in desperate times, and upon a more than ordinary occasion; and that some allegations of criminality have been introduced, as to persons and things, that ought not, in my opinion, to have been adverted to in a case like this.

What, for instance, has this case to do with the motion made by Lord Moira, in the House of Lords in Ireland, in February last, or the accidental conversations with Lord Edward Fitzgerald? If you have a feeling for virtue, I trust that Lord Moira will be revered as a character that adds a dignity to the peerage. What made that noble character forego his great fortune, quit his extensive demesnes and the tranquillity of the philosophic mind, but the great and glorious endeavour to do service to his country? I must repeat, he is an honour to the Irish peerage. Let me ask, why was the name of Lord Moira, or Lord Wycombe (who happened to dine at Duke Giffard's), introduced into this trial? what has that motion which Lord Moira introduced into the House of Lords to do with the trial of Mr. Oliver Bond on a charge of high treason?

Gentlemen, much pains have been taken to warm you, and then you are entreated to be cool; when the fire has been kindled, it has been spoken to, and prayed to be extinguished. What is that?

This question was occasioned by a clash of arms among the military that thronged the court. Some of those who were nearest to the advocate appeared, from their looks and gestures, about to offer him personal violence, upon which, fixing his eye sternly upon them, he exclaimed—

You may assassinate, but you shall not intimidate me.

Here Mr. CURRAN was again interrupted by the tumult of the auditors; it was the third time that he had been obliged to sit down. On rising, he continued:—

I have very little, scarcely any, hope of being able to discharge my duty to my unfortunate client—perhaps most unfortunate in having me for his advocate. I know not whether to impute these inhuman interruptions to mere accident; but I greatly fear they have been excited by prejudice.

The Court said they would punish any person who dared to interrupt the counsel for the prisoner:—"Pray, Mr. CURRAN, proceed in stating your case; we will take care, with the blessing of God, that you shall not be interrupted."

You have been cautioned, gentlemen, against prejudice. I also urge the caution, and not with less sincerity. But what is the prejudice against which I would have you armed? I will tell you: it is that pre-occupation of mind that tries the accused before he is judicially heard—that draws those conclusions from passion which should be founded on proof—and that suffers the temper of the mind to be dissolved and debased in the heat of the season. It is not against the senseless clamour of the crowd, feeling impatient that the idle discussion of fact delays the execution, that I warn you. No; you are too proud, too humane, to hasten the holiday of blood. It is not against any such disgraceful feelings that I warn you. I wish to recall your recollections to your own minds, to guard you against the prejudice of elevated and honest understandings—against the prejudice of your virtues. I shall lay before you the case of my client, to controvert the evidence given on the part of the prosecution, and shall offer to your consideration some observations in point of law, under the judicial control of the Court. I will strip my client's case from the extraneous matter that has been attempted to be fastened on it. I feel myself, gentlemen, warmed, when I speak to you in favour of my client's innocency, and to bring his innocency home to your judgments. I know the honesty and rectitude of your characters, and I know my client has nothing to fear from your understandings.

It is my duty to state to you, we have evidence to prove that the witness on the part of the prosecution is undeserving of credit; and it is my duty to examine into the moral character of the witness that has been produced. It is of the utmost concern you should do this, as your verdict is to decide on the life or death, the fame or dishononr of the prisoner at the bar. With respect to prosecutions brought forward by the state, I have ever been of opinion that the decision is to be by the jury; and that as to any matter of law, the jury do derive information from the court: for jurors have, by the constitution, a fixed and permanent power to decide on matter of fact; while the letter of the law the Sovereign leaves to be expounded by the mouth of the King's judges. Some censure upon past occasions has fallen on former judges, for a breach of this doctrine.

Upon a former occasion I differed in opinion from the learned judge who then presided, as to what I construed to be the law of high treason, touching the compassing or imagining the death of the King. I am not ashamed of the opinion I entertained. As a point of law, I never shall be ashamed of it. I am extremely sorry I should differ from the bench on a point of law; but judges have had different opinions upon the same subject.

Where an overt act is laid, of compassing and imagining the death of the King, it does not mean, in construction of law, the natural dissolution of the King; but where there was not the fact acted upon, but confined merely to the intention a man had, such intention must, according to Lord Coke and Sir M. Foster, be proved by two witnesses. In England, the statute of Edward III. provides against the event of the death of the King by any person levying war, whereby his life might become endangered; and the proof of such overt act must be substantiated by two witnesses; how it comes not to be settled and required in Ireland, is not accounted for.

Before the statute of Edward III., the law relative to high treason was undefined, which tended to oppress and harass the people; for, by the common law of England, it was formerly a matter of doubt whether it was necessary to have two witnesses to prove an overt act of high treason. Lord Coke says, that in England there must be two witnesses to prove an overt act; it seems he was afterwards of a contrary opinion. In the reign of William III. a statute passed, and by that statute in England there must be two witnesses. When that statute came to be enacted here, the clause relative to there being two witnesses to an overt act of high treason was not made the law in Ireland; but why it was not required in Ireland is not explained. By the English act of William III., the overt act must be proved by two witnesses in England, but it does not say in Ireland.

Surely, as the common law of England and the common law of Ireland are the same, the consciences of an Irish jury ought to be fully satisfied by the testimony of two witnesses to an overt act. On this point, however, some of the Irish judges are of opinion, that two witnesses are not, in Ireland, required to substantiate an overt act, therefore their opinion must be acquiesced in.

It has been insinuated, and with artful applications

to your feelings of national independence, that I have advanced, on a former occasion, the doctrine that you should be bound in your decisions by an English act of parliament, the statute of William III. Reject the unfounded accusation; nor believe thad I assail your independence, because I instruct your judgment and excite your justice. No; the statute of William III. does not bind you, but it instructs you upon a point which before was enveloped in doubt. The morality and wisdom of Confucius, of Plato, of Socrates, or of Tully, do not bind you, but they may elevate and illumine you; and in the same way have British acts of parliament reclaimed you from barbarism. By the statute of Wm. III., two witnesses are necessary, in cases of high treason, to a just and equal trial between the Sovereign and the subject; and Sir Wm. Blackstone, one of the wisest and best authorities on the laws of England, states two witnesses to be but a necessary defence of the subject against the profligacy of ministers. In this opinion he fortifies himself with that of Baron Montesquieu, who says, that where one witness is sufficient to decide between the subject and the state, the consequences are fatal to liberty; and a people so circumstanced cannot long maintain their independence. The oath of allegiance, which every subject is supposed to have taken, stands upon the part of the accused against the oath of his accuser; and no principle can be more wise or just than that a third oath is necessary to turn the balance. Neither does this principle merely apply to the evidence of a common and impeached informer, such, as you have heard this day, but to that of any one witness, however high and respectable his character.

And now, gentlemen of the jury, let me state to you, in the clearest point of view, the defence of the prisoner at the bar, and see what has been the nature of the evidence adduced. The prisoner at the bar is accused of compassing or imagining the death of the King, and of adhering to the King's enemies; the evidence against him is parole and written evidence.

Gentlemen of the jury, I will venture to observe to you, that as to the written evidence, if suffered to go before you by the court, it is only as evidence at large; but as to the credibility of it, that is for you to decide upon.

Mr. Reynolds, in his parole testimony, has sworn that he was made a United Irishman by the prisoner at the bar. Mr. Reynolds says, he was sworn to what he considered to be the objects of that society; he stated them to you; but whether true or false, is for you to determine, by the credit you may give to his testimony. This is the third time Mr. Reynolds has appeared in a court of justice, to prosecute prisoners. He says, the objects of the United Irishmen are to overturn the present government, and to establish a republican form of government is its stead, and to comfort and abet the French, on their invading this kingdom, should such an event take place. You have heard his testimony; let me ask, do you think him incapable of being a villain? do you think him to be a villain? You observed with what kind of pride he gave his testimony; do you believe his evidence, by the solemn oath that you have taken? or do you believe it was a blasted perjury? Can you give credit to any man of a blasted character?

It has been the misfortune of many former jurors to have given their verdict founded upon the evidence of a perjured witness, and on their death-bed they repented of their credulity, in convicting a man upon false testimony. The history of former ages is replete with such conduct, as may be seen in the state trials. In the case of Lord Kimbolton and Titus Oates, the then jurors convicted that nobleman; but some time after his death, the jurors discovered they had given implicit credit to a witness unworthy of it; and the lawyers of those times might have said, "I thank God, they have done the deed." Does not the history of human infirmity give many instances of this kind?

Gentlemen, let me bring you more immediately to the case before you.

Had we no evidence against Reynolds, but his own solitary evidence, then, I say, from the whole of his evidence, you cannot establish the guilt of the prisoner at the bar; take the whole of his evidence into your consideration, and it will appear he is unworthy of credit. He told you he got information from M'Cann on the Sunday morning that the meeting was to be on Monday morning, at ten o'clock. Reynolds goes immediately to Mr. Cope, and gives him that information. On Sunday afternoon, he goes to Lord Edward Fitzgerald, and shows him the orders issued by Captain Saurin to the lawyers' corps: then, said Lord Edward, I fear government intend to arrest me; I will go to France, and hasten them to invade this country; government has no information of the meeting of the provincial delegates at Bond's. No, no, says Reynolds that is impossible. Reynolds wrote to Bond, that he could not attend the meeting, as his wife was ill; Reynolds did not go to the meeting. Bond was arrested on the Monday morning; on Monday evening, at eight at night, Reynolds goes to Lord Edward, in Aungier-street, meets him, and goes again to him the next night; and Lord Edward conversed with Reynolds about his (Lord Edward's) going to France. Reynolds then went to Kildare; he gave the most solemn assurances to the delegates at a meeting there, that he never gave information of the meeting at Bond's.

Now see how many oaths Reynolds has taken. He admits he took two of the oaths of the obligations to the society of United Irishmen. He told you Lord Edward advised him to accept the appointment of colonel in the Kildare United Irishmen's army; and yet he says he afterwards went to Bond's, and Bond advised him to be a colonel. It appears in evidence, that Reynolds was treasurer: he took two more oaths, one as colonel, and one as treasurer, and he took the oath of allegiance also, and he took oath to the truth of his testimony, at the two former trials, and at this. On which do you give him credit? Gentlemen, in order to narrow the question under your consideration, I may observe that what Reynolds said, relative to Lord Edward's conversation, is totally out of this case: it can have no weight at all on the trial of Mr. Bond for high treason, in the finding of your verdict. How, or in what manner, is the prisoner at the bar to be affected by it? I submit to your lordship, that the declaration of Lord Edward to Reynolds, when Bond was not present, is not attachable to the prisoner.

Mr. Reynolds has given you a long account of a conversation he had with Mr. Cope, relative to the proceedings of the society of United Irishmen; and Mr. Cope said, if such a man could be found, as described by Mr. Reynolds, who would come forward and give information, he would deserve the epithet of saviour of his country. Thus, by Reynolds' evidence, it would seem that Mr. Cope was the little pony of repentance to bear away the gigantic crimes of the colossus Reynolds. But remember, said Mr. Reynolds, though I give information, I won't sacrifice my morality; I won't come forward to prosecute any United Irishman. No, no; like a bashful girl, higgling about the price of her virginity, I am determined, says Reynolds, to preserve my character; I will give the communications, but do not think I will descend to be an informer, I will acquaint you of every thing against the United Irishmen, but I must preserve my credit; I tell you the design of the United Irishmen is to overturn the constitution, I will lead you to the threshold of discovery, but I won't name any price for reward. "Pray don't mention it at all," says Mr. Cope, "a man would deserve a thousand or fifteen hundred a year, and a seat in parliament, or any thing, if he could give the information you mention." No such thing is required, no such thing, says Reynolds, you mistake me; I will have nothing in the world, but merely a compensation for losses, do you think I would take a bribe? I ask only of you to give me leave to draw a little bit of a note on you for five hundred guineas only by way of indemnity; that is all; merely for indemnity of losses I have sustained, or am liable to sustain.

Gentlemen of the jury, don't you see the vast distinction between a bribe and gratification? What says Foigard?* Consider my conscience; do you think I would take a bribe? it would grieve my conscience, if I was to take a bribe. To be a member of parliament, and declare for the ayes

* A ruffian in one of the vile comedies of that time.

or the noes, I will accept of no bribe. I will only take a little indemnity for claret that may be spilt; for a little furniture that may be destroyed; for a little wear and tear; for boots and for shoes, for plate destroyed, for defraying the expenses of some pleasurable jaunts, when out of this country: for if I become a public informer against the United Irishmen, and should continue here for some time, I may chance at some time to be killed by some of them, for I have sworn to be true to them, although I also took the oath of allegiance to be true to my Sovereign. I have taken all sorts of oaths: if I frequent the company of those who are loyal to the King, they will despise the man who broke his oath of allegiance; and between the loyalist and the United Irishman I may chance to be killed.

As I am in the habit of living in the world, says Mr. Reynolds to Mr. Cope, you will give me leave to draw a bit of paper on you, only for three hundred guineas at present. It will operate like a bandage to a sore leg; though it won't cure the sore, or the rottenness of the bone, it may hide it from the public view. I will, says Mr. Reynolds, be newly baptised for a draft of three hundred guineas; and become a public informer for a further bit of paper, only for another two hundred guineas; yet I trust you will excuse me, I will not positively take any more.

He might, I imagine, be compared to a bashful girl, and say, "What! shall the brutal arms of man attack a country maid?" and when her gown shortens, and her apron bursts asunder, and she shrinks at the view of public prostitution, shall she not stipulate for full wages? Perhaps he practised upon her virtue, when the innocent dupe thought she was gaining his affections. Do you think that Reynolds would touch a bribe, and become an informer? No, no; he said he would be no informer. But did he not consent to do a little business in private, and did he not get money for it? Perhaps, he said, I thought to be no villain—I would not have the world to think me a villain. I can confide in myself; why should I mind what the world says of me, though it should call me villain? Even though I should become the talk of all the porter-houses—though I should become the talk of all the tea-tables—yet perjury is not brought home to me; no—no human being has knowledge of what is rankling within. Has it not been said I was an honest man, to come upon the public board as a public informer? They called me an honest man, and a worthy, a respectable informer; and thus my character is at bay.

Mr. Reynolds was, unfortunately, a United Irishman. He told you there was a provincial meeting of delegates; but he has not ventured to tell you where the provincial committee met—he has simply said, there was a provincial committee. The meeting, he says, was on a question of great concern. I have doubts upon it; it is not stated to me what these important consultations were about. From M'Cann he heard that a baronial meeting was to be at Bond's, on the 12th of March, and that there was material business to transact. He desired Reynolds to attend. That is all that Reynolds heard from M'Cann. M'Cann is now no more, and this part of the case is in doubt and obscurity. For my part, I am not satisfied that any thing criminal passed at the meeting at Bond's, on the 12th of March. No man can say so on the evidence produced: they do not say it—they only suppose there was. If the jury were to judge by their own present view, I do not think they would, or could, come justly to a verdict of condemnation.

The question is not, whether there was any meeting at Bond's, but what was the object of that meeting? Bond was in the warehouse, in the custody of the guard; afterwards he came up to the room with Mr. Swan. At Bond's there was a meeting of the United Irishmen; and though Bond was not taken in that room, yet Bond's charge is mixed with the guilt of that meeting.

The overt act in the indictment is, of conspiring to levy war, &c. It is material to observe, in this part of the case, it is a bare conspiracy to levy war. That is not, as I conceive, high treason. The bare intention does not amount to compassing or imagining the death of the King; it is not adhering to the King's enemies. Under certain circumstances, compassing the death of the King is not high treason. This is the great hinge, as I apprehend, in this case.

Gentlemen, what was the evidence given? That there was a meeting, for a dangerous purpose. M'Cann said, there was to be a meeting of the delegates at Bond's on the 12th of March; he did not tell Reynolds the purport of that meeting. Therefore, gentlemen, my objection is, was that a provincial meeting? It rests on the hearsay of other witnesses. It was M'Cann told Reynolds, "You must be at the Convention, on the 12th of March, to compass the death of the King, and overturn the government." But Bond did not tell him any such thing: Bond only said, M'Cann was able to give information of what was going forward at that meeting. But Bond knew nothing about it.

Admitting a meeting was held in Bond's house for a guilty purpose, yet Bond might be perfectly innocent; he was not in the room till Mr. Swan came. There was to be a watch-word— "Is M'Cann here? From thence, it would seem, it was a meeting at M'Cann's suggestion. Mr. Bond probably did not know the motive why he gave the use of the room, for there was not one word of conversation between Bond and Reynolds. Reynolds says M'Cann told him the watch-word; M'Cann did not get the watch-word from Bond, the prisoner at the bar. The watch-word was, "Is M'Cann here?" It was for the admission of no person that M'Cann did not know; it had no relation to Mr. Bond.

Has this no weight with you, gentlemen of the jury? Do you feel anxious to investigate the truth? If you believe Reynolds, the meeting was for the worst purpose. But was it with the knowledge of Bond?—for Bond said to Reynolds, "I can give you no information; go to M'Cann, he can inform you." Upon the evidence, therefore, of Reynolds rests this man's life; for the written evidence found in the room cannot, in my apprehension, affect Bond, if you be, as no doubt you will be, of opinion, Bond was not in the room where the papers were found. There is not any evidence of the conversation before Mr. Swan came; and he found on the table a paper written on, and the ink not dry, "I, A. B., was duly elected." It was not found upon the prisoner at the bar: the papers found might affect the persons in the room; but, at the time of the seizure of the papers, Bond was in the warehouse, in custody of Sergeant Dugan, and was not brought up stairs until after the arrest. The papers found upon Bond might be read in evidence against him, but I conceive not those found in the room. What was the intention of mentioning the letter from Reynolds, found on the prisoner at the bar? It was stated, but not read in evidence, merely to apologize for Reynolds' not attending the meeting on the 12th of March. Reynolds says he got it again, and burnt it. Reynolds did not pretend to state to you that he knew from Bond what the object of the meeting was; and it is material to observe that Bond's name was not found entered, in the list of the persons who made returns, and attended the meeting,

I know that Reynolds has laboured to establish a connexion between the prisoner and the meeting held at his house. But how does he manage it? He brings forward asserted conversations with persons who cannot confront him—with M'Cann, whom he has sent to the grave—and with Lord Edward Fitzgerald, whose premature death leaves his guilt a matter upon which justice dares not to pronounce. He has never told you that he has spoken to any of these in the presence of the prisoner. Are you then prepared, in a case of life and death—of honour and of infamy—to credit a vile informer, the perjurer of an hundred oaths—a wretch whom pride, honour, or religion could not bind? The forsaken prostitute of every vice calls upon you, with one breath, to blast the memory of the dead, and to blight the character of the living. Do you think Reynolds to be a villain? It is true he dresses like a gentleman; and the confident expression of his countenance, and the tones of his voice, savour strong of growing authority. He measures his value by the coffins of his victims; and, in the field of evidence, appreciates his fame as the Indian warrior does in fight—by the number of scalps with which he can swell his triumphs. He calls upon you, by the solemn league of eternal justice, to accredit the purity of a conscience washed in his own atrocities. He has promised and betrayed —he has sworn and forsworn; and, whether his soul shall go to heaven or to hell, he seems altogether indifferent, for he tells you that he has established an interest in both. He has told you that he has pledged himself to treason and to allegiance, and that both oaths has he contemned and broken.* At this time, when reason is affrighted from her seat, and giddy prejudice takes the reins—when the wheels of society are set in conflagration by the rapidity of their own motion—at such a time does he call upon a jury to credit a testimony blasted by his own accusation. Vile, however, as this execrable informer must feel himself, history, alas! holds out too much encouragement to his hopes; for, however base, and however perjured, I recollect

* The following is the list of Reynold's oaths:—

Q. (By Mr. Curran)—Can you just tott up the different oaths that you took upon either side? *A.* I will give the particulars.

Q. No; you may mention the gross? *A.* No; I will mention the particulars. I took an oath of secrecy in the county meeting—an oath to my captains, as colonel. After this I took an oath, it has been said—I do not deny it, nor do I say I took it, I was so alarmed, but I would have taken one if required—when the United Irishmen were designing to kill me, I took an oath before a county member, that I had not betrayed the meeting at Bond's. After this I took an oath of allegiance.

Q. Had you ever taken an oath of allegiance before? *A.* After this, I took an oath before the Privy Council. I took two, at different times, upon giving informations respecting these trials. I have taken three since—one upon each of the trials; and, before I took any of them, I had taken the oath of allegiance.

If to these we add his oaths on the trials, we may get a glimpse of the conscience whose strength slew so many.

few instances, in cases between the subject and the crown, where informers have not cut keen, and rode a while triumphant on public prejudice. I know of few instances wherein the edge of his testimony has not been fatal, or only blunted by the extent of its execution, and retiring from the public view beneath a heap of its own carnage.

Bond has been resident in this city twenty years; in your walks of life, gentlemen of the jury, you never heard anything to his prejudice before this charge. I know my duty to my client, and must tell you, if you have had prejudices, I know you will discard them. I am not paying you any compliment—I have spoken under the feelings of an Irishman.

During the course of these trials, I have endeavoured to speak to your understandings. I have not ventured to entreat you on behalf of my client, because I am sure you will give your justice and your merits free operation in your minds and consciences at this trial. I am sure you will try the cause fairly, and admit every circumstance into your reflections. In a case between the crown and the prisoner, I have not ventured to address you on the public feelings. At this important crisis, you will preserve the subject for the sake of the law, and preserve the law for the sake of the crown. You are to decide by your sober and deliberate understandings, and hold the balance equal between the crown and the subject.

You have been emphatically called upon to secure the state by a condemnation of the prisoner. I am less interested in the condition and political happiness of this country than you are, for probably I shall be a shorter while in it. I have, then, the greater claim on your attention and your confidence, when I caution you against the greatest and most fatal revolution—that of putting the sceptre into the hands of the informer. These are, probably, the last words I shall ever speak to you; but these last are directed to your salvation, and that of your posterity. I tell you that the reign of the informer is the suppression of the law. My old friends, I tell you, that, if you surrender yourselves to the mean and disgraceful instrumentality of your own condemnation, you will mark yourselves fit objects of martial law—you will give an attestation to the British minister that you are fit for, and have not expectation of any other than, martial law—and your liberties will be flown, never, never to return! Your country will be desolated, or only become the gaol of the living; until the informer, fatigued with slaughter, and gorged with blood, shall slumber over the sceptre of perjury. No pen shall be found to undertake the disgusting office of your historian; and some future age shall ask—What became of Ireland? Do you not see that the legal carnage which takes place day after day has already depraved the feelings of your wretched population, which seems impatient and clamorous for the amusement of an execution? It remains with you—in your determination it lies—whether that population shall be alone composed of four species of men: the informer, to accuse—the jury, to find guilty—the judge, to condemn—and the prisoner, to suffer. It regardeth not me what impressions your verdict shall make on the fate of this country; but you it much regardeth. The observations I have offered—the warning I have held forth—I bequeath you with all the solemnity of a dying bequest; and, oh! may the acquittal of your accused fellow-citizen, who takes refuge in your verdict from the vampire who seeks to suck his blood, be a blessed and happy promise of speedy peace, confidence, and security, to this wretched, distracted, and self-devouring country!

By the common law, no subject can be deprived of life, but by a trial of his fellow-subjects; but, in times when rebellion prevails in any country, men may suffer without the semblance of a trial by their equals. From the earliest period of history down to the present time, there have been seen, in some parts of the earth, instances where jurors have done little more than record the opinions given to them by the then judges; but that is the last scene of departing liberty.

I have read that, in the period of the rebellion, in the last century, in England, jurors on trials, by the common law of the land, have been swayed in their determination by the unsupported evidence of an informer; and after-times have proved their verdict was ill-founded, the innocency of the convicted persons afterwards appearing.

Trials on charges of high treason are of the utmost moment to the country, not merely in respect of any individual, but of the necessity there is that the public should know the blessings of trial by jury, and that the jurors should solely determine on their verdict by the evidence, and maturely weigh the *credit of the witnesses* against any prisoner. At several of these trials of late date some of you have been present, and you know that the object of the court and the jurors is to investigate the truth from the evidence produced. The jurors are sworn to try, and to bring in a true verdict according to the evidence.

One witness has been examined on this trial, who, I think, does not deserve credit; but it is you who are the sole judges whom you will give credit to. Though you know this witness has given evidence on two former trials, and though the then jury did give credit to his testimony; yet you are not to determine on your verdict, on the faith or precedent of any former jurors, but you are to be solely guided by your own consciences. You will observe we have had here two witnesses to impeach the character of Mr. Reynolds, that were not produced on the former trials; and you will no doubt throw out of your minds whatever did not come this day before you in evidence, on the part of the prosecution, and recollect that which will come before you on the part of the prisoner's defence. You will find your verdict flowing from conscious integrity, and from the feelings of honourable minds, notwithstanding the evidence of the witness Reynolds, who has been examined upon the table, and whose testimony I need not repeat to you. Perhaps you may be inclined to think he is a perjured witness; perhaps you will not believe the story he has told against the prisoner at the bar, and of his own turpitude. You will do well to consider it was through a perjured witness that a Russel and a Sydney were convicted in the reign of James II. If juries are not circumspect to determine *only* by the evidence adduced before them, and not from any extraneous matter, nor from the slightest breath of prejudice, then what will become of our boasted trial by jury; then what will become of our boasted constitution of Ireland? In former times, when jurors decided contrary to evidence, it created great effusion of blood. Let me ask, will you, gentlemen, give a verdict through infirmity of body, or through misrepresentation, or through ignorance? You, by your verdict, will give an answer to this.

Gentlemen of the jury, you will weigh in your minds, that many inhuman executions did take place in former times, though the then accused underwent the solemnity of a trial. The verdicts of those jurors are not in a state of annihilation, for they remain on the page of history, as a beacon to future jurors, The judges before whom the then accused were tried, have long since paid the debt of nature; they cannot now be called to account, why they shrunk from their duty.

I call upon you, gentlemen of the jury, to be firm in the exercise of the solemn duty you are now engaged in, Should you be of opinion to bring in a verdict of condemnation against my unfortunate client, for myself I ought to care nothing, what impressions may actuate your minds to find such verdict; it is not for me, it is for you, to consider what kind of men you condemn to die, and before you write his bloody sentence, to weigh maturely whether the charge against the prisoner is fully proved. If you should, on the evidence you have heard, condemn the prisoner to death, and afterwards repent it, I shall not live among you to trace any proof of your future repentance.

I said I rose to tell you what evidence we had to produce on behalf of my client, the prisoner at the bar. We shall lay evidence before you, from which you can infer that the witness produced this day was a perjured man. We have only to show to you, as honest men, that the witness is not deserving of credit on his oath, we have nothing more to offer on behalf of my client, the prisoner at the bar. It is your province to deliberate in your consciences on the evidence you will hear, whether you will believe the witness you have heard, on his oath, or not. And now I ask you, will you, upon the evidence you have heard, take away the life of the prisoner at the bar, separate him from his wife and from his little children for ever?

I told you I was to state to you the evidence which we had to bring forward on behalf of my unfortunate client. I tell you it is to discredit the testimony of Mr. Reynolds. When you have heard our evidence to this point, I cannot suppose you will give your verdict to doom to death the unhappy and unfortunate prisoner at the bar, and entail infamy upon his posterity. We will also produce respectable witnesses to the hitherto unimpeached character of the prisoner at the bar, and prove that he was a man of fair, honest character. You, gentlemen of the jury, have yourselves known him a number of years in this city; let me ask you, do you not know that the prisoner at the bar has always borne the character of a man of integrity, and of honest fame? and, gentlemen of the jury, I call upon you to answer my question by your verdict.

I feel myself impressed with the idea in my bosom, that you will give your verdict of acquittal of the prisoner at the bar; and that, by your verdict, you will declare on your oaths, that you do not believe one syllable that Mr. Reynolds has told you. Let me entreat you to put in one scale, the base, the attainted, the unfounded, the perjured witness; and in the opposite scale, let me advise you to put the testimony of the respectable witnesses produced against Mr. Reynolds, and the witnesses to the prisoner's hitherto unimpeached character; and you will hold the balance with justice, tempered with mercy, so as your consciences in future will approve.

Let me depart from the scene of beholding human misery, should the life of my client by your verdict be forfeited!

Should he live, by your verdict of acquittal, he would rank as the kindest father, and protector of his little children; as the best of husbands and of friends; and ever maintain that irreproachable character he has hitherto sustained in private life. Should our witnesses exculpate the prisoner from the crimes charged on him, to the extent charged in the indictment, I pray to God to give you the judgment and understanding to acquit him. Do not imagine I have made use of any arguments to mislead your consciences, or to distress your feelings: no, but if you conceive a doubt on your minds, that the prisoner is innocent of the crime of high treason, I pray to God to give you firmness of mind to acquit him. I now leave you, gentlemen of the jury, to the free exercise of your own judgments in the verdict you may give. I have not by way of supplication addressed you in argument; I do not wish to distress your feelings by supplications; it would be most unbefitting to your candour and understanding; you are bound by your oaths to find a true verdict according to the evidence; and you do not deserve the station of jurors, in which the constitution has placed you, if you do not discharge the trust the consitution has vested in you, to give your verdict freely and indifferently, according to your consciences.

Mr. Bond was found GUILTY, but died of apoplexy in prison, during the negotiation which followed his conviction.

FOR LADY PAMELA FITZGERALD AND HER CHILDREN.

[AGAINST ATTAINDER BILL.]

BAR OF THE IRISH COMMONS.

IN COMMITTEE.

August 20th, 1798.

Soon after the death of Lord Edward Fitzgerald his brother Henry wrote to Lord Lieutenant Camden a letter ending thus:—"One word more, and I have done, as I alone am answerable for this letter. Perhaps you will still take compassion on his wife and three babes, the eldest not four years old. The opportunity that I offer is to protect their estate for them from violence and plunder. You can do it if you please."

The appeal was vain, and on the 27th of July, a bill was introduced into the Commons, to attaint Lord Edward Fitzgerald, Cornelius Grogan, and Bagenal Harvey. It was read a second time on the 9th of August, and, on the same day, Lord Caulfield presented Lady Pamela Fitzgerald's petition against it. On the 13th Arthur Moore, in a sound and feeling speech, moved a clause to exempt the heirs from attaint. Barrington and Plunket supported him, but the motion was lost. On the 14th the case was gone into against Harvey, and, on the 18th, witnesses were heard at the bar for the bill, the principal one being Reynolds of Kilkea. He proved the same facts as on Bond's trial, with some special ones as to Lord Edward. There was no doubt of the facts or the evidence.

On the 20th CURRAN was heard against the bill, and spoke as follows:—

I appear in support of a petition presented on behalf of Lord Henry Fitzgerald, brother of the deceased Lord Edward Fitzgerald: of Pamela, his widow; Edward, his only son and heir, an infant of the age of four years; Pamela, his eldest daughter, of the age of two years; and Lucy, his youngest child, of the age of three months, against the bill of attainder now before the committee.

The bill of attainder has formed the division of the subject into two parts. It asserts the fact of the late Lord Edward's treason, and, secondly, it purports to attaint him, and to vest his property in the crown. I shall follow the same order.

As to the first part of the bill, I must remark upon the strange looseness of its allegation. The bill states that he had, during his life, and since the 1st of November last, committed several acts of high treason, without stating what, or when, or where, or with whom: it then affects to state the different species of treason of which he had been guilty; namely, conspiring to levy war, and endeavouring to persuade the enemies of the King to invade the country. The latter allegation they did not attempt to prove. The conspiring, without actually levying war, is clearly no high treason, and has been repeatedly so determined.

Upon this previous and important question, namely, the guilt of Lord Edward (without the full proof of which no punishment can be just), I was asked by the committee, if I had any defence to go into?

I was confounded by a question which I could not answer; but upon a very little reflection, I saw in that very confusion the most conclusive proof of the injustice of the bill. For what can be more flagrantly unjust, than to inquire into a fact of the truth or falsehood of which no human being can have knowledge, save the informer who comes forward to assert it.

Sir, I now answer the question.

I have no defensive evidence! I have no case! it is impossible I should: I have often of late gone to the dungeon of the captive, but never have I gone to the grave of the dead, to receive instructions for his defence, nor in truth have I ever before been at the trial of a dead man! I offer, therefore, no evidence upon this inquiry: against the perilous example of which I do protest on behalf of the public, and against the cruelty and injustice of which I do protest in the name of the dead father, whose memory is sought to be dishonoured; and of his infant orphans, whose bread is sought to be taken away.

Some observations, and but a few, upon the assertions of Reynolds, I will make. I do verily believe him in this instance, even though I have heard him assert it upon his oath. By his own confession he is an informer—a bribed informer: a man whom seven respectable witnesses have sworn in a court of justice, upon their oaths, not to be credible on his oath; a man upon whose single testimony no jury ever did, nor ever ought, to pronounce a verdict of guilty; a kind of man to whom the law resorts with abhorrence, and from necessity, in order to set the criminal against the crime; but who is made use of by the law for the same reason that the most noxious poisons are resorted to in medicine.

If such be the man, look for a moment at his story; he confines himself to mere conversation only, with a dead man! He ventures not to introduce any third person, living or even dead! he wishes, indeed, to asperse the conduct of Lady Edward Fitzgerald; but he well knew that, even were she in the country, she could not be adduced as a witness to disprove him. See, therefore, if there be any one assertion to which credit can be given, except this, that he has sworn and forsworn, that he is a traitor; that he has received five hundred guineas to be an informer; and that his general reputation is, to be utterly unworthy of credit.

As to the papers, it is sufficient to say, that no one of them, nor even all of them, were even asserted to contain any positive proof against Lord Edward; that the utmost that could be deduced from them is nothing more than doubt or conjecture, which, had Lord Edward been living, might have been easily explained, to explain which is now impossible, and upon which to found a sentence of guilt would be contrary to every rule of justice or humanity?

Is this bill of attainder warranted by the principles of reason, the principles of forfeiture in the law of treason, or the usage of parliament in bills of attainder? The subject is, of necessity, very long; it has nothing to attract attention, but much to repel it. But I trust that the anxiety of the committee for justice, nothwithstanding any dulness either in the subject or in the speaker, will secure to me their attention.

Mr. CURRAN then went into a minute detail of the principles of the law of forfeiture for high treason, of which no report appears to exist.

The laws of the Persians and Macedonians extended the punishment of a traitor to the extinction of all his kindred. The law subjected the property and life of every man to the most complicated despotism, because the loyalty of every individual of his kindred was as much a matter of wild caprice, as the will of the most arbitrary despot could be.

This principle was never adopted in any period of our law. At the earliest times of the Saxons, the law of treason acted directly only on the person of the criminal; it took away from him what he actually had to forfeit, his life and property. But as to his children, the law disclaimed to affect them directly; they suffered, but they suffered by a necessary consequence of their father's punishment, which the law could not prevent, and never directly intended. It took away the inheritance, because the criminal, at the time of taking it away, had absolute dominion over it, and might himself have conveyed it away from his family. This is proved by the instances of conditional fees at the common law, and estates tail since the statute *de Donis.* In the former case the tenant did not forfeit until he had acquired an absolute dominion over the estate by the performance of the condition. Neither in the latter case is the estate tail made forfeitable, until the tenant in tail has become enabled in two ways to obtain the absolute dominion, by a common recovery, or by a fine. Until then the issue in tail, though not only the children of the tenant, but taking from him his estate by descent, could not be disinherited by his crime. Here is a decisive proof, that even the early law of treason never intended to extend the punishment of the traitor to his children as such; but even this direct punishment upon the traitor himself, is to take effect only upon a condition suggested by the unalterable rules of natural justice, namely, a judgment founded upon conviction, against which he might have made his defence; or upon an outlawry, where he refused to abide his trial. In that case he is punished, because during his life the fact was triable; because during his life the punishment could act directly upon his person; because during his life the estate was his to convey, and therefore his to forfeit.

But if he died without attainder, a fair trial was impossible, because a fair defence was impossible; a direct punishment upon his person was impossible, because he could not feel it; and a confiscation of his estate was equally impossible, because it was then no longer his, but was vested in his heir, to whom it belonged by a title as good as that by which it had ever belonged to him in his lifetime, namely, the known law of the country.

As to a posthumous forfeiture of lands, that appears to have been attempted by inquest after death. But so early as the 8th of Edward III., the legality of such presentments was disallowed by the judges. And there is no lawyer at this day who can venture to deny that, since the 25th and 34th of Edward III., no estate of inheritance can regularly be forfeited, save by attainder in the life of the party; therefore, the law of the country being that, unless the descent is interrupted by an actual attainder in the lifetime of the criminal, it becomes vested in the heir, the moment it did descend, the heir became seized by a title the most favoured in law. He might, perhaps, have been considered as a purchaser for the most valuable consideration, his mother's marriage, of which he was the issue. Why, then, was posthumous attainder excluded from the protective law of treason? Why has it never since been enacted by a prospective law?

Clearly for this reason, that in its own nature it is inhuman, impolitic, and unjust.

But, it is said, this may be done by a bill of attainder; that the parliament is omnipotent, and, therefore, may do it; and that it is a proceeding familiar to our constitution. As to the first, it cannot be denied that the parliament is the highest power of the country, but an argument from the existence of a power to the exercise of it in any particular instance, is ridiculous and absurd. From such an argument it would follow, that it must do whatever it is able to do; and that it must be stripped of the best of all power—the power of abstaining from what is wrong.

Such a bill ought not to pass. First, because every argument against the justice or the policy of a prospective, is tenfold strong against a retrospective law; because every *ex post facto* law is in itself an exercise of despotic power. When it alters the law of property, it is peculiarly dangerous; when it punishes the innocent for the guilty, it is peculiarly unjust; when it affects to do that which the criminal law, as it now stands, could not do, it acts peculiarly against the spirit of the constitution; which is to contract and restrain penal law by the strictest construction, and not to add to it by vindictive innovation. But, I am warranted to go much further, upon the authority of the British legislature itself, and to say, that the principle of forfeiture, even in the prospective law, is altogether repugnant to the spirit of the British constitution.

The statutes of Anne and of George the Second have declared that, after the death of the Pretender and of his sons, no such forfeiture should or ought to exist. In favour of that high authority, every philosophical and theoretic writer, Baron Montesquieu, the Marquis Beccaria, and many others, might be cited; against it, no one writer of credit or character that has come to my hands. Of the late Mr. Yorke I do not mean to speak with disrespect; he was certainly a man of learning and genius; but it must be observed, he wrote for a party and for a purpose; he wrote against the repeal of the law of forfeiture, more than for its principle; of that principle he expressly declines entering into a direct defence. But for the extending of that principle farther than it is already law, the slightest insinuation cannot be found in his treatise.

But it is asserted to be the usage of the constitution in both countries.

Of bills of attainder, the instances are certainly many, and most numerous in the worst times, and rising above each other in violence and injustice. The most tolerable of them was that which attainted the man who fled from justice, which gave him a day to appear, had he chosen to do so, and operated as a legislative outlawry. That kind of act has been passed, though but rarely, within the present century. There have been many acts of attainder when the party was willing but not permitted to appear and take his trial. In these two kinds of bills of attainder, however, it is to be observed, that they do not any violence to the common law, by the declaring of a new crime or a new punishment, but only by creating a new jurisdiction, and a new order of proceedings.

Of the second kind that has been mentioned, many instances are to be found in the violent reigns of the Plantagenets and Tudors, and many of them revised by the wisdom of cooler and juster times. Of such unhappy monuments of human frailty, Lord Coke said, "*auferat oblivio, si non silentium tegat.*" I beg leave to differ in that from the learned judge: I say, let the record upon which they are written be indelible and immortal: I say, let the memory that preserves them have a thousand tongues to tell them; and when justice, even late and slow, shall have robbed their fellow principle of life, let them be interred in a monument of negative instruction to posterity for ever.

A third kind of bill of attainder might be found, which for the first time declared the law, and attainted the criminal upon it: such was the attainder of Strafford. A fourth, which did not change the law as to the crime, but as to the evidence upon which it was to be proved; such was the attainder of Sir John Fenwick.

Of these two last species of attainder, no lawyer

has ever spoken with respect; they were the cruel effect of the rancour and injustice of party spirit; nor could any thing be said in their excuse, except that they were made for the direct punishment of the actual criminals, and whilst they were yet living.

The only other attainder that remains possible to be added to this catalogue, is that of a bill like the present, which affects to try after a party's death, when trial is impossible; to punish guilt, when punishment is impossible; to inflict punishment where crime is not even pretended; change the settled law of property; to confiscate the widow's pittance! to plunder the orphan's cradle! and to violate the religion of the dead man's grave!

For this, too, there was a precedent: but for the honour of humanity let it be remembered, that an hundred and forty years have elapsed in which that precedent has not been thought worthy of imitation in Great Britain. I mean the attainder of the regicides. Upon the Restoration, four of them were included in that bill of attainder, which was passed after their death.

But, what were the circumstances of that period? A king restored, and by his nature disposed to mercy, a ministry of uncommon wisdom, feeling that the salvation of the state could be secured only by mildness and conciliation; a bigoted, irritated, and interested faction in parliament; the public mind in the highest state of division and agitation.

For what, then, is that act of attainder resorted to as a precedent? Surely it cannot be as a precedent of that servile paroxysm of simulated loyalty, with which the same men, who a few days before had shouted after the wheels of the good Protector, now raked out the grave of the traitorous usurper, and dragged his wretched carcase through the streets; that servile and simulated loyalty, which affected to bow in obsequious admiration of the salutary lenity which their vindictive folly was labouring to frustrate: that servile and interested hypocrisy, which gave a hollow and faithless support to the power of the monarch, utterly regardless alike of his character or his safety.

That the example, which this act of attainder held forth, was never respected, appears from this, that it never has been followed in Great Britain, although that country has since that time been agitated by one revolution, and vexed by two rebellions. So far from extending forfeiture or attainder beyond the existing law, the opinion of that wise and reflecting country was gradually maturing into a dislike of the principle altogether; until, at last, by the statutes of Anne and George II., she declared that no forfeiture or attainder for treason should prejudice any other than the actual offender, nor work any injury to the heir or other person, after the death of the pretenders to the throne. Why has Great Britain thus condemned the principle of forfeiture? Because she felt it to be unjust, and because she found it to be ineffectual.

Need I prove the impolicy of severe penal laws? They have ever been found more to exasperate than to restrain. When the infliction is beyond the crime, the horror of the guilt is lost in the horror of the punishment; the sufferer becomes an object of commiseration; and the injustice of the state, of public odium. It was well observed that, in England, the highwayman never murdered, because there the offender was not condemned to torture! But, in France, where the offender was broken on the wheel, the traveller seldom or never escaped!* What, then, is it in England that sends the traveller home with life, but the comparative mildness of English law? What, but the merciless cruelty of the French law, that gives the atrocious aggravation of murder to robbery? The multiplication of penal laws lessens the value of life, and when you lessen the value of life, you lessen the fear of death.

Look to the history of England upon this subject with respect to treason. Notwithstanding all its formidable array of death, of Saxon forfeiture, and of feudal corruption of blood; in what country do you read of more treasons or of more rebellions? And why? Because these terrors do not restrain the traitor. Beyond all other delinquents, he is likely to be a person of that ardent, enthusiastic, and

* Beccaria on Crimes and Punishments.

intrepid spirit that is roused into more decisive and desperate daring by the prospect of peril.

Mr. Yorke thinks the child of the traitor may be reclaimed to his loyalty by the restitution of his estate. Mr. Yorke, perhaps, might have reasoned better if he had looked to the still greater likelihood of making him a deadly enemy to the state by the ignominy inflicted on his father, and by the loss of his own inheritance. How keenly did Hannibal pursue his vengeance which he had sworn against Rome? How much more enthusiastically would he have pursued his purpose, had that oath been taken upon a father's grave, for the avenging of a father's sufferings, for the avenging of a father's wrongs!

If I am called upon to give more reasons why this precedent has not been for more than a century and a half repeated, I will say, that a bill of attainder is the result of an unnatural union of the legislative and judicial functions; in which the judicial has no law to restrain it; in which the legislative has no rule to guide it, unless passion and prejudice, which reject all rule and law, be called rule and law. It puts the lives and properties of men completely at the mercy of an arbitrary and despotic power.

Such were the acts of posthumous attainder in Ireland, in the reign of the arbitrary Elizabeth, who used these acts as a mere mode of robbing an Irish subject, for the benefit of an English minion. Such was the act of the 9th William III., not passed for the same odious and despicable purpose, but for a purpose equally arbitrary and unjust—the purpose of transferring the property of the country from persons professing one religion into the hands of those professing another—a purpose manifested and avowed by the remarkable clause in that act, which saves the inheritance to the heir of the traitor, provided that heir be a Protestant! Nor was it so brutally tyrannical in its operation, inasmuch as it gave a right to traverse and a trial by jury to every person claiming a right; and protected the rights of infants, until they should be of age, and capable to assert those rights.

There are yet other reasons why that precedent of the regicides was not followed in Great Britain. A government that means honestly will appeal to the affections, not to the fears of the people. A state must be at the last gasp, when it is driven to seek protection in the abandonment of the law—that melancholy avowal of its weakness and its fear. Therefore, it was not done in the rebellion of 1715, nor in that of 1745.

I have hitherto abstained from adverting to the late transactions of Ireland: but I could not defraud my clients, or their cause, of so pregnant an example.

In this country, penal laws have been tried beyond any example of any former times. What was the event? The race between penalty and crime was continued, each growing fiercer in the conflict, until the penalty could go no further, and the fugitive turned upon the breathless pursuer.

From what a scene of wretchedness and horror have we escaped!

But I do not wish to annoy you by the stench of those unburied and unrotted examples of the havoc and the impotence of penal law pushed to its extravagance. I am more pleased to turn your attention to the happy consequences of temperate, conciliatory government—of equal law. Compare the latter with the former, and let your wisdom decide between the tempest and the calm. I know it is a delicate subject, but let me presume to suggest what must be the impression upon this grieved and anxious country, if the rigour of the parliament shall seem at war with the mildness of the government, if the people shall have refuge in the mercy of the crown from the rigour of their own representatives. But if, at the same moment, they shall see the convicted and attainted secured in their lives and in their property by the wise lenity of the crown, while the parliament is visiting shame, and misery, and want, upon the cradle of the unprotected infant, who could not have offended—but I will not follow the idea, I will not see the inauspicious omen; I pray that heaven may avert it.

One topic more you will permit me to add. Every act of the sort ought to have a practical morality flowing from its principle. If loyalty and justice require that these infants should be deprived of bread, must it not be a violation of that principle to give them food or shelter? Must not every loyal and just man wish to see them, in the words of the famous Golden Bull, "always poor and necessitous, and for ever accompanied by the infamy of their father, languishing in continued indigence, and finding their punishment in living, and their relief in dying?" If the widowed mother should carry the orphan heir of her unfortunate husband to the gate of any man who might feel himself touched with the sad vicissitudes of human affairs, who might feel a compassionate reverence for the noble blood that flowed in his veins, nobler than the royalty that first ennobled it, that like a rich stream rose till it ran and hid its fountain;—if, remembering the many noble qualities of his unfortunate father, his heart melted over the calamities of the child; if his heart swelled, if his eyes overflowed, if his too precipitate hand were stretched out by his pity or his gratitude to the poor excommunicated sufferers, how could he justify the rebel tear, or the traitorous humanity?

I shall trespass no longer upon the patience for which I am grateful: one word only, and I have done; and that is, once more earnestly and solemnly to conjure you to reflect, that the fact, I mean the fact of guilt or innocence, which must be the foundation of this bill, is not now, after the death of the party, capable of being tried, consistently with the liberty of a free people, or the unalterable rules of eternal justice; and that, as to the forfeiture and the ignominy which it enacts, that only can be punishment which lights upon guilt, and that can be only vengeance which breaks upon innocence!

Though great exertions were made to stop the bill, it reached the Lords, and passed in September.

A final effort was now made by Lady Edward's friends. A memorial was presented to the King, setting out the reasons, from the constitution, from justice, and from clemency, for stopping this bill. The names to the Memorial are "Richmond" (the Duke), "W. Ogilvie" (Lord Edward's step-father), "Henry Fitzgerald," "Charles James Fox," "Henry Edward Fox," "Holland." This document, and many letters written by the Duchess of Leinster to the Royal Family, will be found in the appendix to Moore's touching and simple narrative of "The Life and Death of Lord Edward Fitzgerald." This, too, was for the time unsuccessful, and the bill received the Royal assent in October; but the execution of the attainder was delayed, and the estate was sold in Chancery for a mortgage, and bought for £10,500, by Mr. Ogilvie, who cleared the property, and restored it to Lady Edward. She went to France, and married there imprudently. She separated from her second husband, and after living long in retirement at Toulouse, died in poor lodgings in the Rue Richepanse, Paris, in November, 1831. An application for the reversal of the attainder was made in 1799; Government agreed to bring it forward in the United Parliament; but it did not pass till 1819.

NAPPER TANDY.

[FOR NOT SURRENDERING ON A CHARGE OF HIGH TREASON, UNDER AN ATTAINDER ACT.]

COURT OF KING'S BENCH.

May 19th, 1800.

JAMES NAPPER TANDY was a Dublin merchant, of respectable family, and much civic influence. In 1773—4, he became a Common Councilman, and a member of the Trinity Guild.* He commanded the Volunteer Artillery, and had his guns cast with "Free Trade or else—" on them. He was Secretary to the first Dublin meeting of the United Irish Society, held on November 9th, 1791, at "The Eagle," in Eustace-street, and there Tone's Declaration and Test (which had been first agreed to in Belfast on October 14th, 1791) were adopted.† His signature is to two other documents of theirs.

At the meeting of the Dublin Volunteers, at Pardon's, in Cope-street, and of which so much appears in Rowan's case, Tandy was busy distributing Drennan's "Citizen Soldiers" proclamation; and during the discussions which followed on it in Parliament, Toler spoke insolently of Tandy. For this Tandy challenged him;‡ but Toler would not fight, and complained to the House of Commons. The Speaker issued his warrant

* He then resided in Dorset-street.

† See the proceedings of the "Society of United Irishmen of Dublin," published in Dublin, by the Society, in 1794, with this motto, "Let the Nation stand."

‡ See his letter to Rowan on the subject in Drummond's Life of Rowan, page 164.

against Tandy, who was arrested at his house in Chancery-lane; but he escaped through a window. The Privy Council issued a proclamation, offering £50 reward for Tandy's arrest, and Tandy brought actions against the Lord Lieutenant (Westmoreland) and the Privy Councillors who signed the proclamation; but after long discussions, in which Simon Butler and Thomas Addis Emmet most ably supported Tandy's case, the subpœnas were quashed.* In February, 1793, Tandy and Rowan were prosecuted as Defenders. Tandy fled to America. Francis Graham, a magistrate, was prosecuted for having suborned Corbally, a tailor, to swear this charge against them; but Graham was acquitted, and on his acquittal prosecuted and convicted Corbally for perjury.†

Thus he lived in perpetual turmoil, and enjoyed it. He was employed by the United Irish in the French negotiation, and for this left America in '98, and having been marked out by the Secret Committee, he was the first of fifty-one persons‡ included in an attainder act (38th George III., c. 80), by which it was declared that, unless the persons named in it surrendered on or before the 1st December, 1798, they would be held convict traitors, and suffer death, confiscation of goods, and corruption of blood accordingly. He tried to join Humbert's Expedition in the Autumn of that year, but missed doing so, and after being part of a day on the Donegal coast, sailed safely to Norway. On the 24th of November, he and Harvey Morris§ (Montmorenci), Corbet, and Blackwall, were arrested by English agents in Hamburgh, and brought to Ireland. A

* The proceedings are in the "United Irish" volume, referred to in the last note but one.

† These cases exist in pamphlet reports, and are highly interesting.

‡ Among the 51, were Wolfe Tone, Lewins, Surgeon Lawless, M'Cormick, Michael Reynolds, and several Presbyterian clergymen.

§ Of Knockalton, in the county Tipperary. He became a General Officer in the French Service.—*See O'Connor's "Military Memoirs of the Irish Nation."*

habeas corpus was issued; but it was not until the 10th of February that the parties were brought from Kilmainham to the King's Bench. On that day they were arraigned, and on the 12th pleaded specially that they had been arrested within the time allowed by the act of parliament. Issue was joined on the facts, and after delays, allowed to the prisoners to procure the attendance of Sir James Crawford (British envoy at Hamburgh at the time of the arrest) the trial of both Tandy and Morris took place on the 19th of May, 1800, before Lord Kilwarden. Mr. Ridgeway opened the prisoner's plea, and CURRAN supported it as follows:—

MY Lords, and you, Gentlemen of the Jury, I am in this case of counsel for Mr. Tandy, the prisoner at the bar, I could have wished it had been the pleasure of the gentlemen who conduct this business on the part of the crown, to have gone on first. The subject itself is of a very novel nature in this country; but certainly it is the right of the crown, and which the gentlemen have thought proper to follow, to call on the counsel for the prisoner to begin; and, therefore, it is my duty, my lords, to submit to you, and to explain, under the direction of the court, to you, gentlemen of the jury, what the nature of the question is that you are sworn to try.

An act of parliament was passed in this country, which began to be a law on the 6th of October, 1798. On that day it received the royal assent. By that law it is stated, that the prisoner at the bar had been guilty of acts of treason of many different kinds; and it is enacted, that he shall stand attainted of high treason, except he should, on or before the 1st day of December following, surrender himself to one of the judges of this court, or to one of his Majesty's justices of the peace, for the purpose of becoming amenable to that law from which he was supposed to have fled, in order to abide his trial for any crime that might be alleged against him.

It was a law not passed for the purpose of absolutely pronouncing any judgment whatsoever against him, but for the purpose of compelling him to come in and take his trial; and nothing can show more strongly that that act of Parliament has not established any thing touching the fact of the prisoner's guilt; because it would be absurd, in one and the same breath, to pronounce that he was guilty of high treason, and then call upon him to come in and abide his trial; and the title of the act speaks that it is an act not pronouncing sentence against the prisoner, but that it is an act in order to compel him to come forward.

This act creates a parliamentary attainder, not founded on the establishment of the prisoner's guilt of treason, but on his contumacious avoidance of trial, by standing out against a trial by law. I make this observation to you, gentlemen of the jury, in order that you may, in the first instance, discharge from your minds any actual belief of any criminality in the prisoner at the bar; and that for two reasons: first, because a well-founded conviction of his guilt, on the authority of this statute, might have some impression on the minds of men sitting in judgment on the prisoner; but for a more material reason, I wish to put it from your minds, because his guilt or innocence has nothing to do with the issue you are sworn to try.

Gentlemen, the issue you are called to try is not the guilt or the innocence of the prisoner; it is therefore necessary you should understand exactly what it is.

The prisoner was called on to show cause why he should not suffer death, pursuant to the enacting clause of the statute, and he has put in a plea in which he states that, before the time for surrender had expired, namely, on the 24th of November, 1798, seven days before the day he had for surrendering had expired, he was, by order of his Majesty, arrested, and made a prisoner, in the town of Hamburgh; and, in consequence of such arrest, it became impossible for him to surrender himself, and become amenable to justice within the time prescribed; and the counsel for the crown have rested the case on the denial, in point of fact, of this allegation; and, therefore, the question that you are to try is simplified to this—" I was arrested," says the prisoner, "whereby it became impossible for me to surrender"—to which the counsel for the crown reply—"You were not arrested at the time alleged by you, whereby it would have become impossible for you to surrender." This I conceive to be the issue, in point of fact, joined between the parties, and on which it is my duty to explain the evidence that will be offered.

Mr. Tandy is a subject of this country, and has never been in it from the time this Act of Parliament passed until he was brought into it after his arrest, on the 24th of November, 1798. On that day he was in the town of Hamburgh. He had seven days, in which time it was practicable for him to arrive in this country, and surrender himself, according to the requisitions of the act of attainder. Every thing that could be of value to man, was at stake, and called on him to make that surrender. If he did not surrender, his life was forfeited—if he did not surrender, his fortune was confiscated—if he did not surrender, the blood of his family was corrupted; and he could leave them no inheritance, but the disgrace of having suffered as a traitor.

Your common sense, gentlemen, will show you that, where a man is to forfeit his life, unless he complies with the conditions of an Act of Parliament—your common sense, your common humanity must show you, that a man ought to be suffered to perform the conditions on which his life depends. It can require no argument to impress upon your minds, that to call on a man to surrender himself on pain of death, and by force to prevent him from surrendering, goes to an atrocity of oppression that no human mind can contemplate without horror.

But it seems that the prisoner at the bar was a man of too much consequence to the repose of all civilized nations, to the great moral system—I might almost say, to the great physical system of the universe, to be permitted to act in compliance with the statute that called upon him to surrender himself upon pain of death. The wisdom of the entire Continent was called upon to exercise its mediation on this most momentous circumstance. The diplomatic wisdom of Germany was all put into action on the subject. The englightened humanity of the North was called on to lend its aid. Gentlemen, you know as well as I the princely virtues and imperial qualifications, the consummate wisdom and sagacity of our steadfast friend and ally, the Emperor of all the Russias; you must feel the awe with which he ought to be mentioned; his sacred person has become embodied in the criminal law of England, and it has become almost a misprision to deem of him or speak of him but with reverence. I feel that reverence for him; and I deem of him and conceive him to be a constellation of all virtue, compared with whose radiance the Ursa-major twinkles only as the glow-worm.

And, gentlemen, what was the result of the exercise of this combination of wisdom? That James Napper Tandy ought to be got rid of in the ordinary way. They felt an honest and a proper indignation that a little community like Hamburgh should embezzle that carcase which was the property of a mild and merciful government; they felt a proper indignation that the senate of Hamburgh, under the present sublime system, should defraud the mercy of the government of the blood of the prisoner, cheat the gibbet of his bones, or deprive the good and loyal ravens of this country of his flesh; and, accordingly, by an order issued to these miserable inhabitants of the town of Hamburgh, who were made to feel that common honesty and common humanity can only be sustained by a strength not to be resisted, they were obliged to break the ties of justice and hospitality—to trample on the privileges that every stranger claims; they were obliged to suffer the prisoner to be trampled on, and meanly, and cruelly, and pitiably to give up this unfortunate man to the disposal of those who could demand him at such a price.

If a surrender, in fact, had been necessary on the part of the prisoner, certainly a very material object was achieved by arresting him: because they thereby made it impossible for him to avail himself of the opportunity. They made it impossible for him to avail himself of the surrender, if the reflection of his mind led him to it. If a sense of the duty he owed his family led him to a wish, or to an intention, of availing himself of the remaining time he had to surrender, they determined he should not take advantage of it. He had been guilty of what the law deems a crime, that is, of flying from justice, though it does not go to the extent of working a corruption of blood; but by this act of power, by this act of tyrannic force, he was prevented from doing that which every court of justice must intend he was willing to do—which the law intends he would have done—which the law gave him time to do—which the law supposes he might have done the last hour, as well as the first. He was on his passage to this country: that would not have taken up a third part of the time that was yet to elapse; but by seizing on him in the manner that he was arrested, it became impossible for him to surrender himself, or become amenable to justice.

The prisoner, when he was arrested, was treated in a manner that made it impossible for him to do any act that might have been considered as tantamount to a surrender. He was confined in a dungeon, little larger than a grave: he was loaded with irons; he was chained by an iron that communicated from his arm to his leg; and that so short, as to grind into his flesh. In such a state of restriction did he remain for fifteen days; in such a situation did he lie in a common vault; food was cut into shapeless lumps, and flung to him by his filthy attendants as he lay on the ground, as if he had been a beast; he had no bed to lie on, not even straw to coil himself up in, if he could have slept. In that situation he remained in a foreign country for fifteen days of his long imprisonment; and he is now called to show good cause why he should not suffer death, because he did not surrender himself and become amenable to the law. He was debarred all communication whatsoever: if he attempted to speak to the sentinels that guarded him, they could not understand him; he did make such kind of indications of his misery and his sufferings as could be conveyed by signs, but he made them in vain; and he is now called on to show good cause, wherefore he did contumaciously and traitorously refuse to surrender himself, and become amenable to the law.

Gentlemen of the jury, I am stating facts that happened in a foreign country; will you expect that I should produce witnesses to lay those abominable offences before you in evidence? It was not in the power of the prisoner at the bar to procure witnesses; he was not of importance enough to call on the armed civilization of Europe, or on the armed barbarity of Europe, to compel the inhabitants of the town where he was imprisoned, to attend at the bar of this court to give evidence for the preservation of his life; but though such interposition could not be obtained to preserve his life, it could be procured for the purposes of blood.

And this is an additional reason why the rights of neutral states should be respected; because, if an individual, claiming those privileges, be torn from that sanctuary, he comes without the benefit of the testimony of those that could save his life. It is a maxim of law that no man shall lose any thing, much less his life, by the non-performance of a condition, if that non-performance have arisen by the act of God, or of the party who is to avail himself of the condition, that the impossibility so imposed shall be an excuse for the non-performance of the condition; that is the defence the prisoner relies upon here. "Why did you not surrender, and become amenable to justice? Because I was in chains." "Why did you not come over to Ireland? Because I was in prison, in a grave, in the town of Hamburgh." "Why did you not do something, tant-amount to a surrender? Because I was unpractised in the language of the strangers, who could not be my protectors, because they were also my fellow-sufferers."

But he may push this reasoning much farther: the statute was made for the express purpose of making him amenable. When the crown seized him at Hamburgh, it thereby made him amenable, and so satisfied the law. It could not seize him for execution as an attainted person, for the time had not arrived at which the attainder could attach. The King, therefore, seized him as a man liable to be tried, and yet he calls upon him to suffer death, because he did not make himself amenable by voluntary surrender; that is, because he did not do that which the King was pleased to do for him, by a seizure, which made it at once unnecessary and impossible for him to do so by any voluntary act.

Such is the barbarity and folly that must ever arise, when force and power assume the functions of reason and justice.

As to his intention after the arrest it is clearly out of the question. The idea of intention is not applicable to an impossible act. To give existence to intention, the act must be possible, and the agent must be free. Gentlemen, this, and this only, is the subject on which you are to give a verdict. I do think it is highly honourable to the gentleman who has come over to this country, to give the prisoner at the bar the benefit of his evidence; no process could have compelled him; the inhabitants of foreign countries are beyond the reach of process to bring witnesses to give evidence. But we have a witness, and that of the highest respectability, who was himself at Hamburgh at the time Mr. Tandy was arrested, in an official situation. We will call Sir J. Crawford, who was then the King's representative in the town of Hamburgh. We will show you by his evidence the facts that I have stated; that before the time allowed to the prisoner to surrender had elapsed, Sir J. Crawford did, in his official situation, and by orders from his own government, cause the person of Mr. Tandy to be arrested in Hamburgh. Far am I from suspecting, or insinuating against Sir James Crawford, that any of the cruelties that were practised on that abused and helpless community, or on my abused client, were committed at his instance or personal sanction; certain am I that no such fact could be possible.

I told you before, gentlemen, that the principal question you had to try was, the fact on which the parties had joined issue: the force and arrest alleged by the prisoner; and the denial of that force by the counsel for the crown. There is one consideration that I think necessary to give some attention to. What you may think of the probable guilt or innocence of the prisoner, is not within the question that you are to decide; but if you should have any opinion of that sort, the verdict given in favour of the prisoner can be no preclusion to public justice, if after your verdict they still call for his life; the utmost that can follow from a verdict in his favour would be, that he will be considered as a person who has surrendered to justice, and must abide his trial for any crime that may be charged against him. There are various ways of getting rid of him, if it be necessary to the repose of the world that he should die.

I have said, if he has committed any crime he is amenable to justice, and in the hands of the law; he may be proceeded against before a jury, or he may be proceeded against in another and more summary manner; it may so happen that you may not be called upon to dispose finally of his life or of his character.

Whatever verdict a jury can pronounce upon him can be of no final avail. There was, indeed, a time when a jury was the shield of liberty and life: there was a time when I never rose to address it without a certain sentiment of confidence and pride; but that time is past. I have now no heart to make any appeal to your indignation, your justice, or your humanity. I sink under the consciousness that you are nothing. With us the trial by jury has given place to shorter, and, no doubt, better modes of disposing of life. Even in the sister nation, a verdict can merely prevent the duty of the hangman; but it never can purge the stain which the first malignity of accusation, however falsified by proof, stamps indelibly on the character of an "acquitted felon." To speak proudly of it to you would be a cruel mockery of your condition; but let me be at least a supplicant with you for its memory. Do not, I beseech you, by a vile instrumentality, cast any disgrace upon its memory.

I know you are called out to-day to fill up the ceremonial of a gaudy pageant, and that to-morrow you will be flung back again among the unused and useless lumber of the constitution: but trust me, the good old trial by jury will come round again; trust me, gentlemen, in the revolution of the great wheel of human affairs, though it is now at the bottom, it will re-ascend to the station it has lost, and once more assume its former dignity and respect; trust me, that mankind will become tired of resisting the spirit of innovation, by subverting every ancient and established principle, and by trampling upon every right of individuals and of nations. Man, destined to the grave, nothing that appertains to him is exempt from the stroke of death—his life fleeth as a dream, his liberty passeth as a shadow. So, too, of his slavery; it is not immortal; the chain that grinds him is gnawed by rust, or it is rent by fury, or by accident, and the wretch is astonished at the intrusions of freedom, unannounced even by the harbinger of hope. Let me, therefore, conjure you, by the memory of the past, and the hope of the future, to respect the fallen condition of the good old trial by jury, and cast no infamy upon it. If it be necessary to the repose of the world that the prisoner should die, there are many ways of killing him—we know there are; it is not necessary that you should be stained with his blood. The strange and still more unheard-of proceedings against the prisoner at the bar, have made the business of this day a subject of more attention to all Europe, than is generally excited by the fate or the suffering of any individual. Let me, therefore, advise you seriouly to reflect upon your situation, before you give a verdict of meanness and of blood, that must stamp the character of folly and barbarity upon this already disgraced and degraded country.

AGAINST SIR HENRY HAYES.

[ABDUCTION OF MISS PIKE.]

CORK SPRING ASSIZES.

April 13th, 1801.

Sir Henry Brown Hayes, Knight, was the son of Mr. Attwell Hayes, a wealthy citizen of Cork. At the time of the occurrence for which Curran prosecuted him, Sir Henry was a widower, with several children, and, being a man of address and fortune, was popular in Cork. It is said that his expenses had exceeded his means, and that he was induced to the abduction of Miss Pike to retrieve his affairs. The attempt at such an offence was then a capital felony under the statute law.

Mary Pike was the only child of Mr. Samuel Pike, a Cork banker, of a respectable Quaker family, who had died some time before, leaving her a fortune of over £20,000. Her mother was in weak health, resident in the city of Cork, and maintaining her connexion with the Society of Friends, which Miss Pike and many of her relatives had abandoned.

In 1797, Miss Pike, then twenty-one years old, resided with a relation, Mr. Cooper Penrose, at a beautiful demesne, called Wood-hill, near Cork. Sir Henry Hayes rode there on Sunday, the 2nd July, 1797, and, professing a desire to see the place, it was shown to him by Mr. Penrose, and he was finally (though previously unknown) asked to dinner by Mr. Penrose, and then met Miss Pike for the first time.

Sir Henry was captivated or content with this acquaintance. He wrote to Dr. Gibbings, Mrs. Pike's physician; and having learned Dr. Gibbings' hand-writing from the reply, this letter, in close imitation of that writing, was sent to Wood-hill:—

"TO COOPER PENROSE, ESQ.

"Dear Sir,—Our friend, Mrs. Pike, is taken suddenly ill; she wishes to see Miss Pike. We would recommend dispatch, as we think she has not many hours to live.

"Yours, &c., Robert Gibbings."

This document reached Mr. Penrose after midnight of July the 22nd, and, as soon as possible, Miss Pike, accompanied by Miss Penrose, and a Mrs. Richard Pike, set off in Mr. Penrose's carriage. The night was wet and stormy. They had not gone far when their carriage was stopped by armed men, Miss Pike's name ascertained, and her person identified by a muffled man. The traces of their carriage were then cut; and Miss Pike, placed in a chaise with a lady, who seems to have been a sister of Sir Henry's, was driven off, under a mounted escort, to Mount-Vernon. She was carried from the gate up the steep avenue by the muffled man. Her treatment, then, Miss Pike thus describes in her evidence:—

Q. How did you get into the house? *A.* He took me in his arms into the parlour.

What happened after you got into the house; were there lights in the parlour? There was a snuff of a candle just going out.

Miss Pike, be so good as to tell what happened after you got into the parlour; did any other persons make their appearance? Yes, two women.

Did you see any body else in the house that night, but Sir Henry and the two women? I did not, until the next morning.

Did you see any other persons in that house at any time after? Yes, a man in priest's habits.

Was it that night or next morning? It was next morning.

At break of day, was it? Yes.

Did anything particular happen then? Before that, I was forced up stairs.

By whom? By Sir Henry Hayes and his sister.

After you were forced up stairs, did anything particular happen? Before that, there was a kind of ceremony read, and they forced a ring on my finger; before I was taken up stairs, there was a kind of ceremony of marriage, and a man appeared dressed in the habit of a clergyman.

Court—You said something about a ring? A ring was attempted to be forced on my finger, which I threw away.

After you were forced up stairs, and after this kind of a ceremony of marriage was performed, did anything particular happen above stairs? I was locked into a room.

What sort of a room? A small room with two windows.

What happened after that; do you recollect anything more? There was tea brought up, and after that Sir Henry Hayes came up.

After tea was brought up, and after Sir Henry came up stairs, did anything happen?

Court—It is now about four years ago; and, therefore, mention only what you remember.

I remember his father coming up.

It was after that? Before my uncle came to take me home.

Court—Was the room furnished or unfurnished? There was a bed and a table in it.

Do you recollect anything that passed after Sir Henry's coming up; and if you do, state it to the Court? I recollect perfectly his coming in and out, and behaving in the rudest manner, and saying I was his wife.

Were you restored shortly after? About eight o'clock next morning.

Was or was not any part of that transaction between you and Sir Henry Hayes with your consent or against it? Against it entirely.

Did you write anything while at Mount-Vernon? Yes; I wrote a note, directed to my uncle.

How did you come to write that letter? I was anxious to get to my friends, and repeatedly asked for pen and ink.

It was at length brought to you? Yes; and as well as I can recollect, I wrote to my uncle, to let him know where I was.

Sir Henry Hayes absconded. Government offered £1000 for his apprehension, and Miss Pike's relatives offered another reward—both in vain. He was outlawed, but returned to Cork, and lived there without concealment, and Miss Pike went to reside in Bath. About two years after, Hayes wrote to her a polite letter, offering to stand his trial at the next assizes. Upon this the outlawry was reversed by consent, and an application to remove the venue to Dublin city having failed, the case came on at the Spring assizes of Cork, on the 13th day of April, 1801, before Mr. Justice Day.

There were two indictments, one for the abduction, another for procuring it, but on coming into court the Crown quashed the second indictment. The sustained indictment had two counts, one for abduction, with intent to marry, the other charging a still baser purpose.

The trial excited great interest, and Sir Henry came into court, attended by numerous and influential friends.

Witnesses having been ordered out of court, CURRAN spoke as follows:—

MY Lord and Gentlemen of the Jury—It is my duty, as one of the counsel in this prosecution, to state to your lordship, and to you, gentlemen of the jury, such facts as I am instructed will be established by evidence, in order that you may be informed of the nature of the offence charged by the indictment, and be rendered capable of understanding that evidence, which, without some previous statement, might appear irrelevant or obscure. And I shall make a few such observations, in point of law, on the evidence we propose to adduce, with respect to the manner in which it will support the charge, if you shall believe it to be true, as may assist you in performing that awful duty which you are now called upon to discharge. In doing so, I cannot forget upon what very different ground from that of the learned counsel for the prisoner, I find myself placed. It is the privilege, it is the obligation, of those who have to defend a client on a trial for his life, to exert every force, and to call forth every resource, that zeal, and genius, and sagacity can suggest. It is an indulgence in favour of life—it has the sanction of usage—it has the permission of humanity; and the man who should linger one single step behind the most advanced limit of that privilege, and should fail to exercise every talent that heaven had given him, in that defence, would be guilty of a mean desertion of his duty, and an abandonment of his client.

Far different is the situation of him who is concerned for the crown. Cautiously should he use his privileges—scrupulously should he keep within the duties of accusation. His task is to lay fairly the nature of the case before the court and the jury. Should he endeavour to gain a verdict otherwise than by evidence, he were unworthy of speaking in a court of justice. If I heard a counsel for the crown state anything that I did not think founded in law, I should say to myself, "God grant that the man who has stated this may be an ignorant man, because his ignorance can be his only justification." It shall, therefore, be my endeavour, so to lay the matters of fact and of law before you, as shall enable you clearly to comprehend them, and, finally, by your verdict, to do complete justice between the prisoner and the public.

My Lord, and Gentlemen of the Jury, this is an indictment, found by the grand jury against the prisoner at the bar, for having feloniously carried away Mary Pike, with intent against her will to marry her; there is another charge also, that he did feloniously carry her away with intent to defile her.

There was a former statute made on this subject, enacting the punishment of death against any man that should, by violence, carry away a female, and actually marry or defile her. But it was found that young creatures, the victims of this sort of crime, for their natural timidity, and the awful impression made upon them in an assembly like the present, were often unequal to the task of prosecution, and that offences against that statute often passed unpunished, because the natural delicacy and modesty of the sex shrunk from the revolting details that were unavoidable on such trials. It, therefore, became necessary to enact a new law upon the subject, making the taking away with intent to marry or defile, although, in fact, no such marriage or defilement had taken place, felony of death. Thus was suppressed the necessity of all those shocking, but necessary, details, that were otherwise required.

Of the enormity of the crime, I trust I need say

but little. I trust in God there could not be found in this great city twelve men, to whom it could be necessary to expatiate on the hideous enormity of such an offence. It goes to sap the foundation of all civil society; it goes to check the working of that natural affection, which heaven has planted in the breast of the parent for the child. In fact, gentlemen of the jury, if crimes like this shall be encouraged and multiplied by impunity, why should you defraud your own gratifications of the fruits of your industry?— why lay up the acquisitions of self-denying toil, as an advancement for your child? —why check your own appetites to give her all?— why labour to adorn her person or her mind with useless, with fatal accomplishments? You are only decking her with temptations for lust and rapine; you are refining her heart, only to make her feel more profoundly the agony of violation and of dishonour. Why, then, labour to multiply the inducements of the ravisher?—why labour to augment and to perpetuate the sufferings of the victim? Instead of telling you my opinion of the enormity of this crime, I will tell you that of the legislature upon it:—the legislature has deemed it a crime deserving the punishment of death.

I will now state to you the facts as I am instructed they will appear to you in evidence.

The prisoner at the bar, (and considering his education, his age, his rank, and situation in society, I do regret, from my soul, that he is there,) married many years ago; his wife died, leaving him the surviving parent of, I believe, many children. Miss Mary Pike is the only child of a person, whom, I suppose, you all knew—Mr. Samuel Pike, of this city. He had devoted a long life to a very persevering and successful industry, and died advanced in years, leaving this his only child entitled to all the fruits of his laborious and persevering application. The property she is entitled to, I understand, is very great, indeed. At the time of the transaction, to which your attention must be called, she was living in the house, and under the protection, of an universally respected member of society, Mr. Cooper Penrose. From the moment her mind was susceptible of it, no expense was spared to give her every accomplishment that she was capable of receiving; and in the house of her own father, while he lived, and in the house of Mr. Penrose, when she came under his protection, her mind was formed to the most correct principles of modesty, and delicacy, and decorum, with those additional characteristics, humility and reserve, that belong to that most respectable sect of which her father was a member. The prisoner at the bar, it seems, had heard of her, and had heard of her property; for it is a material circumstance in this case, that he never by any accident had seen her, even for a moment, until he went to see and identify her person, and mark her out the victim of his projected crime.

He was not induced by the common motives

that influence young men—by any individual attachment to the mind or the person of the lady. It will appear, that his first approach to her was meanly and perfidiously contrived, with the single purpose of identifying her person, in order that he might feloniously steal it, as the title-deed of her estate.

Some time before the 22nd of July, in the year 1797, he rode down to the residence of Mr. Penrose. Mr. Penrose has a country-house, built in a very beautiful situation, and which attracts the curiosity of strangers, who frequently go to see it.

The prisoner at the bar went into the grounds as one of these, and seemed to observe every thing with great attention. Mr. Penrose immediately came out to him, and conducted him to whatever objects he supposed might gratify his curiosity. He affected to be much entertained; he lingered about the grounds until the hour of Mr. Penrose's dinner approached. Mr. Penrose, quite a stranger to the prisoner at the bar, was not, I suppose, very anxious to invite a perfect stranger in among his family, more desirous, probably, of enjoying the little exclusive confidential intercourse of that family. However, with that good nature which any man of his cordial and honest turn of mind will feel it his duty to exercise, he did invite Sir Henry Hayes to dinner. The invitation was accepted of; and thus the first step towards the crime he meditated, was an abuse of the sacred duty which the hospitality of his host imposed upon him, as a man, and as a gentleman. He placed himself at the friendly and unsuspecting board, in order to the accomplishment of his design, by the most unfeeling and unextenuated violation of the rights of the host, whom he made his dupe—of the lady, whom he marked as his victim—and of the law, which he determined to trample upon, and disgrace by the commission of a felony of death. There, when the eye of the prisoner could escape from the smiles that were lavished upon him—those honest smiles of respect and cordiality, that come only from the heart—it was to search the room, to find out who probably was the person that he had come to identify. He made his observation, and took his departure; but it was not a departure for the last time.

Mrs. Pike, the widow, mother of the prosecutrix, was then in Cork, in a dangerous state of health. In order to get Miss Pike out of the hands of her protector, a stratagem was adopted. Dr. Gibbings was the attending physician upon her mother; it does not appear that the prisoner knew Dr. Gibbings' handwriting: it was necessary that a letter should be sent, as if from Dr. Gibbings; but to do so with effect, it was necessary that a letter should be written to Mr. Penrose in a hand-writing, bearing such a similitude to the doctor's, as might pass for genuine. To qualify himself for this, the prisoner at the bar made some pretext for sending a written message to Dr. Gibbings, which procured, in return, a written answer from the doctor. Thus was he furnished with the form of the hand-writing of Dr. Gibbings, which he intended to counterfeit; and, accordingly, there was written, on the 22nd day of July, 1797, a letter, so like the character of Dr. Gibbings, that he himself, on a slight glance, would be apt to take it for his own. It was in these words:—"Dear Sir,—Our friend, Mrs. Pike, is taken suddenly ill; she wishes to see Miss Pike; we would recommend despatch, as we think that she has not many hours to live. Your's, Robert Gibbings." Addressed "to Mr. Cooper Penrose." The first step to the crime was a flagrant breach of hospitality, and the second, towards the completion, was the inhuman fraud of practising upon the piety of the child, to decoy her into the trap of the ravisher, to seduce her to destruction by the angelic impulses of that feeling that attaches her to the parent—that sends her after the hour of midnight, from the house of her protector, to pay the last duty, and to receive the parting benediction. Such was the intention with which the prosecutrix, of a rainy night, between one and two o'clock in the morning, rose from her bed; such was her intention; it was not her destination; it was not to visit the sick bed of a parent; it was not to carry a daughter's duty of consolation to her dying mother; it was not for that she came abroad; it was that she might fall into the hands of preconcerted villany; that she should fall into that trap, which was laid for her, with the intention to despoil her of every thing that makes human existence worth the having, by any female who has any feeling of delicacy or honour.

I should state to you, that she left the house of Mr. Penrose, in his carriage, attended by two female relations, one of them his daughter; and when they had advanced about half way to Cork, the carriage was suddenly met by four or five men. They ordered the coachman to stop. One of them was dressed in a great coat, and armed with pistols, and had the lower part of his face concealed, by tying a handkerchief round it.

The ladies, as you may suppose, were exceedingly terrified at such a circumstance as this. They asked, as well as extreme terror would permit, what they sought for; they were answered, "they must be searched." On looking about, they observed another chaise, stationed near the place where they were detained. It will appear to you, that Miss Pike was taken forcibly out of the carriage from her friends; that she was placed in the other chaise which I have mentioned; in which she found, shame to tell it—she found a woman. The traces of Mr. Penrose's chaise were then cut: and the ladies that came in it left, of course, to find their way as well as they could, and return in the dark.

The carriage, into which the prosecutrix was put, drove off towards Cork; the female that was with her will appear to you to have been the sister of the prisoner. Happy! happy for her! that death has taken her away from being the companion of his trial, and of his punishment, as she was the accomplice of his guilt: but she is dead. The carriage drove on to the seat, belonging to the prisoner at the bar, called Mount-Vernon, in the liberties of the city; at the bottom of his avenue, which it seems is a steep ascent, and of considerable length, the horses refused to go on; upon which the prisoner rode up to the chaise, dismounted from his horse, which he gave to one of his attendants, opened the door, took the prosecutrix out, and carried her, struggling in his arms, the whole length of the avenue, to his house. When he arrived there, he carried her up stairs, where she saw a man, attired in somewhat like the dress of a priest; and she was then told that she was brought there to marry the prisoner at the bar. In what frame of mind the miserable wretch must have been, any man that has feelings; must picture to himself. She had quitted the innocent and respectable protection of her friends and family, and found herself —good God! where?—in the power of an inexorable ravisher, and surrounded by his accomplices: she looked in every mean and guilty countenance; she saw the base unfeeling accomplices induced by bribe, and armed for present force, bound and pledged by the community of guilt and danger, by the felon's necessity, to the future perjury of self-defence.

Thus situated, what was she to look to for assistance? What was she to do? Was she to implore the unfeeling heart of the prisoner? As well might she have invoked her buried father, to burst the cerements of the grave, and rise to the protection of his forlorn and miserable child. There, whatever sort of ceremony they thought right to perform, took place; something was muttered in a language which she partly did not hear, and partly could not understand; she was then his wife—she was then Lady Hayes.

A letter was then to be written to apprize her miserable relations of their new affinity. A pen was put into her hand, and she consented to write, in hopes that it might lead to her deliverance; but when the sad scroll was finished, and the subscription only remained, neither entreaties nor menaces could prevail upon her, desolate and forlorn as she was, to write the odious name of the ravisher. She subscribed herself by the surname of her departed father; as if she thought there was some mysterious virtue in the name of her family, to which she could cling in that hour of terror, as a refuge from lawless force and unmerited suffering.

A ceremony of marriage had taken place: a ring was forced upon her finger; she tore it off, and indignantly dashed it from her; she was then forced into an adjoining chamber, and the prisoner brutally endeavoured to push her towards the bed.

My lord, and gentlemen of the jury, you will

soon see this young lady. You will see that whatever grace or proportion her person possesses, it does not seem formed for much power of resistance, or of self-defence. But there is a last effort of sinking modesty, that can rally more than the powers of nature to the heart, and send them to every fibre of the frame, where they can achieve more than mere vulgar strength can do upon any ordinary occasion: that effort she did make, and made it with effect; and in that instance, innocence was crowned with success.

Baffled and frustrated in his purposes of force, he sought to soften, to conciliate. "And do you not know me?" said he. "Don't you know who I am?" "Yes," answered she, "I do know you; I do now remember you did go to my cousin's, as you say you did. I remember your mean intrusion, you are Sir Henry Hayes." How naturally do the parties support their characters! The criminal puts his questions under the consciousness of guilt, as if under the forecast of his present situation. The innocent victim of that guilt regards him already as his prosecutrix; she recognizes him, but it is only to identify him as a malefactor, and to disclaim him as a husband.

Gentlemen, she remained in this captivity, until her friends got intelligence of her situation. Justice was applied to. A party went to the house of the prisoner, for the purpose of enlarging her. The prisoner at the bar had fled. His sister, his accomplice, had fled. They left behind them Miss Pike, who was taken back by her relations. Informations were lodged immediately. The prisoner absconded. It would be base and scandalous to suffer a crime of that kind to pass with impunity, without doing every thing that could be done to bring the offender to justice. Government was apprized of it. Government felt as it ought. There was offered, by proclamation, a reward to a considerable amount for taking the prisoner. The family of Miss Pike did as they ought. They offered a considerable additional sum, as the reward for his apprehension. For some time he kept in concealment; the rewards were offered in vain; the process of the law went on; an indictment, to the honour of this city, to the honour of the national character, was found; they proceeded to the outlawry of the prisoner.

What I have stated hitherto reflects honour upon all persons concerned, except the unhappy man at the bar, and his accomplices; but what I am about to relate, is a circumstance that no man of feeling or humanity can listen to without indignation. Notwithstanding that outlawry; notwithstanding the publicly offered rewards, to the amount of near one thousand pounds, for the apprehension of the prisoner at the bar, (would to God the story could not be told in a foreign country! would to God it were not in the power of those so ready to defame us, to adduce such a circumstance in corroboration of their charge!) for near two years did the prisoner live in public, almost in the heart of your city; reading in every newspaper, over his tea, the miserable proclamation of impotent public justice, of the laws defied and trampled upon. The second city in the nation was made the hiding-place—no! no! not the hiding-place, where guilt hid its head—but the receptacle where it walked abroad, unappalled, and threw your degraded city into the odious predicament of being a sort of public accessory and accomplice in his crime, by giving it that hideous appearance of protection and impunity. Here he stayed, basking in the favour of a numerous kindred and acquaintance, in a widely-extended city.

Sad reverse! It was not for guilt to fly! It was for guilt to stand, and bay at public justice! It was only for innocence to betake itself to flight! It was not the ravisher that fled. It was the helpless female, the object of this crime, the victim of his felony! It was hers to feel that she could despair of even personal protection in that country which harboured and cherished the delinquent! It was she who was hunted, a poor fugitive from her family and her home; and was forced to fling herself at the feet of a foreign nation, a suppliant for personal protection. She fled to England, where she remained for two years.

A few months ago, previous to the last term, a

letter was written and sent to Miss Pike, the prosecutrix, by the prisoner. The purport of it was, to state to her, that his conduct to her had been honourable and delicate, and asserting, that any lady, possessed of the smallest particle of humanity, could not be so sanguinary as to wish for the blood of an individual, however guilty; intimating a threat, that her conduct upon this occasion would mark her fate through life; desiring her to withdraw her advertisements, saying, he would abide his trial at the assizes of Cork; boasting his influence in the city in which he lived, thanking God he stands as high as any man in the regards of rich and poor, of which the inefficacy of her present and former rewards must convince her.

He thought, I suppose, that an interval of two years, during which he had been an outlaw, and had resided among his friends, had brought the public mind to such a state of honourable sympathy in his favour, as would leave any form of trial perfectly safe. After this he thought proper to appear, and the outlawry was reversed without opposition by counsel for the prosecution; because their object was not to take advantage of any judgment of outlawry upon which he might be executed; but to admit him to plead to the charge, and take his trial by a jury of his country. He pleaded to that indictment in the court above, and accordingly he now stands at the bar of this court for the purpose of trial.

The publicity of his living in this city, of his going to festivals and entertainments, during the course of two years, did impress the minds of the friends of this unhappy lady with such a despair of obtaining public justice that they did struggle hard, not, as it is said, to try the offence by a foreign jury; but to try the offence at a distant place, in the capital where the authority of the court might keep public justice in some sort of countenance. That application was refused: and justly did you, my lord, and the learned judges, your brethren, ground yourselves upon the reason which you gave. "We will not," said you, "give a judicial sanction to a reproach of such a scandalous atrocity upon any county in the land, much less upon the second city in it." "I do remember," said one of you, "a case, which happened not twenty years since. A similar crime was committed on two young women of the name of Kennedy; it was actually necessary to guard them through two counties with a military force as they went to prosecute; that mean and odious bias, that the dregs of every community will feel by natural sympathy with every thing base, was in favour of the prisoners. Every means were used to try and baffle justice, by practising upon the modesty and constancy of the prosecutrixes, and their friends; but the infatuated populace, that had assembled together to celebrate the triumph of an acquittal, were the unwilling spectators of the vindication of the law. The court recollected that particular respect is due to the female who nobly comes forward to vindicate the law, and give protection to her sex. The jury remembered what they owed to their oaths, to their families, to their country. They felt as became the fathers of families, and foresaw what the hideous consequence would be of impunity, in a case of manifest guilt. They pronounced that verdict which saved their characters; and the offenders were executed."

I am glad that the Court of King's Bench did not yield to the despair which had taken place in the minds of those who were anxious to bring the prosecution forward. I am glad the prisoner was sent to this bar, in order that you may decide upon it.

I have stated to you, gentlemen of the jury, the facts that I conceive material; I have stated that it was necessary, and my duty, as counsel for the crown, to give you an exact idea of the nature of the offence, of the evidence, and of the law; that you may be enabled to combine the whole case together, and to pronounce such a verdict as shall fairly decide the question, which you are sworn to try, between the public and the prisoner. Any thing I say, either as to the fact, or as to the law, ought not to attract any thing more than bare attention for a single moment; it should make no impression upon your belief, unless confirmed by credible evidence. I am merely stating facts from instruction; but I am not a witness.

I am also obliged, as I told you, to make observations as to the law, but that is wholly submitted to the court; to which it is your duty, as well as mine, to bow with all becoming deference and respect.

My lord, the prisoner is indicted as a principal offender, upon the statute; and, therefore, it is necessary that the jury shall understand what kind of evidence is necessary to sustain that charge. Formerly there was a distinction taken by courts of justice between two species of principals; the one, a principal at the doing of the very act; the other, a principal in the second degree, who was then considered as an accessory at the fact: a distinction in point of law, which, as Mr. Justice Forster observes, was a great inconvenience in the course and order of proceeding against accomplices in felony; tending, as it plainly did, to the total obstruction of justice in many cases, and to great delay in others; and which induced the judges, from a principle of true political justice, to come into the rule now established: "That all persons present, aiding and abetting, are principals."

I now proceed to show what kind of presence it is that will make a man concurring in the crime, in judgment of the law, "present, aiding, and assisting:" which to explain, I shall read the words of the last-mentioned writer, as follows: "When the law requireth the presence of the accomplice at the perpetration of the fact, in order to render him a principal, it doth not require a strict, actual, immediate presence; such a presence as would make him an eye or ear witness of what passeth." And I may thus exemplify this case: "Several persons set out together, or in small parties, upon one common design, be it murder, or other felony; or for any other purpose, unlawful in itself; and each taketh the part assigned him: one to commit the fact, others to watch at proper stations, to prevent a surprise, or favour, if need be, the escape of those who are more immediately engaged; they are all (provided the fact be committed,) in the eye of the law, present at it. For it was made a common cause with them; each man operated in his station, at one and the same instant, towards the same common end: and the part each man took, tended to give countenance, encouragement, and protection, to the whole gang, and to ensure the success of their common enterprise."

If the prisoner at the bar formed a design of doing the illegal act with which he is charged, namely, running away with Miss Pike, in order to marry or defile her; if he projected the perpetration of it by dividing his accomplices in such manner, as that each might contribute his part to its success; that it was made a common cause; that what each man did, tended to secure the success of the common enterprise; then every person so acting, although not an eye or ear witness of what was done, yet in the eye of the law is guilty. He is a principal, and punishable as such.

Suppose, that some should guard at Mr. Penrose's bounds; others guard at different stations on the road; others guard at the bridge; others remain at the house at Mount-Vernon. In that case, I should not hesitate to say, in point of law, that the man stationed at the back door of Mr. Penrose's house (supposing her to be taken out by violence,) the men guarding on the road, and at the bridge; nay, the priest that waited at Mount-Vernon to celebrate the marriage, were all a combination of one common power; acting each man in his station, to produce the intended effect; and, as such, were all equally principals in the offence.

But, in the present case, it is not necessary to argue upon a constructive presence; for here is an actual presence. If what I have stated should be supported by the witnesses, there is full ground to convince the jury, that Sir Henry Hayes was the person in disguise, who put her into his carriage, when taken out of Mr. Penrose's; particularly when the circumstance is considered, that he went to the house in order to identify her person, for that knowledge of her person would have been useless, unless he had been present at the first taking of her.

If the jury believe he was there at such first taking, he was actually present and guilty. But, supposing the jury to doubt, strange as the doubt must be, yet if there shall be evidence to satisfy them that the prisoner, at the bottom of the hill leading to his house, took her out of his carriage, and led her to the house, that is, as to him, a taking and carrying away, clearly within the statute. There cannot be the least doubt, that every step the chaise proceeded from Mr. Penrose's to Mount-Vernon, that every man who joined the cavalcade, and became an assistant in the project, became a principal in the entire transaction, and guilty of carrying her away, contrary to the statute.

In further illustration, suppose this case. A highwayman stops a traveller, and proceeds to rob him; and another comes up to the assistance of that robber; there is not the least doubt, that the man who joins in the robbery a little later, is equally guilty with the former in the eye of the law. This is applicable to the present case.

Thus I have stated the nature of the case, and what I conceive to be the law touching that case. I know not what kind of defence may be set up. There are some defences which, if they can be established clearly, must acquit the prisoner. If he did not do this, if she was not taken away, or if Sir Henry took no share in the transaction, there can be no doubt in the case. It will be for your consciences to say, whether this be a mere tale of the imagination, unsupported by truth, and uncorroborated by evidence. It is material, however, to state to you that, as soon as guilt is once established in the eye of the law, nothing that the party can do can have any sort of retrospect so as to purge that criminality, if once completed. It is out of the power of the expiring victim of a death-blow to give any release or acquittal to his murderer; it is out of the power of any human creature, upon whom an illegal offence has been committed, by any act of forgiveness to purge that original guilt; and, therefore, the semblance of a marriage is entirely out of the case.

In the case of the Misses Kennedy, the young ladies had been obliged to submit to a marriage, and cohabitation for a length of time; yet the offenders were most justly convicted, and suffered death.

It is, therefore, necessary for you to keep your minds and understandings so fixed upon the material points of the charge, as that, in the course of the examination, no sidelong view of the subject may mislead or divert your attention.

The point before you is, whether the crime was once committed; and if so, nothing happening after can make any sort of difference upon the subject. It has been my most anxious wish to abstain, as far as was consistent with my duty, from every the remotest expression of contumely or disrespect to the unhappy prisoner at the bar; or to say or to do anything that might unhinge his mind or distract his recollection, so as to disable him from giving his whole undisturbed reflection to the consideration of his defence; but it is also a sacred duty, which every man placed in my situation owes to public justice, to take care, under the affectation of false humanity, not to suffocate that charge which it is his duty to unfold, nor to frustrate the force of that evidence which it is his duty to develop. Painful must it be to the counsel, to the jury, and the court, who are bound by their respective duties to prosecute, to convict, and to pronounce, and to draw down the stroke of public justice, even upon the guilty head; but despicable would they all be, if, instead of surrendering the criminal to the law, they could abandon the law to the criminal; if, instead of having mercy upon outraged justice and injured innocence, they should squander their disgraceful sympathy upon guilt alone. Justice may weep; but she must strike where she ought not to spare. We, too, may lament; but, when we mourn over crimes, let us take care that there be no crimes of our own upon which our tears should be shed.

Gentlemen, you cannot be surprised that I hold this language to you. Had this case no reference to any country but our own, the extraordinary circumstances attending it, which are known to the whole nation, would well warrant much more than I have said. But you cannot forget that the eyes of another country also are upon you: another country, which is now the source of your legislation. You are not ignorant what sort of character is given of us there; by what sort of men, and from what kind of motive. Alas! we have no power of contradicting the cruel calumnies that are there heaped upon us, in defiance of notorious truth, and of common mercy and humanity; but, when we are there charged with being a barbarous race of savages, with whom no measures can be held, upon whose devoted heads legislation can only pour down laws of fire, we can easily, by our own misconduct, furnish proof that to a much less willing belief may corroborate their base evidence, and turn their falsehood into truth.

Once more, and for the last time, let me say to you, you have heard the charge. Believe nothing upon my statement. Hear and weigh the evidence. If you doubt its truth, acquit without hesitation. By the laws of every country, because by those of eternal justice, doubt and acquittal are synonymous terms. If, on the other hand, the guilt of the prisoner shall unhappily be clearly proved, remember what you owe to your fame, your conscience, and your country. I shall trouble you no further, but shall call evidence in support of the indictment; and I have not a doubt, that there will be such a verdict given, whether of conviction or acquittal, as may hereafter be spoken of, without kindling any shame in yourselves, or your country.

Before the witnesses were called Mr. CURRAN objected to any

person but the prisoner being suffered to stand at the bar. Prisoner's counsel declared they were not anxious about it, but mentioned the case of Mr. Horne Tooke, where the Court allowed him to be attended by his counsel. The Court said, the prisoner here should have that indulgence, when he came to his defence; but, for the present, all other persons, save his attorney, and one of his counsel, were ordered to withdraw from the bar.

Miss Pike proved the facts stated before, but her cross-examination by Mr. Quin contained some inconsistencies:—

Q. Can you swear, that, at that time, you knew any one of the persons who took and carried you away from that part of the Glanmire Road, where you were stopped? *A.* No, I cannot.

Your uncle mentioned something as you went along of the necessity of giving immediate informations—did he not? I said before he did.

When did you give the informations? The Monday morning following.

Do you recollect what day of the week it happened? I believe Saturday.

And you gave informations on Monday? I did.

Where did you swear them? At my aunt's.

Who drew them out? Indeed I do not know who wrote them.

Do you recollect whether you swore in the informations, that Sir Henry took, and carried you away on the Glanmire Road? I believe I did not.

Was there any interposition used with you to induce you to come into court this morning? No, there was not.

Did any person describe the dress or person of Sir Henry to you before you came into court? No, sir.

Will you now say upon your oath, that if, at the time you came into court and sat upon the table, you were asked the question, that you could have said positively you knew Sir Henry Hayes? No, I could not, because he might have been very much disguised.

Mr. and Miss Penrose, Dr. Gibbings, and Mr. Richard Pike proved the other facts. Mr. Quin spoke for the prisoner, but declined to call witnesses, and pressed for an acquittal in law, from the insufficiency of the evidence under the statute of abduction. CURRAN shortly replied, as follows:—

It is the undoubted privilege of the crown to reply in all criminal cases, not only to a point of law, but if the prisoner's counsel speak to evidence, the crown is warranted to reply. I might by law have prevented such speaking altogether; but I will never oppose such indulgence to a prisoner. The evidence adduced upon the part of the crown has not been attempted to be denied by a single witness, and, therefore, I think it would be absurd to go about to establish the credibility of testimony uncontroverted, even by the prisoner. I feel myself, therefore, only called upon to answer the objections in point of law. Much has been said about that indictment which was quashed; the observations on that, as far as they go, are a complete answer to themselves. It is undoubted law, that if a man be indicted as a principal, and acquitted, and afterwards indicted as an accessory before the fact, that the former acquittal is a conclusive plea in bar. The law is clearly settled in that case, and an acquittal upon the present indictment would be a complete bar to any prosecution upon the second; therefore it was, that the second indictment was quashed. We sent up that indictment in fact, because we did not, with precise exactness, know how the evidence would turn out upon the trial. The second indictment was a mere charge of an accessorial offence; but feeling that, to bring forward the real merits of the case, we should go upon the first indictment, we thought it would be an act of unwarrantable vexation not to apprize the prisoner, the court, and the jury, that that was the only charge against him. And therefore it is, that that indictment should be dimissed entirely from the subject. The argument contended for is, that the evidence adduced does not support the indictment; to that, and that alone, it is necessary for me to reply: the only question is, whether there is sufficient evidence to maintain the indictment. [Reads the indictment.] On this a question of law occurs. What is a taking and carrying away? I see no possibility that the jury can disbelieve that the man who took her out of Mr. Penrose's carriage was the prisoner at the bar, who went before to identify her. He could not make use of that knowledge of her person on that occasion, if he was not there; he should have shown that he was then in some other place, but to do so was not attempted. Observe upon the latter part of the transaction, on the carriage proceeding with her in it to the passage leading to Mount-Vernon, that there a man, dressed as the lady describes, alit from his horse; but there has been strong evidence that he did not come from the house; took the handkerchief from his face, took her in his arms, and carried her in his arms from the foot of the hill to Mount-Vernon house, and where that marriage was absolutely solemnized. Upon this part of the question there does, to be sure, arise a question—Was that a taking and carrying away within the statute? I do admit that the taking and carrying away are essential; but it is not being the first taker that is necessary within the act of parliament: for if ten different persons had rescued her from one another, and another had taken her into the place, where, &c., he would be guilty, because he had taken her, and carried her away. The question, therefore, is, Was there a taking within the act or not? Mr. Quin has argued from two cases, that he supposes similar to the present; the one was burglary, the other was murder. They differ materially in this from the present, that they are things done at one moment of time, and, in the present case, a continuance of the force is a continuance of the taking; upon the statute of Henry VII. there must be an actual marriage in order to constitute the offence; but in England, as well as here, there must be a previous taking and carrying away; therefore, what is there considered as such, must be, in this country, a taking and carrying away. 2 Hawkins, 315. Also, if a woman be taken away by force in one county, and carried into another, and there married, the offender may be indicted, and tried in the second county upon the statute of Henry VII., because it is a continuation of force, and of such kind as amounts to forcibly taking within the statute; and so it is, if the prisoner at the bar had taken her by force in an adjoining county, and brought her into this.

You have an unquestionable authority, and a most respectable one, stating that a continuance of force in the county where the indictment is laid, is a sufficient taking and carrying away within the statute.

Suppose a man hires a gang of people to seize a woman in Dublin, and bring her down by force; in the last stage, he goes and takes her in his arms, and carries her into his house; will any one say, that because he had not seized her in the first instance himself, that his seizing her by force, in the last stage, is not a taking within the statute?

The simple question to be decided upon is this, in point of law, whether the taking her out of that chaise, in which she was brought to the avenue of the prisoner, was a sufficient taking, and whether the carrying her up to his house, was such a carrying away, as, added to the taking, brought the present case within the statute.

To support this, I shall cite the case of the King and Lapyard, an indictment on which the facts were,—"That Mrs. Hobart, coming out of the playhouse, had an attempt made by the prisoner to snatch her ear-ring from her ear; it appeared that the snatch at it was so violent, that it tore through her ear. When she went home, she found not only that the ear-ring had not been taken away by the prisoner, but actually found it sticking in the curls of her hair." It was necessary, then, that there should be a taking, and also a carrying away; and the question was, whether the facts did amount to that taking and carrying away. The judge gave in to the doubt proposed by the prisoner's counsel. I shall mention two cases, one where a man turned a cart from a horizontal to a perpendicular position to get at the goods; the other case was, where a person removed a parcel into the head of a waggon in order to steal it, which had been before in the tail of it, and in each case there was judged a sufficient taking and carrying away. A man lodged at an inn, and in the morning took the sheets out of his bed, and carried them into the stable, and another stole them. The jury found the prisoner guilty; but judgment was respited, and the case submitted to the consideration of the twelve judges, who were of opinion, that he was guilty of the charge of felony laid in the indictment. Compare these to the present case. Miss Pike was taken by force out of the chaise; she was carried by force up the avenue; she was taken by force into a room. What would become of the law, if miserable subterfuges of this kind could have any effect? The circumstances of this case make it ridiculous to suppose that the conduct of the prisoner was from any motive of hospitality, as has been insinuated, for she stated other facts inconsistent with such a defence. Every fact, if the jury believed the prosecution, was by force, and against her consent. Let me remind the jury that such an idea as this ought not to go abroad, that a gang may be hired by a man, to force away a woman, and that that man, meeting her in the last stage of the transaction, shall completely commit a felony against the statute, with impunity.

The judge charged fairly, and after an hour's deliberation the jury found the prisoner Guilty, but recommended him to mercy. The law point on the insufficiency of the evidence was referred to the twelve judges, and decided against Sir Henry, but the recommendation to mercy was acceded to, and he was transported.

HEVEY *v.* MAJOR SIRR.

KING'S BENCH.

May 17th, 1802.

As an illustration of the government of Ireland at the time of the trial, and for some years before, this case is most interesting, and CURRAN'S speech equal to the occasion.

Hevey was a brewer in Dublin, and in '98 acted as a yeoman in the Roebuck cavalry. Happening to be in court during a trial, and seeing a rascal whom he had once employed, on the table, he said what he thought of him, and was then obliged to give evidence against the witness's character, and the prisoner was acquitted. For this he was seized on by Major Sirr and his gang, forced into prison, obliged to give up a valuable mare to Sandys, a comrade of Sirr's, was then hurried to Kilkenny, tried by Court-martial, and sentenced to be hanged. Lord Cornwallis saw the report of the trial, and released Hevey. In September, 1801, Major Sirr met Hevey in the Commercial Buildings, threatened him, and when Hevey defied him, Sirr thrust the unfortunate man into the provost prison in the Castle, till he signed a submission. For this the action was brought.

Lord Kilwarden (Arthur Wolfe) and a special jury tried the case. CURRAN opened for the plaintiff:—

THIS is the most extraordinary action I have ever met with. It must proceed from the most unexampled impudence in the plaintiff, if he has brought it wantonly, or the most unparalled miscreancy in the defendant, if it shall appear supported by proof. The event must stamp the most condign and indelible disgrace on the guilty defendant, unless an unworthy verdict should shift the scandal upon another quarter.

On the record the action appears short and simple. It is an action of trespass, *vi et armis,* for an assault, battery, and false imprisonment. But the facts that led to it, that explain its nature, and its enormity, and, of course, that should measure the damages, are neither short nor simple. The novelty of them may surprise, the atrocity must shock your feelings, if you have feelings to be shocked. But I do not mean to address myself to any of your proud feelings of liberty—the season for that is past. There was, indeed, a time when, in addressing a jury upon very inferior violations of human rights, I have felt my bosom glow and swell with the noble and elevating consciousness of being a free-man, speaking to free-men, and in a free country; where, if I was not able to communicate the generous flame to their bosoms, I was not at least so cold as not to catch it from them. But that is a sympathy which I am not now so foolish as to affect either to inspire, or to participate. I shall not insult you by the bitter mockery of such an affectation; buried as they are, I do not wish to conjure up the shades of departed freedom to flutter round their tomb, to taunt or to reproach them. Where freedom is no more, it is a mischievous profanation to use her language; because it tends to deceive the man who is no longer free, upon the most important of all points—that is, the nature of the situation to which he is reduced; and to make him confound the licentiousness of words with the real possession of freedom. I mean not, therefore, to call for a haughty verdict, that might humble the insolence of oppression, or assert the fancied rights of independence. Far from it; I only ask for such a verdict as may make some reparation for the most extreme and unmerited suffering, and may also tend to some probable mitigation of the public and general destiny. For this purpose I must carry back your attention to the melancholy period of 1798. It was at that sad crisis that the defendant, from an obscure individual, started into notice and consequence. It is in the hot-bed of public calamity that such portentous and inauspicious products are accelerated without being matured. From being a town-major, a name scarcely legible in the list of public incumbrances, he became at once invested with all the real powers of the most absolute authority. The life and the liberty of every man seemed to be given up to his disposal. With this gentleman's extraordinary elevation begins the story of the sufferings and ruin of the plaintiff.

It seems, a man of the name of M'Guire was prosecuted for some offence against the state. Mr. Hevey, the plaintiff, by accident was in court; he was then a citizen of wealth and credit, a brewer, in the first line of that business. Unfortunately for him, he had heretofore employed the witness for the prosecution, and found him a man of infamous character. Unfortunately for himself, he mentioned this circumstance in court. The counsel for the prisoner insisted on his being sworn: he was so. The jury were convinced that no credit was due to the witness for the crown, and the prisoner was accordingly acquitted. In a day or two after, Major Sirr met the plaintiff in the street, asked how he dared to interfere in his business, and swore, "By God, he would teach him how to meddle with his people."

Gentlemen, there are two classes of prophets, one that derive their predictions from real or fancied inspiration, and are sometimes mistaken; and another who prophecy what they are determined to bring about themselves. Of this second, and by far the most authentic class, was the Major; for heaven, you see, has no monopoly of prediction.

On the following evening, poor Hevey was dogged in the dark into some lonely alley; there he was seized, he knew not by whom, nor by what authority—and became in a moment to his family and his friends, as if he had never been. He was carried away in equal ignorance of his crime and of his destiny, whether to be tortured, or hanged, or transported. His crime he soon learned; it was the treason which he had committed against the majesty of Major Sirr. He was immediately conducted to a new place of imprisonment in the

Castle-yard, called the Provost. Of this mansion of misery, of which you have since heard so much, Major Sandys was, and I believe yet is, the keeper —a gentleman of whom I know how dangerous it is to speak, and of whom every prudent man will think and talk with all due reverence. He seemed a twin star of the defendant,—equal in honour, in confidence;—equal also (for who could be superior?) in probity and humanity. To this gentleman was my client consigned, and in his custody he remained about seven weeks, unthought of by the world as if he had never existed. The oblivion of the buried is as profound as the oblivion of the dead; his family may have mourned his absence or his probable death; but why should I mention so paltry a circumstance? The fears or the sorrows of the wretched give no interruption to the general progress of things. The sun rose and the sun set, just as it did before—the business of the government, the business of the castle, of the feast, or the torture went on with their usual exactness and tranquillity.

At last Mr. Hevey was discovered among the sweepings of the prison, and was to be disposed of. He was at last honoured with the personal notice of Major Sandys. "Hevey (says the Major), I have seen you ride, I think, a smart sort of a mare; you can't use her here; you had better give me an order for her." The plaintiff, you may well suppose, by this time had a tolerable idea of his situation; he thought he might have much to fear from a refusal, and something to hope from compliance; at all events, he saw it would be a means of apprizing his family that he was not dead;—he instantly gave the order required. The Major graciously accepted it, saying, "Your courtesy will not cost you much: you are to be sent down to-morrow to Kilkenny, to be tried for your life; you will most certainly be hanged; and you can scarcely think that your journey to the other world will be performed on horseback." The humane and honourable Major was equally a prophet with his compeer. The plaintiff on the next day took leave of his prison, as he supposed for the last time, and was sent under a guard to Kilkenny, then the head-quarters of Sir Charles Asgil, there to be tried by a court-martial for such crime as might chance to be alleged against him.

In any other country the scene that took place on that occasion might excite no little horror and astonishment; but with us, these sensations have become extinguished by frequency of repetition. I am instructed that a proclamation was sent forth, offering a reward to any man who would come forward and give any evidence against the traitor Hevey. An unhappy wretch who had been shortly before condemned to die, and was then lying ready for execution, was allured by the proposal. His integrity was not firm enough to hesitate long between the alternative proposed; pardon, favour, and reward, with perjury on one side—the rope and the gibbet on the other. His loyalty decided the question against his soul. He was examined, and Hevey was appointed by the sentence of a mild, and no doubt enlightened court-martial, to take the place of the witness, and succeed to the vacant halter.

Hevey, you may suppose, now thought his labours at an end; but he was mistaken; his hour was not yet come. You, probably, gentlemen, or you, my lords, are accounting for his escape, by the fortunate recollection of some early circumstances that might have smote upon the sensibility of Sir Charles Asgil, and made him believe that he was in debt to Providence for the life of one innocent, though convicted victim. But it was not so; his escape was purely accidental.

The proceedings upon this trial happened to meet the eye of Lord Cornwallis. The freaks of fortune are not always cruel; in the bitterness of her jocularity, you see she can adorn the miscreancy of the slave in the trappings of power, and rank, and wealth. But her playfulness is not always inhuman; she will sometimes in her gambols, fling oil upon the wounds of the sufferer; she will sometimes save the captive from the dungeon and the grave, were it only that she might afterwards re-consign him to his destiny, by the reprisal of capricious cruelty upon fantastic commiseration. Lord Cornwallis read the transmiss of Hevey's condemnation; his heart recoiled from the detail of stupidity and barbarity; he dashed his pen across the odious record, and ordered that Hevey should be forthwith liberated. I cannot but highly honor him for his conduct in this instance; nor, when I recollect his peculiar situation at that disastrous period, can I much blame him for not having acted towards that court with the same vigour and indignation which he hath since shown with respect to those abominable jurisdictions.

Hevey was now a man again—he shook the dust off his feet against his prison gate; his heart beat the response to the anticipated embrace of his family and his friends, and he returned to Dublin. On his arrival here, one of the first persons he met with, was his old friend, Major Sandys. In the eye of poor Hevey, justice and humanity had shorn the Major of his beams—he no longer regarded him with respect or terror. He demanded his mare; observing, that though he might have travelled to heaven on foot, he thought it more comfortable to perform his earthly journeys on horseback. "Ungrateful villain," says the Major; "is this the gratitude you show to his Majesty and to me, for our clemency to you? You shan't get possession of the beast, which you have forfeited by your treason; nor can I suppose, that a noble animal that had been honoured with conveying the weight of duty and allegiance, could condescend to load her loyal loins with the vile burden of a convicted traitor." As to the Major, I am not surprised that he spoke and acted as he did. He was no doubt astonished at the impudence and novelty of one calling the privileges of official plunder into question. Hardened by numberless instances of that mode of unpunished acquisition, he had erected the frequency of impunity into a sort of warrant of spoil and rapine.

One of these instances I feel I am now bringing to the memory of your lordship. A learned and respected brother barrister* had a silver cup; the Major heard that for many years it had borne an inscription of "*Erin go bragh*," which meant "*Ireland for ever.*" The Major considered this perseverance in guilt for such a length of years, as a forfeiture of the delinquent vessel. My poor friend was accordingly robbed of his cup. But upon writing to the then Attorney-General, that excellent officer felt the outrage, as it was his nature to feel everything that was barbarous or base; and the Major's sideboard was condemned to the grief of restitution.

And here, let me say, in my own defence, that this is the only occasion upon which I have ever mentioned this circumstance with the least appearance of lightness. I have often told the story in a way that it would not become me to tell it here. I have told it in the spirit of those feelings which were excited at seeing that one man could

* Mr. M'Nally.

be sober and humane at a crisis when so many thousands were drunk and barbarous. And probably my statement was not stinted by the recollection that I held that person in peculiar respect and regard. But little does it signify, whether acts of moderation and humanity are blazoned by gratitude, by flattery or by friendship; they are recorded in the heart from which they sprung; and in the hour of adverse vicissitude, if it should ever come, sweet is the odour of their memory, and precious is the balm of their consolation.

But to return: Hevey brought an action for his mare. The Major, not choosing to come into court, and thereby suggest the probable success of a thousand actions, restored the property, and paid the costs of the suit to the attorney of Mr. Hevey.

It may perhaps strike you, my lord, as if I were stating what was not relevant to the action. It is materially pertinent; I am stating a system of concerted vengeance and oppression. These two men acted in concert; they were Archer and Aimwell.* You master at Litchfield, and I at Coventry. You are plunderer in the gaol, and I tyrant in the street. And in our respective situations we will co-operate in the common cause of robbery and vengeance. And I state this, because I see Major Sandys in court: and because I feel I can prove the fact beyond the possibility of denial. If he does not dare to appear, so called upon, as I have called

* Two characters in the "Beaux Stratagem."

upon him, I prove it by his not daring to appear. If he does venture to come forward, I will prove it by his own oath, or if he ventures to deny a syllable that I have stated, I will prove it by irrefragable evidence that his denial was false and perjured. Thus far, gentlemen, we have traced the plaintiff through the strange vicissitudes of barbarous imprisonment, of atrocious condemnation, and of accidental deliverance.

Here Mr. CURRAN described the feelings of the plaintiff and of his family upon his restoration; his difficulties on his return, his struggle against the aspersions on his character, his renewed industry, his gradual success, the implacable malignity of Sirr and of Sandys, and the immediate cause of the present action.*

Three years had elapsed since the deliverance of my client; the public atmosphere had cleared—the private destiny of Hevey seemed to have brightened—but the malice of his enemies had not been appeased. On the 8th of September last, Mr. Hevey was sitting in a public coffee-house; Major Sirr was there. Mr. Hevey was informed that the Major had at that moment said, that he (Hevey) ought to have been hanged. The plaintiff was fired at the charge, he fixed his eye on Sirr, and asked, if he had dared to say so? Sirr declared that he had, and had said it truly. Hevey answered that he was a slanderous scoundrel. At the instant, Sirr rushed upon him, and, assisted by three

* So in the Report.

or four of his satellites, who had attended him in disguise, secured him, and sent him to the castle guard, desiring that a receipt might be given for the villain. He was sent thither. The officer of the guard chanced to be an Englishman, but lately arrived in Ireland; he said to the bailiffs,—If this were in England, I should think this gentleman entitled to bail, but I don't know the laws of this country: however, you had better loosen those irons on his wrists, or I think they may kill him.

Major Sirr, the defendant, soon arrived, went into his office, and returned with an order which he had written, and by virtue of which Mr. Hevey was conveyed to the custody of his old friend and gaoler, Major Sandys. Here he was flung into a room of about thirteen feet by twelve—it was called the hospital of the provost. It was occupied by six beds, in which were to lie fourteen or fifteen miserable wretches, some of them sinking under contagious diseases. On his first entrance, the light that was admitted by the opening of the door, disclosed to him a view of the sad fellow-sufferers, for whose loathsome society he was once more to exchange the cheerful haunts of men, the use of open air, and of his own limbs; and where he was condemned to expiate the disloyal hatred and contempt which he had dared to show to the overweening and felonious arrogance of slaves in office, and minions in authority; here he passed the first night, without bed or food.

The next morning his humane keeper, the Major, appeared. The plaintiff demanded "why he was so imprisoned;" complained of hunger, and asked for the goal allowance. Major Sandys replied with a torrent of abuse, which he concluded by saying,— "Your crime is your insolence to Major Sirr; however, he disdains to trample upon you—you may appease him by proper and contrite submission; but unless you do so, you shall rot where you are. I tell you this, that if government will not protect us, by God we will not protect them. You will probably (for I know your insolent and ungrateful hardiness,) attempt to get out by a Habeas Corpus; but in that yon will find yourself mistaken, as such a rascal deserves."

Hevey was insolent enough to issue a Habeas Corpus, and a return was made upon it—"that Hevey was in custody under warrant from General Craig, on a charge of treason." That this return was a gross falsehood, fabricated by Sirr, I am instructed to assert. Let him prove the truth of it if he can. The Judge before whom this return was brought, felt that he had no authority to liberate the unhappy prisoner; and thus, by a most inhuman and malicious lie, my client was again remanded to the horrid mansion of pestilence and famine.

Mr. Curran proceeded to describe the feelings of Mr. Hevey—the despair of his friends—the ruin of his affairs—the insolence

of Sandys—his offer to set him at large, on condition of making an abject submission to Sirr—the indignant rejection of Hevey —the supplication of his father and sister, rather to submit to an enemy, however base and odious, than perish in such a situation; the repugnance of Hevey—the repetition of kind remonstrances; and the final submission of Hevey to their entreaties—his signing a submission dictated by Sandys, and his enlargement from confinement.

Thus was he kicked from his goal into the common mass of his fellow-slaves, by yielding to the tender entreaties of the kindred that loved him, to sign, what was in fact, a release of his claim to the common rights of a human creature, by humbling himself to the brutal arrogance of a pampered slave. But he did suffer the dignity of his nature to be subdued by its kindness: he has been enlarged, and he has brought the present action.

As to the facts I have stated, I shall make a few observations. It might be said for the defendant, that much of what was stated may not appear in proof. To that I answer, that I would not have so stated, if I had not seen Major Sandys in court. I therefore put the facts against him in a way which I thought the most likely to rouse him to a defence of his own character, if he dared to be examined as a witness. I have, I trust, made him feel, that he has no way of escaping universal detestation, but by denying those charges, if false. And if they are not denied, being thus publicly asserted, my entire case is admitted—his original oppression in the provost is admitted—his robbery of the cup is admitted—his robbery of the mare is admitted—the lie so audaciously forged on the Habeas Corpus is admitted—the extortion of the infamous apology is admitted. Again, I challenge this worthy compeer of the worthy Major to make his election between proving his guilt by his own corporal oath, or by the more credible modesty of his silence.

I have now given you a mere sketch of this extraordinary history. No country, governed by any settled laws, or treated with common humanity, could furnish any occurrences of such unparalleled atrocity; and if the author of Caleb Williams,* or of the Simple Story,† were to read the tale of this man's sufferings, it might, I think, humble the vanity of their talents (if they are not too proud to be vain), when they saw how a much more fruitful source of incident could be found in the infernal workings of the heart of a malignant slave, than in the richest copiousness of the most fertile and creative imagination. But it is the destiny of Ireland to be the scene of such horrors, and to be stung by such reptiles to madness and to death.

And now I feel a sort of melancholy pleasure, in getting nearly rid of this odious and nauseous subject. It remains for me only to make a few observations as to the damages you ought to give,

* Godwin, † Mrs. Inchbald.

if you believe the case of the plaintiff to be as I have stated. I told you before, that neither pride nor spirit belong to our situation; I should be sorry to influence you into any apish affectation of the port or stature of freedom or independence.

But my advice to you is, to give the full amount of the damages laid in the declaration; and I will tell you why I give you that advice; I think no damages could be excessive, either as a compensation for the injury of the plaintiff, or as a punishment for the savage barbarity of the defendant; but my reasons for giving you this advice lie much deeper than such considerations; they spring from a view of our present most forlorn and disastrous situation. You are now in the hands of another country; that country has no means of knowing your real condition, except by information that she may accidentally derive from transactions of a public nature. No printer would dare to publish the thousand instances of atrocity which we have witnessed, as hideous as the present, nor any one of them, unless he did it in some sort of confidence, that he could scarcely be made a public sacrifice by brutal force, for publishing what was openly proved in a court of justice.

Mr. Curran here made some pointed observations on the state of a country where the freedom of the press is extinguished, and where another nation, by whose indolent mercy, or whose

instigated fury, it may be spared or sacrificed, can know nothing of the extent of its sufferings, or its delinquency, but by casual hearsay.

I know that those philosophers have been abused, who think that men are born in a state of war. I confess I go further, and firmly think they cannot be reclaimed to a state of peace. When I see the conduct of man to man I believe it. When I see the list of offences in every criminal code in Europe—when I compare the enormity of their crimes with the still greater enormity of their punishments, I retain no doubt upon the subject.

But if I could hesitate as to men in the same community, I have no doubt of the inextinguishable malignity that will for ever inflame nation against nation. Well was it said, that a "nation has no heart." Towards each other, nations are uniformly envious, vindictive, oppressive, and unjust. What did Spain feel for the murders or robberies of the West? nothing. And yet, at that time, she prided herself as much as England ever did on the elevation of her sentiment, and the refinement of her morality. Yet what an odious spectacle did she exhibit! her bosom burning with all the fury of rapine and tyranny; her mouth full of the pious praises of the living God, and her hands red with the blood of his innocent and devoted creatures. When I advise you, therefore, to mark your feeling of the case before you, do not think I mean that you could make any general impression on the morality or tenderness of the country whose property we are become. I am not so foolish as to hope any such effect; practical justice and humanity are virtues that require laborious acts, and mortifying privations; expect not, therefore, to find them,—appeal not to them.

But there are principles and feelings substituted in their place, a stupid preference and admiration of self, an affectation of humanity, and a fondness for unmerited praise; these you may find, for they cost nothing, and upon them you may produce some effect. When outrages of this kind are held up to the world, as done under the sanction of their authority, they must become odious to mankind, unless they let fall some reprobation on the immediate instruments and abettors of such deeds. An Irish Lord Lieutenant will shrink from the imputation of countenancing them. Great Britain will see that it cannot be her interest to encourage such an infernal spirit of subaltern barbarity, that reduces man to a condition lower than that of the beast of the field. They will be ashamed of employing such instruments as the present defendant. When the government of Ireland lately gave up the celebrated O'Brien* to the hands of the executioner, I have no little reason to believe that they suffered as they deserved on the oc-

* See ante, Curran's defence of Finney.

casion. I have no doubt but that your verdict this day, if you act as you ought to do, will produce a similar effect. And as to England, I cannot too often inculcate upon you that she knows nothing of our situation. When torture was the daily and ordinary system of the executive government, it was denied in London, with a profligacy of effrontery equal to the barbarity with which it was exhibited in Dublin; and if the facts that shall appear to-day should be stated on the other side of the water, I make no doubt that very near one hundred worthy persons would be ready to deny their existence upon their honour, or, if necessary, upon their oaths.

I cannot but observe also to you, that the real state of one country is more forcibly impressed on the attention of another by a verdict on such a subject as this, than it could be by any general description. When you endeavour to convey an idea of a great number of barbarians practising a great variety of cruelties upon an incalculable multitude of sufferers, nothing defined or specific finds its way to the heart; nor is any sentiment excited, save that of a general, erratic, unappropriated, commiseration.

If, for instance, you wished to convey to the mind of an English matron the horrors of that direful period, when, in defiance of the remonstrance of the ever-to-be-lamented Abercromby, our poor people were surrendered to the licentious brutality of the soldiery, by the authority of the state, you would vainly endeavour to give her a general picture of lust, and rapine, and murder, and conflagration. By endeavouring to comprehend every thing, you would convey nothing.

When the father of poetry* wishes to pourtray the movements of contending armies, and an embattled field, he exemplifies only, he does not describe; he does not venture to describe the perplexed and promiscuous conflicts of adverse hosts, but by the acts and fates of a few individuals he conveys a notion of the vicissitudes of the fight, and the fortunes of the day.

So should your story to her keep clear of generalities; instead of exhibiting the picture of an entire province, select a single object; and even in that single object do not release the imagination of your hearer from its task, by giving more than an outline. Take a cottage; place the affrighted mother of her orphan daughter at the door, the paleness of death upon her face, and more than its agonies in her heart; her aching eye, her anxious ear struggling through the mist of closing day, to catch the approaches of desolation and dishonour. The ruffian gang arrives; the feast of plunder begins; the cup of madness kindles in its circulation. The wandering glances of the ravisher become concentrated upon the shrinking and devoted victim. You need not

* Homer.

dilate, you need not expatiate; the unpolluted mother, to whom you tell the story of horror, beseeches you not to proceed; she presses her child to her heart, she drowns it in her tears; her fancy catches more than an angel's tongue could describe; at a single view she takes in the whole miserable succession of force, of profanation, of despair, of death.

So it is in the question before us. If any man shall hear of this day's transaction, he cannot be so foolish as to suppose that we have been confined to a single character, like those now brought before you. No, gentlemen; far from it; he will have too much common sense not to know that outrages like this are never solitary; that where the public calamity generates imps like these, their number is as the sands of the sea, and their fury as insatiable as its waves.

I am therefore anxious that our *masters* should have one authenticated example of the treatment which our unhappy country suffers under the sanction of their authority; it will put a strong question to their humanity, if they have any—to their prudence, if their pride will let them listen to it; or, at least, to that anxiety for reputation, to that pretension to the imaginary virtues of mildness and mercy, which even countries the most divested of them are so ready to assert their claim to, and so credulously disposed to believe that claim allowed.

There are some considerations respecting yourselves, and the defendant, to which I should wish to say a word. You may, perhaps, think your persons unsafe, if you find a verdict against so considerable a person. I know his power, as well as you do—I know he might send you to the Provost, as he has done the plaintiff, and forge a return on any writ you might issue for your deliverance—I know there is no spot on the devoted nation (except that on which we now are), where the story of oppression can be told or heard; but I think you can have no well-founded apprehensions. There is a time when cruelty and oppression become satiated and fatigued; in that satiety at least you will find yourselves secure. But there is still a better security for you—the gratitude of the worthy defendant. If anything could add to his honours and his credit, and his claims, it would be your verdict for the plaintiff; for in what instance have you ever seen any man so effectually accredited and recommended, as by the public execration?—what a man, for instance, might not O'Brien have been, if the envy of the gibbet had not arrested the career of his honours and preferments!

In every point of view, therefore, I recommend to you to find, and to find liberally, for the plaintiff; I have founded my advice upon the real circumstances of your situation; I have not endeavoured to stimulate you into any silly hectic of fancied liberty. I do not call upon you to expose yourselves by the affectation of vindicating the cause of freedom and humanity; much less do I wish to exhibit ourselves to those, whose property we are, as indignant or contumacious under their authority. Far from it; they are unquestionably the proprietors of us; they are entitled of right to drive us, and to work us; but we may be permitted modestly to suggest, that for their own sakes, and for their own interest, a line of moderation may be drawn—that there are excesses of infliction that human nature cannot bear.

With respect to her western negroes, Great Britain has had the wisdom and humanity to feel the justice of this observation, and in some degree to act upon it; and I have too high an opinion of that great and philosophic nation, not to hope that she might think us not undeserving of equal mildness—provided it did not interfere with her just authority over us. It would, I should even think, be for her credit, that having the honour of so illustrious a rider, we should be kept in some sort of condition, somewhat bordering upon spirit, which cannot be maintained, if she suffers us to be utterly broken down by the malicious wantonness of her grooms and jockeys.

This cause is of no inconsiderable expectation; and in whatever light you regard it,—whether with respect to the two countries or to Ireland singly, or to the parties concerned, or to your own sense of character and public duty, or to the natural consequences that must flow from the event, you ought to consider it with the most profound attention before you agree upon your verdict.

FOR OWEN KIRWAN.

[HIGH TREASON.]

SPECIAL COMMISSION, GREEN-STREET.

Thursday, 1*st September*, 1803.

THE failure of the risings and invasions of 1798 broke the faith of some, the principles of others, and the hopes of many; but the causes of discontent increased. The horrid revenge which followed the defeat of the rebels—the treachery of Government to the United Irish leaders in 1798, and to the Catholics in 1801—and the extinction of the Constitution of'82, were added to the political slavery of the Catholics, and the desperate poverty of the people. The revival of the war after the short peace of Amiens, and the alienation from England caused by the first blight of the Union, increased the strength and hopes of revolution.

Robert Emmet and his associates accumulated pikes, guns, cartridges, materials for street defences, and considerable camp equipage, in different stores in Dublin, the principal of them being in Mass-lane. He had arranged for the arrival in Dublin of bodies of peasantry from the neighbouring counties, and the commencement of the insurrection there on the 23rd July, 1803; while Thomas Russell was to head another movement in the county Down. Government were in possession of much vague information; yet so conceited and absolute was Mr. Secretary Marsden (then the real governor of Ireland), that he allowed the Lord Lieutenant to go to the Lodge in the Phœnix-Park, late on the 23rd, without an additional guard, and left the public functionaries, military and civil, without distinct instructions. The night was unusually dark for the time of the year, and, favoured by it, a mob assembled about nine o'clock, and at ten (the hour agreed on), a number of them received arms from the depôt in Mass-lane. A signal rocket was then fired—Emmet and some of his friends turned out, and a rush was made towards the Castle. The mob acted like a mob—got confused, violent, and alarmed—paused and wavered—butchered Colonel Brown, Lord Kilwarden, and some others, who could not fight—and ran from the fire of a few small bodies of troops who were first hurried against them. The leaders, in disgust, abandoned them; the insurrection was over long before morning. All that remained was for Government to proclaim, try, hang, and oppress. They did all vigorously.

A Special Commission was issued, and it opened its sittings on the 31st of August, the Judges being Lord Norbury, Mr. Justice Finucane, and Barons George and Daly. Nineteen persons were tried before the Commission:—one, Walter Clare, was respited; another, Joseph Doran, was acquitted; the rest, including Robert Emmet, were hanged. Russell shared the same fate in Downpatrick.

Curran, aided by Ponsonby and M'Nally, was counsel for several of the prisoners; but his only speech was for Owen Kirwan.

Kirwan was tried on the 1st day of September. He was a tailor and clothes dealer, resident at 64, Plunket-street, Dublin, and exercised no influence in the insurrection.

The Attorney-General (O'Grady,* afterwards Viscount Guillamore), stated the case.

The witnesses called were Edward Wilson and Mr. Douglas, who proved the scene in Thomas-street; Lieutenant Coltman, who proved the taking of arms, stores, and especially rockets,

* He was appointed Attorney-General June the 7th, 1803. John Stewart, made Attorney-General on the 6th of December, 1800, came between Toler and O'Grady. James M'Clelland was Solicitor-General during these trials, and continued so till November, when Plunket succeeded him.

in Mass-lane; Thomas Rice, who proved Emmet's proclamations; Benjamin Adams, who swore that, on the firing of the signal rocket, he saw Kirwan turn out from his shop, with a pike on his shoulder, at the head of several men; and Joseph Adams, who confirmed Benjamin's evidence.

CURRAN then, hopeless it would seem of saving the prisoner, but anxious to serve the country, spoke as follows:—

It has become my duty to state to the court and jury the defence of the prisoner at the bar. I was chosen for that very unpleasant task, without my concurrence or knowledge; but as soon as I was apprised of it, I accepted it without hesitation. To assist a human being, labouring under the most awful of all situations—trembling in the dreadful alternative of honourable life or ignominious death—is what no man, worthy of the name, could refuse to man; but it would be peculiarly base in any person who had the honour of wearing the King's gown, to leave the King's subject undefended, until a sentence pronounced upon him had shown, that neither in fact nor in law could any defence avail him.

I cannot, however, but confess, that I feel no small consolation when I compare my present with my former situation upon similar occasions. In those sad times to which I allude, it was frequently my fate to come forward to the spot where I now stand, with a body sinking under infirmity and disease, and a mind broken with the consciousness of public calamity, created and exasperated by public folly. It has pleased heaven that I should live to survive both those afflictions, and I am grateful to its mercy.

I now come here through a composed and quiet city—I read no expression in any face, save such as marks the ordinary feelings of social life, or the various characters of civil occupation—I see no frightful spectacle of infuriated power or suffering humanity—I see no tortures—I hear no shrieks—I no longer see the human heart charred in the flame of its own wild and paltry passions, black and bloodless, capable only of catching and communicating that destructive fire by which it devours, and is itself devoured.

I no longer behold the ravages of that odious bigotry by which we were deformed, and degraded, and disgraced—a bigotry against which no honest man should ever miss an opportunity of putting his countrymen, of all sects and of all descriptions, upon their guard. It is the accursed and promiscuous progeny of servile hypocrisy—of remorseless lust of power—of insatiate thirst of gain, labouring for the destruction of man under the specious pretences of religion. Her banner stolen from the altar of God, and her allies congregated from the abysses of hell, she acts by votaries, to be restrained by no compunctions of humanity, for they are dead to mercy—to be reclaimed by no voice of reason, for refutation is the bread on which their folly feeds: they are outlawed alike from their species and their Creator—the object of their crime is social life, and the wages of their sin is social death.

Though it may happen that a guilty individual should escape from the law that he has broken, it cannot be so with nations—their guilt is too unwieldy for such escape. They may rest assured that Providence has, in the natural connexion between causes and their effects, established a system of retributive justice, by which the crimes of nations are sooner or later avenged by their own inevitable consequences. But that hateful bigotry, that baneful discord, which fired the heart of man, and steeled it against his brother, has fled at last, and, I trust, for ever. Even in this melancholy place, I feel myself restored and re-created, by breathing the mild atmosphere of justice, mercy, and humanity—I feel I am addressing the parental authority of the law—I feel I am addressing a jury of my countrymen, my fellow-subjects, and my fellow-Christians, against whom my heart is waging no ill-concealed hostility—from whom my face is disguising no latent sentiment of repugnance or disgust. I have not now to touch the chords of an angry passion in those that hear me, nor have I the terror of thinking, that if those chords cannot be snapt by the stroke, they will be only provoked into a more instigated vibration. Whatever I address to the Court in point of law, or to the jury in point of fact, will be heard not only with patience, but with an anxious desire to supply what may be defective in the defence.

This happy change in the minds and feelings of all men is the natural consequence of that system of mildness and good temper which has been recently adopted, and which I strongly exhort you, gentlemen of the jury, to imitate, and to improve upon, that you may thereby demonstrate to ourselves, to Great Britain, and to the enemy, that we are not that assemblage of fiends which we have been alleged to be, unworthy of the ordinary privilege of regular justice or the lenient treatment of a merciful government.

It is of the utmost importance to be on your guard against the wicked and mischievous representation of the circumstances which call you now together; you ought not to take from any unauthenticated report those facts which you can have directly from sworn evidence.

I have heard much of the dreadful extent of the conspiracy against this country—of the narrow escape of the government. You now see the fact as it is. By the judicious adoption of a mild and conciliatory system of conduct, what was six years ago a formidable rebellion, has now dwindled down to a drunken riotous insurrection, disgraced, certainly, by some odious atrocities; its objects, whatever they were, were, no doubt, highly criminal, but as an attack upon the state, of the most contemptible insignificance. I do not wonder that the patrons of burning and torture should be vexed that their favourite instruments were not employed in recruiting for the rebellion. I have no doubt that had they been so employed, the effect would have followed; and that an odious, drunken insurrection would have been easily swelled into a formidable rebellion. Nor is it strange that persons so mortified should vent themselves in wanton, exaggerated misrepresentation, and in unmerited censure—in slandering the nation in the person of the Viceroy, and the Viceroy in the character of the nation—and that they should do so, without considering that they were weakening the common resources against the common danger, by making the different parts of the empire odious to each other, and by holding out to the enemy, and falsely holding out, that we were too much absorbed in civil discord to be capable of effectual resistance.

In making this observation, my wish is merely to refute a slander upon my country. I have no pretension to be the vindicator of the Lord Lieutenant of Ireland, whose person I do not know that I have ever seen. At the same time, when I am so necessarily forced upon the subject, I feel no disposition to conceal the respect and satisfaction with which I see the King's representative comport himself as he does, at a crisis of no little anxiety, though of no considerable danger, if we may believe the evidence we have heard. I think it was a proof of his Excellency's firmness and good sense, not to discredit his own opinion of his confidence in the public safety, by an ostentatious display of unnecessary open preparation; and I think he did himself equal honour by preserving his usual temper, and not suffering himself to be exasperated by the event, when it did happen, into the adoption of any violent or precipitate measures.

Perhaps, I may even be excused if I confess that I was not wholly free from some professional vanity, when I saw that the descendant of a great lawyer* was capable of remembering, what, without the memory of such an example, he perhaps might not have done, that even in the moment of peril, the law is the best safeguard of the constitution. At all events, I feel, that a man, who at all times has so freely censured the extravagancies of power and force, as I have done, is justified, if not bound, by consistency of character, to give the fair attestation of his opinion to the exercise of wisdom and humanity, wherever he finds them, whether in a friend or in a stranger.

I hope, that these preliminary observations are not wantonly and irrelevantly delaying you from the question which you are to try, and which I am ready to enter into; but there still remains a circumstance to be observed upon for a moment before you proceed to the real subject of your inquiry, the guilt or innocence of the prisoner, the fact that has been so impressively stated—the never

* Lord Hardwicke.

to be too much lamented fate of that excellent man, Lord Kilwarden, whose character was as marked by the most scrupulous anxiety for justice as by the mildest and tenderest feelings of humanity.

Let us not wantonly slander the character of the nation, by giving any countenance to the notion, that the horror of such a crime could be extended farther than the actual perpetrators of the deed. The general indignation, the tears that were shed at the sad news of his fate, show that we are not that nest of demons on whom any general stigma could attach from such an event; the wicked wretch himself, perhaps, has cut off the very man, through whose humanity he might have escaped the consequences of other crimes; and, by a hideous aggravation of his guilt, has given another motive to Providence to trace the murderer's steps, and secure the certainty of his punishment. But on this occasion, the jury should put it out of their minds, and think nothing of that valuable man, save his last advice, "That no person should perish but by the just sentence of the law;" and that advice I hope you will honour, not by idle praise, but by strict observance.

As to the evidence, give me leave to advert to one circumstance which ought to be removed from your minds; it was adverted to before, and I do not believe it was resisted by the officers of the crown: it occurred in the former case. No act of parliament or commission under the great seal can be evidence in such a case as this.

Mr. Attorney-General—My lord, I hope Mr. CURRAN will excuse me for interrupting him. No allusion was made to the act of parliament or the commission in this case; and although I did advert to them in the former, no attempt was made to rely upon them as evidence.

Mr. CURRAN—I mentioned the circumstance in the confidence that it would be given up as not applicable in evidence, and the learned gentleman will please to recollect, that he referred to the first statement made by him, and even to the verdict found yesterday, and therefore it is right upon my part to take notice of that which might make an impression upon the jury.

Lord Norbury—This much we must say, that no notice has been taken by the Bench of any act of parliament or any other document but what has been proved in evidence before us.

Mr. CURRAN—If I had not been interrupted by the anxiety of the Attorney-General, I should have added, that as the statute, if offered, would not be evidence, much less was the statement evidence. He also suggested that notoriety would be evidence; but however that may be with respect to a grand jury, it can have no influence with a petit jury. It may as well be said, that the notoriety of a man having committed a crime is evidence of his guilt. Notoriety is at best another name for reputation, which cannot even by law be given in evidence in any criminal case, and which, *a fortiori*, could not sustain a verdict of conviction.

Mr. Justice Finucane—Public war is always taken from notoriety.

Mr. CURRAN—But I do not think, that insurrection can take its character of innocence or guilt from notoriety. And I will add to the jury what I am certain will meet the acquiescence of the Bench, that though the jury should leave their homes without any doubt of the fact, yet it is their duty to forget the notoriety, and, attending to their oaths, to decide according to the evidence, the probability of such a conspiracy at the present time.

It is clear from the evidence that it could not be imputed to any particular sect, or party, or faction; because no sect or faction could fail, had they acted in it, of engaging one hundred times the number of deluded instruments in their design.

We may then fairly ask, is it likely that the country at large, setting even apart all moral tie of duty, or allegiance, or the difficulty, or the danger, could see any motive of interest to recommend to them the measure of separating from England, or fraternizing with France? Is there any description of men in Ireland who could expect any advantage from such a change? And this reasoning is more pertinent to the question, because politics are not now, as heretofore, a dead science, in dead language; they have now become the subject of the day, vernacular and universal: and the repose which the late system of Irish government gave the people for reflection, has enabled them to consider their own condition, and what they, or any other country, could have to hope from France, or rather from its present master. I scorn to allude to that personage, merely to scold or to revile him: unbecoming obloquy may show that we do not love the object, but certainly not that we do not fear him. Buonaparte, a stranger, an usurper, getting possession of a numerous, proud, volatile, and capricious people; getting that possession by military force, able to hold it only by force, to secure his power, found, or thought he found, it necessary to abolish all religious establishments, as well as all shadow of freedom. He has completely subjugated all the adjoining nations. Now, it is clear that there are but two modes of holding states, or the members of the same state, together; namely, community of interest, or predominance of force. The former is the natural bond of the British empire; their interest, their hopes, their dangers, can be no other than one and the same, if they are not stupidly blind to their own situation; and stupidly blind indeed must they be, and justly must they incur the inevitable consequences of that blindness and stupidity, if they have not fortitude and magnanimity enough to lay aside those mean and narrow jealousies which have hitherto prevented that community of interest and unity of effort, by which alone we can stand, and without which we must fall together.

But force only can hold the acquisitions of the French Consul. What community of interest can he have with the different nations that he has subdued and plundered? Clearly none. Can he venture to establish any regular and protected system of religion among them? Wherever he erected an altar, he would set up a monument of condemnation and reproach upon those wild and fantastic speculations which he is pleased to dignify with the name of philosophy, but which other men, perhaps, because they are endowed with a less aspiring intellect, conceive to be a desperate anarchical atheism, giving to every man a dispensing power for the gratification of his passions, teaching him that he may be a rebel to his conscience with advantage, and to his God, with impunity.

Just as soon would the government of Britain venture to display the crescent in its churches, as an honorary member of all faiths show any reverence to the cross in his dominions.

Apply the same reasoning to liberty: can he venture to give any reasonable portion of it to his subjects at home, or his vassals abroad? The answer is obvious: sustained merely by military force, his unavoidable policy is to make the army every thing, and the people nothing. If he ventured to elevate his soldiers into citizens, and his wretched subjects into freemen, he would form a confederacy of mutual interest between both, against which he could not exist a moment.

If he relaxed in like manner with Holland, or Belgium, or Switzerland, or Italy, and withdrew his armies from them, he would excite and make them capable of instant revolt. There is one circumstance which just leaves it possible for him not to chain them down still more rigorously than he has done, and that is, the facility with which he can pour military reinforcements upon them, in case of necessity. But destitute as he is of a marine, he could look to no such resource with respect to any insular acquisition; and of course he should guard against the possibility of danger, by so complete and merciless a thraldom as would make an effort of resistance physically impossible.

Perhaps, my lords, and gentlemen, I may be thought the apologist, instead of the reviler of the ruler of France. I affect not either character—I am searching for the motives of his conduct, and not for the topics of his justification. I do not affect to trace those motives to any depravity of heart or of mind, which accident may have occasioned for a season, and which reflection or compunction may extinguish or allay, and thereby make him a completely different man, with respect to France and to the world; I am acting more fairly and more usefully by my country, when I show, that his conduct must be so swayed by the permanent pressure of his situation, by the control of an unchangeable and inexorable necessity, that he cannot dare to relax or relent, without becoming the certain victim of his own humanity or contrition.

I may be asked, are these merely my own speculations, or have others in Ireland adopted them? I answer freely, *non meus hic sermo est.* It is, to my own knowledge, the result of serious reflection in numbers of our countrymen. In the storm of arbitrary sway, in the distraction of torture and suffering, the human mind had lost its poise and its tone, and was incapable of sober reflection; but, by removing those terrors from it, by holding an even hand between all parties, by disdaining the patronage of any sect or faction, the people of Ireland were left at liberty to consider her real situation and interest; and happily for herself, I trust in God, she has availed herself of the opportunity.

With respect to the higher orders, even of those who thought they had some cause to complain, I know this to be the fact; they are not so blind as not to see the difference between being proud, and jealous, and punctilious in any claim of privilege or right between themselves and their fellow-subjects, and the mad and desperate depravity of seeking the redress of any dissatisfaction that they might feel, by an appeal to force, or by the dreadful recourse to treason and to blood.

As to the humbler orders of our people, for whom I confess I feel the greatest sympathy, because there are more of them to be undone, and because, from want of education, they must be more liable to delusion; I am satisfied the topics to which I have adverted, apply with still greater force to them, than to those who are raised above them.

I have not the same opportunity of knowing their actual opinions; but if their opinions be other than I think they ought to be, would to God they were present in this place, or that I had the opportunity of going into their cottages —and they well know I should not disdain to visit them—and to speak to them the language of affection and candour on the subject; I should have little difficulty in showing to their quick and apprehensive minds, how easy it is, when the heart is incensed, to confound the evils which are inseparable from the destiny of imperfect man, with those which arise from the faults or errors of his political situation. I would put a few questions to their candid and unadulterated sense. I would ask them,—Do you think that you have made no advance to civil prosperity within the last twenty years? Are your opinions of modern and subjugated France the same that you entertained of popular and revolutionary France fourteen years ago? Have you any hope, that if the First Consul got possession of your island, he would treat you half so well as he does those countries at his door, whom he must respect more than he can respect or regard you?

And do you know how he treats those unhappy nations? You know that in Ireland there is little personal wealth to plunder, that there are few churches to rob. Can you then doubt that he would reward his rapacious generals and soldiers by parcelling out the soil of the island among them, and by dividing you into lots of serfs, to till the respective lands to which you belong, or sending you as graziers to enjoy the rocks of Malta and Gibraltar? Can you suppose that the perfidy and treason of surrendering your country to an invader, would, to your new master, be any pledge of your new allegiance? Can you suppose that while a single French soldier was willing to accept an acre of Irish ground, that he would leave that acre in the possession of a man, who had shown himself so wickedly and so stupidly dead to the suggestions of the most obvious interest, and to the ties of the most imperious moral obligations?

To what do you look forward with respect to the aggrandizement of your sect? Are you Protestants? he has abolished Protestantism with Christianity. Are you Catholics? do you think he will raise you to the level of the Pope? Perhaps, and I think, he would not; but, if he did, could you hope more privilege than he has left his Holiness? And what privilege has he left him? he has reduced his religion to be a mendicant for contemptuous toleration, and he has reduced his person to beggary and to rags.

Let me ask you a further question. Do you think he would feel any kind-hearted sympathy for you? Answer yourselves by asking, what sympathy does he feel for Frenchmen, whom he is ready by thousands to bury in the ocean, in the barbarous gambling of his wild ambition? What sympathy, then, could bind him to you? He is not your countryman. The scene of your birth and your childhood is not endeared to his heart, by the reflection, that it was also the scene of his: he is not your fellow-Christian; he is not, therefore, bound to you by any similarity of duty in the world, or by any union of hope beyond the grave. What, then, could you suppose the object of his visit, or the consequence of his success? Can you be so foolish as not to see, that he would use you as slaves, while he held you; and that when he grew weary, which he soon would become, of such a worthless and precarious possession, he would carry you to market in some treaty of peace, barter you for some more valuable concession, and surrender you to expiate, by your punishment and degradation, the advantage you had given him by your follies and your crimes.

There is another topic on which a few words might be addressed to the deluded peasant of this country: he might be asked,—What could you hope from the momentary success of any effort to subvert the government by mere intestine convulsion? Could you look forward to the hope of liberty or property? Where are the characters, the capacities, and the motives of those that have embarked in those chimerical projects? you see them a despicable gang of needy adventurers; desperate from guilt and poverty; uncountenanced by a single individual of probity or name; ready to use you as the instruments, and equally ready to abandon you by treachery or flight, as the victims of their crimes. For a short interval, murder and rapine might have their sway; but do not be such fools as to think, that though robbing might make a few persons poor, it could make many rich.

Do not be so silly as to confound the destruction of property with the partition of wealth. Small must be your share of the spoil, and short your enjoyment of it. Soon, trust me, very soon, would such a state of things be terminated by the very atrocities of its authors. Soon would you find yourselves subdued, ruined, and degraded. If you looked back, it would be to character destroyed, to hope extinguished. If you looked forward, you could see only the dire necessity you had imposed upon your governors, of acting towards you with no feelings but those of abhorrence and self-preservation, of ruling you by a system of coercion, of which alone you would be worthy, and of loading you with taxes (that is, selling the food and raiment which your honest labour might earn for your family,) to defray the expense of that force, by which only you could be restrained.

Say not, gentlemen, that I am inexcusably vain when I say, would to God that I had an opportunity of speaking this plain, and, I trust, not absurd, language to the humblest orders of my countrymen. When I see what sort of missionaries can preach the doctrines of villainy and folly with success, I cannot think it very vain to suppose, that they would listen with some attention and some respect to a man who was addressing plain sense to their minds, whose whole life ought to be a pledge for his sincerity and affection, who had never in a single instance deceived, or deserted, or betrayed them, who had never been seduced to an abandonment of their just rights, or a connivance at any of their excesses, that could threaten an injury to their character or their condition.

But perhaps I have trespassed too much upon your patience, by what may appear a digression from the question. The motive of my doing so, I perceive by your indulgent hearing, you perfectly comprehend. But I do not consider what I have said as a mere irrelevant digression, with respect to the immediate cause before you. The reasoning comes to this: the present state of this country shows, that nothing could be so stupidly and perversely wicked as a project of separation, or of French connexion; and, of course, nothing more improbable than the adoption of such a senseless project. If it be then so senseless, and therefore so improbable, how strong ought the evidence to be on which you would be warranted in attesting on your oaths, to England and to France, so odious an imputation on the good sense and loyalty of your country. Let me revert again to the evidence which you have heard to support so incredible a charge. I have already observed on the contemptible smallness of the number, a few drunken peasants, assembled in the outlets; there, in the fury of intoxication, they committed such atrocities as no man can be disposed to defend or to extenuate; and having done so, they flee before a few peace-officers, aided by the gallantry of Mr. Justice Drury, who, even if he did retreat, as has been insinuated, has at least the merit of having no wish to shed the blood of his fellow-Christians, and is certainly entitled to the praise of preserving the life of a most valuable citizen and loyal subject.

In this whole transaction, no attempt, however feeble or ill directed, is made on any place belonging to or connected with the government. They never even approach the barrack, the castle, the magazines. No leader whatsoever appears; nothing that I can see to call for your verdict, except the finding the bill, and the uncorroborated statement of the Attorney-General. In that statement, too, I must beg leave to guard you against mistake in one or two particulars. As to what he said of my Lord Kilwarden, it was not unnatural to feel as he seemed to do at the recollection, or to have stated that sad event as a fact that took place on that occasion, but I am satisfied he did not state it with the least intention of agitating your passions, or of letting it have the smallest influence on your judgment.

In your inquiry into a charge of treason, you are to determine upon evidence; and what is there in this case to connect the prisoner with the general plan or the depôt which was found? I do not say that the account of these matters was not admissible evidence; but I say, that the existence of these things without a design, or proof of a design, without connexion with the prisoner, cannot affect his life; for you cannot found a verdict upon construction or suspicion.

The testimony of Adams seemed to have been brought forward as evidence of greater cogency. He saw the prisoner go out with a bag half full, and return with it empty. I am at a loss to conjecture what they would wish you to suppose was contained in it:—but men are seen at his house;

does it follow that he was connected with the transactions in Thomas-street? The elder Adams does not appear to have stated any thing material but his own fears. The proclamation may be evidence of a treasonable conspiracy existing; but it is no evidence against the prisoner, unless he be clearly connected with it; and in truth when I see the evidence on which you are to decide, reduced to what is legal or admissible, I do not wonder that Mr. Attorney-General himself should, upon the first trial, have treated this doughty rebellion with the laughter and contempt it deserved.

Where now is this providential escape of the government and the castle? why, simply in this, that nobody attacked either the one or the other, and that there were no persons that could have attacked either. It seems not unlike the escape which a young man had of being shot through the head at the battle of Dettingen, by the providential interference by which he was sent twenty miles off on a foraging party, only ten days before the battle.

I wish from my heart that there may be now present some worthy gentlemen, who may transmit to Paris a faithful account of what has this day passed.

If so, I think some loyal absentee may possibly find an account of it in the *Publiciste* or the *Moniteur*, and perhaps somewhat in this way: "On the 23rd of July last, a most splendid rebellion displayed her standard in the metropolis of Ireland, in a part of the city, which, in their language, is called the *Poddle.* The band of heroes that came forth at the call of patriotism, capable of bearing arms, at the lowest calculation must have amounted to little less than two hundred persons. The rebellion advanced with a most intrepid step, till she came to the site of the old Four Courts and Tholsel. There she espied a decayed pillory, on which she mounted, in order to reconnoitre, but she found to her great mortification, that the rebels had staid behind. She therefore judged it right to make her escape, which she effected in a masterly manner down *Dirty Lane;* the rebels at the same time retiring in some disorder from the *Poddle*, being hard pressed by the poles and lanterns of the watchmen, and being additionally galled by Mr. Justice Drury, who came to a most unerring aim on their rear, on which he played without any intermission, with a spy-glass from his dining-room window. *Raro antecedentem scelestum deseruit pœna pede claudo.*

"It is clearly ascertained that she did not appear in her own clothes, for she threw away her regimental jacket before she fled, which has been picked up, and is now to be seen at Mr. Carleton's, at sixpence a head for grown persons, and threepence for a nurse and child. It was thought at first to be the work of an Irish artist, who might have taken measure in the absence of the wearer;

but by a bill and receipt found in one of the pockets, it appears to have been made by the actual body-tailor of her August Highness the Consort of the First Consul. At present it is but poorly ornamented, but is said that the Irish Volunteers have entered into a subscription to *trim* it, if it shall be ever worn again."

Happy, most happy, is it for those islands, that those rumours which are so maliciously invented and circulated, to destroy our confidence in each other, to invite attack, and dispirit resistance, turn out, upon inquiry, to be so ludicrous and contemptible, that we cannot speak of them without laughter, or without wonder that they did not rather form the materials of a farce in a puppet-show, than of a grave prosecution in a court of justice.

There is still, gentlemen, another topic material to remind you of; this is the first trial for treason that has occurred since the union of these islands. No effectual union can be achieved by the mere letter of a statute. Do not imagine that bigotry can blend with liberality, or barbarism with civilization. If you wish to be really united with Great Britain, teach her to respect you, and do so by showing her that you are fit objects of wholesome laws—by showing that you are as capable of rising to a proud equality with her in the exercise of social duties and civil virtues, as every part of the globe has proved you to be in her fleets and her armies; show her that you can try this cause as she would try it; that you have too much sense and humanity to be borne away in your verdict by despicable panic, or brutal fury; show her, that in prosecutions by the state, you can even go a step beyond her, and that you can discover and act upon those eternal principles of justice, which it has been found necessary in that country to enforce by the coercion of law: you cannot but feel that I allude to their statute which requires two witnesses in treason.

Our statute does not contain that provision; but if it were wise to enact it there as a law, it cannot be other than wise to adopt it here as a principle; unless you think it discreet to hold it out as your opinion, that the life of man is not so valuable here, and ought not to be as secure, as in the other part of the empire; unless you wish to prove your capability of equal rights and equal liberty with Britain, by consigning to the scaffold your miserable fellow-subject, who if tried in England on the same charge and the same evidence, would by law be entitled to a verdict of acquittal.

I trust you will not so blemish yourselves—I trust you will not be satisfied even with a cold imitation of her justice, but on this occasion you will give her an example of magnanimity, by rising superior to the passion or the panic of the moment.

If in any ordinary case, in any ordinary time, you have any reasonable doubt of guilt, you are bound by every principle of law and justice to acquit. But I would advise you, at a time like this, rather to be lavish than parsimonious in the application of that principle; even though you had the strongest suspicion of his culpability, I would advise you to acquit; you would show your confidence in your own strength, that you felt your situation too high to be affected in the smallest degree by the fate of so insignificant an individual. Turn to the miserable prisoner himself—tainted and blemished as he possibly may be, even him you may retrieve to his country and his duty, by a salutary effort of seasonable magnanimity. You will inspire him with reverence for that institution which knows when to spare, as well as when to inflict; and which, instead of sacrificing him to a strong suspicion of his criminality, is determined, not by the belief, but by the possibility of his innocence, and dismisses him with indignation and contemptuous mercy.

An attempt was made to prove that Kirwan slept at home on the 23rd; and witnesses were also examined to prove his general loyalty. Baron George then charged, and in five minutes after, the jury found a verdict of GUILTY. He was sentenced on the 2nd of September, and hanged in Thomas-street, on the 3rd.

AGAINST ENSIGN JOHN COSTLEY

[CONSPIRACY TO MURDER.]

SESSIONS-HOUSE, GREEN-STREET.

February 23rd, 1804.

THE following speech is chiefly valuable, as illustrating the placid and just manner in which so vehement an advocate as CURRAN could discharge his duty as prosecutor.

Costley was an ensign in the Roscommon Militia.

He was arraigned before Baron George and Mr. Justice Day at Green-st., Dublin, on the 21st of February, 1804, on an indictment, charging him and Charles Frazer Frizell with having conspired to murder the Rev. William Ledwich, parish priest of Rathfarnham, in the county Dublin. Other indictments charged burglary in the house of Catherine Byrne, with intent to murder. There was one count for a common assault.

On Thursday, the 23rd, the trial came on, and CURRAN stated the case for the crown as follows:—

MY Lords, and Gentlemen of the Jury, I am concerned in this cause as counsel for the crown —that is, as counsel for the law and for the public peace, by putting the charge, that has been found by the indictment, into a course of sober, humane, firm, and dispassionate inquiry, before you, Gentlemen of the Jury, to enable you to fulfil to the public the awful, heavy, aud severe duty of finding the prisoner at the bar guilty, if he be guilty, and that awful, solemn, and equally bounden duty you owe to the prisoner himself, to acquit him, if he shall appear to be innocent of the charges brought against him.

It becomes my duty at present, and painful is that duty, and painful must it be to every man who acts as counsel for the crown against the life of a fellow-subject, painful must it be in proportion to the sad conviction that he feels in his mind that the prosecution must be successful.

It is my duty, gentlemen of the jury, to apprize you of the nature of the charge, as well as to apprize you of the circumstances that will be given in evidence to support that charge, that you may understand, in some previous degree, the law by which you are to be directed, and that you should have some previous knowledge of the nature of the evidence that shall be adduced for the purpose of substantiating that charge.

The prisoner has been given in charge to the jury on an indictment stating, that he, with others, did conspire to kill and murder William Ledwich, who is prosecutor in this cause. That offence is made capital by the statute laws of the country; and, gentlemen, I would be glad to guard you against a mistake, that in common parlance arises on this subject. A conspiracy to kill and murder does not owe it's criminality to the length of time it may occupy in it's progress, from its first conception to it's ultimate adoption—a conspiracy may be formed the very instant before the step is taken to put it into effect. If a number of people meet accidentally in the street, and conspire together to kill and murder at the moment, it is as essentially the crime of conspiracy as if it had been intended for a year before, and hatched for that year to the moment of its accomplishment.

On the charge of burglary alleged against the prisoner at the bar, it becomes requisite to be equally clear and explicit, that you may comprehend how essential it is, that two circumstances shall go to compose this species of crime, which is also made capital, and consequently liable to the punishment of death. It becomes necessary before you can decide on a verdict of guilt on this indictment, that two circumstances shall be proved to your satisfaction. The first of these is, the breaking open of the dwelling or habitation of any of his Majesty's subjects any time after night-fall; and the next essential ingredient is, that such breaking must have been effected with design or intent to commit a felony. These distinct and separate facts you must combine in proof before the charge of burglary can be sustained; so far, that should you be satisfied that a breaking into a dwelling or habitation at a late hour of the night was accomplished, it becomes necessary, in addition, that you should have as strong and forcible a conviction on your minds, that such breaking into the house or dwelling was designed and perpetrated with the intent to commit a felony, before you can venture to bring in a verdict of guilty. As to the burglary charged against the prisoner at the bar, you will perceive that the indictment lays the breaking into the habitation of the prosecutor, with intent to kill and murder him; an act, which, if perpetrated, would constitute a capital felony in itself, and the intention of which, connected with the fact of breaking into the house, forms an indictment on grounds sufficiently firm to form the capital crime of burglary.

It may be equally necessary to hint to you, gentlemen of the jury, that the statute which makes burglary a capital offence, does not lay down a distinct species of felony, the commission of which must previously occupy the intention—it does not discriminate between the intention of committing a murder and committing a robbery; so that, on this principle, if you shall reconcile it to your minds in the course of the evidence which shall be adduced, that the prisoner at the bar broke into the habitation alluded to, with intent to murder, the crime of burglary is effectually constituted; and you are bound, by the sacred oath you have taken, to bring in a sentence of conviction. But if the evidence shall not appear to you sufficiently strong to reconcile your consciences to the belief, that the prisoner at the bar, let the fact of his breaking open the house be ever so incontrovertible, did form the design or intention to commit the murder alleged, then, gentlemen of the jury, your understandings will suggest to you, that it becomes an imperious duty on you to bring in a verdict of acquittal.

I feel it is my duty to make these preliminary observations by which you might at least be directed to that more minute and precise exposition of the law, which you will have the satisfaction of hearing from the court. I also feel, that the man who stands up in a court of justice, owes to the jury whom he addresses, the duty of elucidating any matter of law suggested by the nature of the case in which he becomes an advocate, and a studied anxiety not to aggravate or strain its circumstances beyond a fair and liberal construction of that law. I repeat, gentlemen, that I feel it becomes a duty equally awful and imperious on his conscience, to view the object of explanation in all its points and bearings, with uniform and impartial investigation. The more momentous and important the object of inquiry becomes, the more ardent must his anxiety be not to mislead; and that delicacy, which the advocate must feel in a predicament of this nature, becomes a principle to govern the consciences and the oaths of persons delegated to expound the law in more exalted situations.

I have hitherto stated two material charges against the prisoner at the bar, in which your judgments will be exercised. Those of a less important or inferior nature, I do not think it equally necessary to dilate upon; and will therefore proceed to state the particular circumstances that attended this extraordinary and unfortunate transaction.

I understand, gentlemen of the jury, it will appear in evidence before you, that on the night of the 3rd of the present month of February, about the hour of ten o'clock, this attempt was made on the Rev. William Ledwich, a Roman Catholic clergyman of the parish of Rathfarnham, where he has resided for more than twenty-five years, an edifying and respected pattern of innocence of heart, mildness of manners, of exemplary piety, and conduct the most inoffensive and irreproachable.

As this venerated and innocent man was preparing to seek that undisturbed and calm repose, which he should look for, after a conscientious and precise discharge of the functions and duties of the preceding day, he heard a tumultuous noise under the window of the chamber in which he was about to sleep. He naturally went to the window, which he raised, to see what created the unusual disturbance with which he was annoyed from below, when he recollected a voice, and immediately asked, Is not that Mr. Frizell? He also knew the prisoner by his voice, and asked, "Is not that Ensign Costley?" They answered to their names, and ordered him to come down. Astonished at this kind of proceeding, he asked for what he should come down? The reply was, that he must go to the guard-house. Mr. Ledwich began to expostulate. "You know, Mr. Frizell, that I am an infirm man, and that I am to be at all times found on any occasion for me. I entreat of you not to disturb me this night, and you shall find me punctual in attendance at your guard-house on to-morrow." The party below were still vociferous, urging that he must come to the guard-house. This infirm gentleman then put his head out of the window, to try the effect of further entreaty, on which a stroke of a drawn sword was made at him, which fortunately missed his head, but made a deep cut in the window-frame from which he looked out. On this he retired to his room, unconscious how to act, but at length yielded to the half advice, and half persuasions of a fellow-lodger, who was roused by the tumult in the street, and in suspense what opinion to give, as to the most effectual mode for Mr. Ledwich to adopt, in order to save his life. At length he made his way through a back door, and secured a retreat over Lord Ely's park wall, glassed at the top, the sense of peril giving to his feeble bodily powers that concentrated effort which a hard struggle for life will often produce. Having clambered to the top of this wall, he precipitated himself at the other side to a dangerous and most extraordinary depth. Here, it becomes requisite, gentlemen of the jury, to animadvert, but to do it with candour, and not with a view to stimulate your indignation, on a military officer, wearing his Majesty's garb, entrusted with an armed force, for the important purpose of defending his fellow-subjects, and preserving the public peace, degrading that commission, and disgracing the honour of those forces under his command, by converting the arms given to them for protection into vile instruments of annoyance, seeking by their means to take away a life it was his duty to preserve. Nor is the aggravation of this horrible outrage small, when offered against a man advanced in years, infirm in health, a priest in orders, preaching the same faith with others, upon the same authorized system of social duty on this side of the grave, in order to realize those hopes in the next world, given to Christians to entertain by that wise Redeemer, whose last charge, on leaving this earth, tended most sublimely and emphatically to enforce the obligation of mutual affection between man and man, and whose last awful and divine command was, that we should love one another.

It is not my custom, however, to say any thing that might embitter the voice of accusation. I know the unhappy circumstances under which the young man at the bar labours; and I have endeavoured, in the conduct of this prosecution, to take off the pressure of that peculiar predicament under which he unfortunately stands. But I cannot permit a relaxation of duty so flagrant, from any individual consideration, let the object of that consideration be what it may.

When I perceive those violent struggles to distort and tear asunder all the social ties which bind man to man—not by the wantonness of aggravating description, or offering of cruel taunts at the prisoner's situation—but by some system of conduct operating as a remote but sure cause of so lamentable an effect, I should think myself indeed an unworthy and unfeeling co-operator in the conduct every honest mind must reprobate, and an accessory to the consequences which flow from it, were I, from the affectation of false feelings of humanity, to sink parts of that detail, which it becomes my duty to disclose.

I understood that the conduct attributable, and perhaps justly so, to certain parties labouring under the present accusation, might have indicated something like an excuse under the unhappy pretext of intoxication. If any of you, gentlemen of the jury, have permitted an opinion to get hold of your understanding, that a voluntary privation of reason amounts to an extenuation of a crime committed, permit me to remove so egregious a mistake from your minds, It is the law of this country, touching the subject of intoxication as apology for crimes, that so far from contributing any excuse or apology for the perpetration of crimes, such state of mind is considered as a high aggravation of any offence committed under its influence. This being the law of the land, you are bound most solemnly on your oaths strictly to abide by it—in deciding by the same law, which unequivocally says, that intoxication is no excuse for or palliation of guilt. I am afraid that circumstances will come out in evidence of complicated aggravation in the offence charged against the prisoner at the bar. It will appear that he ordered a party of the military under his command to fire into the windows of the prosecutor's bed-chamber, and that some of the bullets were found lodged in the walls of his apartment, while others passed through the curtains of his bed. It will also appear that other shots took effect in an adjacent apartment, where other lodgers were asleep. If it shall be suggested as a defence of the prisoner's conduct, that he acted, or thought he acted, under the orders of a magistrate, it is a weak pretext and a gross mistake, to suppose that the company even of a real magistrate, which it appears that Mr. Frizell, however qualified, is not, could give a man sanction to break into a habitation in order to commit a murder. On the contrary it is a most hideous aggravation of such offence. The system of our laws uniting a degree of wisdom and a principle of equity not to be equalled, or perhaps found, in the laws of any other country in the world, divides the criminal code into different branches, and on that principle it is left to the judge to expound the law, while the jury are confined to the investigation of facts, on which alone they must decide. There may be cases where a higher authority interferes,—cases for which a wise provision is also made by appealing to a branch of the judicial authority, invested with a power to turn off from a culprit, the bitter edge of the law. A portion of that power is delegated in the first instance to persons who soften the rigour of the law, by the emotions peculiar to kind and sympathetic hearts liberally imbued with the finer feelings of humanity. The judges of the land are therefore wisely permitted to exercise those principles of social affections and compassion towards proper objects, which will ultimately terminate with a higher power, who is bound to administer justice in mercy.

Gentlemen of the Jury, I have endeavoured to state to you those principles and maxims of the criminal laws of your country, by which you cannot fail to perceive the boundaries which the sound policy of our general law has affixed to each department. Finding the facts against the prisoner at the bar, according to the evidence which shall be laid before you, will not preclude him from mercy, should he be conceived a proper subject for it, a consideration which you, as honest and humane men, must feel a superior gratification in contemplating. But, on the other hand, reflect that it is not because you suspect a culprit, that you must find him guilty; for the wise policy of the law itself has it, that the more hideous are the circumstances of the offence, so much the more shall christian charity induce you to be incredulous as to its perpetration. And, on that principle, the practice of the courts is grounded, which requires that solemn and pathetic appeal to God, from the officer, praying to send the culprit a good deliverance. Therefore, unless a true conviction shall remove all rational doubt from your minds before you take upon you to pass a verdict on the life or liberty of your fellow-creature, it will be, as I before have stated, your bounden duty unreservedly to acquit. But if conviction shall supersede all doubt, and clear up all embarrassment, you are equally bound to consider that pardon and mercy to the culprit are lodged in other breasts than yours. I shall conclude, gentlemen of the jury, with only one observation, that is, in your discussion of the several charges exhibited against the prisoner at the bar, you will not permit anything I have said, or any statement of the evidence I have laid before you, to make an exclusive impression on you.

The Rev. William Ledwich proved that on the 3rd of February he was lodging at Catherine Byrne's house at Rathfarnham, that about ten o'clock on that night Frizell and Costley, with a party of their yeomen came to the house, and endeavoured to force him away to the guard-house; that he resisted, was struck at with a sword, and finally escaped over Lord Ely's wall at the back of the house. Other witnesses proved the prisoner and his party fired into the house, and also broke the doors and windows to force their way in.

Mr. Egan opened the defence, using the cross-examination of the prosecutor's witnesses, to prove that Costley was only drunk and intemperate, and had got into a riot, and called Lord Erris and Colonel Caulfield to testify to his character. After a reply from Mr. M'Nally and a charge from Judge Day, the jury acquitted the prisoner on all the charges, except the assault. On that he was found Guilty, and for it he was sentenced to two years' imprisonment, and a trifling fine.

MASSY *v.* HEADFORT.

[FOR CRIMINAL CONVERSATION.]

ENNIS SUMMER ASSIZES.

July 27th, 1804.

The Rev. Charles Massy, second son of Sir Hugh Massy, Bart., was a clergyman, deriving a large income from church livings. In March, 1796, he married, against his father's wish, a Miss Rosslewin, then eighteen years of age, and of remarkable beauty. By her he had one son. He was residing, in 1803, at Doonas, on the Clare bank of the Shannon, about five miles above Limerick. The Marquis of Headfort, with his regiment of Meath Militia, was then quartered in Limerick, his lordship residing in the Earl of Limerick's house. Mr. Massy, when at one time a rector in Meath, had known the dowager Lady Bective and the Headfort family; so, when his wife became acquainted with Lord Headfort in Limerick, he very naturally asked the Marquis to Doonas—his wife was rather fond of society and display, but, then, Lord Headfort was fifty years old.

The result of the visit was, that on a Sunday morning after the Christmas of 1803, while Mr. Massy was performing service in his church, Mrs. Massy eloped with Lord Headfort, and for this the action was brought. Damages were laid at £40,000, and the case was tried at the Clare Summer Assizes before Baron Smith and a special jury.

An immense bar was employed for the plaintiff; they were—John Philpot Curran, Bartholomew Hoare, Henry Deane Grady, Thomas Carey, John White, Amory Hawksworth, William O'Regan, Thomas Lloyd, William M'Mahon, and George Bennet, Esqrs.; agent, Anthony Hogan, Esq. The Counsel for the defence were George Ponsonby, Thomas Quin, Thomas Goold, John Francks, Charles Burton, Richard Pennefather, Esqrs.; agent, James Simms, Esq.

Mr. George Bennet opened the pleadings. Mr. Hoare stated the case, describing Lord Headfort as "this hoary veteran in whom, like Etna, the snow above did not quench the flames below." His speech throughout is masculine, original, and to the point; while his Cornish plunderer has been cited as an instance of the highest eloquence. Here it is:—

"The noble lord proceeded to the completion of his diabolical project, not with the rash precipitancy of youth, but with the most cool and deliberate consideration. The Cornish plunderer, intent on spoil, callous to every touch of humanity, shrouded in darkness, holds out false lights to the tempest-tossed vessel, and lures her and her pilot to that shore upon which she must be lost for ever, the rock unseen, the ruffian invisible, and nothing apparent but the treacherous signal of security and repose; so this prop of the throne, this pillar of the state, this stay of religion, the ornament of the peerage, this common protector of the people's privileges and of the crown's prerogatives, descends from these high grounds of character to muffle himself in the gloom of his own base and dark designs, to play before the eyes of the deluded wife and the deceived husband the falsest lights of love to the one, and of friendly and hospitable regards to the other, until she is at length dashed upon that hard bosom, where her honour and happiness are wrecked and lost for ever; the agonized husband beholds the ruin with those sensations of misery and of horror which you can better feel than I describe; she, upon whom he had embarked all his hopes and all his happiness in this life, the treasure of all his earthly felicities, the rich fund of all his hoarded joys, sunk before his eyes into an abyss of infamy, or if any fragment escape, escaping to solace, to gratify, to enrich her vile destroyer."

Five witnesses proved the marriage and elopement, the happiness of Mr. Massy's home, and the fortune of Lord Headfort.

Mr. Quin opened the defence, not denying the fact, but the injury. He alleged that Mrs. Massy's character was so light that it was gross folly or worse of her husband, to have thrown her into Lord Headfort's way. To prove this he examined Colonel Pepper, Captain Charleton, and Mr. George Evans Bruce.* Mr. Ponsonby followed on the same side, with great skill, and then CURRAN said:—

NEVER so clearly as in the present instance have I observed that safeguard of justice, which Providence hath placed in the nature of man. Such is the imperious dominion with which truth and reason wave their sceptre over the human intellect, that no solicitations, however artful, no talent, however commanding, can reduce it from its allegiance. In proportion to the humility of our submission to its rule, do we rise into some faint emulation of that ineffable and presiding divinity, whose characteristic attribute it is, to be coerced and bound by the inexorable laws of its own nature, so as to be all-wise and all-just from necessity, rather than election. You have seen it in the learned advocate,† who has preceded me, most peculiarly and strikingly illustrated. You have seen even his great talents, perhaps the first in any country, languishing under a cause too weak to carry him, and too heavy to be carried by him. He was forced to dismiss his natural

* Struck at for (amongst other things), his evidence in this case, by Harry Deane Grady in the "Nosegay," a once celebrated, but now happily forgotten satire.

† Mr. Ponsonby.

candour and sincerity, and having no merits in his case, to substitute the dignity of his own manner, the resources of his own ingenuity, against the overwhelming difficulties with which he was surrounded. Wretched client! unhappy advocate! what a combination do you form! But such is the condition of guilt, its commission mean and tremulous, its defence artificial and insincere, its prosecution candid and simple, its condemnation dignified and austere. Such has been the defendant's guilt, such his defence, such shall be my address, and such, I trust, your verdict.

The learned counsel has told you, that this unfortunate woman is not to be estimated at forty thousand pounds. Fatal and unquestionable is the truth of this assertion. Alas! gentlemen, she is no longer worth any thing—faded, fallen, degraded, and disgraced, she is worth less than nothing! But it is for the honour, the hope, the expectation, the tenderness, and the comforts that have been blasted by the defendant, and have fled for ever, that you are to remunerate the plaintiff, by the punishment of the defendant. It is not her present value which you are to weigh, but it is her value at that time, when she sat basking in a husband's love, with the blessing of heaven on her head, and its purity in her heart: when she sat amongst her family, and administered the morality of the parental board: estimate that past value, compare it with its present deplorable diminution, and it may lead you to form some judgment of the severity of the injury, and the requisite extent of the compensation.

The learned counsel has told you, you ought to be cautious, because your verdict cannot be set aside for excess. The assertion is just; but has he treated you fairly by its application? His cause would not allow him to be fair—for, why is the rule adopted in this single action? Because this being peculiarly an injury to the most susceptible of all human feelings—it leaves the injury of the husband to be ascertained by the sensibility of the jury, and does not presume to measure the justice of their determination by the cold and chilly exercise of his own discretion.

In any other action it is easy to calculate. If a tradesman's arm is cut off, you can measure the loss which he has sustained; but the wound of feeling, and the agony of the heart cannot be judged by any standard with which I am acquainted. And you are unfairly dealt with, when you are called on to appreciate the present suffering of the husband, by the present guilt, delinquency, and degradation of his wife. As well might you, if called on to give compensation to a man for the murder of his dearest friend, find the measure of his injury, by weighing the ashes of the dead. But it is not, gentlemen of the jury, by weighing the ashes of the dead, that you would estimate the loss of the survivor.

The learned counsel has referred you to other cases, and other countries, for instances of moderate verdicts. I can refer you to some authentic instances of just ones. In the next country, £15,000 against a subaltern officer. In Travers and M'Carthy, £5,000 against a servant. In Tighe against Jones, £10,000 against a man not worth a shilling.

What then ought to be the rule, where rank, and power, and wealth, and station, have combined to render the example of his crime more dangerous—to make his guilt more odious—to make the injury to the plaintiff more grievous, because more conspicuous? I affect no levelling familiarity, when I speak of persons in the higher ranks of society—distinctions of orders are necessary, and I always feel disposed to treat them with respect—but when it is my duty to speak of the crimes by which they are degraded, I am not so fastidious as to shrink from their contact, when to touch them is essential to their dissection. In this action, the condition, the conduct, and the circumstances of the party, are justly and peculiarly the objects of your consideration.

Who are the parties?

The plaintiff, young, amiable, of family, and education. Of the generous disinterestedness of his heart you can form an opinion even from the evidence of the defendant, that he declined an alliance, which would have added to his fortune and consideration, and which he rejected for an unportioned union with his present wife. She, too, at that time, was young, beautiful and accomplished; and felt her affection for her husband increase in proportion as she remembered the ardour of his love, and the sincerity of his sacrifice.

Look now to the defendant!—I blush to name him! I blush to name a rank which he has tarnished—and a patent that he has worse than cancelled. High in the army—high in the state—the hereditary councillor of the king—of wealth incalculable:—and to this last I advert with an indignant and contemptuous satisfaction, because, as the only instrument of his guilt and shame, it will be the means of his punishment, and the source of compensation for his guilt.

But let me call your attention, distinctly, to the questions you have to consider. The first is the fact of guilt. Is this noble lord guilty? His counsel knew too well how they would have mortified his vanity, had they given the smallest reason to doubt the splendour of his achievement. Against any such humiliating suspicion he had taken the most studious precaution by the publicity of the exploit. And here, in this court, and before you, and in the face of the country, has he the unparalleled effrontery of disdaining to resort even to a profession of innocence.

His guilt established, your next question is, the

damages you should give. You have been told, that the amount of damages should depend on circumstances. You will consider these circumstances, whether of aggravation or mitigation.

His learned counsel contend, that the plaintiff has been the author of his own suffering, and ought to receive no compensation for the ill consequences of his own conduct. In what part of evidence do you find any foundation for that assertion? He indulged her, it seems, in dress—generous and attached, he probably indulged her in that point beyond his means; and the defendant now impudently calls on you to find an excuse for the adulterer in the fondness and liberality of the husband.

But you have been told, that the husband connived. Odious and impudent aggravation of injury, to add calumny to insult, and outrage to dishonour. From whom, but a man hackneyed in the paths of shame and vice—from whom, but from a man having no compunctions in his own breast to restrain him, could you except such brutal disregard for the feelings of others; from whom, but from the cold-blooded veteran seducer—from what, but from the exhausted mind, the habitual community with shame—from what, but the habitual contempt of virtue and of man, could you have expected the arrogance, the barbarity, and folly of so foul, because so false an imputation? He should have reflected, and have blushed, before he suffered so vile a topic of defence to have passed his lips.

But ere you condemn him, let him have the benefit of the excuse, if the excuse be true.

You must have observed how his counsel fluttered and vibrated, between what they call connivance and injudicious confidence; and how, in affecting to distinguish, they have confounded them both together.

If the plaintiff has connived, I freely say to you, do not reward the wretch who has prostituted his wife, and surrendered his own honour; do not compensate the pander of his own shame, and the willing instrument of his own infamy. But as there is no sum so low to which that defence, if true, ought not to reduce your verdict, so neither is any so high to which such a charge ought not to inflame it, if the charge be false.

Where is the single fact in this case on which the remotest suspicion of connivance can be hung? Odiously has the defendant endeavoured to make the softest and most amiable feelings of the heart the pretext of his slanderous imputations. An ancient and respectable prelate, the husband of his wife's sister, is chained down to the bed of sickness, perhaps to the bed of death; in that distressing situation, my client suffered that wife to be the bearer of consolation to the bosom of her sister; he had not the heart to refuse her, and the softness of his nature is now charged on him as a crime. He is now insolently told, that he connived at his dishonour, and that he ought to have foreseen, that the mansion of sickness and sorrow would have been made the scene of assignation and of guilt. On this charge of connivance I will not further weary you or exhaust myself; I will add nothing more, than that it is as false as it is impudent, that in the evidence it has not a colour of support; and that by your verdict you should mark it with reprobation.

The other subject, namely, that he was indiscreet in his confidence, does, I think, call for some discussion, for I trust you see that I affect not any address to your passions, by which you may be led away from the subject—I presume merely to separate the parts of this affecting case, and to lay them item by item before you, with coldness of detail and not with any colouring or display of fiction or of fancy. Honourable to himself was his unsuspecting confidence, but fatal must we admit it to have been, when we look to the abuse committed upon it. But where was the guilt of this indiscretion? He did admit this noble lord to pass his threshold as his guest. Now the charge which this noble lord builds on this indiscretion is, "Thou fool! thou hadst confidence in my honour, and that was a guilty indiscretion: thou simpleton! thou thoughtest that an admitted and cherished guest would have respected the laws of honour and hospitality, and thy indiscretion was guilt: thou thoughtest that he would have shrunk from the meanness and barbarity of requiting kindness with treachery, and thy indiscretion was guilt."

Gentlemen, what horrid alternative in the treatment of wives would such reasoning recommend? Are they to be immured by worse than eastern barbarity? Are their principles to be depraved, their passions sublimated, every finer motive of action extinguished by the inevitable consequences of thus treating them like slaves? Or is a liberal and generous confidence in them to be the passport of the adulterer, and the justification of his crimes?

Honourably, but fatally for his own repose, he was neither jealous, suspicious nor cruel. He treated the defendant with the confidence of a friend, and his wife with the tenderness of a husband. He did leave to the noble Marquis the physical possibility of committing against him the greatest crime which can be perpetrated against a being of an amiable heart and refined education. In the middle of the day, at the moment of divine worship, when the miserable husband was on his knees, directing the prayers and thanksgiving of his congregation to their God, that moment did the remorseless adulterer choose to carry off the deluded victim from her husband, from her child, from her character, from her happiness, as if not content to leave his crime confined to its miserable aggravations, unless he gave it a cast and colour of factitious sacrilege and impiety.

Oh! how happy had it been when he arrived at the bank of the river with the ill-fated fugitive, ere yet he had committed her to that boat, of which, like the fabled bark of Styx, the exile was eternal, how happy at that moment, so teeming with misery and with shame, if you, my lord, had met him, and could have accosted him in the character of that good genius which had abandoned him. How impressively might you have pleaded the cause of the father, of the child, of the mother, and even of the worthless defendant himself. You would have said: "Is this the requital that you are about to make for respect and kindness, and confidence in your honour? Can you deliberately expose this young man, in the bloom of life, with all his hopes before him—can you expose him, a wretched outcast from society, to the scorn of a merciless world? Can you set him adrift upon the tempestuous ocean of his own passions, at this early season, when they are most headstrong; and can you cut him out from the moorings of those domestic obligations by whose cable he might ride at safety from their turbulence? Think of, if you can conceive it, what a powerful influence arises from the sense of home, from the sacred religion of the heart in quelling the passions, in reclaiming the wanderings, in correcting the discords of the human heart; do not cruelly take from him the protection of these attachments.

"But if you have no pity for the father, have mercy at least upon his innocent and helpless child; do not condemn him to an education scandalous or neglected; do not strike him into that most dreadful of all human conditions, the orphanage that springs not from the grave, that falls not from the hand of Providence, or from the stroke of death, but comes before its time, anticipated and inflicted by the remorseless cruelty of parental guilt."

For the poor victim herself, not yet immolated, while yet balancing upon the pivot of her destiny, your heart could not be cold, nor your tongue be wordless. You would have said to him: "Pause, my lord, while there is yet a moment for reflection. What are your motives, what your views, what your prospects from what you are about to do? You are a married man, the husband of the most amiable and respectable of women; you cannot look to the chance of marrying this wretched fugitive; between you and such an event there are two sepulchres to pass. What are your inducements? Is it love, think you? No, do not give that name to any attraction you can find in the faded refuse of a violated bed. Love is a noble and generous passion; it can be founded only on a pure and ardent friendship, on an exalted respect—on an implicit confidence in its object. Search your heart, examine your judgment, do you find the semblance of any one of these sentiments to bind you to her? What could degrade a mind to which nature or education had given port, or stature, or character, into a friendship for her? Could you repose upon her faith? Look in her face, my lord; she is at this moment giving you the violation of the most sacred of human obligations as the pledge of her fidelity. She is giving you the most irrefragable proof, that as she is deserting her husband for you, so she would without a scruple abandon you for another. Do you anticipate any pleasure you might feel in the possible event of your becoming the parents of a common child? She is at this moment proving to you that she is as dead to the sense of parental as of conjugal obligation; and that she would abandon your offspring to-morrow, with the same facility with which she now deserts her own. Look then at her conduct, as it is, as the world must behold it, blackened by every aggravation that can make it either odious or contemptible, and unrelieved by a single circumstance of mitigation, that could palliate its guilt, or retrieve it from abhorrence.

"Mean, however, and degraded as this woman must be, she will still (if you take her with you,) have strong and heavy claims upon you. The force of such claims does certainly depend upon circumstances; before, therefore, you expose her fate to the dreadful risk of your caprice or ingratitude, in mercy to her, weigh well the confidence she can place in your future justice and honour: at that future time, much nearer than you think, by what topics can her cause be pleaded to a sated appetite, to a heart that repels her, to a just judgment in which she never could have been valued or respected? Here is not the case of an unmarried woman, with whom a pure and generous friendship may insensibly have ripened into a more serious attachment, until at last her heart became too deeply pledged to be reassumed. If so circumstanced, without any husband to betray, or child to desert, or motive to restrain, except what related solely to herself, her anxiety for your happiness made her overlook every other consideration, and commit her history to your honour; in such a case, the strongest and the highest that man's imagination can suppose, in which you at least could see nothing but the most noble and disinterested sacrifice; in which you could find nothing but what claimed from you the most kind and exalted sentiment of tenderness, and devotion, and respect; and in which the most fastidious rigour would find so much more subject for sympathy than blame; let me ask you, could you even in that case, answer for your own justice and gratitude?

"I do not allude to the long and pitiful catalogue of paltry adventures, in which it seems your time has been employed; the coarse and vulgar succession of casual connexions, joyless, loveless, and unendeared: but do you not find upon your memory some trace of an engagement of the character I have sketched? Has not your sense of what you would owe in such a case, and to such a woman, been at least once put to the test of experiment? Has it not once, at least, happened that such a woman, with all the resolution of strong faith, flung her youth, her hope, her beauty, her talent, upon your bosom, weighed you against the world, which she found but a feather in the scale, and took you as an equivalent? How did you then acquit yourself? Did you prove yourself worthy of the sacred trust reposed in you? Did your spirit so associate with hers, as to leave her no room to regret the splendid and disinterested sacrifice she had made? Did her soul find a pillow in the tenderness of yours, and support in its firmness? Did you preserve her high in her own consciousness, proud in your admiration and friendship, and happy in your affection? You might have so acted; and the man that was worthy of her would have perished rather than not so act, as to make her delighted with having confided so sacred a trust to his honour. Did you so act? Did she feel that, however precious to your heart, she was still more exalted and honoured in your reverence and respect? Or did she find you coarse and paltry, fluttering and unpurposed, unfeeling, and ungrateful? You found her a fair and blushing flower, its beauty and its fragrance bathed in the dew of heaven. Did you so tenderly transplant it, as to preserve that beauty and fragrance unimpaired? Or did you so rudely cut it, as to interrupt its nutriment, to waste its sweetness, to blast its beauty, to bow its faded and sickly head? And did you at last fling it like 'a loathsome weed away?' If then to such a woman, so clothed with every title that could ennoble, and exalt, and endear her to the heart of man, you would be cruelly and capriciously deficient, how can a wretched fugitive like this, in every point her contrast, hope to find you just? Send her then away. Send her back to her home, to her child, to her husband, to herself."

Alas! there was no one to hold such language to this noble defendant; he did not hold it to himself. Bnt he paraded his despicable prize in his own carriage, with his own retinue, his own servants; this veteran Paris hawked his enamoured Helen from this western quarter of the island to a sea-port in the eastern, crowned with the acclamations of a senseless and grinning rabble, glorying and delighted, no doubt, in the leering and scoffing admiration of grooms, and ostlers, and waiters, as he passed.

In this odious contempt of every personal feeling, of public opinion, of common humanity, did he parade this woman to the sea-port, whence he transported his precious cargo to a country, where her example may be less mischievous than in her own; where I agree with my learned colleague in heartily wishing he may remain with her for ever. We are too poor, too simple, too unadvanced a country, for the example of such achievements. When the relaxation of morals is the natural growth and consequence of the great progress of arts and wealth, it is accompanied by a refinement that makes it less gross than shocking; but for such palliations we are at least a century too young. I advise you, therefore, most earnestly to rebuke this budding mischief, by letting the wholesome vigour and chastisement of a liberal verdict speak what you think of its enormity.

In every point of view in which I can look at the subject, I see you are called upon to give a verdict of bold, and just, and indignant, and exemplary compensation. The injury of the plaintiff demands it from your justice; the delinquency of the defendant provokes it by its enormity. The rank on which he has relied for impunity calls upon you to tell him, that crime does not ascend to the rank of the perpetrator, but the perpetrator sinks from his rank, and descends to the level of his delinquency. The style and mode of his defence is a gross aggravation of his conduct, and a gross insult upon you.

Look upon the different subjects of his defence as you ought, and let him profit by them as he deserves. Vainly presumptuous upon his rank, he wishes to overawe you by that despicable consideration. He next resorts to a cruel aspersion upon the character of the unhappy plaintiff, whom he had already wounded beyond the possibility of reparation: he has ventured to charge him with connivance. As to that, I will only say, gentlemen of the jury, do not give this vain boaster a pretext for saying, that if her husband connived in the offence, the jury also connived in the reparation.

But he has pressed another curious topic upon you. After the plaintiff had cause to suspect his designs, and the likelihood of their being fatally successful, he did not then act precisely as he ought. Gracious God! what an argument for him to dare to advance! It is saying this to him:—"I abused your confidence, your hospitality; I laid a base plan for the seduction of the wife of your bosom; I succeeded at last, so as to throw in upon you that most dreadful of all suspicions to a man fondly attached, proud of his wife's honour, and tremblingly alive to his own; that you were possibly a dupe to the confidence in the wife, as much as in the guest. In this so pitiable distress, which I myself had studiously and deliberately contrived for you, between hope and fear, and doubt and love, and jealousy and shame; one moment shrinking from the cruelty of your suspicion; the next, fired with indignation at the facility and credulity of your acquittal; in this labyrinth of doubt, in this frenzy of suffering, you were not collected and composed; you did not act as you might have done, if I had not worked you to madness; and upon that very madness which I have inflicted upon you, upon the very completion of my guilt, and of your misery, I will build my defence. You will not act critically right, and therefore are unworthy of compensation."

Gentlemen, can you be dead to the remorseless atrocity of such a defence! And shall not your honest verdict mark it as it deserves.

But let me go a little further; let me ask you, for I confess I have no distinct idea—What should be the conduct of a husband so placed, and who is to act critically right? Shall he lock her up, or turn her out, or enlarge or abridge her liberty of acting as she pleases? Oh, dreadful Areopagus of the tea-table! how formidable thy inquests, how tremendous thy condemnations! In the first case, he is brutal and barbarous; an odious eastern despot. In the next; what! turn an innocent woman out of his house, without evidence or proof, but merely because he is vile and mean enough to suspect the wife of his bosom, and the mother of his child! Between these extremes, what intermediate degree is he to adopt? I put this question to you—Do you at this moment, uninfluenced by any passion as you now are, but cool and collected, and uninterested as you must be, do you see clearly this proper and exact line, which the plaintiff should have pursued? I much question if you do. But if you did or could, must you not say, that he was the last man from whom you should expect the coolness to discover, or the steadiness to pursue it? And yet this is the outrageous and insolent defence that is put forward to you. My miserable client, when his brain was on fire, and every fiend of hell was let loose upon his heart, should then, it seems, have placed himself before his mirror; he should have taught the stream of agony to flow decorously down his forehead; he should have composed his features to harmony; he should have writhed with grace, and groaned in melody.

But look farther to this noble defendant, and his honourable defence. The wretched woman is to be successively the victim of seduction, and of slander. She, it seems, received marked attentions. Here, I confess, I felt myself not a little at a loss. The witnesses could not describe what these marked attentions were, or are. They consisted, not, if you believe the witness that swore to them, in any personal approach, or contact whatsoever, nor in any unwarrantable topics of discourse. Of what materials, then, were they composed? Why, it seems a gentleman had the insolence at table to propose to her a glass of wine; and she, oh, most abandoned lady! instead of flying like an angry parrot at his head, and besmirching and bescratching him for his insolence, tamely and basely replies, "Port, sir, if you please."

But, gentlemen, why do I advert to this folly, this nonsense? Not surely to vindicate from censure the most innocent and the most delightful intercourse of social kindness, or harmless and cheerful courtesy, "where virtue is, these are most virtuous." But I am soliciting your attention, and your feeling, to the mean and odious aggravation, to the unblushing and remorseless barbarity, of falsely aspersing the wretched woman he had undone.

One good he has done, he has disclosed to you the point in which he can feel; for how imperious must that avarice be, which could resort to so vile an expedient of frugality? Yes, I will say, that, with the common feelings of a man, he would have rather suffered his thirty thousand a year to go as compensation to the plaintiff, than have saved a shilling of it by so vile an expedient of economy. He would rather have starved with her in a gaol, he would rather have sunk with her into the ocean, than have so vilified her—than have so degraded himself.

But it seems, gentlemen, and indeed you have been told, that long as the course of his gallantries has been, and he has grown grey in the service, it is the first time he has been called upon for damages. To how many might it have been fortunate, if he had not that impunity to boast? Your verdict will, I trust, put an end to that encouragement to guilt, that is built upon impunity.

The devil, it seems, has saved the noble Marquis harmless in the past; but your verdict will tell him the term of that indemnity is expired—that his old friend and banker has no more effects in his hands—and that if he draws any more upon him, he must pay his own bills himself. You will do much good by doing so: you may not enlighten his conscience, nor touch his heart; but his frugality will understand the hint. It will adopt the prudence of age, and deter him from pursuits, in which, though he may be insensible of shame, he will not be regardless of expense. You will do more—you will not only punish him in his tender point, but you will weaken him in his strong one, his money. We have heard much of this noble Lord's wealth, and much of his exploits, but not much of his accomplishments or his wit; I know not that his verses have soared even to the "poet's corner." I have heard it said, that an ass laden with gold could find his way through the gate of the strongest city. But, gentlemen, lighten the load upon his back, and you will completely curtail the mischievous faculty of a grave animal, whose momentum lies, not in his agility, but his weight; not in the quantity of his motion, but the quantity of his matter.

There is another ground on which you are called upon to give most liberal damages, and that has been laid by the unfeeling vanity of the defendant. This business has been marked by the most elaborate publicity. It is very clear that he has been allured by the glory of the chase, and not the value of the game. The poor object of his pursuit could be of no value to him, or he could not have so wantonly, and cruelly, and unnecessarily abused her. He might easily have kept this unhappy intercourse an unsuspected secret. Even if he wished for elopement, he might easily have so contrived it, that the place of her retreat would be profoundly undiscoverable.

Yet, though even the expense, a point so tender to his delicate sensibility, of concealing, could not be one-fortieth of the cost of publishing her, his vanity decided him in favour of glory and publicity. By that election, he has, in fact, put forward the Irish nation, and its character, so often and so variously calumniated, upon its trial before the tribunal of the empire; and your verdict will this day decide whether an Irish jury can feel with justice and spirit upon a subject that involves conjugal affection and comfort, domestic honour and repose, the certainty of issue, the weight of public opinion, the gilded and presumptuous criminality of overweening rank and station.

I doubt not but he is at this moment reclined on a silken sofa, anticipating that submissive and modest verdict, by which you will lean gently on his errors; and expecting from your patriotism, no doubt, that you will think again, and again, before you condemn any great portion of the immense revenue of a great absentee, to be detained in the nation that produced it, instead of being transmitted, as it ought, to be expended in the splendour of another country. He is now probably waiting for the arrival of the report of this day, which I understand a famous note-taker has been sent hither to collect. Let not the gentleman be disturbed.

Gentlemen, let me assure you, it is more, much more the trial of you, than of the noble Marquis, of which this imported recorder is at this moment collecting materials. His noble employer is now expecting a report to the following effect:—"Such a day came on to be tried at Ennis, by a special jury, the cause of Charles Massy against the most noble the Marquis of Headfort. It appeared that the plaintiff's wife was young, beautiful, and captivating; the plaintiff himself, a person fond of this beautiful creature to distraction, and both doating on their child. But the noble Marquis approached her; the plume of glory nodded on his head. Not the goddess Minerva, but the goddess Venus, had lighted up his casque with 'the fire that never tires, such as many a lady gay had been dazzled with before.' At the first advance she trembled; at the second, she struck to the redoubted son of Mars, and pupil of Venus. The jury saw it was not his fault (it was an Irish jury); they felt compassion for the tenderness of the mother's heart, and for the warmth of the lover's passion. The jury saw on the one side, a young, entertaining gallant; on the other, a beauteous creature, of charms irresistible. They recollected that Jupiter had been always successful in his amours, although Vulcan had not always escaped some awkward accidents. The jury was composed of fathers, brothers, husbands, but they had not the vulgar jealousy, that views little things of that sort with rigour; and, wishing to assimilate their country in every respect to England, now that they are united to it, they, like English gentlemen, returned to their box, with a verdict of 6*d.* damages, and 6*d.* costs."

Let this be sent to England. I promise you, your odious secret will not be kept better than that of the wretched Mrs. Massy. There is not a bawdy chronicle in London, in which the epitaph which you would have written on yourselves will not be published; and our enemies will delight in the spectacle of our precocious depravity, in seeing that we can be rotten before we are ripe. I do not suppose it; I do not, cannot, will not believe it; I will not harrow up myself with the anticipated apprehension.

There is another consideration, gentlemen, which I think most imperiously demands even a vindictive award of exemplary damages—and that is, the breach of hospitality.

To us peculiarly does it belong to avenge the violation of its altar. The hospitality of other countries is a matter of necessity or convention—in savage nations, of the first: in polished, of the latter: but the hospitality of an Irishman is not the running account of posted and ledgered courtesies, as in other countries; it springs like all his qualities, his faults, his virtues, directly from his heart. The heart of an Irishman is by nature bold, and he confides; it is tender, and he loves; it is generous, and he gives; it is social, and he is hospitable. This sacrilegious intruder has profaned the religion of that sacred altar so elevated in our worship, so precious to our devotion: and it is our privilege to avenge the crime. You must either pull down the altar, and abolish the worship; or you must preserve its sanctity undebased. There is no alternative between the universal exclusion of all mankind from your threshold, and the most rigorous punishment of him who is admitted and betrays. This defendant has been so trusted, has so betrayed, and you ought to make him a most signal example.

Gentlemen, I am the more disposed to feel the strongest indignation and abhorrence at this odious conduct of the defendant, when I consider the deplorable condition to which he has reduced the plaintiff, and perhaps the still more deplorable one that the plaintiff has in prospect before him. What a progress has he to travel through, before he can attain the peace and tranquillity which he has lost? How like the wounds of the body are those of the mind! how burning the fever! how painful the suppuration! how slow, how hesitating, how relapsing the process to convalescence! Through what a variety of suffering, what new scenes and changes must my unhappy client pass, ere he can re-attain, should he ever re-attain, that health of soul of which he has been despoiled by the cold and deliberate machinations of this practised and gilded seducer?

If, instead of drawing upon his incalculable wealth for a scanty retribution, you were to stop the progress of his despicable achievements, by reducing him to actual poverty, you could not even so punish him beyond the scope of his offence, nor reprise the plaintiff beyond the measure of his suffering. Let me remind you, that in this action, the law not only empowers you, but that its policy commands you to consider the public example, as well as the amount of your verdict. I confess I am most anxious that you should acquit yourselves worthily upon this important occasion. I am addressing you as fathers, husbands, brothers. I am anxious that a feeling of those high relations should enter into, and give dignity to your verdict.

But I confess, I feel a ten-fold solicitude when I remember that I am addressing you as my countrymen, as Irishmen, whose characters as jurors, as gentlemen, must find either honour or degradation in the result of your decision. Small as must be the distributive share of that national estimation, that can belong to so unimportant an individual as myself, yet I do own I am tremblingly solicitous for its fate. Perhaps it appears of more value to me, because it is embarked on the same bottom with yours; perhaps the community of peril, of common safety, or common wreck, gives a consequence to my share of the risk, which I could not be vain enough to give it, if it were not raised to it by that mutuality. But why stoop to think at all of myself, when I know that you, gentlemen of the jury—when I know that our country itself are my clients on this day, and must abide the alternative of honour or of infamy, as you shall decide. But I will not despond, I will not dare to despond. I have every trust, and hope, and confidence in you. And to that hope I will add my most fervent prayer to the God of all truth and justice, so to raise, and enlighten, and fortify your minds, that you may so decide, as to preserve to yourselves while you live, the most delightful of all recollections—that of acting justly; and to transmit to your children the most precious of all inheritances—the memory of your virtue.

Baron Smith charged, and after a trial of twelve hours' duration, the jury at midnight found for the plaintiff, £10,000 damages, with costs.

FOR JUDGE JOHNSON.

[HABEAS CORPUS.]

COURT OF EXCHEQUER.

BEFORE CHIEF BARON LORD AVONMORE AND THE OTHER BARONS.

February 4th, 1805.

Robert Johnson was called to the Irish Bar in Michaelmas Term, 1776, and obtained an early reputation for ability. In June, 1800, he was made one of the Justices of the Court of Common Pleas in Ireland.

On the 5th of November, 1803, a letter, signed "Juverna," was published in *Cobbett's Political Register*. It was written in a bold and bitter style, and having narrated the story of the Trojan Horse, applied it to Lord Hardwicke's rule in Ireland. In that and subsequent papers Lord Hardwicke was described as "a very eminent breeder of sheep in Cambridgeshire;" Lord Chancellor Redesdale is called "a very able and strong-built Chancery pleader from Lincoln's Inn;" Mr. Secretary Marsden appears as "a corrupt, unprincipled, rapacious plunderer, preying upon the property of the state;" and Justice Osborne as "the most corrupt instrument of a debased and degraded government, lending himself as a screen to conceal them from the disgrace their actions would naturally bring upon them."

These are the strongest passages, and the ones that were relied on in the prosecution.

Cobbett was prosecuted for these publications, as libelling Lords Hardwicke and Redesdale, Mr. Marsden, and Judge Osborne; he was tried at Westminster, before Lord Ellenborough, on the 4th of May, 1804. The Attorney-General prosecuted; Mr. Adam defended Cobbett, and called Lord Minto.

Charles Yorke, Windham, Lord Henry Stewart, &c., to swear to Cobbett's ultra loyalty; but in ten minutes the jury found him guilty of the libel.

In one of the "Juverna" articles (that published on the 10th of December), Plunket, then Solicitor-General for Ireland, was attacked on many grounds, but especially for his speech in reply on Emmet's trial. "Juverna" represents Emmet as describing Plunket thus: "That viper, whom my father nourished! He it was from whose lips I first imbibed those principles and doctrines which now by their effects drag me to my grave, and he it is who is now brought forward as my prosecutor, and who, by an unheard-of exercise of the prerogative, has wantonly lashed with a speech to evidence the dying son of his former friend, when that son had produced no evidence, had made no defence; but, on the contrary, had acknowledged the charge, and submitted to his fate."

For publishing this libel, Plunket brought a civil action against Cobbett; the case was heard by Lord Ellenborough on the 26th of May, 1804. Erskine opened for the plaintiff; Adam defended Cobbett ably, quoting Plunket's words on the nullity of the Union; but the jury, after twenty minutes' deliberation, found a verdict for the plaintiff, and £500 damages.

These verdicts were not enforced. Cobbett gave up the manuscript of the libellous articles, alleging that they were written by Mr. Justice Johnson. The offended parties believed the statement, and it was resolved to ruin Johnson.

For this purpose a vast machinery was resorted to.

On the 20th of July, 1804, an act was passed, entitled, "an act to render more easy the apprehending and bringing to trial offenders *escaping* from one part of the united kingdom to the other, and also from one county to another," by which, amongst other things, it was enacted, that a warrant from a court in Great Britain might be transmitted to Ireland, be endorsed and executed there by a Justice of the Peace, and the accused party transferred for trial to the court from which the warrant issued.

That all the persons concerned in pushing this act knew its object it would be wrong to say; but it was brought in by Perceval, Lord Redesdale's brother-in-law, and by Charles Yorke, the brother of Lord Hardwicke, and was mainly and speedily used against Johnson—a case for strong suspicion, at least, against the Irish Government.

The act was soon used. Bills were found against Johnson for Libel by the Middlesex Grand Jury, and on the 24th of November, 1804, a warrant was issued against him from the King's Bench at Westminster, founded on a charge of libel; this warrant was endorsed by Robert Bell, Esq., J. P. for the county Dublin, and under it the Judge was conditionally arrested at his house at Milltown, on the 17th, and absolutely on the 18th of January, 1805. Johnson procured delay,* a Habeas Corpus was at once issued, and on the 19th of January he was brought before the Chief Justice and six other Judges, at the Chief's house, and the case immediately gone into. Johnson was ill and sought delay, but O'Grady, (the Attorney-General) refused it, and Johnson read a statement showing that he had sought to go to Bath for his health (then very feeble) and had obtained leave, though warned that he would be held to bail, and that the whole proceeding was a tyrannical and illegal contrivance. Counsel argued the case, the Attorney-General replied on the 22nd, and an eighth judge having come in that day, their lordships divided, three for and three against allowing the cause shown on the writ of Habeas Corpus, and two were neuter. The question, therefore, went into the King's Bench, and was there argued, on the 26th, 28th, and 29th of January, by CURRAN, M'Cartney, William Johnson, for the judge, and by Arthur Browne (the Prime-Sergeant) and the Attorney-General O'Grady, for the crown. Justice Day decided for release, Chief Justice Downes and Justice Daly against it.

* The fact that he was communicated with on the 17th, negatives the charge against government, of having tried to kidnap him—expedition they were bound under the act to use.

CURRAN'S speech contains nothing of argument additional to the speech he afterwards made in the Exchequer, on the same subject; nor has it any pretensions to brilliant eloquence, except, perhaps, in the concluding passage, which is as follows:—

BUT suppose him arrived in London. What defence can he make there? Yes, I think there is one; there is an inborn enthusiasm for liberty—an innate love of freedom—a hatred of oppression and tyranny, that would redeem the victim and secure him from the attack of the oppressor. But give such a power to a prosecutor, as the construction put upon this statute would give, and there is not a man in England, from the Archbishop of Canterbury to the lowest mechanic, who may not be brought here under colour of this statute, and *vice versa*, and tried upon trivial accusations without the possibility of giving bail. The minister going to the House of Commons may be arrested upon the information of an Irish chairman, and a warrant granted by a trading justice. Mr. Pitt is brought over here *in vinculis*. What to do?—to see whether he should be bailed or not. I remember Mr. Fox was here during the life-time of this country: in the same way he might be brought over. It may facilitate the intercourse between the islands—any man may travel at the public expense. Suppose I gave an Irishman in London a small assault in trust; when the vacation arrives, he knocks at the door of a trading justice, and tells him he wants a warrant against the counsellor. „What counsellor?"

"Oh, sure every body knows the counsellor." "Well, friend, and what is your name?" "Thady O'Flanagan, please your honour." "What countryman are you?" "An Englishman, by construction." "Very well, I'll draw upon my correspondent in Ireland for the body of the counsellor."

What! my lords, is there no apprehension of an outrage of that kind? There is nothing against it but the great expense. The two warrants cannot be obtained for less than five shillings of our money. But the expense of journey must be defrayed by the public; and can it be supposed that the legislature intended, that the public money should be thus drawn upon at the good will of every petty prosecutor, either to gratify his malice or supply his necessities?

Lord Chief Justice Downes—Give me leave to ask, whether this mischief might not arise in the case of an unfounded charge of felony?

Mr. Curran—No, my lord; accusers are not so easily found in such cases. The atrocity of the charge deters the party from making it. I have witnessed many trials, and I seldom knew a false charge of a capital crime; but there are a thousand instances of false charges of petty misdemeanors.

I shall add to that head of observation, that this is a state prosecution. Yet it must be proceeded upon as every common case between subject and subject. But if anything can impress this particular case more upon the Court than any other, it is the circumstance that it is a prosecution by the state for a libel; see then what a power is put into the hands of a minister, or the rival of a minister. An experiment must first be made in the province, remote from the seat of government, where it may be supposed to pass *sub silentio.* They would not venture to try it in London, to give up an inhabitant of England to an Irish catchpole, and send him upon a voyage to Ireland to know whether he should be bailed or not. It would appal the English nation to have such an artillery opened upon them; it would be to stand before a loaded cannon, while a child with a lighted torch was sitting at the touch-hole. If my client must undertake this voyage, let the messenger perform the obsequies by night, and take him to the water-edge in the dark, that his countrymen may not see his last look upon his native shore, which he is never to see again. Let not his wife or children witness his departure. He is to be taken to a place, where his innocence cannot appear, for there is no process to produce the witness who can attest it.

My lords, this is an odious experiment. It is of late that this perplexed doctrine of constructions has been revived; it flourished before science had attained its full maturity, and when there was nothing but commentators, and scholiasts, and constructors. Are acknowledged principles to be explained away by some godfather, producing his adopted manuscript—"nullus liber homo capiatur, vel imprisonetur, nisi per legale judicium parium suorum, vel per legem terræ." A manuscript is produced—it came into the hands of a grandfather's executor—by which it appears, that *lex terræ* is for the common people, but *judicium parium* means something more; it means the judgment of the upper house—the judgment of the peers. This exposes the freedom of the subject, and his dearest rights, to the uncertainties of caprice and the vagaries of speculation. It is admitted there are real hardships imposed by this statute; but it is suggested it may be amended. Perhaps it may—perhaps it may not. But under the construction contended for by the prosecuter, they are desperate and formidable. If you see one construction which is destructive of former rights, and another which is sanative of those rights, I hope you will adopt the latter. I hope that you will not think this a doubtful case—that it will be understood abroad that it is not—that the prosecutor will be pleased with his failure—that he will feel a gratifying consciousness at going out of court mercifully triumphant. If there be any latent motive against the accused, it will be defeated by persisting in the present measure; they will exhibit him as a persecuted man, rousing and arming every principle of the human heart to pity and protect him. If they have any object, they will lose it by an odious and abominable prosecution. But grieved should I be to look to the compunction of humanity, or await the satiated vengeance of the prosecutor, instead of the honourable and upright justice of the Court, which is to pass sentence one way or the other.

Therefore, I leave my client with you. He has fled to the temple of justice—he has fallen upon its steps. I trust in Divine Providence, that he will find there a sanctuary, and that your lordships will order him to be discharged from the custody in which he is now detained.

Pending this, another writ had been issued from the Exchequer. Under it Johnson was brought up on the 4th of February, before Barry Viscount Yelverton, Barons George, (William) Smith, and M'Cleiland. Mr. Peter Burrowes shortly and argumentatively moved the release of Judge Johnson, and then CURRAN rose and said:—

My Lords, it has fallen to my lot, either fortunately or unfortunately, as the event may be, to rise as counsel for my client, on this most important and momentous occasion. I appear before you, my lords, in consequence of a writ issued by his Majesty, commanding that cause be shown to this his court, why his subject has been deprived of his liberty; and upon the cause shown in obedience to this writ, it is my duty to address you on the most awful question—if awfulness is to be judged by consequences and events—on which you have ever been called upon to decide. Sorry am I that the task has not been confided to more adequate powers; but, feeble as mine are, they will, at least, not shrink from it. I move you, therefore, that Mr. Justice Johnson be released from illegal imprisonment.

I cannot but observe the sort of scenic preparation with which this sad drama is sought to be brought forward. In part, I approve it; in part, it excites my disgust and indignation. I am glad to find that the Attorney-General and the Solicitor-General, the natural and official prosecutors for the state, do not appear; and I infer from their absence, that his Excellency the Lord Lieutenant disclaims any personal concern in this execrable transaction. I think it does him much honour; it is a conduct that equally accords with the dignity of his character and the feelings of his heart. To his private virtues, whenever he is left to their influence, I willingly concur in giving the most unqualified tribute of respect. And I do firmly believe, it is with no small regret that he suffers his name to be even formally made use of, in avowing for a return of one of the judges of the land, with as much indifference and *nonchalance*, as if he were a beast of the plough.

I observe, too the dead silence into which the public is frowned by authority for the sad occasion. No man dares to mutter, no newspaper dares to whisper, that such a question is afloat. It seems an inquiry among the tombs, or rather in the shades beyond them.

"Ibant sola sub nocte per umbram."

I am glad it is so—I am glad of this factitious dumbness: for if murmurs dared to become audible, my voice would be too feeble to drown them. But when all is hushed, when nature sleeps—

"Cum quies mortalibus ægris"—

the weakest voice is heard—the shepherd's whistle shoots across the listening darkness of the interminable heath, and gives notice that the wolf is upon his walk; and the same gloom and stillness that tempt the monster to come abroad, facilitate the communication of the warning to beware. Yes, through that silence the voice shall be heard; yes, through that silence the shepherd shall be put upon his guard; yes, through that silence shall the felon savage be chased into the toil. Yes, my lords, I feel myself impressed and cheered by the composed and dignified attention with which I see you are disposed to hear me on the most important question that has ever been subjected to your consideration—the most important to the dearest rights of the human being—the most deeply interesting and animating that can beat in his heart, or burn upon his tongue.

Oh! how recreating is it to feel that occasions may arise, in which the soul of man may resume her pretensions—in which she hears the voice of nature whisper to her, "*os homini sublime dedi coelumque tueri*"—in which even I can look up with calm security to the court, and down with the most profound contempt upon the reptile I mean to tread upon! I say, reptile; because, when the proudest man in society becomes so much the dupe of his childish malice, as to wish to inflict on the object of his vengeance the poison of his sting, to do a reptile's work, he must shrink into a reptile's dimension; and, so shrunk, the only way to assail him is to tread upon him.

But to the subject. This writ of habeas corpus has had a return. That return states, that Lord Ellenborough, Chief Justice of England, issued a warrant, reciting the foundation of this dismal transaction, that one of the clerks of the crown office had certified to him, that an indictment had been found at Westminster, charging the Honourable Robert Johnson, late of Westminster, one of the Justices of his Majesty's Court of Common Pleas in Ireland, with the publication of certain slanderous libels against the government of that country; against the person of his Excellency Lord Hardwicke, Lord Lieutenant of that country; against the person of Lord Redesdale, the Chancellor of Ireland; and against the person of Mr. Justice Osborne, one of the Justices of the Court of King's Bench in Ireland. One of the clerks of the crown-office, it seems, certified all this to his lordship. How many of those there are, or who they are, or which of them so certified, we cannot presume to guess, because the learned and noble lord is silent as to those circumstances. We are only informed that one of them made that important communication to his lordship.

It puts me in mind of the information given to one of Fielding's justices: "Did not," says his worship's wife, "the man with the valet make his *fidavy* that you was *a vagram?*" I suppose it was some such petty-bag officer who gave Lord Ellenborough to understand that Mr. Justice Johnson was indicted.

And being thus given to understand and be informed, he issued his warrant to a gentleman, no doubt of great respectability, a Mr. Williams, his tipstaff, to take the body of Mr. Justice Johnson, and bring him before a magistrate, for the purpose of giving bail to appear within the first eight days of this term, so that there might be a trial within the sittings after; and if, by the blessing of God, he should be convicted, then to appear on the return of the *postea,* to be dealt with according to law.

Perhaps it may be a question for you to decide, whether that warrant, such as it may be, is not now absolutely spent; and if not, how a man can contrive to be hereafter in England on a day that is past? And high as the opinion may be in England of Irish understanding, it will be something beyond even Irish exactness, to bind him to appear in England, not a fortnight hence, but a fortnight ago. I wish, my lords, we had the art of giving time this retrograde motion. If possessed of the secret, we might possibly be disposed to improve it from fortnights into years.

There is something not incurious in the juxtaposition of signatures. The warrant is signed by the Chief Justice of all England. In music, the ear is reconciled to strong transitions of key, by a preparatory resolution of the intervening discords; but here, alas! there is nothing to break the fall: the august title of Ellenborough is followed by the unadorned name of brother Bell, the sponsor of his lordship's warrant. Let me not, however, be suffered to deem lightly of the compeer of the noble and learned lord. Mr. Justice Bell ought to be a lawyer; I remember him myself long a crier,* and I know his credit with the state; he has had a *noli prosequi.* I see not, therefore, why it may not be fairly said, "*fortunati ambo!*" It appears by this return, that Mr. Justice Bell endorses this bill of lading to another consignee, Mr. Medlicot, a most respectable gentleman; he describes himself upon the warrant, and he gives a delightful specimen of the administration of justice, and the calendar of saints in office; he describes himself a justice and a peace-officer, that is, a magistrate and a catchpole. So he may receive informations as a justice; if he can write, he may draw them as a clerk; if not, he can execute the warrant as a bailiff; and, if it be a capital offence, you may see the

* This gentleman was formerly crier to the late Baron Hamilton, when the Baron went circuit as a Judge.

culprit, the justice, the clerk, the bailiff, and the hangman, together in the same cart; and, though he may not write, he may "ride and tie." What a pity that their journey should not be further continued together! That, as they had been "lovely in their lives, so in their deaths they might not be divided!" I find, my lords, I have undesignedly raised a laugh: never did I less feel merriment. Let not me be condemned—let not the laugh be mistaken. Never was Mr. Hume more just than when he says, that "in many things the extremes are nearer to one another than the means." Few are those events that are produced by vice and folly, that fire the heart with indignation, that do not also shake the sides with laughter. So, when the two famous moralists of old beheld the sad spectacle of life, the one burst into laughter, the other melted into tears; they were each of them right, and equally right.

"Si credas utrique
"Res sunt humanæ flebile iudibrium."

But these are the bitter ireful laughs of honest indignation—or they are laughs of hectic melancholy despair.

It is stated to you, my lords, that these two justices, if justices they are to be called, went to the house of the defendant. I am speaking to judges, but I disdain the paltry insult it would be to them, were I to appeal to any wretched sympathy of situation. I feel I am above it. I know the bench is above it. But I know, too, that there are ranks, and degrees, and decorums to be observed, and, if I had a harsh communication to make to a venerable judge, and a similar one to his crier, I should certainly address them in very different language indeed. A judge of the land, a man not young, of infirm health, has the sanctuary of his habitation broken open by these two persons, who set out with him for the coast, to drag him from his country, to hurry him to a strange land by the "most direct way," till the King's writ stopped the malefactors, and left the subject of the king a waif dropped in the pursuit.

Is it for nothing, my lords, I say this? Is it without intention, I state the facts in this way? It is with every intention. It is the duty of the public advocate not so to put forward the object of public attention, as that the skeleton only shall appear, without flesh, or feature, or complexion. I mean every thing that ought to be meant in a court of justice. I mean not only that this execrable attempt shall be intelligible to the court as a matter of law, but shall be understood by the world as an act of state. If advocates had always the honesty and the courage, upon occasions like this, to despise all personal considerations, and to think of no consequence but what may result to the public from the faithful discharge of their sacred trust, these frenetic projects of power, these atrocious aggressions on the liberty and happiness of men, would not be so often attempted; for, though a certain class of delinquents may be screened from punishment, they cannot be protected from hatred and derision.

The great tribunal of reputation will pass its inexorable sentence upon their crimes, their follies, or their incompetency; they will sink themselves under the consciousness of their situation; they will feel the operation of an acid so neutralizing the malignity of their natures, as to make them at least harmless, if it cannot make them honest. Nor is there any thing of risk in the conduct I recommend. If the fire be hot, or the window cold, turn not your back to either; turn your face. So, if you are obliged to arraign the acts of those in high stations, approach them not in malice, nor favour, nor fear. Remember, that it is the condition of guilt to tremble, and of honesty to be bold; remember, that your false fear can only give them false courage; that while you nobly avow the cause of truth, you will find her shield an impenetrable protection; and that no attack can be either hazardous or inefficient, if it be just and resolute. If Nathan had not fortified himself in the boldness and directness of his charge, he might have been hanged for the malice of his parable.

It is, my lords, in this temper of mind—befitting every advocate who is worthy of the name, deeply and modestly sensible of his duty, and proud of his privilege, equally exalted above the meanness of temporizing or of offending, most averse from the unnecessary infliction of pain upon any man or men whatsoever—that I now address you on a question, the most vitally connected with the liberty and well-being of every man within the limits of the British empire; which being decided one way, he may be a freeman; which being decided the other, he must be a slave.

It is not the Irish nation only that is involved in this question; every member of the three realms is equally embarked: and would to God all England could listen to what passes here this day! They would regard us with more sympathy and respect, when the proudest Briton saw that his liberty was defended in what he would call a provincial court, and by a provincial advocate.

The abstract and general question for your consideration is this. My Lord Ellenborough has signed with his own hand a warrant, which has been endorsed by Mr. Bell, an Irish Justice, for seizing the person of Mr. Justice Johnson, in Ireland, for conveying his person by the most direct way, in such manner as these bailiffs may choose, across the sea, and afterwards to the city of Westminster, to take his trial for an alleged libel against the persons entrusted with the government of Ireland, and to take that trial in a country where the supposed offender did not live at the time of the supposed offence, nor, since a period of at least eighteen months previous thereto, has ever resided;

where the subject of his accusation is perfectly unknown; where the conduct of his prosecutors, which has been the subject of the supposed libel, is equally unknown; where he has not the power of compelling the attendance of a single witness for his defence.

Under that warrant, he has been dragged from his family; under that warrant, he was on his way to the water's edge; his transportation has been interrupted by the writ before you, and upon the return of that writ arises the question upon which you are to decide the legality or illegality of so transporting him for the purpose of trial. I am well aware, my lords, of the limits of the present discussion; if the law were clear in favour of the prosecutors, a most momentous question might arise—how far they may be delinquents, in daring to avail themselves of such a law for such a purpose? But I am aware that such is not the present question; I am aware that this is no court of impeachment; and, therefore, that your inquiry is, not whether such a power hath been criminally used, but whether it doth in fact exist?

The arrest of the defendant has been justified by the advocates of the crown, under the forty-fourth of his present Majesty. I have had the curiosity to inquire into the history of that act, and I find that in the month of May, 1804, the brother-in-law of one of the present prosecutors obtained leave to bring in a bill, to "render more easy the apprehending and bringing to trial offenders escaping from one part of the United Kingdom to another, and also from one county to another:" that bill was brought in; it travelled in the caravan of legislation unheeded and unnoticed, retarded by no difficulties of discussion or debate, and in due fulness of season it passed into a law, which was to commence from and after the 1st of August, 1804.

This act, like a young Hercules, began its exploits in the cradle. In the November following, the present warrant was issued, under its supposed authority. Let me not be understood to say that the act has been slided through an unsuspecting legislature, under any particular influence, or for any particular purpose: that any such man could be found, or any such influence exist, or any such lethargy prevail, would not, perhaps, be decent to suppose. Still less do I question the legislative authority of parliament. We all know that a parliament may attaint itself; and that its omnipotence may equally extend in the same way to the whole body of the people. We know also that most unjust and cruel acts of attainder have been obtained by corrupt men in bad times; and if I could bring myself to say, which I do not, that this act was contrived for the mere purpose of destroying an obnoxious individual, I should not hesitate to call it the most odious species of attainder that could be found upon the records of legislative degradation; because, for the simple purpose of extinguishing an individual, it would sweep the liberty of every being in the state into the vortex of general and undistinguished destruction.

But these are points of view upon which the minds of the people of Ireland and England may dwell with terror, or indignation, or apathy, according as they may be fitted for liberty or for chains: but they are not points for the court; and so I pass them by. The present arrest and detention are defended under the forty-fourth of the King: are they warranted by that act? That is the only question for you to decide; and you will arrive at that decision in the usual course, by inquiring, first, how the law stood before upon the subject; next, what the imperfection or grievance of that law was; and, thirdly, what is the remedy intended to be applied by the act in question?

First, then, how stood the law before? Upon this part, it would be a parade of useless learning to go farther back than the statute of Charles, the Habeas Corpus Act, which is so justly called the second Magna Charta of British liberty: what was the occasion of the law? the arbitrary transportation of the subject beyond the realm; that base and malignant war, which the odious and despicable minions of power are for ever ready to wage against all those who are honest and bold enough to despise, to expose, and to resist them.

Such is the oscitancy of man, that he lies torpid for ages under these aggressions, until at last some signal abuse—the violation of Lucrece, the death of Virginia, the oppression of William Tell—shakes him from his slumber. For years had those drunken gambols of power been played in England; for years had the waters of bitterness been rising to the brim; at last, a single drop caused them to overflow,—the oppression of a single individual raised the people of England from their sleep. And what does that great statute do? It defines and asserts the right, it points out the abuse, and it endeavours to secure the right, and to guard against the abuse, by giving redress to the sufferer, and by punishing the offender.

For years had it been the practice to transport obnoxious persons out of the realm into distant parts, under the pretext of punishment, or of safe custody. Well might they have been said, to be sent "to that undiscovered country, from whose bourne no traveller returns;" for of these wretched travellers, how few ever did return?

But of that flagrant abuse, this statute has laid the axe to the root. It prohibits the abuse; it declares such detention or removal illegal; it gives an action against all persons concerned in the offence, by contriving, writing, signing, countersigning, such warrant, or advising or assisting therein.

That you may form a just estimate of the rights which were to be secured, examine the means by which the infringement was in future to be prevented and punished. The injured party has a civil action against the offenders; but the legislature recollected, that the sneaking unprincipled humility of a servile packed jury might do homage to ministerial power, by compensating the individual with nominal damages. The statute does that, of which I remember no other instance—it leaves the jury at liberty to give damages to any extent, above five hundred pounds; but expressly forbids them to find a verdict of damages below it. Was this sufficient? No. The offenders incur a *praemunire*. They are put out of the king's protection; they forfeit their lands and goods; they are disabled from bearing any office of trust or profit. Did the statute stop there? The legislature saw, in their prospective wisdom, that the profligate favourite, who had committed treason against the King by the oppression of his subjects, might acquire such a dominion over the mind of his master, as by the exertion of prerogative to interrupt the course of justice, and prevent the punishment of his crime; if, therefore, the guilty minister of such abuse should attempt to pour poison into the sovereign's ear, and talk to him of mercy, this statute dashes the phial from his hand—it takes away the prerogative of pardon. Are bulwarks like these ever constructed to repel the incursions of a contemptible enemy? Was it a trivial and ordinary occasion which raised this storm of indignation in the parliament of that day? Is the ocean ever lashed by the tempest, to waft a feather, or to drown a fly?

Thus haughtily and jealously does the statute restrain the abuses that may be committed against the liberty of the subject by the judge, the jury, or the minister.

One exception, and one exception only, does it contain: it excepts from its protection, by the sixteenth section, persons who may have committed any capital offence in Scotland or Ireland. If the principle of that exception were now open to discussion, sure I am, that much might be said against its policy. On the one side, you would have to consider the mischief of letting this statute protect a capital offender from punishment, by prohibiting his transmission to that jurisdiction where his crime was committed, and where alone he could be tried. On the other, you would have to weigh the danger to be feared from the abuse of such a power, which, as the Habeas Corpus Act stood, could not be resorted to in any ordinary way, but was confined to the sole and exclusive exercise of the advisers of the prerogative. You would have to consider whether it was more likely that it would be used against the guilty or the obnoxious; whether it was more likely to be used as an instrument of justice against the bad, or a pretext of oppression against the good; and, finally, whether you might not apply to the subject the humane maxim of our law, that better it is that one hundred guilty men should escape, than that one innocent, and, let me add, meritorious man, should suffer. But our ancestors have considered the question; they have decided; and, until we are better satisfied than I fear we can be, that we have not degenerated from their virtue, it can scarcely become us to pass any light or hasty condemnation upon their wisdom.

In this great statute, then, my lords, you have the line of demarcation between the prerogative and the people, as well as between the criminal law and the subject, defined with all the exactness, and guarded by every precaution, that human prudence could devise. Wretched must that legislature be, whose acts you cannot trace to the first unchangeable principles of rational prerogative, of civil liberty, of equal justice! In this act you trace them all distinctly.

By this act you have a solemn legislative declaration, "that it is incompatible with liberty to send any subject out of the realm, under pretence of any crime supposed or alleged to be committed in a foreign jurisdiction, except that crime be capital." Such were the bulwarks which our ancestors placed about the sacred temple of liberty, such the ramparts by which they sought to bar out the ever-toiling ocean of arbitrary power; and thought (generous credulity!) that they had barred it out from their posterity for ever. Little did they foresee the future race of vermin that would work their way through those mounds, and let back the inundation; little did they foresee that their labours were so like those frail and transient works that threatened for a while the haughty crimes and battlements of Troy, but so soon vanished before the force of the trident and the impulse of the waters; or that they were still more like the forms which the infant's finger traces upon the beach, the next breeze, the next tide, erases them, and confounds them with the barren undistinguished strand. The ill-omened bird that lights upon it, sees nothing to mark, to allure, or to deter, but finds all one obliterated unvaried waste:—

"Et sola secum sicca spatiatur arena."

Still do I hope that this sacred bequest of our ancestors will have a more prosperous fortune, and be preserved by a more religious and successful care, a polar star to the wisdom of the legislator, and the integrity of the judge.

As such will I suppose its principle not yet brought into disgrace; and as such, with your permission, will I still presume to argue upon that principle.

So stood the law, till the two acts of the twenty-third and twenty-fourth of George II. which relates wholly to cases between county and county in England. Next followed the act of the thirteenth of his present Majesty, which was merely a regulation between England and Scotland. And next came the act of the forty-fourth of the present reign, upon which you are now called on to decide, which, as between county and county, is an incorporation of the two acts of George II.; and as between England, Scotland, and Ireland, is nearly a transcript of the thirteenth of the King.

Under the third and fourth section of this last act, the learned counsel for the learned prosecutors (for really I think it candid to acquit the Lord Lieutenant of the folly or the shame of this business, and to suppose that he is as innocent of the project, from his temper, as he must, from his education, be ignorant of the subject) endeavour to justify this proceeding.

The construction of this act they broadly and expressly contend to be this:—First, they assert that it extends not only to the higher crimes, but to all offences whatsoever. Secondly, that it extends not only to persons who may have committed offences within any given jurisdictions, and afterwards escaped or gone out of such jurisdictions, but to all persons, whether so escaping or going out, or not. Thirdly, that it extends to constructive offences, that is, to offences committed against the laws of certain jurisdictions, committed in places not within them, by persons that never put their feet within them, but, by construction of law, committing them within such jurisdiction, and of course triable therein. Fourthly, that it extends peculiarly to the case of libels against the persons entrusted with the powers of government, or with offices in the state. And, fifthly, that it extends not only to offences committed after the commencement of the act, but also to offences at any period, however remotely, previous to the existence of the statute; that is, that it is to have an *ex post facto* operation.

The learned prosecutors have been forced into the necessity of supporting these last monstrous positions, because, upon the return of the writ, and upon the affidavits, it appears, and has been expressly admitted in the argument: First, that the supposed libel upon those noble and learned prosecutors relates to the unhappy circumstances that took place in Ireland, on the twenty-third of July, 1803, and of course must have been published subsequent thereto. And, secondly, that Mr. Justice Johnson, from the beginning of 1802 to the present hour, was never for a moment in England, but was constantly a resident in Ireland; so that his guilt, whatever it be, must arise from some act, of necessity committed in Ireland, and by no physical possibility committed, or capable of being committed, in England.

These are the positions upon which a learned chancellor and a learned judge come forward to support their cause, and to stake their character, each in the face of his country, and both in the face of the British empire; these are the positions, which, thank God, it belongs to my nature to abhor, and to my education to despise, and which it is this day my most prompt and melancholy duty to refute and to resist—most prompt in obeying, most grieved at the occasion that calls for such obedience.

We must now examine this act of the forty-fourth of the King, and in doing so, I trust you will seek some nobler assistance than can be found in the principles or the practice of day-rules or side-bar motions; something more worthy a liberal and learned court, acting under a religious sense of their duty to their King, their country, and their God, than the feeble and pedantic aid of a stunted verbal interpretation, straining upon its tip-toe to peep over the syllable that stands between it and meaning. If your object was merely to see if its words could be tortured into a submission to a vindictive interpretation, you would have only to endorse the construction that these learned prosecutors have put upon it, and that with as much grave deliberation as Mr. Justice Bell has vouchsafed to endorse the warrant, which my Lord Ellenborough has thought fit to issue under its authority. You would then have only to look at it, *"ut leguleius quidam cautus atque acutus, praecentor."*

Lord Avonmore—No, Mr. Curran, you forget; it is not *praecentor;* it is, *"leguleius quidam cautus atque acutus, præco actionum cantor formarum, auceps syllabarum."*

Mr. CURRAN.—I thank you, my lord, for the assistance; and I am the more grateful, because, when I consider the laudable and successful efforts that have been made of late to make science domestic and familiar, and to emancipate her from the trammels of scholarship, as well as the just suspicion under which the harbourers and abettors of those outlawed classics have fallen; I see at what a risk you have ventured to help me out. And yet see, my lord, if you are prudent in trusting yourself to the honour of an accomplice. Think, should I be prosecuted for this misprision of learning, if I could resist the temptation of escaping, by turning evidence against so notorious a delinquent as you, my good lord, and so confessedly more criminal than myself, or perhaps than any other man in the empire.

To examine this act, then, my lords, we must revert to the three English statutes, of which it is a transcript. The first of these is the 23rd of Geo. II., cap. 26, sec. 11.

So much of the title as relates to our present inquiry is, "for the apprehending of persons in any other county or place upon warrants granted by justices of the peace in any other county or place."

See now sect. 11, that contains the preamble and enactment as to this subject:—

"And, whereas, it frequently happens that persons, against whom warrants are granted by justices of the peace, for the several counties within this kingdom, escape into other counties or places out of the jurisdiction of the justices of the peace, granting such warrants, and thereby avoid being punished for the offences wherewith they are charged: for remedy whereof, be it enacted by the authority aforesaid, that from and after the 24th day of June, 1750, in case any person against whom legal warrant shall be issued by any justice or justices of the peace for any county, riding, division, city, liberty, town, or place, within this kingdom, shall escape or go into any other county, riding, division, city, liberty, town, or place, out of the jurisdiction of the justice or justices granting such warrant, as aforesaid, it shall and may be lawful for any justice of the peace of the county, riding, division, city, liberty, town, or place, to which such person shall have gone or escaped, to endorse such warrant, upon application made to him for that purpose, and to cause the person against whom the same shall have been issued to be apprehended and sent to the justice or justices who granted such warrant, or some other justice or justices of the county, riding, division, city, liberty, town, or place, from whence such person shall have gone or escaped, to the end that he or she may be dealt with according to law, any law or usage to the contrary notwithstanding."

This act was amended by the 24th of the same reign, the title of which was, "An act for amending and making more effectual a clause in an act passed in the last session of parliament, for the apprehending of person in any county or place, upon warrants granted by justices of the peace of any county or place."

It then recites the 11th section of the 23d of George II., and proceeds, "And whereas such offender or offenders may reside or be in some other county, riding, division, city, liberty, town, or place, out of the jurisdictions of the justice or justices granting such warrant as aforesaid, before the granting such warrant, and without escaping or going out of the county, riding, division, city, liberty, town, or place, after such warrant granted."

I shall reserve a more particular examination of these two acts, for that head of my argument which will necessarily require it. At present I shall only observe—First, that they are manifestly prospective; Secondly, that they operate only as between county and county in England; Thirdly, that they clearly and distinctly go to all offenders whatsoever, who may avoid trial and punishment of their offences by escaping from the jurisdiction in which they were committed, and were of course triable and punishable; and, Fourthly, that provision is made for bailing the persons so arrested in the place where taken, if the offences charged upon them were bailable by law.

In the 13th of his present Majesty, it was thought fit to make a law with respect to criminals escaping from England to Scotland, and *vice versa*; of that act, the present statute of the 44th is a transcript. And upon this statute arises the first question made by the prosecutors; namely, whether, like the acts of the 23rd and 24th of George II. which were merely between county and county, it extended indiscriminately to the lowest as well as the highest offences? or whether the 13th and 44th, which go to kingdom and kingdom, are not confined to some and to what particular species of offences? The preamble to these two statutes, so far as they bear upon our present question, is contained in the third section of the 44th, the act now under consideration; and there is not a word in it that is not most material.

It says, "Whereas, it may frequently happen that felons and other malefactors in Ireland, may make their escape into Great Britain, and also that felons and other malefactors in Great Britain may make their escape into Ireland, whereby their crimes remain unpunished." There being no sufficient provision by the laws now in force in Great Britain and Ireland respectively, for apprehending such offenders, and transmitting them into that part of the United Kingdom in which their offences were committed. "For remedy whereof, &c., and if any person against whom a warrant shall be issued by any justice of the peace in Ireland for any crime or offence against the laws of Ireland, shall escape, go into, reside, or be in any place in England or Scotland, it shall be lawful for any justice of the peace for the place whither or where such persons shall escape, &c., to endorse his name on such warrant; which warrant so endorsed shall be a sufficient authority to the person bringing it to execute the same, by apprehending the person against whom it is granted, and to convey him by the most direct way into Ireland, and before a justice living near the place where he shall land, which justice shall proceed with regard to him as if he had been legally apprehended in such county of Ireland."

The fourth section makes the same provision for escapes from England or Scotland into Ireland. The statute goes on and directs that the expenses of such removal shall be repaid to the person defraying the same, by the treasurer of the county in which the crime was committed, and the treasurer is to be allowed for it in his accounts.

To support the construction that takes in all possible offences of all possible degrees, you have been told, and upon the grave authority of notable cases, that the enacting part of a statute may go beyond its preamble; that it cannot be restrained by the preamble, and still less by the title: that here the enacting clause has the words "any offence," and that "any offence" must extend to every offence, and of course to the offence in question. If the question had been of the lighter kind, you might perhaps have smiled at the parade of authorities produced to establish what no lawyer ever thinks of denying. The learned gentlemen would have acted with more advantage to the justice of the country, though perhaps not to the wishes of their clients, if they had reminded your lordships, that in the construction of a statute, the preamble and even the title itself may give some assistance to the judge in developing its meaning and its extent; if they had reminded you, that remedial laws are to be construed liberally, and penal laws with the utmost strictness and caution.

And when they contended that a supposed libel is within the letter of this law, they would have done well to have added, that it is a maxim that there may be cases within the letter of a statute, which, notwithstanding, the judge is bound to reject from its operation, as being incompatible with its spirit.

They would have done well in adding, that the judge is bound so to construe all laws, as not to infringe upon any of the known rules of religion or morality, any of the known rules of distributive justice, any of the established principles of the liberties and rights of the subject; and that it is no more than a decent and becoming deference to the legislator, to assume as certain, that whatever words he may have used, he could not possibly have meant anything that upon the face of it was palpably absurd, immoral, or unjust.

These are the principles on which I am persuaded this court will always act, because I know them to be the principles on which every court of justice ought to act. And I abstain studiously from appealing to any judicial decisions in support of them; because to fortify them by precedent or authority would be to suppose them liable to be called in question. There is another rule which I can easily excuse the learned gentlemen from adverting to, and that is, that when many statutes are made in *pari materia*, any one of them is to be construed, not independently of the others, but with a reference to the entire code, of which it is only a component part.

On these grounds, then, I say the 44th was not, and could not be intended to go to all offences whatsoever.

First, because the acts of 23d and 24th George II. had already described "all persons" by words of the most general and comprehensive kind. If the framers of the 13th and 44th meant to carry these acts to the same length, they had the words of the former acts before their eyes, and yet they have used very different words: a clear proof, in my mind, that they meant to convey a very different meaning.

In these latter acts they use very singular words, "felons and other malefactors;" that these words are somewhat loose and indefinite, I make no difficulty of admitting; but will any man who understands English deny, that they describe offences of a higher and most enormous degree? You are told, that felon does not necessarily mean a capital offender, because there are felonies not capital, the name being derived from the forfeiture, not of life, but of property. You are also told that malefactor means generally an ill-doer, and in that sense, that every offender is a malefactor; but the 13th and 44th state this class to be felons and malefactors, for whose transmission from kingdom to kingdom "no sufficient provision was made by the laws now in force."

Now I think it is not unfair reasoning to say, that this act extends to a class of offenders whose transmission was admitted to be not incompatible with the just liberty of the subject of England; but for whose transmission the legislature could not say there was no provision: but for whose transmission it was clear that there was not a sufficient provision, though there was some provision. If you can find any class so circumstanced, that is exclusively liable by law to be so transmitted, the meaning of the words "felons and other malefactors" becomes fixed, and must necessarily refer to such class.

Now that class is expressly described in the Habeas Corpus Act, because it declares the transmission of all persons to be illegal, except only persons charged with capital crimes; for their apprehension and transmission there was a provision, the *mandatum regis;* that is, the discretionary exercise of the prerogative. That power had, therefore, been used in cases of treason, as in Lundy's case. So in the case of Lord Sanquhar; Carliel, the principal in the murder of Turner, committed in London by the procurement of Lord Sanquhar, was arrested in Scotland, whither he had fled, by the order of King James I., and brought back to England, where he was executed for the crime, as was Lord Sanquhar, the accessory before the fact. But such interference of the prerogative might be granted or withheld at pleasure, could be applied for only with great difficulty and expense, and therefore might well be called an insufficient provision. No provision for such a purpose can be sufficient, unless, instead of depending on the caprice of men in power, it can be resorted to in the ordinary course of law.

You have, therefore, my lords, to elect between two constructions; one, which makes an adequate provision for carrying the exception in the 16th section of the Habeas Corpus Act into effect; and the other, a complete and radical repeal of that sacred security for the freedom of Englishmen.

But further, the spirit and the letter of the Habeas Corpus law is, that the party arrested shall, without a moment's delay, be bailed, if the offence be bailable; but if misdemeanours are within this act, then an English subject arrested under an Irish warrant, cannot be bailed within any part of the realm of England, but must be carried forward in the custody of Irish bailiffs, to the sea-shore of his country, where he is to be embarked in such vessel as they think proper; and, if it should be the good pleasure of his guardians to let him land alive in any part of Ireland, then, and not till then, may he apply to an Irish justice to admit him to bail in a foreign country, where he is a perfect stranger, and where none but an idiot could expect to find any man disposed to make himself responsible for his appearance.

Can you, my lords, bring your minds easily to believe that such a tissue of despotism and folly could have been the sober and deliberate intention of the legislature? but further, under the acts of George II., even from one county to the next, the warrant by the first justice must be authenticated upon oath, before it can be endorsed by the second; but in this act, between, perhaps, the remotest regions of different kingdoms, no authentication is required; and, upon the endorsement of, perhaps, a forged warrant, which the English justice has no means of inquiring into, a British subject is to be marched through England, and carried over sea to Ireland, there to learn in the county of Kerry, or Galway, or Derry, that he has been torn from his family, his friends, his business, to the annihilation of his credit, the ruin of his affairs, the destruction of his health, in consequence of a mistake, or a practical joke, or an inhuman or remorseless project of vindictive malice; and that he is then at liberty to return, if he be able; that he may have a good action at law against the worthy and responsible bailiff that abused him, if he is foolish enough to look for him, or unfortunate enough to find him. Can you, my lords, be brought seriously to believe, that such a construction would not be the foulest aspersion upon the wisdom and justice of the legislature?

I said, my lords, that an Englishman may be taken upon the endorsement of a forged warrant. Let me not be supposed to be such a simpleton as to think that the danger of forgery makes a shade of difference in the subject. I know too well that calendar of saints, the Irish justices; I am too much in the habit of prosecuting and defending them every term and every commission not to be able to guess at what price a customer might have real warrants by the dozen; and, without much sagacity, we might calculate the average expense of their endorsement at the other side of the water. But further yet, the act provides that the expense of such transmission shall be paid at the end of the journey, by the place where the crime has been committed, but, who is to supply the expenses by the way? what sort of prosecutors do you think the more likely to advance those expenses,—an angry minister or a vindictive individual?

I can easily see that such a construction would furnish a most effectual method of getting rid of a troublesome political opponent; or a rival in trade; or a rival in love; or of quickening the undutiful lingering of an ancestor that felt not the maturity of his heir; but I cannot bring myself to believe, that a sober legislature, when the common rights of humanity seem to be beaten into their last entrenchment, and to make their last stand,—I trust in God, a successful one,—in the British empire, would choose exactly that awful crisis for destroying the most vital principles of common justice and liberty, or of showing to these nations, that their treasure and their blood were to be wasted in struggling for the noble privilege of holding the right of freedom, of habitation, and of country, at the courtesy of every little irritable officer of state, or of our worshipful Rivets, and Bells, and Medlicots, and their trusty and well-beloved cousins and catchpoles.

But, my lords, even if the prosecutor should succeed, which for the honour and character of Ireland I trust he cannot, in wringing from the bench an admission that all offences whatsoever are within this act, he will have only commenced his honourable cause—he will only have arrived at the vestibule of atrocity. He has now to show that Mr. Johnson is within the description of a malefactor, making his escape into Ireland, whereby his offence may remain unpunished, and liable to be arrested under a warrant endorsed in that place whither or where such person escape, go into, reside, or be. For this inquiry you must refer to the 23d and 24th of George II. The first of these, 23d, cap. 11, recites the mischief, "that persons against whom warrants are granted, escape into other countries, and thereby avoid being punished." The enacting part then gives the remedy: "the justice for the place into which such person shall have gone or escaped, shall endorse the original warrant, and the person accused shall thereunder be sent to the justice who granted it, to be by him dealt with," &c.

If words can be plain, these words are so, they extend to persons actually committing crimes within a jurisdiction, and actually escaping into some other, after warrant granted, and thereby avoiding trial. In this act there were found two defects: first, it did not comprehend persons changing their abode before warrant issued, and whose removing, as not being a direct flight from pursuit, could scarcely be called an escape; secondly, it did not give the second justice a power to bail. And here you see how essential to justice it was deemed, that the person arrested should be bailed on the spot and at the moment of arrest, if the charge was bailable.

Accordingly, the 24th of George II., cap. 55, was made: after reciting the former act, and the class of offenders thereby described, namely, actual offenders actually escaping, it recites, that "whereas, such offenders may reside, or be in some other county before the warrant granted, and without escaping or going out of the county after such a warrant granted;" it then enacts, "that the justice for such place where such person shall escape, go into, reside, or be, shall endorse, &c. and may bail, if bailable, or transmit," &c.

Now the construction of these two acts taken together is manifestly this: it takes in every person, who being in any jurisdiction, and committing an offence therein, escaping after warrant, or without escaping after warrant, going into some other jurisdiction, and who shall there reside, that is, permanently abide, or shall be, that is permanently, so as to be called a resident.

Now here it is admitted, that Mr. Johnson was not within the realm of England since the beginning of 1802, more than a year before the offence existed; and therefore you are gravely called upon to say that he is the person who made his escape from a place where he never was, and into a place which he had never left. To let in this wise and humane construction, see what you are called upon to do; the statute makes such persons liable to arrest if they shall have done certain things; to wit, "if they shall escape, go into, reside, or be;" but if the fact of simply being, *i. e.*, existing in another jurisdiction, is sufficient to make them so liable, it follows of course, that the only two verbs that imply doing any thing, that is *escape or go into*, must be regarded as superfluous; that is, that the legislature had no idea whatsoever to be conveyed by them when they used them, and, therefore, are to be altogether expunged and rejected.

Such, my lords, are the strange and unnatural

monsters that may be produced by the union of malignity and folly. I cannot but own, that I feel an indignant, and perhaps ill-natured satisfaction, in reflecting that my own country cannot monopolize the derision and detestation that such a production must attract. It was originally conceived by the wisdom of the east; it has made its escape, and come into Ireland, under the sanction of the first criminal judge of the empire; here, I trust in God, we shall have only to feel shame or anger at the insolence of the visit, without the melancholy aggravation of such an execrable guest continuing to reside or to be among us. On the contrary, I will not dismiss the cheering expectation from my heart, that your decision, my lords, will show the British nation, that a country, having as just and as proud an idea of liberty as herself, is not an unworthy ally in the great contest for the rights of humanity; is no unworthy associate in resisting the progress of barbarity and military despotism, and in defending against its enemies that great system of British freedom, in which we have now a common interest, and under the ruins of which, if it should be overthrown, we must be buried in a common destruction.

I am not ignorant, my lords, that this extraordinary construction has received the sanction of another court, nor of the surprise and dismay with which it smote upon the general heart of the bar. I am aware that I may have the mortification of being told in another country of that unhappy decision, and I foresee in what confusion I shall hang down my head when I am told it.

But I cherish, too, the consolatory hope, that I shall be able to tell them that I had an old and learned friend, whom I would put above all the sweepings of their hall, who was of a different opinion; who had derived his ideas of civil liberty from the purest fountains of Athens and of Rome; who had fed the youthful vigour of his studious mind with the theoretic knowledge of their wisest philosophers and statesmen; and who had refined that theory into the quick and exquisite sensibility of moral instinct, by contemplating the practice of their most illustrious examples;—by dwelling on the sweet-souled piety of Cimon—on the anticipated Christianity of Socrates;—on the gallant and pathetic patriotism of Epaminondas;—on that pure austerity of Fabricius, whom to move from his integrity would have been more difficult than to have pushed the sun from his course.

I would add, that if he had seemed to hesitate, it was but for a moment; that his hesitation was like the passing cloud that floats across the morning sun, and hides it from the view, and does so for a moment hide it, by involving the spectator, without even approaching the face of the luminary. And this soothing hope I draw from the dearest and tenderest recollections of my life; from the remembrance of those attic nights and those refections of the gods which we have partaken with those admired, and respected, and beloved companions who have gone before us; over whose ashes the most precious tears of Ireland have been shed.

Here Lord Avonmore could not refrain from bursting into tears.

Yes, my good lord, I see you do not forget them; I see their sacred forms passing in sad review before your memory; I see your pained and softened fancy recalling those happy meetings, where the innocent enjoyment of social mirth became expanded into the nobler warmth of social virtue, and the horizon of the board became enlarged into the horizon of man; where the swelling heart conceived and communicated the pure and generous purpose, where my slenderer and younger taper imbibed its borrowed light from the more matured and redundant fountain of yours. Yes, my lord, we can remember those nights, without any other regret than that they can never more return; for

"We spent them not in toys; or lust, or wine;
But search of deep philosophy,
Wit, eloquence, and poesy;
Arts which I lov'd, for they, my friend, were thine."*

* Lord Avonmore, in whose breast political resentment was easily subdued, by the same noble tenderness of feeling which distinguished Fox, upon a more celebrated occasion, could not withstand this appeal to his heart. At this period there was a suspension of intercourse between him and Mr. Curran; but the moment the court rose, his lordship sent for his friend, and

But, my lords, to return to a subject from which to have thus far departed, I think may not be wholly without excuse. The express object of the 44th was to send persons from places where they were not triable by law, back to the places that had jurisdiction to try them. And in those very words does Mr. Justice Blackstone observe on the 13th of the King, that it was made to prevent impunity by escape, by giving a power of "sending back" such offenders as had so escaped.

This topic of argument would now naturally claim its place in the present discussion. I mention it now, that it might not be supposed that I meant to pretermit so important a consideration. And I only mention it, because it will connect itself with a subsequent head of this inquiry in a manner more forcibly applicable to the object; when I think I may venture to say it will appear to demonstration, that if the offence charged upon the defendant be triable at all, it is triable in Ireland, and no where else; and, of course, that the prosecutors are acting in direct violation of the statute, when they seek to transport him from a place where he can be tried, into another country which can have no possible jurisdiction over him.

Let us now, my lords, examine the next position contended for by these learned prosecutors. Hav-

threw himself into his arms, declaring that unworthy artifices had been used to separate them, and that they should never succeed in future.—*Life of Curran by his Son*, Vol. i., p. 148, *note*.

ing laboured to prove that the act applies not merely to capital crimes, but to all offences whatsoever; having laboured to show that an act for preventing impunity by escape extends to cases not only where there was no escape, but where escape in fact was physically impossible, they proceeded to put forward boldly a doctrine which no lawyer, I do not hesitate to say it, in Westminster-hall would have the folly or the temerity to advance: that is, that the defendant may, by construction of law, be guilty of an offence in Westminster, though he should never have passed within its limits, till he was sent thither to be tried.

With what a fatal and inexorable uniformity do the tempers and characters of men domineer over their actions and conduct! How clearly must an Englishman, if by chance there be any now listening to us, discern the motives and principles that dictated the odious persecutions of 1794 re-assuming their operations; forgetting that public spirit by which they were frustrated; unappalled by fear, undeterred by shame, and returning again to the charge; the same wild and impious nonsense of constructive criminality—the same execrable application of the ill-understood rules of a vulgar, clerk-like, and illiterate equity, to the sound, and plain, and guarded maxims of the criminal law of England!—the purest, the noblest, the chastest system of distributive justice that was ever venerated by the wise, or perverted by the foolish, or that the children of men in any age or climate of the world have ever yet beheld—the same instruments, the same movements, the same artists, the same doctrines, the same doctors, the same servile and infuriated contempt of humanity, and persecution of freedom!—the same shadows of the varying hour that extend or contract their length, as the beam of a rising or sinking sun plays upon the gnomon of self-interest! How demonstratively does the same appetite for mice authenticate the identity of the transformed princess that had been once a cat.

But it seems as if the whole order and arrangement of the moral and the physical world had been contrived for the instruction of man, and to warn him that he is not immortal. In every age, in every country, do we see the natural rise, advancement, and decline of virtue and of science. So it has been in Greece, in Rome; so it must be, I fear, the fate of England. In science, the point of its maturity and manhood is the commencement of its old age; the race of writers, and thinkers, and reasoners, passes away, and gives place to a succession of men who can neither write, nor think, nor reason. The Hales, the Holts, and the Somerses, shed a transient light upon mankind, but are soon extinct and disappear, and give place to a superficial and overweening generation of laborious and strenuous idlers, of silly scholiasts, of wrangling mooters, of prosing garrulists, who explore their darkling ascent upon the steps of science, by the balustrade of cases and manuscripts —who calculate their depth by their darkness, and fancy they are profound, because they feel they are perplexed. When the race of the Palladios is extinct, you may expect to see a clumsy hod-man collected beneath the shade of his shoulders—

——————"ανηρ ηυστε μεγαστε
Εξοχος ανθρωπων κεφαλην και ευρεας ωμυς"—

affecting to fling a builder's glance upon the temple, on the proportion of its pillars; and to pass a critic's judgment on the doctrine that should be preached within them.

Let it not, my lords, be considered amiss, that I take this up as an English rather than an Irish question. It is not merely because we have no habeas corpus law in existence (the antiquarian may read of it, though we do not enjoy it); it is not merely because my mind refuses itself to the delusion of imaginary freedom, and shrinks from the meanness of affecting an indignant haughtiness of spirit that belongs not to our condition, that I am disposed to argue it as an English question; but it is because I am aware that we have now a community of interest and of destiny that we never had before—because I am aware, that, blended as we now are, the liberty of man must fall where it is highest, or rise where it is lowest, till it finds its common level in the common empire—and because, also, I wish that Englishmen may see, that we are conscious that nothing but mutual benevolence and sympathy can support the common interest that should bind us against the external or the intestine foe—and that we are willing, whenever that common interest is attacked, to make an honest and animated resistance, as in a common cause, and with as cordial and tender anxiety for their safety as for our own.

Let me now briefly, because no subject can be shorter or plainer, consider the principle of local jurisdictions, and constructive crimes.

A man is bound to obedience, and punishable for disobedience of laws:—first, because, by living within their jurisdiction, he avails himself of their protection—and this is no more than the reciprocity of protection, and allegiance on a narrower scale; and, secondly, because, by so living within their jurisdiction, he has the means of knowing them, and cannot be excused because of his ignorance of them.

I should be glad to know upon the authority of what manuscript, of what pocket-case, the soundness of these principles can be disputed? I should be glad to know upon what known principle of English law a Chinese, or a Laplander, can be kidnapped into England, and arraigned for a crime which he committed under the pole, to the injury of a country which he had never seen—in violation of a law which he had never known, and to which he could not owe obedience—and, perhaps, for an act, the non-performance of which, might have forfeited his liberty or his life to the laws of that country which he was bound to know, and was bound to obey?

Very differently did our ancestors think of that subject. They thought it essential to justice, that the jurisdiction of criminal law should be local and defined—that no man should be triable but there, where he was accused of having actually committed the offence; where the character of the prosecutor, where his own character was known, as well as the characters of the witnesses produced against him, and where he had the authority of legal process to enforce the attendance of witnesses for his defence. They were too simple to know any thing of the equity of criminal law. Poor Bracton or Fleta would have stared if you had asked them, "What, gentlemen, do you mean to say that such a crime as this shall escape from punishment?" Their answer would have been no doubt, very simple, and very foolish: they would have said, "We know there are many actions that we think bad actions, which yet are not punishable, because not triable by law; and which are not triable, because of the local limits of criminal jurisdictions."

And, my lords, to show with what a religious scrupulosity the locality of jurisdictions was observed, you have an instance in the most odious of all offences, treason only excepted—I mean the crime of wilful murder. By the common law, if a man in one county procured a murder to be committed, which was afterwards actually committed in another, such procuror could not be tried in either jurisdiction, because the crime was not completed in either. This defect was remedied by the act of Edward VI. which made the author of the crime amenable to justice. But in what jurisdiction did it make him amenable? Was it there where the murder was actually perpetrated? By no means; but there only where he had been guilty of the procurement, and where alone his accessorial offence was completed.

And here you have the authority of Parliament for this abstract position, that where a man living in one jurisdiction does an act, in consequence of which, a crime is committed within another jurisdiction, he is by law triable only where his own personal act of procurement was committed, and not there where the procured or projected crime actually took effect. In answer to these known authorities of common law, has any statute, has a single decision, or even dictum of a Court, been adduced? Or, in an age in which the pastry-cooks and snuff-shops have been defrauded of their natural right to those compositions that may be useful without being read, has even a single manuscript been offered to show the researches of these learned prosecutors, or to support their cause? No, my lords; there has not.

I said, my lords, that this was a fruit from the

same tree that produced the stupid and wicked prosecutions of 1794; let me not be supposed to say it is a mere repetition of that attempt, without any additional aggravation. In 1794, the design —and odious enough it was—was confined to the doctrine of constructive guilt; but it did not venture upon the atrocious outrage of a substituted jurisdiction. The Englishman was tried on English ground where he was known, where he could procure his witnesses, where he had lived, and where he was accused of a crime, whether actual or constructive; but the locality of the trial defeated the infernal malice of these prosecutions. The speeches of half the natural day, where every juryman had his hour, were the knell of sleep, but they were not the knell of death. The project was exposed, and the destined victims were saved. A piece so damned could not safely be produced again on the same stage. It was thought wise, therefore, to let some little time pass, and then to let its author produce it on some other distant, provincial theatre, for his own benefit, and at his own expense and hazard.

To drag an English judge from his bench, or an English Member of Parliament from the senate, and in the open day, in the city of London, to strap him to the roof of a mail-coach, or pack him up in a waggon, or hand him over to an Irish bailiff, with a rope tied about his leg, to be goaded forward like an ox, on his way to Ireland, to be there tried for a constructive misdemeanor, would be an experiment, perhaps not very safe to be attempted. These Merlins, therefore, thought it prudent to change the scene of their sorcery:—

"Modo Romæ, modo ponit Athenis!"

The people of England might, perhaps, enter into the feelings of such an exhibition with an officiousness of sympathy not altogether for the benefit of the contrivers:—

"Nec coram populo natos Medea trucidet"—

and it was thought wise to try the second production before spectators whose necks were pliant, and whose hearts were broken: where every man who dared to refuse his worship to the golden calf, would have the furnace before his eyes, and think that it was at once useless and dangerous to speak, and discreet at least, if it was not honest, to be silent. I cannot deny that it was prudent to try an experiment, which if successful, must reduce an Englishman to a state of slavery, more abject and forlorn than that of the helots of Sparta, or the negroes of your plantations.

For see, my lords, the extent of the construction now broadly and directly contended for at your bar:—The King's peace in Ireland, it seems, is distinct from his peace in England, and both are distinct from his peace in Scotland; and, of course, the same act may be a crime against each distinct peace, and severally and successively punishable in each country—so much more inveterate is the criminality of a constructive than of an actual offence.

So that the same man for the same act, against laws that he never heard of, may be punished in Ireland, be then sent to England, by virtue of the warrant of Mr. Justice Bell, endorsed by my Lord Ellenborough; and after having his health, his hopes, and his property destroyed, for his constructive offences against his Majesty's peace in Ireland, and his Majesty's peace in England, he may find, that his Majesty's peace in the Orkneys, has, after all, a vested remainder in his carcass; and, if it be the case of a libel, for the full time and term of fourteen years from the day of his conviction before the Scottish jurisdiction, to be fully completed and determined.

Is there, my lords, can there be, a man who hears me, that does not feel that such a construction of such a law would put every individual in society under the despotical dominion, would reduce him to be the despicable chattel, of those most likely to abuse their power, the profligate of the higher, and the abandoned of the lower orders; to the remorseless malice of a vindictive minister; to the servile instrumentality of a trading justice? Can any man who hears me, conceive any possible case of abduction, of rape, or of murder, that may not be perpetrated, under the construction now shamelessly put forward.

Let us suppose a case:—By this construction a

person in England, by procuring a misdemeancur to be committed in Ireland, is constructively guilty in Ireland, and, of course, triable in Ireland. Let us suppose that Mr. Justice Bell receives, or says he receives, information, that the lady of an English nobleman wrote a letter to an Irish chambermaid, counselling her to steal a row of pins from an Irish pedlar, and that the said row of pins was, in consequence of such advice and counsel, actually stolen, against the Irish peace of our Lord the King; suppose my Lord Ellenborough, knowing the signature, and reverencing the virtue of his tried and valued colleague, endorses this warrant; is it not clear as the sun, that this English lady may, in the dead of the night, be taken out of her bed and surrendered to the mercy of two or three Irish bailiffs, if the captain who employed them should happen to be engaged in any contemporary adventure nearer to his heart, without the possibility of any legal authority interposing to save her, to be matronized in a journey by land, and a voyage by sea, by such modest and respectable guardians, to be dealt with during the journey as her companions might think proper, and to be dealt with afterward by the worshipful correspondent of the noble and learned lord, Mr. Justice Bell, according to law?

I can without much difficulty, my lords, imagine, that after a year or two had been spent in accounts current, in drawing and re-drawing for human flesh, between our worthy Bells and Medlicots on this side of the water, and their noble or their ignoble correspondents on the other, that they might meet to settle their accounts and adjust their balances. I can conceive that the items might not be wholly destitute of curiosity.—Brother B. I take credit for the body of an English patriot—Brother E. I set off against it that of an Irish judge—Brother B. I charge you in account with three English bishops—Brother E. I set off Mrs. M'Lean and two of her chickens; petticoat against petticoat—Brother B. I have sent you the body of a most intractable disturber, a fellow that has had the impudence to give a threshing to Bonaparte himself: I have sent you Sir Sidney—Dearest Brother E.—But I see my learned opponents smile—I see their meaning. I may be told, that I am putting imaginary and ludicrous, but not probable, and therefore, not supposable cases. But I answer, that that reasoning would be worthy only of a slave, and disgraceful to a freeman. I answer, that the condition and essence of rational freedom is, not that the subject probably will not be abused, but that no man in the state shall be clothed with any discretionary power, under the colour and pretext of which he can dare to abuse him.

As to probability, I answer, that in the mind of man there is no more instigating temptation to the most remorseless oppression, than the rancour and malice of irritated pride and wounded vanity.

To the argument of improbability, I adduce in answer, the very fact, the very question in debate; nor to such answer can I see the possibility of any reply, save that the prosecutors are so heartily sick of the point of view into which they have put themselves by their prosecution, that they are not likely again to make a similar experiment. But when I see any man fearless of power, because it possibly or probably may not be exercised upon him, I am astonished at his fortitude; I am astonished at the tranquil courage of any man who can quietly see that a loaded cannon is brought to bear on him, and that a fool is sitting at its touch-hole with a lighted match in his hand.

And yet, my lords, upon a little reflection, what is it, after what we have seen, that should surprise us, however it may shock us? What have the last ten years of the world been employed in, but in destroying the land-marks of rights, and duties, and obligations; in substituting sounds in the place of sense; in substituting a vile and canting methodism in the place of social duty and practical honour; in suffering virtue to evaporate into phrase, and morality into hypocrisy and affectation? We talk of the violations of Hamburgh or of Baden; we talk of the despotic and remorseless barbarian, who tramples on the common privileges of the human being; who, in defiance of the most known and sacred rights, issues the brutal mandate of usurped authority; who brings his victim by force within the limits of a jurisdiction to which he never owed obedience, and there butchers him for a constructive offence. Does it not seem as if it were a contest whether we should be more scurrilous in invective, or more atrocious in imitation? Into what a condition must we be sinking, when we have the front to select as the subjects of our obloquy, those very crimes which we have flung behind us in the race of profligate rivalry!

My lords, the learned counsel for the prosecutors have asserted that this act of the 44th of the King extends to all offences, no matter how long or previously to it they may have been committed. The words are, "That from and after the 1st day of August, 1804, if any person, &c. shall escape, &c." Now certainly nothing could be more convenient for the purpose of the prosecutors, than to dismiss, as they have done, the words "escape and go into," altogether. If those words could have been saved from the ostracism of the prosecutors, they must have designated some act of the offenders, upon the happening or doing of which the operation of the statute might commence; but the temporary bar of these words they wave by the equity of their own construction, and thereby make it a retrospective law; and having so construed it a manifestly *ex post facto* law, they tell you it is no such thing, because it creates no new offence, and only makes the offender amenable who was not so before. The law professes to take effect only from and after the 1st of August, 1804; now, for eighteen months before that day, it is clear that Mr. Johnson could not be removed by any power existing from his country and his dwelling; but the moment the act took effect, it is made to operate upon an alleged offence, committed, if at all, confessedly eighteen months before.

But another word as to the assertion, that it is not *ex post facto*, because it creates no new crime, but only makes the party amenable.

The force of that argument is precisely this:—If this act inflicted deportation on the defendant by way of punishment after his guilt had been established by conviction, that would, no doubt, be tyrannical, because *ex post facto:* but here he suffers the deportation, while the law is bound to suppose him perfectly innocent; and that only by way of process to make him amenable, not by way of punishment: and surely he cannot be so unreasonable as not to feel the force of the distinction.

How naturally, too, we find similar outrages resort to similar justifications! Such exactly was the defence of the forcible entry into Baden. Had that been a brutal violence committed in perpetration of the murder of the unfortunate victim, perhaps very scrupulous moralists might find something in it to disapprove of; but his Imperial Majesty was too delicately tender of the rights of individuals and of nations, to do any act so flagrant as that would be if done in that point of view; but his Imperial Majesty only introduced a clause of *ne omittas* into his warrant, whereby the worshipful Bells and Medlicots that executed it were authorised to disregard any supposed fantastical privilege of nations that gave sanctuary to traitors; and he did that from the purest motives, from as disinterested a love of justice as that of the present prosecutors; and not at all in the way of an *ex post facto* law, but merely as process to bring him in, and make him amenable to the competent and unquestionable jurisdiction of the *Bois de Boulogne.*

Such are the wretched sophistries to which men are obliged to have recourse, when their passions have led them to do what no thinking man can regard without horror, what they themselves cannot look at without shame; and for which no legitimate reason can suggest either justification or excuse. Such are the principles of criminal justice on which the first experiment is made in Ireland; but I venture to pledge myself to my fellow-subjects of Great Britain, that if the experiment succeeds, they shall soon have the full benefit of that success. I venture to promise them, they shall soon have their full measure of this salutary system for making men "amenable," heaped and running over into their bosoms.

There now remains, my lords, one, and only one topic of this odious subject, to call for observation. The offence here appears by the return and the affidavits, to be a libel upon the Irish government, published by construction in Westminster. Of the constructive commission of a crime in one place by an agent, who, perhaps at the moment of the act, is in another hemisphere, you have already heard enough. Here, therefore, we will consider it simply as an illegal libel upon the Irish government; and whether, as such, it is a charge coming within the meaning of the statute, and for which a common justice of peace in one kingdom, is empowered to grant a warrant for conveying the person accused for trial into the other.

Your lordships will observe, that in the whole catalogue of crimes for which a justice of peace may grant a warrant, there is not one that imposes upon him the necessity of deciding upon any matter of law, involving the smallest doubt or difficulty whatsoever. In treason the overt act; in felony, whether capital or not, the act; in misdemeanors, the simple act. The dullest justice can understand what is a breach of the peace, and can describe it in his warrant. It is no more than the description of a fact, which the informer has seen and sworn to. But no libel comes within such a class; for it is decided over and over, that a libel is no breach of the peace, and upon that ground it was that Mr. Wilkes, in 1763, was allowed the privilege of parliament, which privilege does not extend to any breach of the peace.

See, then, my lords, what a task is imposed upon a justice of the peace, if he is to grant such a warrant upon such a charge: he, no doubt, may easily comprehend the allegation of the informer, as to the fact of writing the supposed libel; in deciding whether the facts sworn amounted to a publication or not, I should have great apprehension of his fallibility; but if he got over those difficulties, I should much fear for his competency to decide what given facts would amount to a constructive publication.

But even if he did solve that question—a point on which, if I were a justice, I should acknowledge myself most profoundly ignorant—he would then have to proceed to a labour, in which I believe no man could expect him to succeed; that is, how far the paper sworn to was, in point of legal construction, libellous or not. I trust this court will never be prevailed upon to sanction, by its decision, a construction that would give to such a set of men a power so incompatible with every privilege of liberty or of law. To say it would give an irresistible power of destroying the liberty of the press in Ireland, would, I am well aware, be but a silly argument, where such a thing has long ceased to exist; but I have, for that very reason, a double interest now, as a subject of the empire, in that noble guardian of liberty in the sister nation. When my own lamp is broken, I have a double interest in the preservation of my neighbour's.

But if every man in England, who dares to observe, no matter how honestly and justly, upon the conduct of Irish ministers, is liable to be torn from his family, and dragged hither by an Irish bailiff, for a constructive libel against the Irish government, and upon the authority of an Irish warrant, no man can be such a fool as not to see the consequence. The inevitable consequence is this, that at this awful crisis, when the weal, not of this empire only, but of the whole civilized world, depends on the steady faith and consolidated efforts of these two countries, when Ireland is become the right arm of England, when every thing that draws the common interest and affection closer gives the hope of life, when every thing that has even a tendency to relax that sentiment is a symptom of death, even at such a crisis may the rashness or folly of those entrusted with its management, so act as to destroy its internal prosperity and repose, and lead it into the two-fold fatal error, of mistaking its natural enemies for its friends, and its natural friends for its natural enemies; without any man being found so romantically daring, as to give notice of the approaching destruction.

My lords, I suppose the learned counsel will do here what they have done in the other court: they will assert that this libel is not triable here; and they will argue that so false and heinous a production surely ought to be triable somewhere.

As to the first position, I say the law is directly against them.

From a very early stage of the discussion, the

gentlemen for the prosecution thought it wise for their clients to take a range into the facts much more at large than they appeared on the return to the writ, or even by the affidavits that have been made; and they have done this to take the opportunity of aggravating the guilt of the defendant, and at the same time of panegyrising their clients; they have, therefore, not argued upon the libel generally as a libel, but they have thought it prudent to appear perfectly acquainted with the charges which it contains: they have, therefore, assumed, that it relates to the transactions of the 23rd of July, 1803; and that the guilt of the defendant was, that he wrote that letter in Ireland, which was afterwards published in England, not by himself, but by some other persons.

Now, on these facts, nothing can be clearer than that he is triable here.

If it be a libel, and if he wrote it here, and it was published in England, most manifestly there must have been a precedent publication, not merely by construction of law, in Ireland, but a publication by actual fact. And for this plain reason, if you for a moment suppose the libel in his possession (and if he did in fact write it, I can scarcely conceive that it was not, unless he wrote it perhaps by construction), there were no physical means of transmitting it to England, that would not amount to a publication here. Because, if he put it into the post-office, or gave it to a messenger to carry thither, that would be complete evidence of publication against him.

So would the mere possession of the paper, in the hands of the witness who appeared and produced it, be perfect evidence, if not accounted for, or contradicted, to charge him with the publication; so that really I am surprised how gentlemen could be betrayed into positions so utterly without foundation.

They would have acted just as usefully for their clients, if they had admitted, what every man knows to be the fact, that is, that they durst not bring the charge before an Irish jury. The facts of that period were too well understood. The Irish public might have looked at such a prosecution with the most incredulous detestation; and if they had been so indiscreet as to run the risk of coming before an Irish jury, instead of refuting the charges against them as a calumny, they would have exposed themselves to the peril of establishing the accusation, and of raising the character of the man whom they had the heart to destroy, because he had dared to censure them.

Let not the learned gentlemen, I pray, suppose me so ungracious as to say, that this publication, which has given so much pain to their clients, is actually true; I cannot personally know it to be so, nor do I say so, nor is this the place or the occasion to say that it is so. I mean only to speak positively to the question before you, which is matter of law. But as the gentlemen themselves thought it meet to pronounce an eulogy on their clients, I thought it rather unseemly not to show that I attended to them; I have most respectfully done so; I do not contradict any praise of their virtues or their wisdom, and I only wish to add my very humble commendation of their prudence and discretion, in not bringing the trial of the present libel before a jury of this country.

The learned counsel have not been contented with abusing this libel as a production perfectly known to them, but they have wandered into the regions of fancy. No doubt the other judges, to whom those pathetic flights of forensic sensibility were addressed, must have been strongly affected by them. The learned gentlemen have supposed a variety of possible cases. They have supposed cases of the foulest calumniators aspersing the most virtuous ministers. Whether such supposed cases have been suggested by fancy or by fact, is not for me to decide; but I beg leave to say, that it is as allowable to us as to them to put cases of supposition:—

—"Cur ego si fingere pauca
Possum, invidear?"

Let me, then, my lords, put an imaginary case of a different kind: let me suppose that a great personage, entrusted with the safety of the citadel (meaning and wishing perhaps well, but misled by those lacquered vermin that swarm in every great hall), leaves it so loosely guarded, that nothing but the gracious interposition of Providence has saved it from the enemy. Let me suppose another great personage, going out of his natural department, and under the supposed authority of high station, disseminating such doctrines as tend to root up the foundation of society, to destroy all confidence between man and man, and to impress the great body of the people with a delusive and desperate opinion, that their religion could dissolve or condemn the sacred obligations that bind them to their country, that their rulers have no reliance upon their faith, and are resolved to shut the gates of mercy against them.

Suppose a good and virtuous man saw that such doctrines must necessarily torture the nation into such madness and despair, as to render them unfit for any system of mild or moderate government: that if on one side bigotry or folly shall inject their veins with fire, such a fever must be kindled, as can be allayed only by keeping a stream of blood perpetually running from the other; and that the horrors of martial law must become the direful but inevitable consequence. In such a case, let me ask you, what would be his indispensable duty? It would be, to avert such dreadful dangers, by exposing the conduct of such persons, by holding up the folly of such bigoted and blind enthusiasm to condign derision and contempt; and painfully would he feel that on such an occasion he must dismiss all forms and ceremonies; and that to do his duty with effect, he must do it without mercy. He should also foresee, that a person so acting, when he returned to those to whom he was responsible, would endeavour to justify himself by defaming the country which he had abused, for calumny is the natural defence of the oppressor: he should therefore so reduce his personal credit to its just standard, that his assertions might find no more belief than they deserved.

Were such a person to be looked on as a mere private individual, charity and good-nature might suggest not a little in his excuse.

An inexperienced man, new to the world, and in the honeymoon of preferment, would run no small risk of having his head turned in Ireland. The people in our island are by nature penetrating, sagacious, artful, and comic, "*natio comœda est.*" In no country under heaven would an ass be more likely to be hood-winked, by having his ears drawn over his eyes, and acquire that fantastical alacrity that makes dullness disposable to the purposes of humourous malice, or interested imposture.

In Ireland, a new great man could get the freedom of a science as easily as of a corporation, and become a doctor, by construction, of the whole Encyclopædia; and great allowance might be made under such circumstances for indiscretions and mistakes, as long as they related only to himself; but the moment they become public mischiefs, they lose all pretensions to excuse; the very ambition of incapacity is a crime not to be forgiven; and however painful it may be to inflict punishment, it must be remembered, that mercy to the delinquent would be treason to the public.

I can the more easily understand the painfulness of the conflict between charity and duty, because at this moment I am labouring under it myself; and I feel it the more acutely, because I am confident, that the paroxysms of passion that have produced these public discussions have been bitterly repented of. I think, also, that I should not act fairly if I did not acquit my learned opponents of all share whatsoever in this prosecution; they have too much good sense to have advised it; on the contrary, I can easily suppose Mr. Attorney-General sent for to give counsel and comfort to his patient; and after hearing no very concise detail of his griefs, his resentments, and his misgivings, methinks I hear the answer that he gives, after a pause of sympathy and reflection: "No, sir, do not proceed in such a business; you will only expose yourself to scorn in one country, and to detestation in the other. You know you durst not try him here, where the whole kingdom would be his witness. If you should attempt to try him there, where he can have no witness, you will have both countries upon your back. An English jury would never find him guilty. You will only confirm the charge against yourself, and be the victim of an impotent abortive malice. If you should have any ulterior project against him, you will defeat that also; for they who might otherwise concur in the design, will be shocked and ashamed of the violence and folly of such a tyrannical proceeding, and will make a merit of protecting him, and of leaving you in the lurch. What you say of your own feelings, I can easily conceive. You think you have been much exposed by those letters; but then remember, my dear sir, that a man can claim the privilege of being made ridiculous or hateful by no publication but his own. Vindictive critics have their rights, as well as bad authors. The thing is bad enough at best; but, if you go on, you will make it worse. It will be considered an attempt to degrade the Irish bench and the Irish bar. You are not aware what a nest of hornets you are disturbing. One inevitable consequence you do not foresee: you will certainly create the very thing in Ireland that you are so afraid of—a newspaper. Think of that, and keep yourself quiet. And, in the meantime, console yourself with reflecting, that no man is laughed at for a long time; every day will procure some new ridicule that must supersede him."

Such, I am satisfied, was the counsel given; but I have no apprehension for my client, because it was not taken.

Even if it should be his fate to be surrendered to his keepers—to be torn from his family—to have his obsequies performed by torch-light—to be carried to a foreign land, and to a strange tribunal, where no witness can attest his innocence—where no voice that he ever heard can be raised in his defence—where he must stand mute, not of his own malice, but the malice of his enemies—yes, even so, I see nothing for him to fear. That all-gracious Being that shields the feeble from the oppressor will fill his heart with hope, and confidence, and courage: his sufferings will be his armour, and his weakness will be his strength. He will find himself in the hands of a brave, a just, and a generous nation; he will find that the bright examples of her Russells and her Sidneys have not been lost to her children. They will behold him with sympathy and respect, and his persecutors with shame and abhorrence. They will feel, too, that what is then his situation, may to-morrow be their own; but their first tear will be shed for him, and the second only for themselves—their hearts will melt in his acquittal. They will convey him kindly and fondly to their shore; and he will return in triumph to his country—to the threshold of his sacred home—and to the weeping welcome of his delighted family. He will find that the darkness of a dreary and lingering night hath at length passed away, and that joy cometh in the morning.

No, my lords, I have no fear for the ultimate safety of my client. Even in these very acts of brutal violence that have been committed against him, do I hail the flattering hope of final advantage to him, and not only of final advantage to him, but of better days and more prosperous fortune for his afflicted country—that country, of which I have so often abandoned all hope, and which I have been so often determined to quit for ever.

> "Sæpe vale dicto multa sum deinde locutus,
> Et quasi discedens oscula summa dabam,
> Indulgens animo, pes tardus erat."

But I am reclaimed from that infidel despair. I am satisfied that while a man is suffered to live, it is an intimation from Providence that he has some duty to discharge, which it is mean and criminal to decline. Had I been guilty of that ignominious flight, and gone to pine in the obscurity of some distant retreat, even in that grave I should have been haunted by those passions by which my life had been agitated—

> ————"vivis quæ cura
> Eadem sequitur tellure repostos."

And if the transactions of this day had reached me, I feel how my heart would have been agonized by the shame of the desertion: nor would my sufferings have been mitigated by a sense of the feebleness of that aid, or the smallness of that service which I could render or withdraw. They would have been aggravated by the consciousness that, however feeble or worthless they were, I should not have dared to thieve them from my country. I have repented—I have stayed—and I am at once rebuked and rewarded by the happier hopes that I now entertain.

In the anxious sympathy of the public—in the anxious sympathy of my learned brethren—do I catch the happy presage of a brighter fate for Ireland. They see, that within these sacred walls the cause of liberty and of man may be pleaded with boldness and heard with favour. I am satisfied they will never forget the great trust, of which they alone are now the remaining depositories. While they continue to cultivate a sound and literate philosophy—a mild and tolerating Christianity—and to make both the sources of a just, and liberal, and constitutional jurisprudence, I see everything for us to hope. Into their hands, therefore, with the most affectionate confidence in their virtue, do I commit these precious hopes. Even I may live long enough yet to see the approaching completion, if not the perfect accomplishment of them. Pleased shall I then resign the scene to fitter actors; pleased shall I lay down my wearied head to rest, and say:—"Lord, now lettest thou thy servant depart in peace, according to thy word, for mine eyes have seen thy salvation."

On the 7th of February, the judgment of the Court was given against the release.

Mr. James Fitzgerald brought the case before the English Commons, on the 8th of February, without effect. On the 27th of May, a bill was brought into the English Commons, to amend the act of the former year, and enabling parties arrested to give bail, and granting subpœnas for witnesses in Ireland. When this bill reached the Lords, Johnson petitioned against it, and was heard by counsel; but it passed.

Pursuant to the decision of the Irish Courts, Judge Johnson was, therefore, removed to England; and having there pleaded specially to the indictment, the non-jurisdiction of the Court under the act, the Crown demurred, and on the 1st of July his plea was quashed.

On the 23rd of November, 1805, the trial took place before the full Court of King's Bench, in Westminster, and a special jury. Erskine, Garrow, &c., were with the law officers of the Crown. Cobbett swore to the documents, and four Irish officials swore that they were in Johnson's writing. After an argument on non-proof of publication in Middlesex, Mr. Adams spoke for the defence, and called Sir Henry Jebb, Dr. Hodgkinson (S. F. T. C. D.), Mr. Archdall, Mr. John Gifford, and Mr. Cassidy, to prove the handwriting not Judge Johnson's. After a quarter of an hour's deliberation, the jury found a verdict of GUILTY. A *nolle prosequi* was entered on this by the Whig Government in Trinity Term, 1806, and Johnson retired upon his pension.

www.ingramcontent.com/pod-product-compliance
Lightning Source LLC
LaVergne TN
LVHW021100110826
845150LV00001B/135

* 9 7 8 1 4 2 5 5 6 6 0 4 3 *